A Guide and Reference

HOW TO
WRITE
ANYTHING

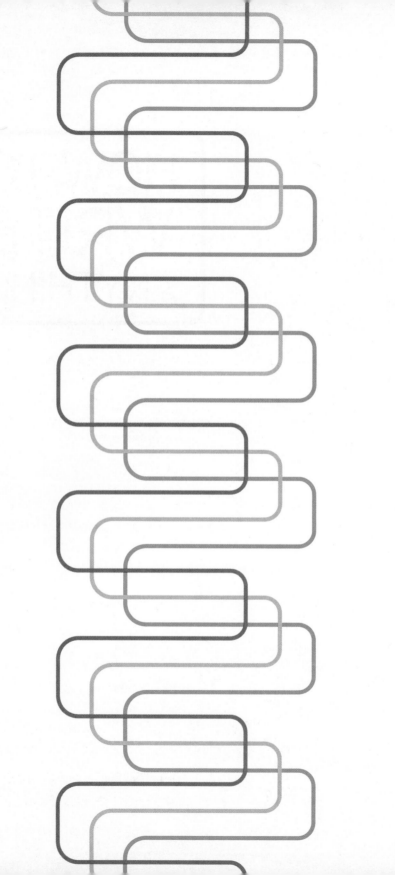

SECOND EDITION

HOW TO WRITE ANYTHING

A Guide and Reference

John J. Ruszkiewicz

UNIVERSITY OF TEXAS AT AUSTIN

BEDFORD/ST. MARTIN'S

Boston ◆ New York

For Bedford/St. Martin's

Senior Executive Editor: Leasa Burton
Senior Development Editor: Ellen Darion
Senior Production Editor: Rosemary R. Jaffe
Assistant Production Manager: Joe Ford
Senior Marketing Manager: Molly Parke
Editorial Assistant: Alyssa Demirjian
Copyeditor: Jennifer Brett Greenstein
Indexer: Mary White
Permissions Manager: Kalina K. Ingham
Senior Art Director and Text Design: Anna Palchik
Cover Design: Marine Miller
Composition: Cenveo Publisher Services
Printing and Binding: RR Donnelley and Sons

President: Joan E. Feinberg
Editorial Director: Denise B. Wydra
Editor in Chief: Karen S. Henry
Director of Marketing: Karen R. Soeltz
Director of Production: Susan W. Brown
Associate Director, Editorial Production: Elise Kaiser
Managing Editor: Elizabeth M. Schaaf

Library of Congress Control Number: 2011934582

Manufactured in the United States of America.

6   5   4   3
f   e   d

For information, write: Bedford/St. Martin's, 75 Arlington Street, Boston, MA 02116 (617-399-4000)

ISBN: 978-0-312-67490-8 (adhesive version)
ISBN: 978-1-4576-0243-6 (spiral version)

Acknowledgments

Preface

How to Write Anything: A Guide and Reference is not a humble title. You might wonder whether any book, especially one designed expressly as a guide for college writers, should promise so much. The simple answer is *no*; the more intriguing one is *maybe*.

What, after all, do writers do when they face an assignment? They try to grasp what the project requires; they look for examples of the genre; they wrestle with basic language and research skills. *How to Write Anything* guides college writers through these stages for their most common academic and professional assignments. In doing so, it lays out strategies to follow in any situation that requires purposeful writing.

But rarely do different writers work in the same order, and the same writer is likely to follow different paths for different projects. *How to Write Anything* doesn't define a single process of writing or imagine that all students using it will have the same skills and interests. Instead, a modular chapter organization and an innovative system of cross-references encourage students to navigate the book's materials to find exactly the information they want at the level of specificity they need—which pretty much sums up the rationale for the book. *How to Write Anything* is both focused and flexible, marrying the rich perspectives of a full rhetoric to the efficiency of a brief handbook. Building on these principles, this second edition includes more genres, defines genres more precisely, and offers students more tools for exploring them.

A Guide and Reference

The Guide, in Parts 1 and 2, covers the genres of writing that instructors frequently assign in composition classes or that students encounter in other undergraduate courses. Each chapter lays out the basics of a genre, such as narrative or argument, then presents the writing process as a flexible series of rhetorical choices—Exploring Purpose and Topic; Understanding Your Audience; Finding and Developing Materials; Creating a Structure; and Choosing a Style and Design. These choices provide students with a framework for writing in any situation and in any genre, and encourage writers to explore the range of possibilities within genres. The explanations here are direct, practical, and economical. If writers do need more help with a particular topic, targeted cross-references make it easy to find in the Reference section.

The Reference section (Parts 3 through 9) covers key aspects of the writing process—with separate parts devoted to Ideas; Shaping and Drafting; Style; Revising and Editing; Research and Sources; Media and Design; and Common Errors. While the topics will seem familiar to most writing instructors, the fresh and lively material here is designed to expand points introduced in the Guide. For instance, a writer might turn to these sections to find specific techniques for generating ideas or arguments or guidance for making a formal style feel more friendly. The organization of *How to Write Anything* lets students quickly find what they need without getting bogged down in other material.

Key Features

A Flexible Writing Process

Writers get started, develop ideas, and revise in different ways. *How to Write Anything* acknowledges this by asking students to think about their *own* processes and what they need help with. At the beginning of each Guide chapter, "How to Start" questions anticipate where students get stuck when writing and direct them to specific materials within the chapter for help. For example, one writer might need advice about finding a topic, while another will already have a topic but need assistance with audience, or developing or organizing ideas.

In this hyperlinked era, it is important for information to be intuitive, easy to find, and, above all, relevant and useful. With this in mind, the cross-references between the Guide and Reference sections target only the topics that students are most likely to need help with for the assignment at hand. The simple language and unobtrusive design of the cross-references make it easy for students to find the exact help they need and to stay focused on their own writing.

Professional and Student Writing

How to Write Anything: A Guide and Reference contains over forty readings carefully chosen to illustrate key principles and show how genres change in response to different contexts and audiences. Every chapter in the Guide includes many complete examples of the genres under discussion, most of these texts annotated to show how they meet criteria set down in *How to Write Anything*. The assignments at the end of these chapters are closely tied to the chapter readings, so students can use the sample texts both as models and as springboards for discussion and exploration.

Just as important, the models in *How to Write Anything* are approachable. The readings—some by published professionals and others by student writers—reveal the diversity of contemporary writing being done in these genres. The student samples are especially inventive—chosen to motivate undergraduates to take comparable risks with their own writing. Together, the readings and exercises suggest to writers not just the rules for each genre, but also the many creative possibilities of working in these genres.

"How To" Visual Tutorials

Throughout the book, students will recognize a world they already live in, one which assumes that composing occurs in more than just words. But learning occurs in more than just words too. Savvy readers of telegraphic text messages, quick-cut visuals, and blogs will no doubt appreciate the direct yet context-rich advice in the book's "How To" Visual Tutorials. Through drawings, photographs, and screenshots, these tutorials offer step-by-step instructions for challenging topics, ranging from how to browse the Internet for ideas to how to cite a variety of materials in both MLA and APA formats.

New to This Edition

How to Write Anything remains a uniquely flexible text: It works with any writing process, any genre, anywhere. In this revision we added reference chapters at the heart of academic writing—critical thinking, genre, and strategies. And to give students more support for academic skills, there are new chapters on synthesis and annotated bibliography, along with a new emphasis on multimodal composing.

More Support for Academic Writing

Three brief new chapters focus on important academic skills. **"Synthesis Papers"** shows students how to summarize, compare, and assess materials from different sources. **"Critical Thinking"** lays out rhetorical appeals and logical fallacies, and an **"Annotated Bibliographies"** chapter provides guidelines for this popular research assignment.

Another new chapter, "Strategies," explores rhetorical tools that work across genres, including comparison and contrast, classification, description, definition, and division.

New Visual Tutorials show how to document a wider range of electronic sources.

New Genre Chapter and a Wider Range of Genres

The new reference chapter, "Genre," defines this key concept, discusses why it matters, and shows students how genres help writers accomplish the work they want to do. New genres covered in this edition of *How to Write Anything* include annotated bibliographies and synthesis papers. New model readings engage students with fresh topics, including the pros and cons of cell phones and iPads, zombies, and what we can learn about a politician from his clothes. Many more readings can be found in the e-library and the e-book (see pp. xv and xvi for more information).

More Advice for Students Using Multimedia

Two new reference chapters, "Understanding Digital Media" and "Digital Elements," explore audio, video, blogs, and wikis.

All genre chapters now feature multimodal assignment options, for example, preparing an evaluation in which a visual comparison plays a major role.

New "Your Turn" Activities

The "Your Turn" activities encourage students to apply the advice in the book, letting them try out genres and strategies before tackling a complete assignment. For example, one prompt asks students to transform a popular song title (consider "Taxman," "Waiting on the World to Change," or "Concrete and Barbed Wire") into a thesis statement that would be suitable for an academic paper. Additional "Your Turn" activities are available both on the free student site and in the e-book. For more on the e-book, see page xv.

Invitation to Write

How to Write Anything was designed and edited to be compact and readable. But it retains a personal voice, frank and occasionally humorous, on the grounds that a textbook without character won't convince students that their own prose should have a style adapted to real audiences. And if some chapters operate like reference materials, they still aren't written coldly or dispassionately—not even the section on Common Errors.

So if *How to Write Anything* seems like an ambitious title, maybe it's because learning to write should be a heady enterprise, undertaken with confidence and optimism. My hope is that this book will encourage students to grasp the opportunities that the writing affords and gain the satisfaction that comes from setting ideas (and words) into motion.

Acknowledgments

The following reviewers were very helpful through several drafts of this book: Angela K. Albright, NorthWest Arkansas Community College; Ellen Arnold, Coastal Carolina University; Diann L. Baecker, Virginia State University; Lisa Baird, Flagler College; Sandie McGill Barnhouse, Rowan-Cabarrus Community College; Bethany Joy Bear, Baylor University; Andrea L. Beaudin, Southern Connecticut State University; Quinton Blackwell, Towson University; Glenn Blalock, Baylor University; Patricia Boyd, Arizona State University; Kevin F. Boyle, College of Southern Nevada; Bob Brown, Chippewa Valley Technical College; Jon Byrne, Itasca Community College; Giselle Muñoz Caro, University of Puerto Rico; Frankie Chadwick, University of Arkansas at Little Rock; Miriam Chirico, Eastern Connecticut State University; Ron Christiansen, Salt Lake Community College; Tara Cole, Oklahoma State University–Oklahoma City; Z. Katherine Combiths, Virginia

Tech; Michelle Cox, Bridgewater State College; Mark Crane, Utah Valley State College; Linsey Cuti, Kankakee Community College; Tracy L. Dalton, Missouri State University; Cathy Decker, Chaffey College; Lauren DeGraffenreid, University of Nevada, Reno; Jim Dervin, Winston-Salem State University; Anthony Edgington, University of Toledo; Caroline L. Eisner, University of Michigan; Jennie Enger, North Dakota State University; Ruth Fair, Winston-Salem State University; Maureen Fitzpatrick, Johnson County Community College; Shawnee Fleenor, Asbury University; Amy Foley, Roberts Wesleyan College; Hank Galmish, Green River Community College; John Gides, California State University–Northridge; Maura Grady, University of Nevada, Reno; Christine Grossman, North Dakota State University; Steffen Guenzel, The University of Alabama; Mark Helm, The Art Institute of Tennessee–Nashville; Virginia Scott Hendrickson, Missouri State University; Kathryn Owen Hix, Greenville Technical College; Jordynn Jack, University of North Carolina at Chapel Hill; Karen Jobe, Oklahoma State University–Oklahoma City; Judith Angelique Johnson, Minnesota State University, Mankato; Jessica Fordham Kidd, University of Alabama; Noreen Lace, California State University–Northridge; Mark Lanting, Kankakee Community College; Lynn Lewis, University of Oklahoma; Mary Libertin, Shippensburg University of Pennsylvania; Amy Locklear, Auburn University–Montgomery; Paula Makris, Wheeling Jesuit University; Cynthia K. Marshall, Wright State University; Leigh A. Martin, Community College of Rhode Island; Kit McChesney, University of Colorado at Boulder; Miles McCrimmon, J. Sargeant Reynolds Community College; Erica Messenger, Bowling Green State University; Mary Ellen Muesing, University of North Carolina–Charlotte; Bryan Peters, Jefferson College; Valarie Phelps, Western Kentucky University; Elizabeth Porto, University of Massachusetts–Amherst; Shay Rahm-Barnett, University of Central Oklahoma; Jennifer A. Rea, Rockford College; Rachel Reed, Auburn University–Montgomery; Juliann Reineke, Greenville Technical College; Mark Reynolds, Jefferson Davis Community College; Rob Roensch, Towson University; Abby Rotstein, College of Southern Nevada; Bridget F. Ruetenik, Penn State Altoona; Jim Schrantz, Tarrant County College; Wendy Sharer, Eastern Carolina University; Marti Singer, Georgia State University; Marian Smith, Chippewa Valley Technical College; David Sorrells, Lamar State

College–Port Arthur; William H. Thelin, University of Akron; James G. Van Belle, Edmonds Community College; Carol Westcamp, University of Arkansas–Fort Smith; Darren Wieland, Minnesota State University, Mankato; Rita Wisdom, Tarrant County College–Northeast Campus; Kelli Wood, El Paso Community College; Mary K. Zacharias, San Jacinto College Central.

All books are collaborations, but I have never before worked on a project that more creatively drew upon the resources of an editorial team and publisher. *How to Write Anything* began with the confidence of Joan Feinberg, president of Bedford/St. Martin's, that I could develop a ground-breaking brief rhetoric. She had the patience to allow the idea to develop at its own pace and then assembled an incredible team to support it. I am grateful for the contributions of Denise Wydra, Editorial Director; Karen Henry, Editor in Chief; and Leasa Burton, Senior Executive Editor. I am also indebted to Anna Palchik, Senior Art Director and designer of the text, and Rosemary Jaffe, Senior Production Editor. Special thanks to Sarah Macomber, who conceived the original Visual Tutorials, to Peter Arkle and Anna Veltfort for their drawings, Christian Wise for his photographs, and to Allie Goldstein, Sophia Snyder, and Shannon Walsh for their help with art research. They all deserve credit for the distinctive and accessible visual style of *How to Write Anything*.

For their marketing efforts, I am grateful to the guidance offered by Karen R. Soeltz, Karita dos Santos, and Molly Parke. And for all manner of tasks, including updating the Visual Tutorials, coordinating permissions and reviews, and manuscript preparation, I thank Alyssa Demirjian.

But my greatest debt is to Ellen Darion, who was my splendid editor on this lengthy project: always confident about what we could accomplish, patient when chapters went off-track, and perpetually good-humored. If *How to Write Anything* works, it is because Ellen never wavered from our original high aspirations for the book. Her hand is in every chapter, every choice of reading, and every assignment.

Finally, I am extraordinarily grateful to my former students whose papers or paragraphs appear in *How to Write Anything*. Their writing speaks for itself, but I have been inspired, too, by their personal dedication and character. These are the sort of students who motivate teachers, and so I am very proud to see their work published in *How to Write Anything*: Jordyn Brown, Marissa Dahlstrom, Manasi Deshpande, Micah T. Eades, Lynn Ehlers, Kyu-heong Kim, Wade Lamb, Cheryl Lovelady, Shane McNamee, Matthew Nance, Miles Pequeno, Heidi Rogers, Kanaka Sathasivan, Kelsi Stayart, J. Reagan Tankersley, Katelyn Vincent, and Annie Winsett.

John J. Ruszkiewicz

Get More Digital Choices for *How to Write Anything,* Second Edition

How to Write Anything doesn't stop with a book. Online, you'll find both free and affordable premium resources to help students get even more out of the book and your course. To learn more about or order any of the products below, contact your Bedford/St. Martin's sales representative, e-mail sales support (**sales_support@bfwpub.com**), or visit the Web site at **bedfordstmartins.com/ howtowrite/catalog**.

Student Site for How to Write Anything
bedfordstmartins.com/howtowrite

Send students to free and open resources, choose flexible premium resources, or upgrade to an expanding collection of innovative digital content.

Free and open resources for *How to Write Anything* provide students with easy-to-access reference materials, visual tutorials, and support for working with sources.

- Checklists for writing different genres
- Links to more models
- Five free videos of real writers from *VideoCentral*
- Three free tutorials from *ix visualizing composition* by Cheryl Ball and Kristin Arola
- *Research and Documentation Online* by Diana Hacker

A free *E-Library for How to Write Anything*. Because there are some things you can't do in print, the second edition of *How to Write Anything* is available with a digital collection of multimodal readings, including a video featuring the writer Michael Pollan encouraging people to see the world from "a plant's-eye view" and an online newspaper's product review of the Rosetta Stone language instruction system. The e-library also includes student models, video tutorials about documenting sources, and assignment options, all packaged for free with the print book. This extra content is also integrated into the *How to Write Anything e-Book*. To order the *E-Library for How to Write Anything* packaged with the print book, use ISBN 978-1-4576-2265-6 (adhesive version) or 978-1-4576-2283-0 (spiral version).

VideoCentral: English is a growing collection of videos for the writing class that captures real-world, academic, and student writers talking about how and why they write. Writer and teacher Peter Berkow interviewed hundreds of people—from Michael Moore to Cynthia Selfe—to produce fifty brief videos about topics such as revising and getting feedback. *VideoCentral* can be packaged for free with *How to Write Anything*. An activation code is required. To order *VideoCentral* packaged with the print book, use ISBN 978-1-4576-1127-8 (adhesive version) or 978-1-4576-2286-1 (spiral version).

E-book Options

bedfordstmartins.com/howtowrite/catalog

With a Bedford e-book, you get the complete text in an interactive online version, plus additional content in the *E-Library for How to Write Anything* and more options for customizing the book to suit your course. **You can** move or hide chapters to match your syllabus and add notes and links that build on the text and engage students in conversation. **Students can** find the book online anytime, anywhere; highlight and add notes to make the text their own; and watch videos and complete practice exercises while they're online. An activation code is required. To order the *How to Write Anything e-Book,* use ISBN 978-0-312-62996-0. To order it packaged with the print book, use ISBN 978-1-4576-1132-2 (adhesive version) or 978-1-4576-2285-4 (spiral version).

Students can also purchase *How to Write Anything* in other popular e-book formats for computers, tablets, and e-readers. For more details, visit **bedfordstmartins.com/ebooks**.

CompClass for How to Write Anything
yourcompclass.com

An easy-to-use online course space designed for composition, *CompClass for How to Write Anything* comes preloaded with the *How to Write Anything e-Book* and the *E-Library for How to Write Anything* as well as the complete Bedford e-library for composition, including *VideoCentral* and *i•cite visualizing research*. *CompClass for How to Write Anything* can be purchased separately at **yourcompclass.com** or packaged with the print book at a significant discount. An activation code is required. To order *CompClass for How to Write Anything* with the print book, use ISBN 978-1-4576-1136-0 (adhesive version) or 978-1-4576-2278-6 (spiral version).

Instructor Resources
bedfordstmartins.com/howtowrite/catalog

You have a lot to do in your course. Bedford/St. Martin's wants to make it easy for you to find the support you need—and to get it quickly. Request a print copy of any of these resources through our online catalog or your sales representative.

Teaching with How To Write Anything is available both in print and as a PDF that can be downloaded from the Bedford/St. Martin's online catalog. In addition to chapter overviews and teaching tips, the Instructor's Manual includes sample syllabi, correlations to the Council of Writing Program Administrators' Outcomes Statement, and classroom activities.

Portfolio Teaching, **Second Edition, by Nedra Reynolds and Rich Rice** provides all the information instructors and writing program directors need to use portfolio assessment successfully in a writing course. *Portfolio Keeping,* Second Edition, is a companion guide for students. Bedford *Bits* at

bedfordbits.com collects creative ideas for teaching a range of composition topics in an easily searchable blog format.

Free Bedford Coursepacks for the most common course management systems—Blackboard, WebCT, Angel, and Desire2Learn—allow you to easily download our most popular digital materials for your course. For details, visit **bedfordstmartins.com/coursepacks**.

Correlation to the Council of Writing Program Administrators' (WPA) Outcomes Statement

How to Write Anything helps students build proficiency in the five categories of learning that writing programs across the country use to assess their work: rhetorical knowledge; critical thinking, reading, and writing; writing processes; knowledge of conventions; and composing in electronic environments. A detailed correlation follows.

Features of *How to Write Anything, A Guide and Reference,* Second Edition, Correlated to the WPA Outcomes Statement

Desired Student Outcomes	Relevant Features of *How to Write Anything*
Rhetorical Knowledge	
Respond to the needs of different audiences.	Each assignment chapter in the Guide has a section called "Understanding Your Audience"; the need to consider one's audience is covered in the discussion of every genre.
	Chapter 3, "Arguments," includes a section on responding to opposing claims and points of view, and Chapters 2 and 4, "Reports" and "Evaluations," discuss writing for experts, general audiences, novices, or peers.
Respond appropriately to different kinds of rhetorical situations.	Each assignment chapter in the Guide offers detailed advice on responding to a particular rhetorical situation, from arguing a claim and proposing a solution to writing an e-mail or a résumé.
	Chapter 25, "Genre," explains how genres help writers accomplish the work they want to do.
Use conventions of format and structure appropriate to the rhetorical situation.	Each chapter in Part 1 includes sections on both "Creating a Structure" and "Choosing a Style and Design" appropriate for the genre covered there. See also "Getting the Details Right" sections in Part 2 chapters.
	Structure is also covered in Part 4, "Shaping and Drafting," in Chapters 25–34: "Genre," "Thesis," "Strategies," "Organization," "Outlines," "Paragraphs," "Transitions," "Introductions," "Conclusions," and "Titles."
	Document design is covered in Chapter 54, "Designing Print and Online Documents."
Adopt appropriate voice, tone, and level of formality.	See the "Choosing a Style and Design" sections in Part 1 chapters, and the "Getting the Details Right" sections in Part 2 chapters.
	Part 5 features chapters on "High, Middle, and Low Style" (35); "Inclusive and Culturally Sensitive Style" (36), and "Vigorous, Clear, and Economical Style" (37).
Understand how genres shape reading and writing.	Each chapter in Part 1 offers student and professional readings accompanied by annotations and commentary about the key features of the genre. Each chapter also begins with a list of examples of the genre that will be familiar to students, followed by a section on understanding the genre covered in that chapter.
	Chapter 25, "Genre," explains how genres help writers accomplish the work they want to do.

Desired Student Outcomes	Relevant Features of *How to Write Anything*
Rhetorical Knowledge (*continued*)	
Write in several genres.	Chapters 1–18 in the Guide (Parts 1 and 2) cover the following genres and assignments: Narratives, Reports, Arguments, Evaluations, Proposals, Causal, Literary, and Rhetorical Analyses, Essay Examinations, Annotated Bibliographies, Synthesis Papers, Position Papers, E-mails, Business Letters, Résumés, Personal Statements, Lab Reports, and Oral Reports. Chapter 25, "Genre," explains how genres help writers accomplish the work they want to do. Part 7 covers research strategies students will use while writing these genres, while Part 8 addresses digital media and strategies students will need for public writing such as brochures and newsletters.
Critical Thinking, Reading, and Writing	
Use writing and reading for inquiry, learning, thinking, and communicating.	The assignment chapters in the Guide emphasize the connection between reading and writing a particular genre: each chapter includes model readings whose annotations address the key features of the genre. Each Part 1 chapter shows students the rhetorical choices they need to consider when writing their own papers in these genres and offers assignments to actively engage them in these choices. Chapter 22, "Critical Thinking," explains rhetorical appeals and logical fallacies. Reference chapters in Parts 3 through 8 cover invention, reading, writing, research, and design strategies that work across all genres.
Understand a writing assignment as a series of tasks, including finding, evaluating, analyzing, and synthesizing appropriate primary and secondary sources.	Each chapter in Part 1 includes a section on "Finding and Developing Ideas." Chapter 12, "Synthesis Papers," shows students how to summarize, compare, and assess the views offered by different sources. Chapter 21 introduces close reading and logical fallacies, while Part 7, "Research and Sources," includes Chapters 41, "Finding Print and Online Sources"; 42, "Doing Field Research"; 43, "Evaluating Sources"; 44, "Annotating Sources"; 45, "Summarizing Sources"; and 46, "Paraphrasing Sources."
Integrate their own ideas with others.	Chapter 47, "Integrating Sources into Your Work," provides detailed advice on integrating and introducing quotations, paraphrasing, summarizing, and avoiding plagiarism.

Desired Student Outcomes	Relevant Features of *How to Write Anything*
Processes	
Be aware that it usually takes multiple drafts to create and complete a successful text.	Chapter 38, "Revising Your Own Work," discusses the importance of revising and gives detailed advice on how to approach different types of revision. Targeted cross-references throughout the text help students get the revision help they need when they need it.
Understand the collaborative and social aspects of writing processes.	Chapter 20 covers collaboration as a strategy of invention; Chapter 23 encourages students to consult experts such as an instructor, a librarian, or a tutor at the writing center. Chapter 39 teaches students to give constructive feedback to other writers. Chapter 42 provides thorough coverage of field research.
Learn to critique their own and others' work.	Chapter 38 focuses students on revising their own work, while Chapter 39 guides students to give useful feedback to other writers. Chapter 22 helps students uncover logical fallacies, while Chapter 44 shows them how to identify claims, assumptions, and evidence.
Use a variety of technologies to address a range of audiences.	Chapters 51 and 52 cover digital media, including blogs, Web sites, wikis, podcasts, videos, and remixes. Chapter 54 covers creating visuals on a computer and downloading them from the Web. Each assignment chapter includes at least one visual example of the genre that the chapter focuses on, and many of the reference chapters include Visual Tutorials featuring photographs and illustrations that provide students with step-by-step instructions for challenging topics, such as using the Web to browse for ideas. This emphasis on visuals, media, and design helps students develop visual literacy they can use in their own work. Chapter 13 covers e-mail; Chapter 18 addresses presentation software; Chapter 38 covers spelling and grammar checkers; and Chapters 41 and 43 cover finding, evaluating, and using print and electronic resources for research.
Knowledge of Conventions	
Learn common formats for different kinds of texts.	Each assignment chapter in the Guide covers a format specific to the genre covered there; see sections "Choosing a Style and Design" in the Part 1 chapters and "Getting the Details Right" in the Part 2 chapters. Sample e-mails, business letters, résumés, and lab reports all appear in Part 2; Chapters 49 and 50 include sample MLA and APA research paper pages. Chapter 51 covers general design principles; Chapter 52 addresses understanding and using images, and Chapter 53 focuses on tables, graphs, and infographics.

Desired Student Outcomes	Relevant Features of *How to Write Anything*
Knowledge of Conventions (*continued*)	
Develop knowledge of genre conventions ranging from structure and paragraphing to tone and mechanics.	Each assignment chapter in Part 1 presents key features of a specific genre, both in the introductory sections and via annotated models. Structure, paragraphing, tone, and mechanics are addressed in these chapters and in targeted cross-references integrated throughout the Guide. These cross-references neatly link the assignment chapters to the reference chapters, helping students choose their own best path through the material. Structure and paragraphing, for example, are covered in Part 4, "Shaping and Drafting"; tone is covered in Part 5, "Style"; and mechanics in Part 9, "Common Errors."
Control such surface features as syntax, grammar, punctuation, and spelling.	Chapters 38 and 39 provide editing and proofreading advice. Part 9, "Common Errors," includes chapters on grammar, punctuation, and mechanics. Targeted cross-references throughout the text send students to these chapters as needed.
Composing in Electronic Environments	
Use electronic environments for drafting, reviewing, revising, editing, and sharing texts.	Chapters 51 and 52 focus on digital media, including blogs, Web sites, wikis, podcasts, videos, and remixes. Chapter 13 covers e-mails; Chapter 18 covers presentation software, and Chapters 38 and 39 address word-processing programs.
Locate, evaluate, organize, and use research material collected from electronic sources, including scholarly library databases, other official databases (e.g., federal government databases), and informal electronic networks and Internet sources.	Part 7, "Research and Sources," includes thorough coverage of finding and using online sources in Chapters 40, 41, 43, and 48. Chapters 49 and 50 provide instruction and models for documenting online sources in both MLA and APA formats. Visual Tutorials also address these tasks; see How to Cite from a Web Site in MLA (pp. 526–27) and in APA (pp. 556–57) and How to Cite from a Database in MLA (pp. 528–29) and in APA (pp. 558–59).
Understand and exploit the differences in the rhetorical strategies and in the affordances available for both print and electronic composing processes and texts.	The text and e-book include a wide range of print and multimodal genres, from essays and scholarly articles to photographs, infographics, Web sites, and audio and video presentations. Rhetorical choices that students make in each genre are covered in the Guide chapters and appear in discussions of the writing context and in abundant models in the book.

Contents

2   Reports   44

3 | **Arguments** 72

4   Evaluations   106

6   Proposals   176

7   **Literary Analyses**   206

8   Rhetorical Analyses   250

10   **Position Papers**   290

11   **Annotated Bibliographies**   296

reference

guide

Genres

Need a form that you don't see here? Try "Special Assignments," p. 282.

How to start
- Need a **topic**? See page 10.
- Need to choose the right **details**? See page 14.
- Need to **organize the events** in your story? See page 16.

1 Narratives

chronicle
events in
people's lives

Chances are you've shared bits and pieces of your life story in writing many times. In doing so, you've written personal narratives. *Personal* does not necessarily mean that writers of personal narratives are always baring their souls. Instead, it implies that they are telling stories from a unique perspective, providing details only they could know and insights only they could have.

REFLECTION
For a scholarship application, you include a *personal reflection*, explaining how a summer job in a drugstore made you first consider a career in pharmacy.

LITERACY NARRATIVE
To work at the campus writing center, you must prepare a *literacy narrative* detailing your own experiences with writing and language.

STUDENT MEMOIR
You direct your grandparents to a community group that is collecting *memoirs* from local citizens so that they can describe their experiences as immigrants.

GRAPHIC NARRATIVE
You want more people to think about bicycling to work, so you create a *visual narrative* about your own experiences as an urban cyclist, posting both photographs and videos on a blog.

DECIDING TO WRITE A NARRATIVE   Narratives may describe almost any human activity that writers want to share with readers: school, family, work experiences, personal tragedies, travel, sports, growing up, relationships, and so on. Stories can be told in words or through other media, including photographs, film, songs, cartoons, and more. ○ Expect a narrative you write to do the following.

Tell a story.   In a narrative, something usually happens. Maybe all you do in the piece is reflect on a single moment when something peculiar caught your attention. Or your story could follow a simple sequence of events—the classic road-trip script. Or you might spin a tale complicated enough to seem like an actual plot, with a connected beginning, middle, and end. In every case, though, you need to select specific events that serve your purpose in writing, whatever it may be. Otherwise you're just rambling.

StoryCorps Story-Booth   StoryCorps is a national project of Sound Portraits Productions meant to inspire people to record one another's stories in sound. And, yes, there's an iPhone app.

(Photo of the StoryCorps Story-Booth, courtesy of StoryCorps. Learn more at www.storycorps.net.)

choose a genre
p. 390

Make a point — usually. Your point may depend on your specific reason for writing a narrative. If your insurance agent asks about your recent auto wreck, she probably just wants to know who hit whom and how you are involved in the incident. But most narratives will be less cut-and-dry and more reflective, enabling you to connect with audiences more subtly — to amuse, enlighten, and, perhaps, even to change them. ○ Some narratives are therapeutic too, enabling you to confront personal issues or to get a weight off your chest.

Observe details closely. What makes a narrative memorable and brings it to life are its details — the colors, shapes, textures, sounds, and smells that you share with readers through language or other media. Those physical impressions go a long way toward convincing people that a story is credible and honest. They prove that you were close enough to an experience to have an insider's perspective. So share your sensory reactions with readers, conveying specific information as events unfurl. But don't fall back on clichés to make your points. Give readers evidence that the story really belongs to you.

Sara Smith, a college student, keeps a journal both to explore ideas that are important to her and so she'll have a reservoir of events and memories for writing assignments. Does this journal entry suggest any paper topics to you?

> My Dad friended me last night. How lame is that? Last month he didn't know how to send an e-mail and all of a sudden he has his own page on Facebook. It's really sad, it's worse than sad, it's pathetic. He's lonely. Has no friends. So he puts up a picture of us — a father and his very happy daughter, both with the Albert Einstein crazy hair except his is grey and mine is brown, both beaming — to show people what a good family guy he is. There should be an age limit or something, for Facebook.

develop a statement
p. 393

Reflection

Mark Edmundson, a professor of English at the University of Virginia, tells a lengthy tale about an odd job he had after graduating from college as a lesson to students today not to rush into their professional careers without first experiencing the world. The narrative is key to his argument—it engages readers with details about working on a concert for the band Pink Floyd, but then leads up to a splendid climax. The article may seem like a story, but it is tightly organized to make a point.

The Pink Floyd Night School

Mark Edmundson

May 2, 2010

"So, what are you doing after graduation?"

In the spring of my last year in college I posed that question to at least a dozen fellow graduates-to-be at my little out-of-the-way school in Vermont. The answers they gave me were satisfying in the extreme: not very much, just kick back, hang out, look things over, take it slow. It was 1974. That's what you were supposed to say.

My classmates weren't, strictly speaking, telling the truth. They were, one might even say, lying outrageously. By graduation day, it was clear that most of my contemporaries would be trotting off to law school and graduate school and to cool and unusual internships in New York and San Francisco.

But I did take it slow. After graduation, I spent five years wandering around doing nothing—or getting as close to it as I could manage. I was a cab driver, an obsessed moviegoer, a wanderer in the mountains of Colorado, a teacher at a crazy grand hippie school in Vermont, the manager of a movie house (who didn't do much managing), a crewman on a ship and a doorman at a disco.

The most memorable job of all, though, was a gig on the stage crew for a rock production company in Jersey City. We did our shows at Roosevelt Stadium, a grungy behemoth that could hold 60,000, counting seats on the grass. I humped amps out of the trucks and onto the stage; six or so hours later I humped them back. I did it for the Grateful Dead and Alice Cooper and the Allman Brothers and Crosby, Stills & Nash on

This opening question will be repeated again later in the narrative, giving a tight structure to the story.

The paragraph is full of authentic details about the 1970s. Note the word choices too: gig, grungy, humped.

the night that Richard Nixon resigned. But the most memorable night of that most memorable job was the night of Pink Floyd.

Pink Floyd demanded a certain quality of sound. They wanted their amps stacked high, not just on stage, where they were so broad and tall and forbidding that they looked like a barricade in the Paris Commune. They also wanted amp clusters at three highly elevated points around the stadium, and I spent the morning lugging huge blocks of wood and circuitry up and up and up the stairs of the decayed old bowl.

There was one other assignment: a parachute-like white silken canopy roof that Pink Floyd required over the stage. It took about six hours to get the thing up and in position. We were told that this was the first use of the canopy and Pink's guys were unsteady. They had some blueprints, but those turned out not to be of much use. Eventually the roof did rise and inflate, with American know-how applied. Such know-how involved a lot of spontaneous knot-tying and strategic rope tangling.

Pink Floyd went on at about 10 that night and the amp clusters that we'd expended all that servile sweat to build didn't work—people had sat on them, kicked them or cut the cords. So Pink made its noise, the towers stayed mute, the mob flicked on lighters at the end and then we spent three hours breaking the amps down and loading the truck. We refused to go after the speakers all the way up the stadium steps and, after some sharp words, Pink's guys had to scramble up and retrieve them.

There was, for the record, almost always tension between the roadies and the stage crew. One time, at a show by (if memory serves) Queen, their five roadies got into a brawl with a dozen of our stage crew guys; then the house security, mostly Jersey bikers and black-belt karate devotees, heard the noise and jumped in. The roadies held on for a while, but finally they saw it was a lost cause. One of them grabbed a case of champagne from the truck cab and opened a bottle and passed it around—all became drunk and happy. Pink's road manager wanted the inflatable canopy brought down gently, then folded and packed securely in its wooden boxes. The problem was that the thing was full of helium and no one knew where the release valve was; we'd also secured it to the stage with so many knots of such foolish intricacy that their disentanglement would have given a gang of sailors pause. Everyone was tired. Those once intoxicated were no longer. It was 4 a.m. and time to go home.

Edmundson must digress here to explain the tensions between roadies and stage crews so the key incident in his story makes sense.

An hour went into concocting strategies to get the floating billowy roof down. It became a regular seminar. Then came Jim — Jimbo — our crew chief, who looked like a good-natured Viking captain and who defended the integrity of his stage crew at every turn, even going so far as to have screamed at Stevie Nicks, who was yelling at me for having dropped a guitar case, that he was the only one who had the right to holler at Edmundson. Faced with the Pink Floyd roof crisis, Jimbo did what he always could be counted on to do in critical circumstances, which is to say, he did something.

Jimbo walked softly to a corner of the stage, reached into his pocket, removed a buck knife and with it began to saw one of the ropes attaching the holy celestial roof to the earth. Three or four of us, his minions, did the same. "Hey, what are you doing?" wailed Pink's head roadie. "I'll smash your —" Only then did he realize that Jimbo had a knife in his hand, and that some of the rest of us did, too. In the space of a few minutes, we sawed through the ropes.

There came a great sighing noise as the last thick cord broke apart. For a moment there was nothing; for another moment, more of the same.

Then the canopy rose into the air and began to float away, like a gorgeous cloud, white and soft. The sun at that moment burst above the horizon and the silk bloomed into a soft crimson tinge. Jimbo started to laugh his big bear-bellied laugh. We all joined. Even Pink's guys did. We were like little kids on the last day of school. We stood on the naked stage, watching the silk roof go up and out, wafting over the Atlantic. Some of us waved.

"So, what are you doing after graduation?" Thirty-five years later, a college teacher, I ask my students the old question. They aren't inclined to dissimulate now. The culture is on their side when they tell me about law school and med school and higher degrees in journalism and business; or when they talk about a research grant in China or a well-paying gig teaching English in Japan.

I'm impressed, sure, but I'm worried about them too. Aren't they deciding too soon? Shouldn't they hang out a little, learn to take it slow? I can't help it. I flash on that canopy of white silk floating out into the void. I can see it as though it were still there. I want to point up to it. I'd like for my students to see it, too.

The details here about Jimbo keep readers amused and engaged by the story.

Here's the one major point of the story, the reason Edmundson has offered his personal experience to readers.

The opening question is repeated, but note the difference now in the students' answers.

Exploring purpose and topic

▶ topic

When writing a narrative on your own, you usually don't have to search for a topic. You already know what to record in a journal or diary, or what portion of your life to share in e-mails with friends. You understand your audience well enough, too, to tailor your story to the people likely to read it.

Assigned to write a narrative in school, however, you face different choices. Typically, such an assignment asks you to describe an event that has changed or shaped you. Or perhaps an instructor requests a story that explores an aspect of your personality or reveals something about the communities to which you belong. But when no topic ideas present themselves, consider the following strategies.

For example, this picture of Niki de Saint Phalle's sculpture *Sun God* got one student writing about her very colorful trip to San Diego, California.

Brainstorm, freewrite, build lists, and use memory prompts to find a topic for a narrative. It might help, for example, to scroll through some old photographs on your computer or even to pick up your yearbook. Talk with others, too, about their choices of subjects or share ideas on a class Web site. Trading ideas might jog your own memory about an incident or moment worth retelling.

Choose a manageable subject. You may be tempted to write about life-changing events so dramatic that they can seem clichéd: deaths, graduations, car wrecks, winning hits, or first love. But understand that to make such topics work, you have to make them fresh for readers who've likely undergone similar experiences—or seen the movie. If you find an angle on such familiar events that belongs specifically to you and can express it originally, you might take the risk. ○

Alternatively, you can narrate a slice of life rather than the whole side of beef—your toast at a wedding rather than the three-hour reception, a single encounter on a road trip rather than the entire cross-country adventure, or the scariest part of the night you were home alone when the power went out, rather than a minute-by-minute description. Most big adventures contain within them dozens of more manageable tales.

get an idea
p. 356

Understanding your audience

People like to read other people's stories, so the audiences for narratives are large, diverse, and receptive. (Even many diarists secretly hope that someone someday will find and read the confidential story of their lives.) Most of these eager readers probably expect a narrative to make some point or reveal an insight. Typically, they hope to be moved by the piece, to learn something from it, or perhaps to be amused by it.

You can capitalize on those expectations, using stories to introduce ideas that readers might be less eager to entertain if presented more formally. Here's a writer for *Automobile* magazine using a brief anecdote to introduce a piece about electric cars:

> I took two semesters of physics in college. The first concerned the physical world – objects smashing into one another, mass, momentum – concepts that made intuitive sense. I got a B. The second focused on electromagnetic fields, which are invisible and have something to do with calculus. I got a D+. So it's perhaps understandable that I'm a bit apprehensive about the brave new world of the electric car.
>
> – Ezra Dyer, "On the Juice," July 2010

Sometimes, however, your audience is already attuned to a subject. For instance, people within well-defined social, political, ethnic, or religious groups are often eager to read and share their life experiences. Women and members of minority groups have used such narratives to document the adversities they face or to affirm their solidarity. Similarly, members of religious groups recall what it was like to grow up Jewish or Catholic or Baptist—and their readers appreciate when a story hits a familiar note. The best of these personal narratives, naturally, attract readers from outside the target audience too. ○

Of course, you might decide that the target audience of a narrative is ultimately yourself: You write about personal experiences to understand them. Even then, be demanding. Think about how your story might sound ten or twenty years from now. Whatever the audience, you have choices to make.

respect your readers
p. 440

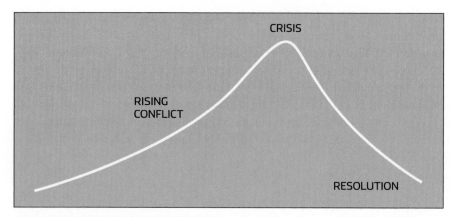

A Classic Narrative Arc   You'll need to decide where to start your story and where to stop. The plan shown in this illustration is effective because the action unfolds in a way that meets audience expectations.

Select events that will keep readers engaged.   Consider what parts of your topic will matter to readers. Which events represent high points in the action or moments that could not logically be omitted? Select those and consider cutting the others. Build toward a few major events in the story that support one or two key themes—in Edmundson's narrative (see p. 7) it's the canopy floating away.

Pace the story effectively.   Readers do want the story to move ahead, but not always at the same speed. Early on, they may want to learn about the characters involved in the action or to be introduced to the setting. You can slow the narrative to fill in these details and also to set up expectations for what will follow. For instance, if a person plays a role later in the story, introduce him or her briefly in the early paragraphs. If a cat matters, introduce the cat. But don't dwell on incidentals: Keep the story moving.

Tailor your writing to your intended readers.   An informal story written for peers may need brisk action as well as slang and dialogue to sound convincing—though you shouldn't use rough language for cheap effects. In a narrative written for an academic audience, you might slow the pace and use more neutral language. But don't be too cautious. You still want the story to have enough texture to make your experiences seem authentic.

For instance, when writing a personal statement for an application to an academic program, keep a tight rein on the way you present yourself. O Here, for example, is a serious anecdote offered in an application to graduate school. You could easily imagine it told much more comically to friends.

> During my third year of Russian, I auditioned for the role of the evil stepsister Anna in a stage production of *Zolushka*. Although I welcomed the chance to act, I was terrified because I could not pronounce a Russian *r*. I had tried but was only able to produce an embarrassing sputter. Leading up to the play, I practiced daily with my professor, repeating "ryba" with a pencil in my mouth. When the play opened, I was able to say "*Kakoe urodstvo!*" with confidence. This experience gave me tremendous pride, because through it I discovered the power to isolate a problem, seek the necessary help, and ultimately solve it. I want to pass this power along to others by becoming a Russian language instructor.
>
> —Melissa Miller

refine your tone
p. 432

Finding and developing materials

▶ develop details

Photographs such as this one taken at a Fourth of July parade may recall not only the scene but also the moment the photo was taken, who was there, and so on.

When you write about an event soon after it occurs—for instance, an accident report for an insurance claim—you might have the facts fresh in your mind. Yet even in such cases, evidence helps back up your recollections. That's why insurance companies encourage drivers to carry a disposable camera in their cars in case they have a collision. The photo freezes details that human memory, especially under pressure, could ignore or forget. Needless to say, when writing about events in the more distant past, other aids to memory will help.

Consult documents.   A journal, if you keep one, provides a handy record for personal narratives such as a job history or family chronicle. Even a daily planner or electronic calendar might hold the necessary facts to reconstruct a series of events: Just knowing when important meetings occurred may refresh your memory.

Consult images.   Photographs and videos provide material for personal narratives of all sorts. Not only do they document people and places, but they may also generate ideas, calling to mind far more than just what appears in the images. In writing a personal narrative, such prompts may stimulate your recall of past events and, just as important, the feelings those events generated. Visual images also remind you of physical details—shapes, colors, and textures—that can add authenticity to a narrative and assure readers you're a sharp observer.

Trust your experiences.   In gathering material for a narrative (or looking for a subject), you might doubt your credentials: "What have I done worth writing about"? ○ Most people underestimate the quality of their own experience. First-year college students, for example, are usually knowl-edgeable about high school or certain kinds of music or working minimum-wage jobs or dealing with difficult parents. You don't have to be an expert to observe life or have something to say about it.

Here's humorist David Sedaris—who has made a career writing about his very middle-class life from his unique personal perspective—describing the insecurity of many writers:

> When I was teaching—I taught for a while—my students would write as if they were raised by wolves. Or raised on the streets. They were middle-class kids and they were ashamed of their background. They felt like unless they grew up in poverty, they had nothing to write about. Which was interesting because I had always thought that poor people were the ones who were ashamed. But it's not. It's middle-class people who are ashamed of their lives. And it doesn't really matter what your life was like, you can write about anything. It's just the writing of it that is the challenge. I felt sorry for these kids, that they thought that their whole past was absolutely worthless because it was less than remarkable.
>
> —David Sedaris, interviewed in *January Magazine*, June 2000

Your Turn   Where might you search for ideas if you were writing a tale about some slice of your life? Obviously, relatives and friends might be good resources, as would photo albums and memory books. But how about some off-the-wall resources—your list of bookmarked Web sites, for example, or a hometown map, or maybe your clothes closet? List other offbeat memory prompts and compare your ideas with those your classmates suggest.

find a topic
p. 356

Creating a structure

▶ organize events

Don't be intimidated by the idea of organizing a narrative. ○ You know a great deal about narrative structure from watching films or TV. All the complex plot devices you see in dramas or comedies—from foreshadowing to flashback—can be adapted to narratives you create in prose. But you need to plan ahead, know how many words or pages you have to tell your story, and then be sure you connect your incidents with effective transitional words and phrases.

Consider a simple sequence.   In a simple sequence, one event follows another chronologically. This structure has its complications, but it's a natural choice for narrative. Journals and diaries probably have the simplest sequential structures, with writers just recording one event after another without connecting them by anything much more than a date.

> **First event**
> **Next event**
> **Next event**
> **Final event**

Build toward a climax.   Narratives become more complex if you want to present a set of incidents that lead to a *climax* or an *epiphany*. A climax is the moment when the action of a story peaks, takes an important turn, or is resolved. An epiphany is a moment of revelation when a writer or character suddenly sees events in a new light.

> **First event**
> **Next event**
> **Next event**
>
> **Climax and/or epiphany**
>
> **Final event**

connect ideas
p. 416

Narratives can have both structural features and often do—it's only logical that a major event in life would trigger heightened awareness or new understanding. In creating a structure for this kind of narrative, you can begin by deciding what that important event will be and then choosing other elements and incidents that lead up to or explain it. Omit everything not connected to that moment from the story. ○

Similarly, when you want a narrative to make a specific point, include only events and incidents that reinforce your theme, directly or indirectly. Delete any actions that don't contribute to that point, however much you love them. Or refocus your narrative on a moment that you do love.

If every picture tells a story, what narrative does this image suggest? Consider the missing windmill blade, the worker's posture, the quiet sky, and any other details that seem important.

revise and edit
p. 452

Choosing a style and design

Narratives are usually written in middle or low styles. That's because both styles nicely mimic the human voice through devices such as contractions and colloquialisms. Both styles are also comfortable with *I*, the point of view of many stories. A middle style may be safe for reaching academic or professional audiences. But a low style, dipping into slang and unconventional speech, can more accurately capture many moments in life and thus feel more authentic. It's your choice.

Style is important because narratives get their energy and textures from sentence structures and vocabulary choices. In general, narratives require tight but expressive language—*tight* to keep the action moving, *expressive* to capture the gist of events. In a first draft, run with your ideas and don't do much editing. Flesh out the skeleton as you have designed it and then go back to see if the story works technically: Characters should be introduced and developed, locations identified and colored, events clearly explained and sequenced, key points made memorably and emphatically. You'll likely need several drafts to get these major items into shape.

Then look at your language and allow plenty of time for it. Begin with Chapter 37, "Vigorous, Clear, Economical Style." When the language is right, your readers get the impression that you have observed events closely. Here are some options for your narrative.

Don't hesitate to use first person—*I*.   Most personal narratives are about the writer, so first-person pronouns are used without apology. ○ (Third-person perspective tends to be used by essayists and humorists.)

A narrative often must take readers where the *I* has been, and using the first-person pronoun helps make writing authentic. Consider online journalist Michael Yon's explanation of why he reported on the Iraq War using *I* rather than a more objective third-person perspective:

> I write in first person because I am actually there at the events I write about. When I write about the bombs exploding, or the smell of blood, or the bullets snapping by, and I say *I*, it's because I was there. Yesterday a sniper shot at us, and seven of my neighbors were injured by a large bomb. These are my neighbors. These are soldiers. . . . I feel the fire from the explosions, and am lucky, very lucky, still to be alive. Everything here is first person.
>
> – Glenn Reynolds, *An Army of Davids*

define your style
p. 432

Use figures of speech such as similes, metaphors, and analogies to make memorable comparisons.   *Similes* make comparisons by using *like* or *as*: *He used his camera* like *a rifle*. *Metaphors* drop the *like* or *as* to gain even more power: *His camera was a rifle aimed at enemies*. An *analogy* extends the comparison: *His camera became a rifle aimed at his imaginary enemies, their private lives in his crosshairs*.

People use comparisons eagerly. Some are so common they've been reduced to invisible clichés: *hit me like a ton of bricks; dumb as an ox; clear as a bell*. You want to use similes and metaphors in your narratives that are fresher than these and yet not contrived or strained. Here's science writer Michael Chorost effortlessly deploying both a metaphor (*spins up*) and a simile (*like riding a roller coaster*) to describe what he experiences as he awaits surgery.

> I can feel the bustle and clatter around me as the surgical team spins up to take-off speed. It is like riding a roller coaster upward to the first great plunge, strapped in and committed.
>
> *— Rebuilt: How Becoming Part Computer Made Me More Human*

In choosing verbs, favor active rather than passive voice.   Active verbs propel the action (*Estela signed the petition*), while passive verbs slow it down by an unneeded word or two (*The petition was signed by Estela*). ◯

Since narratives are all about movement, build sentences around strong and unpretentious verbs. Edit until you get down to the bone of the action and produce sentences as effortless as these from Joseph Epstein, describing the pleasures of catching plagiarists. ◯ Verbs are highlighted in this passage; you'll find only one passive verb (*is followed*) in the mix.

> In thirty years of teaching university students I never encountered a case of plagiarism, or even one that I suspected. Teachers I've known who have caught students in this sad act report that the capture gives one an odd sense of power. The power derives from the authority that resides behind the word *gotcha*. This is followed by that awful moment — a veritable sadist's Mardi Gras — when one calls the student into one's office and points out the odd coincidence that he seems to have written about existentialism in precisely the same words Jean-Paul Sartre used fifty-two years earlier.
>
> *— "Plagiary, It's Crawling All Over Me,"* Weekly Standard, *March 6, 2006*

> Need help seeing the big picture? See "How to Revise Your Work" on pp. 456–57.

improve your sentences
p. 444

avoid plagiarism
p. 497

The difference between the almost right word and the right word is really a large matter—it's the difference between the lightning bug and the lightning.

—Mark Twain

Use powerful and precise modifiers. In most cases, one strong word is better than several weaker ones (*freezing* rather than *very cold; doltish* rather than *not very bright*). Done right, proper modifiers can even make you hungry.

> My friend Barbara got the final stretch of the trip, a southwestern route of burritos and more burritos: with and without rice, with and without sour cream, planned burritos and serendipitous burritos.
>
> We pulled off the highway near Odessa, Texas, to hunt down a Taco Villa and, across the street, espied something called JumBurrito, an even smaller Texas chain. Taco Villa's grilled chicken burrito had a profusion of chicken that indeed tasted grilled, while JumBurrito's combination burrito redeemed dull beef with vibrant avocado.
>
> Neither approximated the majesty of the burrito I loved most, which I ate in Dallas, at a Taco Cabana. A great burrito is a balancing act, and the proportions of ground beef, beans, sour cream, and diced tomatoes in Taco Cabana's plump, heavy Burrito Ultimo (three Wet Naps) were spot on.
>
> —Frank Bruni, "Life in the Fast-Food Lane," *New York Times*, May 24, 2006

Use dialogue to propel the narrative and to give life to your characters. What people say and how they say it can reveal a great deal about them without much commentary from you. But be sure the words your characters speak sound natural: *No* dialogue is better than awkward dialogue. Dialogue ordinarily requires quotation marks and new paragraphs for each change of speaker. But keep the tags simple: You don't have to vary much from *he said* or *she said*.

> "My dear Mr. Bennet," said his lady to him one day, "have you heard that Netherfield Park is let at last?"
>
> Mr. Bennet replied that he had not. "But it is," returned she; "for Mrs. Long has just been here, and she told me all about it."
>
> Mr. Bennet made no answer.
>
> "Do not you want to know who has taken it?" cried his wife, impatiently.
>
> "*You* want to tell me, and I have no objection to hearing it." This was invitation enough.
>
> —Jane Austen, *Pride and Prejudice*

> **Your Turn** Good dialogue is hard to write. So practice. Write a one-page story mostly in dialogue, like the brief excerpt from *Pride and Prejudice*. Tell readers what you must about your characters, but let most of the action occur within their words. Then read your story aloud over and over and revise it until the dialogue sounds authentic. Get feedback from your classmates, and give them suggestions on their stories as well.

Develop major characters through language and action. Search for the precise adjectives and adverbs to describe your characters' looks (*cheery, greedily*) and manners (*tight, conceitedly, smarmy*) or, even better, have them reveal their natures by their actions (*glancing in every mirror; ignoring the staff to fawn over the bigwigs*). In fact, you'll probably need to do both. Here's how one writer describes a classmate (ouch!) with whom she is partnered on a group project:

> If you are using dialogue—say it aloud as you write it. Only then will it have the sound of speech.

—John Steinbeck

> Jane dragged me to her dorm one weekend to help her crunch the numbers. Her phone started ringing, but she told me to ignore it. The answering machine clicked on as a whiny, southern voice pleaded, "Jane, Honey, where *are* yew? Daddy and I have been trying to reach you for three days, but you haven't answered your dorm or cell phones. Please, call us so we'll know that you're okay. We love you very much, Sweetie."
> Jane's annoyance rivaled the desperation in her mother's voice. She had always claimed to love her family, but she barely batted an eye at her mom's concern for her well-being. "I don't have time for her right now," Jane stated coldly as she continued typing.
>
> —Bettina Ramon, "Ambition Incarnate"

Develop the setting to set the context and mood. Show readers where and when events are occurring if the setting makes a difference—and that will be most of the time. Location (Times Square; dusty street in Gallup, New Mexico; your bedroom), as well as climate and time of day (cool dawn, exotic dusk, broiling afternoon), will help readers get a fix on the story. But don't churn out paragraphs of description ○ just for their own sake; readers will skate right over them.

develop a draft
p. 398

Use images to tell a story.   Consider whether photographs attached to the narrative might help readers grasp the setting and situation. Or use images simply to brighten your narrative or to illustrate a sequence of events. An illustrated timeline is a simple form of this kind of narrative, as are scrapbooks or high school yearbooks. More complex stories about your life or community can be told by combining your words and pictures in photo-essays or other media environments. ◯

Don't, however, use images as an excuse to avoid descriptive writing; rather, consider how they complement your text, and so may have a legitimate place in your story.

Fisherman with His Catch, a 32-inch, 18-pound Striped Bass   Note how the photograph conveys far more than the statistics alone would.

think visually
p. 592

Examining models

Such a piece typically narrates the processes by which a person learns to read or write or acquires an intellectual skill or ability. In "Strange Tools," author Richard Rodriguez explains how he developed his habits of reading. The selection is from *Hunger of Memory* (1981), in which Rodriguez explains how his life has followed the pattern of "the scholarship boy," described by Richard Hoggart as a youth from a lower-class background whose pursuit of education separates him from his community.

Strange Tools

RICHARD RODRIGUEZ

Sets the scene.

From an early age I knew that my mother and father could read and write both Spanish and English. I had observed my father making his way through what, I now suppose, must have been income tax forms. On other occasions I waited apprehensively while my mother read onion-paper letters airmailed from Mexico with news of a relative's illness or death. For both my parents, however, reading was something done out of necessity and as quickly as possible. Never did I see either of them read an entire book. Nor did I see them read for pleasure. Their reading consisted of work manuals, prayer books, newspapers, recipes.

Richard Hoggart imagines how, at home,

> . . . [The scholarship boy] sees strewn around, and reads regularly himself, magazines which are never mentioned at school, which seem not to belong to the world to which the school introduces him; at school he hears about and reads books never mentioned at home. When he brings those books into the house they do not take their place with other books which the family are reading, for often there are none or almost none; his books look, rather, like strange tools.

Hoggart's "scholarship boy" is a key theme in Rodriguez's work.

In our house each school year would begin with my mother's careful instruction: "Don't write in your books so we can sell them at the end of

23

the year." The remark was echoed in public by my teachers, but only in part: "Boys and girls, don't write in your books. You must learn to treat them with great care and respect."

OPEN THE DOORS OF YOUR MIND WITH BOOKS, read the red and white poster over the nun's desk in early September. It soon was apparent to me that reading was the classroom's central activity. Each course had its own book. And the information gathered from a book was unquestioned. READ TO LEARN, the sign on the wall advised in December. I privately wondered: What was the connection between reading and learning? Did one learn something only by reading it? Was an idea only an idea if it could be written down? In June, CONSIDER BOOKS YOUR BEST FRIENDS. Friends? Reading was, at best, only a chore. I needed to look up whole paragraphs of words in a dictionary. Lines of type were dizzying, the eye having to move slowly across the page, then down, and across. . . .The sentences of the first books I read were coolly impersonal. Toned hard. What most bothered me, however, was the isolation reading required. To console myself for the loneliness I'd feel when I read, I tried reading in a very soft voice. Until: "Who is doing all that talking to his neighbor?" Shortly after, remedial reading classes were arranged for me with a very old nun.

At the end of each school day, for nearly six months, I would meet with her in the tiny room that served as the school's library but was actually only a storeroom for used textbooks and a vast collection of *National Geographics*. Everything about our sessions pleased me: the smallness of the room; the noise of the janitor's broom hitting the edge of the long hallway outside the door; the green of the sun, lighting the wall; and the old woman's face blurred white with a beard. Most of the time we took turns. I began with my elementary text. Sentences of astonishing simplicity seemed to me lifeless and drab: "The boys ran from the rain. . . . She wanted to sing. . . . The kite rose in the blue." Then the old nun would read from her favorite books, usually biographies of early American presidents. Playfully she ran through complex sentences, calling the words alive with her voice, making it seem that the author somehow was

---

Narrates early experiences as a reader.

Details give Rodriguez's experiences impact.

speaking directly to me. I smiled just to listen to her. I sat there and sensed for the very first time some possibility of fellowship between a reader and a writer, a communication, never *intimate* like that I heard spoken words at home convey, but one nonetheless *personal*.

One day the nun concluded a session by asking me why I was so reluctant to read by myself. I tried to explain; said something about the way written words made me feel all alone—almost, I wanted to add but didn't, as when I spoke to myself in a room just emptied of furniture. She studied my face as I spoke; she seemed to be watching more than listening. In an uneventful voice she replied that I had nothing to fear. Didn't I realize that reading would open up whole new worlds? A book could open doors for me. It could introduce me to people and show me places I never imagined existed. She gestured toward the bookshelves. (Bare-breasted African women danced, and the shiny hubcaps of automobiles on the back covers of the *Geographic* gleamed in my mind.) I listened with respect. But her words were not very influential. I was thinking then of another consequence of literacy, one I was too shy to admit but nonetheless trusted. Books were going to make me "educated." *That* confidence enabled me, several months later, to overcome my fear of the silence.

In fourth grade I embarked upon a grandiose reading program. "Give me the names of important books," I would say to startled teachers. They soon found out that I had in mind "adult books." I ignored their suggestion of anything I suspected was written for children. (Not until I was in college, as a result, did I read *Huckleberry Finn* or *Alice's Adventures in Wonderland*.) Instead, I read *The Scarlet Letter* and Franklin's *Autobiography*. And whatever I read I read for extra credit. Each time I finished a book, I reported the achievement to a teacher and basked in the praise my effort earned. Despite my best efforts, however, there seemed to be more and more books I needed to read. At the library I would literally tremble as I came upon whole shelves of books I hadn't read. So I read and I read and I read: *Great Expectations*; all the short stories of Kipling; *The Babe Ruth Story*; the entire first volume of the

Most action occurs in Rodriguez's thoughts.

Encyclopaedia Britannica (A–ANSTEY); the *Iliad; Moby-Dick; Gone with the Wind; The Good Earth; Remond; Forever Amber; The Lives of the Saints; Crime and Punishment; The Pearl.* . . . Librarians who initially frowned when I checked out the maximum ten books at a time started saving books they thought I might like. Teachers would say to the rest of the class, "I only wish the rest of you took reading as seriously as Richard obviously does."

But at home I would hear my mother wondering, "What do you see in your books?" (Was reading a hobby like her knitting? Was so much reading even healthy for a boy? Was it the sign of "brains"? Or was it just a convenient excuse for not helping around the house on Saturday mornings?) Always, "What do you see . . . ?"

Growing skill as a reader causes conflict for Rodriguez.

What *did* I see in my books? I had the idea that they were crucial for my academic success, though I couldn't have said exactly how or why. In the sixth grade I simply concluded that what gave a book its value was some major idea or theme it contained. If that core essence could be mined and memorized, I would become learned like my teachers. I decided to record in a notebook the themes of the books that I read. After reading *Robinson Crusoe*, I wrote that its theme was "the value of learning to live by oneself." When I completed *Wuthering Heights,* I noted the danger of "letting emotions get out of control." Rereading these brief moralistic appraisals usually left me disheartened. I couldn't believe that they were really the source of reading's value. But for many more years, they constituted the only means I had of describing to myself the educational value of books.

Getting older, Rodriguez examines why he reads.

In spite of my earnestness, I found reading a pleasurable activity. I came to enjoy the lonely good company of books. Early on weekday mornings, I'd read in my bed. I'd feel a mysterious comfort then, reading in the dawn quiet—the bluegray silence interrupted by the occasional churning of the refrigerator motor a few rooms away or the more distant sound of a city bus beginning its run. On weekends I'd go to the public library to read, surrounded by old men and women. Or, if the weather was fine, I would take my books to the park and read in the shade of a tree. A warm summer evening was my favorite reading time. Neighbors would leave for vacation and I would water their lawns. I would sit through the twilight on the front porches or in backyards, reading to the cool, whirling sounds of the sprinklers.

I also had favorite writers. But often those writers I enjoyed most I was least able to value. When I read William Saroyan's *The Human Comedy*, I was immediately pleased by the narrator's warmth and the charm of his story. But as quickly I became suspicious. A book so enjoyable to read couldn't be very "important." Another summer I determined to read all the novels of Dickens. Reading his fat novels, I loved the feeling I got—after the first hundred pages—of being at home in a fictional world where I knew the names of the characters and cared about what was going to happen to them. And it bothered me that I was forced away at the conclusion, when the fiction closed tight, like a fortune-teller's fist—the futures of all the major characters neatly resolved. I never knew how to take such feelings of a novel's meaning. Still, there were pleasures to sustain me after I'd finish my books. Carrying a volume back to the library, I would be pleased by its weight. I'd run my fingers along the edge of the pages and marvel at the breadth of my achievement. Around my room, growing stacks of paperback books reinforced my assurance.

I entered high school having read hundreds of books. My habit of reading made me a confident speaker and writer of English. Reading also enabled me to sense something of the shape, the major concerns, of Western thought. (I was able to say something about Dante and Descartes and Engels and James Baldwin in my high school term papers.) In these various ways, books brought me academic success as I hoped that they would. But I was not a good reader. Merely bookish, I lacked a point of view when I read. Rather, I read in order to acquire a point of view. I vacuumed books for epigrams, scraps of information, ideas, themes—anything to fill the hollow within me and make me feel educated. When one of my teachers suggested to his drowsy tenth-grade English class that a person could not have a "complicated idea" until he

Rodriguez concludes by raising doubts about the skills he has acquired.

had read at least two thousand books, I heard the remark without detecting either its irony or its very complicated truth. I merely determined to compile a list of all the books I had ever read. Harsh with myself, I included only once a title I might have read several times. (How, after all, could one read a book more than once?) And I included only those books over a hundred pages in length. (Could anything shorter be a book?)

There was yet another high school list I compiled. One day I came across a newspaper article about the retirement of an English professor at a nearby state college. The article was accompanied by a list of the "hundred most important books of Western Civilization." "More than anything else in my life," the professor told the reporter with finality, "these books have made me all that I am." That was the kind of remark I couldn't ignore. I clipped out the list and kept it for the several months it took me to read all of the titles. Most books, of course, I barely understood. While reading Plato's *Republic*, for instance, I needed to keep looking at the book jacket comments to remind myself what the text was about. Nevertheless, with the special patience and superstition of a scholarship boy, I looked at every word of the text. And by the time I reached the last word, relieved, I convinced myself that I had read *The Republic*. In a ceremony of great pride, I solemnly crossed Plato off my list.

STUDENT MEMOIR   In the following essay, Miles Pequeno uses a narrative about a chess match to describe a changing relationship with his father and preserve an important memory. The paper was written in response to an assignment in an upper-division college writing class.

Pequeno 1

Miles Pequeno

Professor Mitchell

English 102

May 12, 20--

Check. Mate?

"Checkmate! Right? You can't move him anywhere, right? I got you again!" I couldn't control my glee. For good measure, I even grabbed my rook, which stood next to his king, and gave him a posthumous beating. The deposed king tumbled from the round table and onto the hardwood floor with a thud. The sound of sure victory. Being eight, it was easy to get excited about chess. It gave me not only at least a few minutes of Dad's attention and approval, but the comfort of knowing I'd taste victory every time. Either Dad was letting me always win, or I was the prodigy he wanted me to be. I always liked to believe it was the latter.

The relationship I had with my father was always complicated. I loved him and he loved me; that much was understood. But his idea of fatherhood was a little unorthodox (or maybe too orthodox, I'm not sure which). We didn't play catch in the yard, but he did make flash cards to teach me my multiplication tables when I was still in kindergarten. He didn't take me to

Narrative opens with dialogue and action.

Uses particular details to explain relationship with father.

Pequeno 2

Astros games, but he made sure I knew lots of big words from the newspaper. We were close, but only on his terms.

Save for the ever-graying hair near his temples, he looks much the same now as he did when I was little: round belly, round face, and big brown eyes that pierced while they silently observed and inwardly critiqued. His black hair, coarse and thick, and day-or-two-old beard usually gave away his heritage. He came to our suburb of Houston from Mexico when he was a toddler, learned English watching Spider-Man cartoons, and has since spent his life catching up, constantly working at moving up in the world. Even more was expected of me, the extension of his hard work and dreams for the future. I had no idea at the time, but back when I was beating him at chess as a kid, I myself was a pawn. He was planning something.

Then a funny thing happened. After winning every game since age eight, the five-year winning streak ended. I lost. This time, Dad had decided to take off the training wheels. Just as he was thrust into the real world unceremoniously with my birth when he was but eighteen years old, I was forced to grow up a little early too. The message was clear: Nothing is being handed to you anymore, Son.

This abrupt lesson changed my outlook. I no longer wanted to make Dad proud; I wanted to equal or better him. I'd been conditioned to seek his attention and approval, and then the rug was pulled from beneath my feet. I awoke to the

Using first person, Pequeno draws on personal experience to describe and characterize his father.

Notice how a metaphor here (training wheels) blossoms into an analogy about growing up.

Pequeno 3

realization that it was now my job to prove that the student could become the teacher.

Provides
background
information
that is
important
later in story.

I spent time after school every day playing chess against the artificial intelligence of my little Windows 95 computer. I knew what problems I had to correct because Dad was sure to point them out in the days after forcing that first loss. I had trouble using my queen. Dad always either knocked her out early or made me too afraid to put her in play. The result was my king slaughtered time and time again as his bride, the queen, sat idle on the far side of the board.

Paragraph
sets the
physical scene
for climactic
chess match.

Our chess set was made of marble, with green and white hand-carved pieces sitting atop the thick, round board. Dad kept the set next to the TV and, most nights, we'd take it down from the entertainment center and put it on the coffee table in front of the sofa, where we sat side by side and played chess while halfway paying attention to the television. One night after Mom's spaghetti dinner, I casually walked into the living room to find Dad sitting sipping a Corona and watching the Rockets game. Hakeem Olajuwon was having a great night. Usually, if Dad was really into something on TV, we'd go our separate ways and maybe play later. This night, I picked up the remote control from the coffee table. Off.

First dialogue
since opening
signals rising
action.

"Let's play," I said resolutely. I grabbed the marble chess set, with all the pieces exactly where I had put them in anticipation of this game. The board seemed heavier than usual as I carried it to the coffee table. I sat down next to him

Pequeno 4

on the sofa and stared at the pieces, suddenly going blank. The bishops might as well have been knights. I froze as Dad asked me what color I wanted. Traditionally, this had been merely a formality. I'd always picked white before because I wanted to have the first move. That was the rule: *White moves first, green next.*

"Green."

Then it all came back to me. The certainty of my declaration surprised him. He furrowed his brows slightly and leaned back just enough to show good-natured condescension.

"You sure? That means I go first."

"I'm sure. Take white."

So he began his attack. He started off controlling one side of the board, slowly advancing. The knights led the charge, with the pawns waiting in the wings to form an impenetrable wall around the royal family, who remained in their little castle of two adjacent spaces.

Every move was made with painful precision. Now and then after my moves, he'd sigh and sink a little into the sofa. He'd furrow those big black brows, his eyes darting quickly from one side of the board to the other, thinking two or three moves ahead. Some of his mannerisms this time were completely new, like the hesitation of his hand as he'd reach for a piece and then jerk it back quickly, realizing that my strategy had shut more than a few doors for him.

"Combat" metaphor in next few paragraphs moves story forward.

Pequeno 5

Eventually I worked up the courage to thrust the queen into action. She moved with great trepidation at first, never attacking, merely sneaking down the board. In the meantime, Dad's advancing rooks and knights were taking out my line of pawns, which I'd foolishly put too far into play. Every risk either of us took was clearly calculated. Sometimes he'd mutter to himself, slowly realizing this game wasn't as usual.

Things were looking good. Even if I didn't win, I'd already won a victory by challenging him. But that wasn't what I had practiced for. It wasn't why I'd turned off the television, and it certainly wasn't why I was concentrating so hard on these white and green figurines.

I was locked in. This was more than father and son. This was an epic battle between generals who knew each other well enough to keep the other at bay. But I was advancing. Sure, there were losses, but that was the cost of war. I had a mission.

My queen finally reached his king unharmed.

"Check."

I uttered the word silently. As the game had progressed, gaining intensity and meaning, there was no conversation. In its place were sporadic comments, muttered with deference. So when I said "check," I made sure not to make a big deal of it. I said it quietly, softly. I didn't want to jinx myself with bragging, and I certainly didn't want to get too excited and break my own concentration. As his king scrambled for a safe hiding place, my knights continued their advance. I had

Another extended analogy.

Pequeno 6

planned for this stage of the game several moves before, which was apparently at least one move more than Dad was thinking ahead. Check again. More scrambling, and another check. It seemed I had him cornered. Then . . .

"Check." It wasn't the first time I had him in check, and I didn't expect it to be the last in this game.

"Mate," he whispered, faint hints of a smile beginning to show on the corners of his mouth, pushing his cheeks up slightly. I hadn't realized that I had won until he conceded defeat with that word. Raising his eyebrows, he leaned back into the cushion of the sofa. He looked a little tired.

"Mate?" I wasn't sure he was right. I didn't let myself believe it until I stared at these little marble men. Sure enough, his desperate king was cornered.

"Good game, Son."

And that was it. There was his approval right there, manifesting itself in that smile that said "I love you" and "you sneaky son of a bitch" at the same time. But I didn't feel like any more of a man than I had an hour before. In fact, I felt a little hollow. So I just kept my seat next to him, picked up the remote control again, and watched the Rockets finish off the Mavericks. Business as usual after that. I went back to my room and did some homework, but kept the chess game at the forefront of my mind.

Wait a second. Had he let me win? Damn it, I'd worked so hard just for him to toy with me again, even worse than

Note that story climax occurs mostly through dialogue.

Father's smile signals change in father-son relationship.

Pequeno 7

when he'd let me beat him before. No, there's no way he let me win. Or maybe he did. I don't know.

I walked back into the living room.

"Rematch?"

So we played again, and I lost. It didn't hurt, though. It didn't feel nearly as bad as when he first took off the training wheels. This was a different kind of defeat, and it didn't bother me one bit. I had nothing left to prove. If I'd lost, so what? I'd already shown what I could do.

But what if he'd let me win?

Again, so what? I had made myself a better player than I was before. I didn't need him to pass me a torch. I'd taken the flame myself, like a thirteen-year-old Prometheus. After that night, I was my own man, ready for everything: high school, my first girlfriend, my parents' divorce, my first job, moving away to college, starting a career. I never lost the feeling that I could make everything work if I just chose the right moves. I still live by that principle.

Initial doubts about follow-up match lead to epiphany in final paragraph — sudden moment of insight.

GRAPHIC NARRATIVE (EXCERPT)   In *Persepolis* (2003), Marjane Satrapi uses the medium of the graphic novel to narrate the story of her girlhood in Iran. As she grew up, she witnessed the overthrow of the shah and the Islamic Revolution, and the subsequent war with Iraq. The selection on the following pages describes life under the shah.

HE TOOK PHOTOS EVERY DAY. IT WAS STRICTLY FORBIDDEN. HE HAD EVEN BEEN ARRESTED ONCE BUT ESCAPED AT THE LAST MINUTE.

TODAY I WENT TO REY HOSPITAL WITH MY CAMERA.

PEOPLE CAME OUT CARRYING THE BODY OF A YOUNG MAN KILLED BY THE ARMY. HE WAS HONORED LIKE A MARTYR. A CROWD GATHERED TO TAKE HIM TO THE BAHESHTE ZAHRA CEMETERY.

THEN THERE WAS ANOTHER CADAVER, AN OLD MAN CARRIED OUT ON A STRETCHER. THOSE WHO DIDN'T FOLLOW THE FIRST ONE WENT OVER TO THE OLD MAN, SHOUTING REVOLUTIONARY SLOGANS AND CALLING HIM A HERO.

HERE IS ANOTHER MARTYR.

WELL, I WAS TAKING MY PHOTOS WHEN I NOTICED AN OLD WOMAN NEXT TO ME. I UNDERSTOOD THAT SHE WAS THE WIDOW OF THE VICTIM. I HAD SEEN HER LEAVE THE HOSPITAL WITH THE BODY.

PLEASE! STOP IT! STOP IT!

WHAT? WHAT IS IT?

STOP IT!

WHO ARE YOU?

HIS WIDOW!

ARE YOU A ROYALIST?

NO, BUT MY HUSBAND DIED OF CANCER...

Assignments

1. **Reflection:** Using Mark Edmundson's "The Pink Floyd Night School" as your model (p. 7), write a narrative about an event in your life that changed you and that might make some readers reconsider their choices in life too. While Edmundson is happy with the decision he made (to put off professional school for a while), your narrative might move in a different direction. If appropriate, supplement your story with photographs. (Wouldn't you like to see the canopy described in "The Pink Floyd Night School" as it floats away?)

2. **Literacy Narrative:** After reading Richard Rodriguez's "Strange Tools" (p. 23), write a literacy narrative of your own, recalling teachers or assignments that helped (or hindered) you in learning to read or write. Describe books that changed you or ambitions you might have to pursue a writing or media career. However, you don't have to be an aspiring writer to make sense of this assignment. Remember that there are many kinds of literacy. The narrative you write may be about your encounters with paintings, films, music, fashion, architecture, or maybe even video games.

3. **Student Memoir:** Using Miles Pequeno's "Check. Mate?" as a model (p. 29), compose a short narrative describing how an individual (like Pequeno's father) changed your life or made you see the world differently. Give readers a strong sense both of this person and your relationship to him or her. Make this a paper you might want to keep.

4. **Graphic Narrative:** *Persepolis* (p. 35) demonstrates that a story can be told in various media: This graphic novel even became an animated film in 2007. Using a medium other than words alone, tell a story from your own life or from your community. Draw it, use photographs, craft a collage, create a video, record interviews, or combine other media suited to your nonfiction tale.

5. **Your Choice:** Compose a personal narrative about a subject and for an audience of your choosing, perhaps using the assignment to serve some other purpose. Perhaps you have to prepare a personal statement for a scholarship application or you'd like to turn some blog entries you wrote while traveling in South America into a more coherent tale. You may experiment with media too, combining prose and images in a Web project or trying your hand at creating a photo narrative.

How to start
- Need a **topic**? See page 49.
- Need to **find information**? See page 52.
- Need to **organize that information**?
  See page 54.

2

Reports

provide
readers
with reliable
information

You've been preparing reports since the second grade when you probably used an encyclopedia to explain why volcanoes erupt or who Franklin Roosevelt was. Today, the reports you write may be more ambitious.

NEWS REPORT
You write a *news report* for a stargazers' Web site, describing the discovery of a Martian cave by amateur astronomers at a high school.

INVESTIGATIVE REPORT
You write an *investigative report* to compare the case for and against allowing more oil drilling in shallow waters near American coastlines.

ACADEMIC REPORT
You research an *academic report* on countries that are competing for international attention by building skyscrapers or other signature buildings.

FLOWCHART
You draw a *flowchart* to highlight the tangled process street merchants in your community must endure to get a vendor's permit.

INFOGRAPHIC
You design an *infographic* to present recent data on the gender and ethnic makeup of students graduating from local high schools.

DECIDING TO WRITE A REPORT   As you might guess, reports make up one of the broadest genres of writing. If you use Google to search the term online, you will turn up an unwieldy 1.5 billion items, beginning with the *Drudge Report* and moving on to sites that cover everything from financial news to morbidity studies. Such sites may not resemble the term papers, presentations, and lab reports you'll typically prepare for school. But they'll share at least some of the goals you'll have when drafting academic reports. ○

Present information.   Obviously, people read reports to discover what they don't already know or confirm what they do. They expect what they read to be timely and accurate. And sometimes, the information or data you present *will* be new (as in *news*), built from recent events or the latest

 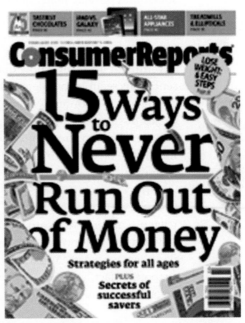

Stephen Colbert parodies the concept of the news report in his nightly putdown of cable-TV pundits, *The Colbert Report*. Treating the genre more conventionally is *Consumer Reports*, which offers objective assessments of consumer products and services in its widely read monthly magazine.

○
choose a genre
p. 390

research. But just as often, your reports will repackage data from existing sources. *Are dogs really color-blind?* The answer to such a question is already out there for you to find — if you know where to look.

Find reliable sources.   The heart and soul of any report will be reliable sources that provide or confirm information — whether they are "high government officials" quoted anonymously in news stories or scholarly articles listed in the bibliographies of college term papers. If asked to write a report about a topic new to you, immediately plan to do library and online research. O

Just as often, the information in reports is generated by careful experiments and observations — as you acknowledge whenever you prepare a lab report for a biology or chemistry course. But even personal experience may sometimes provide material for reports, though anecdotes usually need corroboration to be convincing.

Aim for objectivity.   Writers and institutions (such as newspapers or government agencies) know that they'll lose credibility if their factual presentations seem incomplete or biased. Of course, smart readers understand that reports on contentious subjects — global warming, stem cell research, or health-care reform, for example — may lean one way or another. In fact, you may develop strong opinions based on the research you've done and be inclined to favor certain ideas. But readers of reports usually prefer to draw their own conclusions.

Present information clearly.   Readers expect material in reports and reference material to be arranged (and perhaps illustrated) for their benefit. O So when you put forward information, state your claims quickly and support them with data. You'll gain no points for surprises, twists, or suspense in a report. In fact, you'll usually give away the game on the first page of most reports by announcing not only your thesis but also perhaps your conclusions.

find a topic p. 356

think visually p. 592

This very brief report — actually a news item — from *Astronomy* magazine explains an astronomical discovery. Brief as it is, it shows how reports work.

Uranus's Second Ring-Moon System

LAURA LAYTON

Saturn isn't the only planet to harbor a complex ring structure. In 1986, NASA's *Voyager 2* spacecraft sent back images of a family of ten moons and a system of rings orbiting Uranus. New images from the Hubble Space Telescope (HST) increase those numbers.

The Hubble telescope imaged Uranus's two newly discovered rings in 2003 and 2005. (*NASA, ESA, and M. Showalter of the SETI Institute.*)

On December 22, planetary astronomer Mark Showalter of the SETI Institute and Jack Lissauer of the NASA Ames Research Center announced the discovery of two additional moons and two large outer rings. HST's Advanced Camera for Surveys (ACS) imaged new moons Cupid and Mab as well as two faint, dusty rings from July 2003 through August 2005.

Newly discovered moon Cupid orbits in the midst of a swarm of inner moons known as the Portia group, so named after the group's largest moon. The Portia group lies just outside Uranus's inner ring system and inside the

Title is simple, factual.

Opening paragraphs present new information and sources.

Facts are presented clearly and objectively.

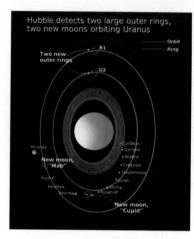

Hubble detects two large outer rings, two new moons orbiting Uranus

The features and locations of Uranus's known moons and rings.   *(NASA, ESA, and A. Field of STScI.)*

Images and captions illustrate discovery.

planet's larger, classical moon group of Belinda, Perdita, Puck, and Miranda. Mab, the smaller of the two newly detected moons, orbits outside the inner moon group and Cupid, but interior to Uranus's four outer moons.

A second ring system was also detected around Uranus and imaged by Hubble. Rings R/2003 U 1 and R/2003 U 2 (R1 and R2, respectively) both lie outside the orbit of the inner ring system. Researchers believe micron-size dust is a main constituent of these rings.

What is not clear is how these rings formed. Meteoroid impacts on Uranus's moons that eject fine dust may feed the rings or collisions among existing rings may produce new ones. Either way, the moons' small sizes and surface areas keep any ejected material from falling back to their surfaces and reaccreting. According to Showalter, "Dust material is coming off of Mab and spreading out to make this [R1] ring." It's not apparent what body provides the material for the inner (R2) ring. Lissauer theorizes that a disrupted moon may have been a source.

Authorities are quoted.

Showalter believes Uranus's ring-moon system is unstable and exhibits chaotic evolution. Since the last observations were made, Uranus's moons changed orbit. This has long-term implications for Uranus's ring-moon system. "Long-term changes to the system include collisions and crossing ring systems," adds Lissauer.

One thing is for sure, says Lissauer — "Our solar system is a dynamic place."

—*Astronomy*, December 28, 2005

Exploring purpose and topic

topic ◀

When assigned a report, think about the kinds of information you need to present and the subgenre of report you are preparing. Will your report merely answer a factual question about a topic and deliver basic information? Or are you expected to do a more in-depth study or compare different points of view, as you would in an investigative report? Or might the report deliver new information based on your own recent research or experiments? Consider your various options as you select a topic.

Answer questions. For this kind of report, include basic facts and, perhaps, an overview of key features, issues, or problems. Think of an encyclopedia as a model: When you look up an article there, you usually aren't interested in an exhaustive treatment of a subject.

Assigned a report intended to answer basic questions, you can choose topics that would otherwise seem overly ambitious. So long as all that readers expect is an overview, not expertise, you could easily write two or three fact-filled pages on "Memphis and the Blues" or "The Battle of Marathon" by focusing on just a few key figures, events, and concepts. Given this opportunity, select a topic that introduces you to new ideas or perspectives — this could, in fact, be an instructor's rationale for this type of assignment.

Review what is already known about a subject. Instructors who ask you to write five- or ten-page reports on specific subjects in a field — for example, to compare banking practices in Japan and the European Union or to describe current trends in museum architecture — doubtless know plenty about those subjects already. They want you to look at the topic in some depth to increase what *you* know. But the subject may also be evolving rapidly because of current events, technological changes, or ongoing research.

So consider updating an idea introduced in a lecture or textbook: You might be surprised by how much you can add to what an instructor has presented. If workers are striking in Greece again, make that a focal point of your general report on European Union economic policies; if your course covers globalism, consider how a world community made smaller by jet travel complicates the response to epidemic diseases. In considering topics for in-depth reports, you'll find "research guides" especially helpful. ○ You may also want to consult librarians or experts in the field you're writing about. ○

plan a project p. 466 | ask for help p. 379

Field research is one way to acquire new information.

Report new knowledge.   Many schools encourage undergraduates to conduct original research in college. In most cases, this work is done under the supervision of an instructor in your major field, and you'll likely choose a topic only after developing expertise in some area. For a look at the types of research topics students from different schools have explored, search "undergraduate research journal" on the Web.

If you have trouble finding a subject for a report, try the brainstorming techniques suggested in Chapter 19, both to identify topic ideas and to narrow them to manageable size.

Your Turn   Having trouble finding a fresh topic for a report? Let your own curiosity guide you. Make a list of things you'd simply like to know more about within the general area of your topic. If you need prompts, check out HowStuffWorks.com, especially its blogs and podcasts, such as "Stuff You Missed in History Class." You'll see that almost any subject or topic area is filled with interesting nooks and crannies.

Understanding your audience

You probably know that you should tailor any report to its potential readers. Well-informed audiences expect detailed reports that use technical language, but if your potential audience includes a range of readers, from experts to amateurs, design your work to suit them all. Perhaps you can use headings to ease novices through your report while simultaneously signaling to more knowledgeable readers what sections they might skip. ○ Make audience-sensitive moves like this routinely, whenever you are composing.

However, sometimes it's not the content that you must tailor for potential readers, but their perceptions of *you*. They'll look at you differently, according to the expertise you bring to the project. What are the options?

Suppose you are the expert. This may be the typical stance of most writers of professional reports, who smoothly present material they know well enough to teach. But knowledgeable people still often make two common mistakes in presenting information. Either they assume an audience is as informed as they are, and so omit the very details and helpful transitions that many readers need, or they underestimate the intelligence of their readers and consequently bore them with trivial and unnecessary explanations. ○ Readers want a confident guide but also one who knows when — *and when not* — to define a term, provide a graph, or supply some context.

Suppose you are the novice. In a typical report for school, you're likely dealing with material relatively new to you. Your expertise on language acquisition in childhood may be only a book chapter and two journal articles thick, but you may still have to write ten pages on the topic to pass a psychology course. Moreover, you not only have to provide information in a report, but you also have to convince an expert reader — your instructor — that you have earned the credentials to write about this subject.

Suppose you are the peer. For some reports, your peers may be your primary audience. That's especially true of oral presentations in class. You know that an instructor is watching and likely grading the content — including your topic, organization, and sources. But that instructor may also be watching how well you adapt that material to the interests and capabilities of your classmates. ○

Tips for Writing Credible Reports

- Choose a serious subject you know you can research.
- Model the project on professional reports in that area.
- Select sources recognized in the field.
- Document those sources correctly.
- Use the discipline's technical vocabulary and conventions.

think visually
p. 592

respect your
readers p. 440

understand oral
reports p. 346

Finding and developing materials

▶ find information

Once you have settled on a research topic and thesis, plan to spend time online, in a library, or in the field gathering the data you need for your report. Look beyond reference works such as dictionaries and encyclopedias toward resources used or created by experts in the field, including scholarly books published by university presses, articles in professional journals, government reports (also known as white papers), oral histories, and so on. Deliberately seek out materials that push you well beyond what you knew at the outset of the project. The level of the works you read may intimidate you at first, but that's a signal that you are learning something new — an outcome your instructor probably intended.

Sometimes, you will write reports based on information you discover yourself, either under the controlled conditions of a scientific experiment or through interviews, fieldwork, polling, or news gathering. ○ It's not easy to summarize all the rules that govern such work. They vary from field to field and major to major, and some you will learn in courses devoted to research methods. But even informal field research requires systematic procedures and detailed record keeping so that you can provide readers with data they can verify. To get reports right, follow these basic principles.

Need help finding relevant sources? See "How to Browse for Ideas" on pp. 360–61.

Base reports on the best available sources.   You can't just do an online search on a topic and hope for the best. The quality of material on Web sites (and in libraries, for that matter) varies widely. You will embarrass yourself quickly if you don't develop procedures and instincts for evaluating sources. Look for materials — including data such as statistics and photographic reproductions — presented by reliable authors and experts and supported by major institutions in government, business, and the media. For academic papers, take your information whenever possible from journals and books published by university presses and professional organizations. ○

With Web materials, track them back to their original sources. Use the Google search engine for "Korean War," for instance, and you might find an item that seems generic — except that its URL indicates a military location (.mil). Opening the URL, however, you discover that a government institution — the Naval Historical Center — supports the site. So its

interview and observe
p. 478

find reliable sources
p. 482

information is likely to be credible but will reflect the perspectives of the Department of the Navy. That's information you need to know as you read material from the site.

Base reports on multiple sources.   Don't rely on a limited or narrow selection of material. Not all ideas or points of view deserve equal coverage, but neither should you take any particular set of claims for granted. Above all, avoid the temptation to base a report on a single source, even one that *is* genuinely excellent. You may find yourself merely paraphrasing the material, not writing a report of your own. ○

Fact-check your report.   It's a shame to get the big picture in focus in a report and then lose credibility because you slip up on a few easily verifiable facts. In a lengthy project, these errors might seem inevitable or just a nuisance. But misstatements can take on a life of their own and become lore — like the initial and exaggerated reports of crime and mayhem during Hurricane Katrina. So take the extra few minutes required to get the details right.

Some Online Sites for Locating Facts and Information

- **Alcove 9: An Annotated List of Reference Sites** A collection of online reference sites maintained by the Library of Congress.
- **Bartleby.com: Great Books Online** Includes online versions of key reference and literary works, from *Gray's Anatomy* to the *Oxford Shakespeare.*
- **Biography.com** A collection of twenty-five thousand brief biographies, from Julius Caesar to Miley Cyrus.
- **FedStats** *The* site for finding information gathered by the federal government. Also check out USA.gov.
- **Internet Public Library** Provides links to material on most major academic fields and subjects. Includes reference collections as well.
- **The World Factbook** Check here for data about any country – compiled by the CIA.

restate ideas
p. 494

Creating a structure

▶ organize
   information

How does a report work? Not like a shopping mall — where the escalators and aisles are designed to keep you wandering and buying, deliberately confused. Not like a mystery novel that leads up to an unexpected climax, or even like an argument, which steadily builds in power to a memorable conclusion. Instead, reports lay all their cards on the table right at the start and hold no secrets. They announce what they intend to do and then do it, providing clear markers all along the way.

Clarity doesn't come easily; it only seems that way when a writer has been successful. You have to know a topic intimately to explain it to others. Then you need to choose a pattern that supports what you want to say. Among structures you might choose for drafting a report are the following, some of which overlap. ○

Organize by date, time, or sequence.   Drafting a history report, you may not think twice about arranging your material chronologically: In 1958, the USSR launched *Sputnik*, the first Earth satellite; in 1961, the USSR launched a cosmonaut into Earth orbit; in 1969, the United States put two men on the moon. This structure puts information into a relationship readers understand immediately as a competition. You'd still have blanks to fill in with facts and details to tell the story of the race to the moon, but a chronological structure helps readers keep complicated events in perspective.

By presenting a simple sequence of events, you can use time to organize reports involving many kinds of information, from the scores in football games to the movement of stock markets to the flow of blood through the human heart. ○

Organize by magnitude or order of importance.   Many reports present their subjects in sequence, ranked from biggest to smallest (or vice versa), most important to least important, most common/frequent to least, and so on. Such structures assume, naturally, that you have already done the research to position the items you expect to present. At first glance, reports of this kind might seem tailored to the popular media: "Ten Best Restaurants in Seattle," "One Hundred Fattest American Cities." But you might also use such a structure to report on the disputed causes of a war, the multiple effects of a stock market crash, or even the factors responsible for a disease.

develop a draft
p. 398

shape your work
p. 406

Organize by division. It's natural to organize some reports by division — that is, by breaking a subject into its major parts. A report on the federal government, for example, might be organized by treating each of its three branches in turn: executive, legislative, and judicial. A report on the Elizabethan stage might examine the separate parts of a typical theater: the heavens, the balcony, the stage wall, the stage, the pit, and so on. Of course, you'd then

The Swan Theatre
The architectural layout of this Elizabethan theater, shown in this 1596 sketch by Johannes de Witt, might suggest the structure of a report describing the theater.

have to decide in what order to present the items, perhaps spatially or in order of importance. You might even use an illustration to clarify your report.

Organize by classification.   Classification is the division of a group of concepts or items according to specified and consistent principles. Reports organized by classification are easy to set up when you borrow a structure that is already well established — such as those below. A project becomes more difficult when you try to create a new system — perhaps to classify the various political groups on your campus or to describe the behavior of participants in a psychology experiment.

- **Psychology** (by type of study): abnormal, clinical, comparative, developmental, educational, industrial, social
- **Plays** (by type): tragedy, comedy, tragicomedy, epic, pastoral, musical
- **Nations** (by form of government): monarchy, oligarchy, democracy, dictatorship
- **Passenger cars** (by engine placement): front engine, mid engine, rear engine
- **Dogs** (by breed group): sporting, hound, working, terrier, toy, nonsporting, herding

Organize by position, location, or space.   Organizing a report spatially is a powerful device for arranging ideas — even more so today, given the ease with which material can be illustrated. O A map, for example, is a report organized by position and location. But it is only one type of spatial structure.

You use spatial organization in describing a painting from left to right, a building from top to bottom, a cell from nucleus to membrane. A report on medical conditions might be presented most effectively via cutaways that expose different layers of tissues and organs. Or a report on an art exhibition might follow a viewer through a virtual 3-D gallery.

Organize by definition.   Typically, definitions begin by identifying an object by its "genus" and "species" and then listing its distinguishing

think visually p. 592

features, functions, or variations. This useful structure is the pattern behind most entries in dictionaries, encyclopedias, and other reference works. It can be readily expanded too, once the genus and species have been established: *Ontario* is a *province of Canada* between Hudson Bay and the Great Lakes. That's a good start, but what are its geographical features, history, products, and major cities — all the things that distinguish it from other provinces? You could write a book, let alone a report, based on this simple structure.

Organize by comparison/contrast.   You've probably been comparing and contrasting since the fourth grade, but that doesn't make this principle of organization any less potent for college-level reports. ○ You compare and contrast to highlight distinctions that might otherwise not be readily apparent. Big differences are usually uninteresting: That's why *Consumer Reports* doesn't

If you're looking for transportation, you're unlikely to opt for a horse. But you might compare a small car to a pickup.

understand evaluation p. 106

test Nikon SLRs against disposable cameras. But the differences between Nikons and Canons? That might be worth exploring.

Organize by thesis statement.   Obviously, you have many options for organizing a report; moreover, a single report might use several structural patterns. So it helps if you explain early in a report what its method of organization will be. That idea may be announced in a single thesis sentence, a full paragraph (or section), or even a PowerPoint slide. ○

SENTENCE ANNOUNCES STRUCTURE

In the late thirteenth century, Native Puebloans may have abandoned their cliff dwellings for several related reasons, including an exhaustion of natural resources, political disintegration, and, most likely, a prolonged drought.

– Kendrick Frazier, *People of Chaco: A Canyon and Its Culture*

PARAGRAPH EXPLAINS STRUCTURE

In order to detect a problem in the beginning of life, medical professionals and caregivers must be knowledgeable about normal development and potential warning signs. Research provides this knowledge. In most cases, research also allows for accurate diagnosis and effective intervention. Such is the case with cri du chat syndrome (CDCS), also commonly known as cat cry syndrome.

– Marissa Dahlstrom, "Developmental Disorders: Cri Du Chat Syndrome"

develop a statement p. 393

Choosing a style and design

Reports are typically written in a formal or *high* style—free of emotional language that might make them sound like arguments. ○ To separate fact from opinion, scientific and professional reports usually avoid personal references as well as devices such as contractions and dialogue. Reports in newspapers, magazines, and even encyclopedias may be less formal: You might detect a person behind the prose. But the style will still strive for impartiality, signaling that the writer's opinions are (or, at least, *should* be) less important than the facts reported.

Why tone down the emotional, personal, or argumentative temper of the language in reports? It's a matter of audience. The moment readers suspect that you are twisting language to advocate an agenda or moving away from a sober recital of facts, they will question the accuracy of your report. So review your drafts to see if a word or phrase might be sending the wrong signals to readers. Give your language the appearance of neutrality, balance, and perspective.

Present the facts cleanly.   Get right to the point and answer key questions directly: *Who? What? Where? When? How? Why?* Organize paragraphs around topic sentences so readers know what will follow. Don't go off on tangents. Keep the exposition controlled and focus on data. When you do, the prose will seem coolly efficient and trustworthy.

Keep out of it.   Write from a neutral, third-person perspective, avoiding the pronouns *I* and *you*. Like all guidelines, this one has exceptions, and it certainly doesn't apply across the board to other genres of writing. But when perusing a report, readers don't usually care about the writer's personal opinion unless that writer's individual experiences are part of the story.

Avoid connotative language.   Maintaining objectivity is not easy because language is rife with *connotations*—the powerful cultural associations that may surround words, enlarging their meanings and sometimes imposing value judgments. Connotations make *shadowy* and *gloomy* differ from *dark*; *porcine* and *tubby*, from *overweight*. What's more, the connotations of individual words are not the same for every reader. One person may have no problem with a term like *slums*, but another person living in *low-income*

define your style p. 432

housing may beg to differ. Given the minefield of potential offenses that writing can be, don't use loaded words when more neutral terms are available and just as accurate. Choose *confident*, not *overweening* or *pompous*; try *corporate official* rather than *robber baron*—unless, of course, the more colorful term fits the context. ⭕

Cover differing views fairly, especially those you don't like. The neutrality of reports is often a fiction. You need only look at the white papers or fact sheets on the Web sites of various groups to appreciate how data presentation can sometimes be biased. But a report you prepare for a course or a professional situation should represent a good-faith effort to run the bases on a subject, touching all its major points. An upbeat report on growth in minority enrollment on your campus might also have to acknowledge areas where achievements have been lagging. A report on the economic boom that occurred during Bill Clinton's presidency (1993–2001) might also have to cover the dot-com bust and slide into recession at the end of his term.

Pay attention to elements of design. Clear and effective design is particularly important in reports. ⭕ If your paper runs more than a few pages and can be readily divided into parts, consider using headings or section markers to help readers follow its structure and locate information. Documents such as term papers and lab reports may follow specific formulas, patterns, and templates that you will need to learn.

Many types of factual information are best presented graphically. This is especially the case with numbers and statistics. So learn to create or incorporate charts, graphs, photos, and illustrations, and also captions, into your work. Software such as Microsoft Word can create modest tables and simple graphics; generate more complex tables and graphs with software such as Excel, OmniGraffle or VectorDesigner. And remember that any visual items should be purposeful, not ornamental.

Many reports these days are, in fact, oral presentations that rely on presentation software such as PowerPoint, Keynote, or Prezi. You'll want to learn how to use these tools effectively.

improve your
sentences p. 444

think visually p. 592

Examining models

INVESTIGATIVE REPORT In "The Running Shoe Debate: How Barefoot Runners Are Shaping the Shoe Industry," an article published in *Popular Mechanics* (April 22, 2009), writer Tyghe Trimble looks into claims by some runners that they actually perform better without shoes because human beings were designed to run barefoot.

The Running Shoe Debate: How Barefoot Runners Are Shaping the Shoe Industry

TYGHE TRIMBLE

The Boston Marathon, one of the world's most competitive 26.2-mile races, had the best runners from Kenya, Ethiopia, the U.S. and around the globe churning out 5-minute miles on Monday for over two hours. While all eyes were on the front-runners—notably the United States' Ryan Hall (third) and Kara Goucher (third among female racers)—way back in the pack there was one person, Rick Roeber, who stole headlines with his unique running style. One glance at Roeber's feet and you can see what all the fuss is about: he isn't wearing shoes. And a number of people—ultra-marathoners, biomechanics experts and doctors included—think that's probably the best way to run. Some go so far as to say running shoes are in fact causing injuries.

While entry into the Boston Marathon is a feat in itself—Roeber needed to have about an 8-minute-mile pace over 26 miles to qualify—attempting the race barefoot is something most runners would find an absurd, even obscene, gesture. Runners are hooked on shoes. For good reason, it would appear: Ranging from 5 mm to 22 mm thick and made mostly of polymer, running shoes are engineered to support feet for mile after mile of rough asphalt and rocky terrain. They protect vulnerable soles from glass and debris, provide padding and, shoe companies claim, help correct problematic twists and turns of our ankles and legs caused by excessive pronation.

Opening paragraph grabs readers' attention by getting right to the point.

The rationale for running shoes is explained.

61

But to barefoot advocates such as Chris McDougall, author of *Born to Run*, Knopf, . . . Roeber is one of the few in Monday's race not drinking the shoe industry's Kool-Aid. In his book, McDougall follows the Tahumara, a Mexican tribe of ultrarunners who race from 50 to 200 miles straight without shoes, yet remain healthy and injury-free. Science doesn't support the shoe industry's claim that "humans are born broken," McDougall tells *PM*, [*Popular Mechanics*] and that running shoes exist to fix our stride. Humans have been barefoot for nearly 2 million years, but have had running shoes for only a little more than 40—when Nike-founder Bill Bowerman cobbled together the modern-day running shoe with glues, plastic and a waffle iron in his basement. Shoes cause runners to lose musculature in their feet, McDougall argues, and take away the natural cushion in their stride.

> Trimble provides a brief history of running shoes.

Could shoes—and shoe companies—be part of a $25 billion snake oil industry, covering hundreds of thousands of perfectly able bare feet? Or is barefoot running dangerous for marathoners and weekend joggers alike? That's the debate now brewing in the running community. The answer depends in part on a classic chicken and egg question: Do we run the way we do because of running shoes, or do running shoes support the way we now run?

> This brief paragraph identifies the questions the report will examine.

Taking It in Stride

In a back room at the $2 million New Balance running shoe research and development lab in Lawrence, Mass., the MTS 858 Mini Bionix II—a giant hydraulic piston with the cast of a foot attached—loudly pounds into the heel of a light blue, cushioned running shoe. This stress-testing machine, made by the same company that builds earthquake simulators, can apply 5620 pounds of force to a shoe 30 times every second (although researchers at New Balance tend to be gentler on the footwear). Down the hall, a glass plate sitting in the middle of a polished wooden floor conceals a camera that measures the impact of the shoe on the ground. Cameras also capture the light reflected by tiny silver dots worn by a runner on a treadmill, tracking hundreds of points on the body during each stride. Across the room, an outline of feet projected onto the wall conveys the treadmill runner's footstrike in real time.

Meanwhile, a computer records streams of data relaying angle and force, to be interpreted and analyzed by researchers later. This is high-tech biomechanics, all in the service of designing the perfect running shoe.

Some researchers and runners think this ideal shoe will be cushioned and wide, with high-tech gels, plastics and perhaps even moving parts to better absorb shock. To others, the perfect shoe looks more like a sock, with only a thin cover to protect feet from glass and other ground hazards. The two design camps split cleanly between catering to different strides: While the barefoot runner's gait tends to strike on the forefoot, a significant amount of shoe technology is aimed toward a heel-to-toe motion. A study from 1980, which was repeatedly cited by shoe experts at the New Balance labs, reveals how much more prevalent heel-to-toe running is. Analyzing the form of 753 runners, biomechanical researcher Benno Nigg found that 80 percent of runners (videotaped in two races) ran with a heel-to-toe motion; 45 percent of the faster runners (those with a 5-minute, 18-second-mile pace or better) ran heel-to-toe-step; the rest ran with what he calls a midfoot strike, in which the heel and forefoot strike the ground simultaneously.

> Trimble provides detailed information about the design of running shoes, but does not bury readers in technical language.

Shoe companies design shoes for the vast majority—the 80 percent of heel-to-toe runners—and their goal is to prevent excessive rolling movement of the foot. "There are people who will pronate a lot but will not get injured," says Keith Williams, a senior lecturer at the University of California, Davis, who has consulted in the footwear industry for 30 years. "Then there are those who will pronate a little and get injured." To play it safe, shoe companies bulk up the heel, the arch and extend the sides of shoes, which stabilizes the foot as it rolls from heel to toe.

> Here and elsewhere, Trimble carefully identifies the credentials of any authority he quotes.

While there are as many ways to do this as there are shoes for sale, Sean Murphy, manager of advanced product engineering at New Balance, says shoe companies often fall back on what he calls the 22-12 solution—placing 22 millimeters of material under the heel of the shoe and 12 millimeters under the forefoot. "Shoe companies have been stuck in the paradigm of the 22-12 for years," Murphy says, and people buy them in part because it's the feel they've grown accustomed to. "We're just now building products for people who tend to run more on their forefoot, like many ultramarathoners."

But according to McDougall, all shoes with cushioned heels, however spare, encourage heel-to-toe running, which he says leads to excessive pronation. "Take the heel off the shoe and those problems will be solved," McDougall says. In other words: Run barefoot. He points to a 2008 paper in the *British Journal of Sports Medicine*, in which the author, a researcher at the University of Newcastle in Australia, "revealed that there are no evidence-based studies—not one—that demonstrate that running shoes make you less prone to injury."

Murphy agrees. "The studies on injuries just aren't there," he says. However, there is also a dearth of studies demonstrating that running shoes make runners more prone to injury.

> An important research question remains unresolved: Do shoes help runners?

The More Perfect Shoe

With or without shoes, humans are evolved to run. In a 2004 study published in *Nature*, Dennis Bramble and Daniel Lieberman provide clear physiological evidence of this: Humans are efficient sweaters, for one. We also have tall bodies with ample surface area to cool ourselves, large buttocks with muscles critical for stabilization in running, and long legs that include Achilles tendons—ideal for storing and releasing mechanical energy. These features, the authors argue, allowed us to be superior scavengers and even hunters (by tracking sprinting animals).

> Trimble gets to the crux of the issues: Humans probably need shoes to run on man-made surfaces.

The problem modern-day runners face, according to Hugh Herr, *Popular Mechanics* 2005 Breakthrough Award winner and head of the biomechatronics group at MIT, isn't presented by our bodies but by the evolution of running surfaces. Humans that ran to scavenge or hunt for their food weren't pounding concrete. Herr is in a unique position to weigh in on shoe technology. He defended the double-prosthetic sprinter, Oscar Pistorius, in his appeal to the International Association of Athletics Federations board last year against charges that his Cheetah prosthetics provided a mechanical advantage. Herr also invented the iWalk Power-foot One, the most advanced robotic ankle in existence.

Bare feet just aren't meant to support running on modern day hard-top surfaces, Herr says. In his research, Herr focused on two problems with both shod and barefoot running—pronation angle and impact force. While barefoot running is best for a natural, stress-free pronation angle, Herr says, it is not ideal for coping with roads and sidewalks that can lead to stress-impact injuries. Shoes, on the other hand, excel at diminishing the force of impact on hard ground. But they do so at the cost of the natural stride — all the padding added to the shoe exaggerates the foot's rotation. "It's hard to design a shoe with pronation as small as what exists naturally," Herr says. "When you're barefoot, you have the advantage of the heel being very thin [and thus diminishing rotation]."

Herr's solution to the problem of shoe design is to start from scratch and fundamentally redesign the running shoe. His first-stage prototype looks nothing like any shoe for sale today. Called the SpringBuck, Herr's shoe is form fitting, taking advantage of the barefoot runner's naturally low pronation, while a spring-like heel diminishes the impact of feet on hard surfaces. This shoe even shows a metabolic reduction for the runner, Herr says, thanks to the optimized stride. Though no doubt radical to barefoot advocates and shoe labs alike, a running shoe that rethinks humans' relationship with their environment may fill the vacuum of science on the great shoe debate and finally provide a one-size-fits-all solution.

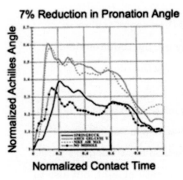 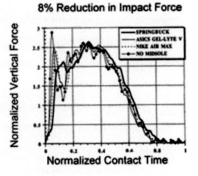

Pronation angle and force for bare feet, two supportive pairs of industry shoes, and Hugh Herr's SpringBuck design.

ACADEMIC REPORT   Academic reports often support clear and straightforward thesis statements. The following short report does that in explaining the dual mission of Frank Gehry's celebrated Guggenheim Museum Bilbao. The paper below is based not only on sources but also on information gathered at the museum, in Spain's Basque Country.

Winsett 1

Annie Winsett

Professor Sidor

Writing 200

December 5, 20--

Inner and Outer Beauty

The Guggenheim Bilbao, designed by North American architect Frank Gehry (b. 1929), is a recent addition to the Solomon R. Guggenheim Foundation, a conglomeration of museums dedicated to modern American and European art. Home to several permanent works and host to visiting expositions, the Guggenheim Bilbao is itself an artistic wonder, perhaps more acclaimed than any of the art it houses. In design, the building meets the requirements of a proper museum, but it also signifies the rejuvenation of Spain's Basque Country.

Like any museum, the Guggenheim Bilbao is dedicated to preserving and presenting works of art. Paintings and sculptures are here to be protected. So the thick glass panes of the Bilbao serve not only to let in natural light, but also to provide escape for the heat generated by the titanium

> Thesis suggests a paper with two parts.

Winsett 2

outsides of the structure. The unconventional metal plating of the Guggenheim, guaranteed to last up to one hundred years, actually ensures its survival as well. Similarly, the floor material will be able to withstand the many visitors to come.

Even though the outside of the Guggenheim Bilbao appears to be composed of irregular forms only, the interior houses nineteen functional galleries. The alternating rooms and curving walkways around a central atrium provide an extensive journey through the world of art. So the unusual exterior structure actually allots a vast amount of wall and floor display space and serves the wide variety of art it houses more than adequately.

First section of paper explains how the avant-garde building functions as a museum.

Winsett offers a photograph to convey Bilbao's extraordinary design.

Fig. 1. The Guggenheim Museum Bilbao

Winsett 3

"But" at beginning of paragraph signals that report is moving into its second section.

But the Guggenheim Bilbao was created to do more. In 1991, having noted the economic depression facing one of its main industrial cities, the Basque Country government proposed that the Solomon R. Guggenheim Foundation locate its next museum in Bilbao ("History" 1). As part of a massive revitalization involving the city's port, railways, and airport, the new museum would enhance the cultural identity of the city. Perhaps a conventional structure would have met the need for societal enrichment.

Yet the Basque government achieved much more by selecting a design by Frank Gehry. Designed with computers, the museum presents an original and striking three-dimensional form not possible using conventional design methods. From above, it appears that its metal-coated solids extend from a central skylight in the shape of a flower ("Guggenheim"). The building also suggests a ship on the river's shore with edges that swoop upward in a hull-like fashion. The "scales" of metal that surround the structure's steel frame are like those of a fish. Undoubtedly, the design references the museum's coastal and riverside environment.

Report explains how museum represents city of Bilbao.

Whatever its intended form, Gehry's building captures the spirit of a renewed Bilbao in the twenty-first century. For instance, Gehry managed to incorporate the city's mining industries in the structural materials. The titanium plates reflect both the beautiful Basque sky and the core of the

Winsett 4

Basque economy. Also crucial is the tourism such an incomparable structure might generate. Though most of Gehry's works incorporate the unique materials and forms seen in Bilbao, the Guggenheim is individual and original. And travelers have flocked here to experience the futuristic titanium masterpiece. As hoped, Bilbao and the Basque Country have earned a revived place in the international community. At the 2004 Venice Biennial, the Basque Country was recognized for the most successful urban regeneration project in the world, at the heart of which was the Guggenheim museum ("Culture").

Winsett 5

Works Cited

"Culture." *Euskadi.net*. Eusko Jaurlaritza-Gobierno Vasco
    (Basque Govt.), 17 Mar. 2005. Web. 7 Nov. 2006.

"Guggenheim Bilbao Museum." *Bilbao Metropoli-30*. Assn.
    for the Revitalization of Metropolitan Bilbao, 2006. Web.
    30 Oct. 2006.

"History of the Guggenheim Museum Bilbao." *Guggenheim
    Bilbao*. Solomon R. Guggenheim Foundation, 26 Oct.
    2006. Web. 29 Oct. 2006.

Paper uses several online sources.

FLOWCHART   This flowchart, created by Mike Wirth and Suzanne Cooper-Guasco, was a winner of the Sunlight Foundation's 2010 Design for America contest. The Foundation's goal with the contest was "to inspire the design community to tell great stories about how our government works, what our government does, and what it could do." The chart faithfully depicts the difficulty of moving bills through the U.S. Congress, but makes the process seem at least thought-provoking. The sequence, presented in bright — perhaps optimistic — colors, seems dynamic and plausible. To see this flowchart at full size, go to http://www.mikewirthart.com/wp-content/uploads/2010/05/howlawsmadeWIRTH2.jpg.

Passing a bill is complicated and so is the visual text.

Bill passage is pictured as a thick arc with a few smaller pathways. Key stages are marked by color.

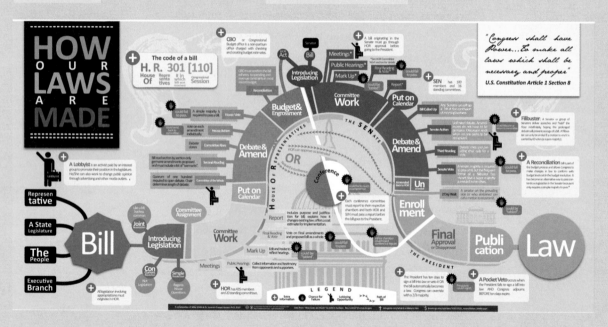

A legend explains how to interpret elements of the infographic.

Impediments are highlighted in red, including the critical budget stage.

1. **News Report:** Imagine that you've been asked to prepare a factual report on some natural phenomena (like the rings of Uranus, see p. 47) to a group of ninth graders — one of the toughest audiences in the world. In a brief article, engage them with a topic of your choosing, perhaps reflecting your own interest in an offbeat subject. You might design the report as a paper, oral presentation, or Web site. Be sure to base it on reliable sources, which you should cite in some form within the report.

2. **Investigative Report:** In "The Running Shoe Debate" (p. 61), Tyghe Trimble presents both sides of a controversy without taking a position himself. Prepare a similar report, preferably on a subject you already know something about. Draw upon your own experience to correct false impressions readers less knowledgeable than you might have about the topic. But be certain to look for new information to keep the report fresh, and to base all claims you make on reputable sources and authorities, which you should acknowledge in the paper itself (as Trimble does) or cite in the proper academic style. (For MLA style, see p. 503; for APA style, see p. 540.)

3. **Academic Report:** Write a factual report based on a topic from a course outside your major — in

other words, on a subject generally new to you. Like Annie Winsett in "Inner *and* Outer Beauty" (p. 66), narrow your subject to a specific claim you can explore in several pages. Use trustworthy sources and document them correctly.

4. **Flowchart:** "How Our Laws Are Made" (see p. 70) is a schematic example of an important genre of report that explains how things work or get done. Sometimes called "process analyses," such reports include instruction manuals, handbooks, guidebooks, cookbooks, technical schematics, and so on. Choose a process you know well or want to learn more about, break it into stages, and then describe it accurately in a flowchart, a traditional paper, or some combination of these media.

5. **Your Choice:** Begin a project with a topic you would love to know more about. Do the necessary research to find out much more about your subject, narrowing it down to manageable size for a paper or oral presentation. Then either prepare a written version of the report to submit to your instructor or an oral version to share with a wider audience, perhaps your classmates if you can have the opportunity.

How to start ▶
- Need a **topic**? See page 79.
- Need **support for your argument**? See page 85.
- Need to **organize your ideas**? See page 88.

3

Arguments

ask readers
to consider
debatable
ideas

It doesn't take much to spark an argument these days—a casual remark, a political observation, a dumb joke that hurts someone's feelings. Loud voices and angry gestures may follow, leaving observers upset and frustrated. But arguments aren't polarizing or hostile by nature, not when people more interested in generating light than heat offer them. Arguments should make us smarter and better able to deal with problems in the world. In fact, you probably make such constructive arguments all the time without raising blood pressures, at least not too much.

ARGUMENT TO ADVANCE A THESIS
In an op-ed for the local paper, you *argue the thesis* that people who talk on cell phones while driving are a greater hazard than drunk drivers because they are more numerous and more callous.

EXPLORATORY ARGUMENT
At a conference, you *explore the argument* that high school officials have adopted "zero tolerance" disciplinary policies to avoid the tough decisions that administrators are paid to make. You decide that they have.

REFUTATION ARGUMENT
In a term paper, you use facts and logic to *refute the argument* that students with college degrees will likely earn more in their lifetimes than students with only a high school diploma.

VISUAL ARGUMENT
Rather than write a letter to the editor about out-of-control salaries for NCAA football coaches, you create a *visual argument*—an editorial cartoon—suggesting that a local coach is paid more than the entire faculty.

DECIDING TO WRITE AN ARGUMENT   Arguments come in many shapes to serve different purposes. Subsequent chapters in this section cover some genres often assigned in the classroom, including *evaluations, proposals,* and *literary analyses*. ○ But even less specialized arguments have distinctive features. In your projects, you'll aim to do the following.

Offer levelheaded and disputable claims.   You won't influence audiences by making points no one cares about. Something clear and specific ought to be at stake in any argument. Maybe you want to change readers' minds about an issue or shore up what they already believe. In either case, you'll need a well-defined and carefully qualified point, either stated or implied, if you hope to influence levelheaded people. ○

Poster by Ben Shahn, 1968
This poster illustrates the words of British pacifist and parliamentarian John Morley (1838–1923). Note how the style of Shahn's typography and crayon figure complement each other to make a memorable argument out of Morley's sober observation.

(Ben Shahn, "You have not converted a man because you have silenced him." 1968. Copyright © Estate of Ben Shahn / Licensed by VAGA, New York, NY. Photo copyright ©: Smithsonian American Art Museum, Washington, D.C. / Art Resource, NY.)

choose a genre
p. 390

develop a statement
p. 393

Offer good reasons to support a claim.   Without evidence and supporting reasons, a claim is just an assertion—and little better than a shout or a slogan. Slogans do have their appeal in advertising and politics. But they don't become arguments until they are developed through full-bodied thinking and supported by a paper trail of evidence.

Understand opposing claims and points of view.   You won't be able to make a strong case until you can *honestly* paraphrase ○ the logic of those who see matters differently. And, in your own arguments, you will seem smarter and more fair when you acknowledge these other *reasonable* opinions even as you refute them. Also be prepared to address less rational claims calmly, but firmly.

Use language strategically—and not words only.   Sensible opinions still have to dress for the occasion: You need to find the right words and images to carry a case forward. Fortunately, there are many ways to make words memorable. Design is increasingly important too. You may want to use images to influence readers or choose various media for your thoughts to reach different audiences. ○

It goes without saying that many appeals you encounter daily do not measure up to the criteria of serious argument. We've all been seduced by claims just because they are stylish, hip, or repeated so often that they begin to seem true. But if much persuasion doesn't seem fair or sensible, that's all the more reason to reach for a higher standard.

CARS HAVE BUMPERS. BIKERS HAVE BONES.

DRIVE AWARE.   **RIDE AWARE.**

UTAH DEPARTMENT OF PUBLIC SAFETY

What claim does this ad from the Utah Department of Public Safety actually make? Might anyone dispute it? Do you find the ad effective visually?

restate ideas
p. 494

think visually
p. 592

Here's a *Chronicle of Higher Education* article by Scott Keyes, a 2009 Stanford University graduate, who offers good reasons in support of a clear thesis—that parents and others should allow students to choose their own careers. Like the familiar five-paragraph essay you may have learned in high school, Keyes's essay offers the conventional three points to back up its claim. But "Stop Asking Me My Major" doesn't read like an article just going through the motions thanks to its fully developed introduction, careful attention to opposing arguments, and agreeable style.

The Chronicle of Higher Education

Commentary: January 10, 2010
Scott Keyes

Stop Asking Me My Major

Introductory section lays out the problem of choosing a major systematically, adding to Keyes's credibility.

One of my best friends from high school, Andrew, changed majors during his first semester at college. He and I had been fascinated by politics for years, sharing every news story we could find and participating in the Internet activism that was exploding into a new political force. Even though he was still passionate about politics, that was no longer enough. "I have to get practical," he messaged me one day, "think about getting a job after graduation. I mean, it's like my mom keeps asking me: What can you do with a degree in political science anyway?"

I heard the same question from my friend Jesse when students across campus were agonizing about which major was right for them. He wasn't quite sure what he wanted to study, but every time a field sparked his interest, his father would pepper him with questions about what jobs were available for people in that discipline. Before long, Jesse's dad had convinced him that the only way he could get a job and be successful after college was to major in pre-med.

My friends' experiences were not atypical.

Choosing a major is one of the most difficult things students face in college. There are two main factors that most students consider when making this decision. First is their desire to study what interests them. Second is the fear that a particular major will render them penniless after graduation and result in that dreaded postcollege possibility: moving back in with their parents.

All too often, the concern about a major's practical prospects are pushed upon students by well-intentioned parents. If our goal is to cultivate students who are happy and successful, both in college as well as in the job market, I have this piece of advice for parents: Stop asking, "What can you do with a degree in (fill in the blank)?" You're doing your children no favors by asking them to focus on the job prospects of different academic disciplines, rather than studying what interests them.

It is my experience, both through picking a major myself and witnessing many others endure the process, that there are three reasons why parents (and everyone else) should be encouraging students to focus on what they enjoy studying most, rather than questioning what jobs are supposedly available for different academic concentrations.

Keyes spends five paragraphs developing his subject before offering his thesis.

The first is psychological. For his first two years of college, Jesse followed his dad's wishes and remained a pre-med student. The only problem was that he hated it. With no passion for the subject, his grades slipped, hindering his chances of getting into medical school. As a result his employability, the supposed reason he was studying medicine in the first place, suffered.

The second reason to stop asking students what they can do with a major is that it perpetuates the false notion that certain majors don't prepare students for the workplace. The belief that technical majors such as computer science are more likely to lead to a job than a major such as sociology or English is certainly understandable. It's also questionable. "The problem," as my friend José explained to me, "is that even as a computer-science major, what I learned in the classroom was outdated by the time I hit the job market." He thought instead that the main benefit of his education, rather than learning specific skills, was gaining a better way of thinking about the challenges he faced. "What's more," he told me, "no amount of education could match the specific on-the-job training I've received working different positions."

Finally, it is counterproductive to demand that students justify their choice of study with potential job prospects because that ignores the lesson we were all taught in kindergarten (and shouldn't ignore the closer we get to employment): You can grow up to be whatever you want to be. The jobs people work at often fall within the realm of their studies, but they don't have to. One need look no further than some of the most prominent figures in our society to see illustrations. The TV chef Julia Child studied English in college. Author Michael Lewis, whose best sellers focus on sports and the financial industry, majored in art history. Matt Groening, creator of *The Simpsons*, got his degree in philosophy, as did the former Hewlett-Packard chief executive Carly Fiorina. Jeff Immelt, chief executive of General Electric, focused on mathematics. Indeed, with the Department of Labor estimating that on average people switch careers (not just jobs) two or three times in their lives, relying on a college major as career preparation is misguided.

I'm not saying any applicant can get any job. Job seekers still need marketable skills if they hope to be hired. However, in a rapidly changing economy, which majors lead to what jobs is not so clear cut. Many employers look for applicants from a diverse background — including my friend who has a degree in biochemistry but was just hired at an investment consulting firm.

That doesn't mean that majors no longer matter. It is still an important decision, and students are right to seek outside counsel when figuring out what they want to study. But questioning how a particular major will affect their employability is not necessarily the best approach. Although parents' intentions may be pure — after all, who

---

Three reasons are offered to support the thesis, each more complex and fully developed.

An informal style, using "I" and even "you" when necessary, reaches out to audiences.

The specific examples here illustrate Keyes's point.

doesn't want to see their children succeed after graduation? — that question can hold tremendous power over impressionable freshmen. Far too many of my classmates let it steer them away from what they enjoyed studying to a major they believed would help them get a job after graduation.

Objections are anticipated and treated as reasonable. But they are answered sensibly too.

One of those friends was Andrew. He opted against pursuing a degree in political science, choosing instead to study finance because "that's where the jobs are." Following graduation, Andrew landed at a consulting firm. I recently learned with little surprise that he hates his job and has no passion for the work.

Jesse, on the other hand, realized that if he stayed on the pre-med track, he would burn out before ever getting his degree. During his junior year he changed tracks and began to study engineering. Not only did Jesse's grades improve markedly, but his enthusiasm for the subject recently earned him a lucrative job offer and admission to a top engineering master's program.

Jesse and Andrew appear in the opening paragraphs as well, tying the argument together structurally.

Andrew and Jesse both got jobs. But who do you think feels more successful?

Exploring purpose and topic

topic ◀

In a college assignment, you could be asked to write an argument about a general topic area related to a course, but you likely won't be told what your claim should be. That decision has to come from you, drawing on your knowledge, experiences, and inclinations. So choose subjects about which you genuinely care—not issues the media or someone else defines as controversial. You'll do a more credible job defending your defiant choice *not* to wear a helmet when cycling than explaining, one more time, why the environment should concern us all. And if environmental matters do roil you, stake your claim on a well-defined ecological problem—perhaps from within your community—that you might actually influence by the power of your rhetoric. ○

If you really are stumped, the Yahoo Directory's list of "Issues and Causes"—with topics from *abortion* to *zoos*—offers problems enough to keep both Janeane Garofalo *and* Ann Coulter busy to the end of the century. To find it, search "Society and Culture" or "Issues and Causes" on the site's main Web directory. ("Society and Culture" itself offers a menu of intriguing topic areas.) Once you have an issue or even a specific claim, your real work begins.

Learn much more about your subject.   Your first task is to do basic library and online research to get a better handle on your topic—*especially* when you think you already have all the answers. Chances are, you don't.

State a preliminary claim, if only for yourself.   Some arguments fail because writers never focus their thinking. Instead, they wander around their potential subjects, throwing out ideas or making contradictory assertions, and leaving it to readers to assemble the random parts. To avoid this misdirection, begin with a *claim*—a *complete* sentence that states a position you will then have to defend. Though you will likely change this initial claim, such a statement will keep you on track as you explore a topic. Even a simple sentence helps:

> The college rankings published annually by *U.S. News & World Report* do more harm than good.
>
> Westerners should be less defensive about their cultures.
>
> People who oppose gay marriage don't know what they are talking about.

Arguments take many different forms, but finger-pointing is rarely a good persuasive tool.

Qualify your claim to make it reasonable.   As you learn more about a subject, revise your topic idea to reflect the complications you encounter. ○ Your tentative thesis will likely grow longer, but the topic will actually narrow because of the issues and conditions you've specified. You'll also have less work to do, thanks to qualifying expressions such as *some, most, a few, often, under certain conditions, occasionally, when necessary,* and so on. Other qualifying expressions are highlighted below.

> The **statistically unreliable** college ratings published by *U.S. News & World Report* **usually** do more harm than good to students **because** some claim that they lead admissions officers to award scholarships on the basis of merit rather than need.

> Westerners should be **more** willing to defend their **cultural** values and **intellectual** achievements **if** they hope to **defend freedom** against its enemies.

> **Many conservative critics** who oppose gay marriage **unwittingly** undermine their own core principles, **especially monogamy and honesty.**

Examine your core assumptions.   Claims may be supported by reasons and evidence, but they are based on assumptions. *Assumptions* are the principles and values on which we ground our beliefs and actions. Sometimes these assumptions are controversial and stand right out. At other times, they're so close to us, they seem invisible—they are part of the air we breathe. Expect to spend a paragraph defending any assumptions your readers might find controversial. ○

think critically
p. 372

develop ideas
p. 412

CLAIM

The statistically unreliable college ratings published by *U.S. News & World Report* usually do more harm than good to students because some people claim that they lead admissions officers to award scholarships on the basis of merit rather than need.

ASSUMPTION

Alleviating need in our society is more important than rewarding merit.
[Probably controversial]

CLAIM

Westerners should be more willing to defend their cultural values and intellectual achievements if they hope to defend freedom against its enemies.

ASSUMPTION

Freedom needs to be defended at all costs.
[Possibly controversial for some audiences]

CLAIM

Many conservative critics who oppose gay marriage unwittingly undermine their own core principles, especially monogamy and honesty.

ASSUMPTION

People should be consistent about their principles.
[Probably noncontroversial]

> **Your Turn** Many writers have a tough time expressing their topic in a complete sentence. They will offer a tentative word or phrase or sentence fragment instead of making the commitment that a full sentence demands, especially one with subordinators and qualifiers that begin to tie their ideas together. So give it a try. Take a topic you might write about and turn it into a full-bore sentence that tells readers what your claim is and how you intend to support it. Scott Keyes's topic sentence has fifty-one words (see p. 76); aim for at least twenty.

Understanding your audience

Retailers know audiences. In fact, they go to great lengths to pinpoint the groups most likely to buy their fried chicken or video games. They then tailor their images and advertising pitches to those specific customers. You'll play to audiences the same way when you write arguments—if maybe a little less cynically.

Understand that you won't ever please everyone in a general audience, even if you write bland, colorless mush—because some readers will then regard you as craven and spineless. In fact, how readers imagine you, *as the person presenting an argument*, may determine their willingness to consider your claims at all.

Readers do react differently to specific topics, so you will need to consider a variety of approaches when imagining the audiences for your arguments.

Consider and control your ethos.   People who study persuasion describe the character that writers create for themselves within an argument as their *ethos*—the voice and attitude they choose to give their appeal. It is a powerful concept, worth remembering. Surely you recognize when writers are coming across as, let's say, ingratiatingly confident or stupidly obnoxious. And don't you respond in kind, giving ear to the likable voice and dismissing the malicious one? A few audiences—like those for political blogs—may actually prefer a writer with a snarky ethos. But most readers respond better when writers seem reasonable, knowledgeable, and fair—neither insulting those who disagree with them nor making those who share their views embarrassed to have them on their side.

Control your ethos by adjusting the style, tone, and vocabulary of your argument: For instance, contractions can make you seem friendly (or too casual); an impressive vocabulary suggests that you are smart (or maybe just pompous); lots of name-dropping makes you seem hip (or perhaps pretentious). You may have to write several drafts to find a suitable ethos for a particular argument. ○ And, yes, your ethos may change from paper to paper, audience to audience.

revise and edit
p. 452

> **Your Turn**   Chances are you have some favorite Web sites or blogs you consult daily. Choose one of those sites, find an entry in it that expresses the *ethos* of the contributor(s) or the site itself, and then analyze that ethos. Is the character of the site friendly and down-to-earth? Arrogant and authoritative? Serious and politically concerned? Point to specific features of the site that help to create its ethos. If you don't consult blogs or Web sites, apply your analysis to a printed or oral text, perhaps an op-ed by a favorite columnist or a political speech by a public figure.

Consider your own limits.   If you read newspapers and magazines that mostly confirm your own political views, you might be in for a wake-up call when you venture an opinion beyond your small circle of friends. Tread softly. There are good reasons why people don't talk politics at parties. When you do argue about social, political, or religious issues, be respectful of those who work from premises different from your own.

Consider race and ethnicity.   The different lives people live as a result of their heritage play a role in many claims you might make about education, politics, art, religion, or even athletics. Be sensitive without being gutless. ○

Consider gender and sexual orientation.   These issues almost always matter, often in unexpected ways. Men and women, whether straight or gay, don't inhabit quite the same worlds. But, even so, you shouldn't argue, either, as if all men and all women think the same way—or should. False assumptions about gender can lead you into a minefield.

Consider income and class.   People's lives are often defined by the realities of their economic situations—and the assumptions that follow from privilege, poverty, or something in between. Think it would be just dandy to have an outdoor pool on campus or a convenient new parking garage? You may find that not everyone is as eager or as able as you to absorb the costs of such proposals to improve campus life. And if you intend to complain about

> Need help supporting your argument? See "How to Use the Writing Center" on pp. 382–83.

respect your readers p. 440

fat cats, ridicule soccer moms, or poke fun at rednecks, is it because you can't imagine them among your readers?

Consider religion and spirituality.   Members of different organized religions manage to insult each other almost without trying, more so now perhaps as religion routinely takes center stage in the political and diplomatic arena. People within the same denomination often hold incompatible views. And the word *atheist* can engender negative reactions in certain audiences. It takes skill and good sense to keep the differences in mind when your topic demands it.

Consider age.   Obviously, you'd write differently for children than for their parents on almost any subject, changing your style, vocabulary, and allusions. But consider that people at different ages really have lived different lives. The so-called Greatest Generation never forgot the Great Depression; teens today will remember the destruction of the World Trade Center towers on September 11, 2001, and perhaps the school shootings in Columbine, Colorado. They'll grow up with different attitudes, values, heroes, and villains. A writer has to be savvy enough to account for such differences when constructing an argument.

Gender attitudes develop early, along with some argument strategies.

Finding and developing materials

develop support ◀

You could write a book from the materials you'll collect researching some arguments. Material is out there on every imaginable subject, and the research techniques you use to prepare a report or term paper should work for arguments too. Since arguments often deal with current events and topics, start with a resource such as the Yahoo "Issues and Causes" directory mentioned earlier. Explore your subject, too, in *LexisNexis,* if your library gives you access to this huge database of newspaper articles. ○

As you gather materials, though, consider how much space you have to make your argument. Sometimes a claim has to fit within the confines of a letter to the editor, an op-ed column in a local paper, or a fifteen-minute PowerPoint lecture. Aristotle, still one of the best theorists on persuasion, thought arguments *should* be brief, with speakers limiting examples to the *minimum* necessary to make a case—no extra points for piling on. So gather big, and then select only the best stuff for your argument.

List your reasons.   You'll come up with reasons to support your claim almost as soon as you choose a subject. Write those down. Then start reading and continue to list new reasons as they arise, not being too fussy at this point. Be careful to paraphrase these ideas so that you don't inadvertently plagiarize them later.

Then, when your reading and research are complete, review your notes and try to group the arguments that support your position. It's likely you'll detect patterns and relationships among these reasons, and an unwieldy initial list of potential arguments may be streamlined into just three or four—which could become the key reasons behind your claim. Study these points and look for logical connections or sequences. Readers will expect your ideas to converge on a claim or lead logically toward it. ○

The whole is greater than the sum of its parts.

— Aristotle

ORIGINAL

<u>Why ethanol won't solve our energy problems</u>

- Using ethanol in cars actually increases NO_x emissions.
- Ethanol requires more energy to make than it produces.
- Ethanol reduces range: You can't drive as far on a gallon.
- Ethanol can plug up fuel systems of older cars.
- Ethanol produces much less energy per gallon than gas.
- Creating ethanol contributes to global warming.
- Ethanol is cheaper than gas only because of massive government subsidies.
- Ethanol harms performance in cars.

refine your search
p. 472

shape your work
p. 406

- Ethanol damages engines.
- Everyone's just on another eco bandwagon.
- Ethanol drives up crop prices, and thus food prices.

STREAMLINED

Why ethanol won't solve our energy problems

- Ethanol hurts performance of vehicles significantly.
- Ethanol is expensive to produce.
- Ethanol harms the environment.

Assemble your hard evidence.   Gather examples, illustrations, testimony, and numbers to support each main point. Record these items as you read, photocopying the data or downloading it carefully into labeled files. Take this evidence from the most reputable sources and keep track of all bibliographical information (author, title, publication info, URL) just as you would when preparing a term paper—even if you aren't expected to document your argument. You want that data on hand in case your credibility is later challenged.

If you borrow facts from a Web site, do your best to track the information down to its actual source. For example, if a blogger quotes statistics from the U.S. Department of Agriculture, take a few minutes to find the table or graph on the USDA Web site itself and make sure the numbers are reported accurately. ○

Think of hard evidence as a broad category that might also include photographs, video clips, or physical objects. Audiences do have a fondness for smoking guns—those pieces of indisputable evidence that clinch an argument. If you find one, use it.

Cull the best quotations.   You've done your homework for an assignment, reading the best available sources. So prove it in your argument by quoting from them intelligently. Choose quotations that do one or more of the following:

- Put your issue in focus or context.
- Make a point with exceptional power and economy.
- Support a claim or piece of evidence that readers might doubt.
- State an opposing point well.

analyze claims and evidence p. 487

Copy passages that appeal to you, but don't plan on using all of them. An argument that is a patchwork of quotations reads like a patchwork of quotations—which is to say, *boring*.

Be scrupulous about getting the quotations right. That's easier now than in the past because files can be copied and downloaded electronically. But you still need to use such passages fairly and be prepared to cite and document them. ○

Find counterarguments.   If you study your subject thoroughly, you'll come across plenty of honest disagreement. List all the reasonable objections that you can find to your claim, either to your basic argument or to any controversial evidence you expect to cite. When possible, cluster these objections to reduce them to a manageable few. Decide which you must refute in detail, which you might handle briefly, and which you can afford to dismiss. ○

> Ethanol counterarguments
>
> • Ethanol is made from corn, a renewable resource.
> • Ethanol is available today.
> • Ethanol is locally made, not imported.
> • Using ethanol decreases CO emissions.

Consider emotional appeals.   Nuclear power plants produce electricity without contributing significantly to global warming. But don't expect Americans who watched the Japanese deal with a nuclear crisis in 2011 following a tsunami to put aside their fears about atomic power readily, even to preserve the environment. Emotions play a powerful role in many arguments, a fact you cannot afford to ignore when a claim you make stirs up strong feelings. Questions to answer include the following:

● What emotions might be raised to support my point?

● How might I responsibly introduce such feelings: through words, images, color, sound?

● How might any feelings my subject arouses work contrary to my claims or reasons?

Well-chosen visuals add power to an argument.   A writer trying to persuade readers not to buy fur might include this photo in an article. How would this image influence you, as a reader?

understand citation styles p. 501

develop ideas p. 412

Creating a structure

It's easy to sketch a standard structure for arguments: one that leads from claim to supporting reasons to evidence and even accommodates a counter-argument or two.

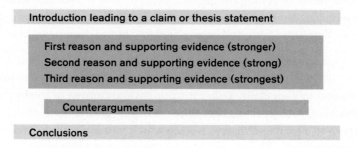

Introduction leading to a claim or thesis statement

First reason and supporting evidence (stronger)
Second reason and supporting evidence (strong)
Third reason and supporting evidence (strongest)

Counterarguments

Conclusions

The problem is that you won't read many effective arguments, either in or out of school, that follow this template. The structure isn't defective, just too simple to describe the way arguments really move when ideas matter. Some controversies need lots of background to get rolling, some require detours to resolve other issues first, and a great many arguments work best when writers simply lay out the facts and allow readers to draw their own conclusions—or be nudged toward them.

You won't write a horrible paper if you use the traditional model because all the parts will be in place. Thesis? Check. Three supporting reasons? Check. Counterarguments? Check. But you will sound exactly like what you are: A writer going through the motions instead of engaging with ideas. Here's how to get your ideas to breathe in an argument—while still hitting all the marks.

Spell out what's at stake.   When you write an argument, you start a disagreement, so you'd better explain why—as Scott Keyes does in "Stop Asking Me My Major" earlier in this chapter. Do you hope to fix a looming problem? Then describe what your concern is and make readers share it. Do you intend to correct a false notion or bad reporting? Then be sure to tell readers what setting the record straight accomplishes. Appalled by the apathy of voters, the dangers of global warming, the infringements of free speech on campus? Then explain what makes such issues matter today and why readers should pay attention. ○

Don't just jump into a claim: Take a few sentences or paragraphs to set up the situation. Quote a nasty politician or tell an eye-popping story or two. Get readers invested in what's to come.

Make a point or build toward one.   Arguments can unfurl just as reports do, with unmistakable claims followed by reams of supporting evidence. But they can also work like crime dramas, in which the evidence in a case builds toward a compelling conclusion—your thesis perhaps. Consider the ethanol issue. You could argue straight up that this fuel causes more problems than it solves. Or you could open by wondering if ethanol really is the miracle fuel some claim it to be and then offer evidence that contradicts the media hype. In both cases, readers get the same claim and reasons. But the first approach might work better for readers already interested in environmental issues, while the second might grab those who aren't by arousing their curiosity. This is your call. ○

Address counterpoints when necessary, not in a separate section.   *Necessary* is when your readers start thinking to themselves, "Yeah, but what about . . . ?" Such doubts likely surface approximately where your own do—and, admit it, you have *some* misgivings about your argument. So take them on. Strategically, it rarely makes sense to consign major objections to a lengthy section near the end of a paper. That's asking for trouble. Do you really want to offer a case for the opposition just when your readers are finishing up?

On the plus side, dealing with opposing arguments (or writing a refutation itself—see p. 101) can be like caffeine for your prose, sharpening your attention and reflexes. Here's Ann Hulbert, for example, eager to take on those who now argue that it's boys who are being shortchanged in schools by curriculums and modes of teaching that favor girls:

> Other complaints about boy-averse pedagogy also don't quite add up – in part because they contradict one another. Sommers blamed a touchy-feely, progressive ethos for alienating boys in the classroom; males, she argued,

develop a statement
p. 393

order ideas
p. 408

thrive on no-nonsense authority, accountability, clarity, and peer rivalry. But now *Newsweek* blames roughly the opposite atmosphere for boy trouble: the competitive, cut-and-dried, standardized-test-obsessed (and recess-less) pedagogical emphasis of the last decade. So much speculative certainty doesn't really shed much light on the puzzle of what's deterring young men from college.

—"Will Boys Be Boys?" *Slate.com*, February 1, 2006

Hold your best arguments for the end.   Of course, you want strong points throughout the paper. But you need a high note early on to get readers interested and then another choral moment as you finish to send them out the door humming. If you must summarize an argument, don't let a dull recap of your main points squander an important opportunity to influence readers. End with a rhetorical flourish that reminds readers how compelling your arguments are. ○

A pithy phrase, an ironic twist, and a question to contemplate can also lock down your case. Here's Maureen Dowd, bleakly—and memorably—concluding an argument defending the job journalists had done covering the Iraq War:

Journalists die and we know who they are. We know they liked to cook and play Scrabble. But we don't know who killed them, and their killers will never be brought to justice. The enemy has no face, just a finger on a detonator.

—"Live from Baghdad: More Dying," *New York Times*, May 31, 2006

Journalists undergo training to prepare for the dangers they are likely to face in conflict zones.

shape an ending
p. 425

Choosing a style and design

Arguments vary widely in style. An unsigned editorial you write to represent the opinion of a newspaper might sound formal and serious. Composing an op-ed under your own name, you'd likely ease up on the dramatic metaphors and allow yourself more personal pronouns. Arguing a point in an alternative newsletter, you might even slip into the lingo of its vegan or survivalist subscribers. Routine adjustments like these really matter when you need to attract and hold readers.

You should also write with sensitivity since some people reading arguments may well be wavering, defensive, or spoiling for a fight. There's no reason to distract them with fighting words if you want to offer a serious argument. Here's how political commentator Ann Coulter described a politically active group of 9/11 widows who she believed were using their status to shield their anti–Iraq War opinions from criticism:

> These broads are millionaires, lionized on TV and in articles about them, reveling in their status as celebrities and stalked by grief-arazzis. I have never seen people enjoying their husbands' death so much.
>
> – *Godless: The Church of Liberalism* (2006)

Any point Coulter might make simply gets lost in her breathtaking idiom of attack.

There are many powerful and aggressive ways to frame an argument without resorting to provocative language or fallacies of argument. ○ Some of these strategies follow.

Invite readers with a strong opening.   Arguments—like advertisements— are usually discretionary reading. People can turn away the moment they grow irritated or bored. So you have to work hard to keep them engrossed by your ideas. You may need to open with a little surprise or drama. Try a blunt statement, an anecdote, or a striking illustration if it helps—maybe an image too. Or consider personalizing the lead-in, giving readers a stake in the claim you are about to make. The following is a remarkable opening paragraph from an argument by Malcolm Gladwell on the wisdom of banning dogs by breed. When you finish, ask yourself whether Gladwell has earned your attention. Would you read the remainder of the piece?

avoid fallacies
p. 372

One afternoon last February, Guy Clairoux picked up his two-and-a-half-year-old son, Jayden, from day care and walked him back to their house in the west end of Ottawa, Ontario. They were almost home. Jayden was straggling behind, and, as his father's back was turned, a pit bull jumped over a backyard fence and lunged at Jayden. "The dog had his head in its mouth and started to do this shake," Clairoux's wife, JoAnn Hartley, said later. As she watched in horror, two more pit bulls jumped over the fence, joining in the assault. She and Clairoux came running, and he punched the first of the dogs in the head, until it dropped Jayden, and then he threw the boy toward his mother. Hartley fell on her son, protecting him with her body. "JoAnn!" Clairoux cried out, as all three dogs descended on his wife. "Cover your neck, cover your neck." A neighbor, sitting by her window, screamed for help. Her partner and a friend, Mario Gauthier, ran outside. A neighborhood boy grabbed his hockey stick and threw it to Gauthier. He began hitting one of the dogs over the head, until the stick broke. "They wouldn't stop," Gauthier said. "As soon as you'd stop, they'd attack again. I've never seen a dog go so crazy. They were like Tasmanian devils." The police came. The dogs were pulled away, and the Clairouxes and one of the rescuers were taken to the hospital. Five days later, the Ontario legislature banned the ownership of pit bulls. "Just as we wouldn't let a great white shark in a swimming pool," the province's attorney general, Michael Bryant, had said, "maybe we shouldn't have these animals on the civilized streets."

– "Troublemakers," *New Yorker*, February 6, 2006

Write vibrant sentences.   You can write arguments full throttle, using a complete range of rhetorical devices, from deliberate repetition and parallelism to dialogue and quotation. Metaphors, similes, and analogies fit right in too. The trick is to create sentences with a texture rich enough to keep readers hooked, yet lean enough to advance an argument. In the following three paragraphs, follow the highlighting to see how Thomas L. Friedman uses parallelism and one intriguing metaphor after another to argue in favor of immigration legislation after witnessing the diversity in a high school graduation class in Maryland. ○

improve your
sentences p. 444

There is a lot to be worried about in America today: a war in Iraq that is getting worse not better, an administration whose fiscal irresponsibility we will be paying for for a long time, an education system that is not producing enough young Americans skilled in math and science, and inner cities where way too many black males are failing. We must work harder and get smarter if we want to maintain our standard of living.

But if there is one reason to still be optimistic about America it is represented by the stunning diversity of the Montgomery Blair class of 2006. America is still the world's greatest human magnet. We are not the only country that embraces diversity, but there is something about our free society and free market that still attracts people like no other. Our greatest asset is our ability to still cream off not only the first-round intellectual draft choices from around the world but the low-skilled—high-aspiring ones as well, and that is the main reason that I am not yet ready to cede the twenty-first century to China. Our Chinese will still beat their Chinese.

This influx of brainy and brawny immigrants is our oil well—one that never runs dry. It is an endless source of renewable human energy and creativity. Congress ought to stop debating gay marriage and finally give us a framework to maintain a free flow of legal immigration.

—"A Well of Smiths and Xias," *New York Times*, June 7, 2006

Ask rhetorical questions.   The danger of rhetorical questions is that they can seem stagy and readers might not answer them the way you want. But the device can be very powerful in hammering a point home. Good questions also invite readers to think about an issue in exactly the terms that a writer prefers. Here's George Will using rhetorical questions to conclude a piece on global warming.

In fact, the earth is always experiencing either warming or cooling. But suppose the scientists and their journalistic conduits, who today say they were so spectacularly wrong so recently, are now correct. Suppose the earth is warming and suppose the warming is caused by human activity. Are we sure there will be proportionate benefits from whatever climate change can be purchased at the cost of slowing economic growth and spending trillions? Are we sure the consequences of climate change—remember, a thick sheet of ice once covered the Midwest—must be bad? Or has the science-journalism complex decided that debate about these questions, too, is "over"?

—"Let Cooler Heads Prevail," *Washington Post*, April 2, 2006

Use images and design to make a point.   If we didn't know it already (and we did), the video and photographic images from 9/11, Hurricane Katrina, and the oil spill in the Gulf of Mexico clearly prove that persuasion doesn't occur by words only. We react powerfully to what we see with our own eyes. Consider, for example, this mug shot of Jared Loughner, the man charged in the January 2011 shooting of U.S. Representative Gabrielle Giffords. Claims that the attack was motivated by political rhetoric receded once the public got a look at the picture.

And yet words still play a part because most images become *focused* arguments only when accompanied by commentary—as commentators routinely prove when they put a spin on news photographs or video. And because digital technology now makes it so easy to incorporate nonverbal media into texts, whether on a page, screen, or Prezi whiteboard, you should always consider how just the right image might enhance the case you want to make. And now you don't always have to start with words. A series of photographs might be shaped into a photo-essay every bit as powerful as a conventional op-ed piece.

In fact, you already have the tools on your computer to create posters, advertisements, slides, and brochures, all of which may be instruments of persuasion. ○

think visually
p. 592

Examining models

In "Play 'Free Bird'!" Lynn Ehlers draws on her personal feelings and experiences to question whether musicians in concert have an ethical obligation to play their fans' favorite songs. Although most of her classmates disagreed with her claim when she first offered it as a topic proposal, Ehlers learned from their objections how to strengthen her case. Watch as she builds up toward her claim, which isn't made explicitly until the final paragraph. See if you agree with the conclusion she comes to in this argument.

Ehlers 1

Lynn Ehlers

Prof. John Ruszkiewicz

Advanced Expository Writing

May 8, 20--

"Play 'Free Bird'!"

There aren't a lot of reasons I'd choose to be here, melting in the unsympathetic humidity of Austin in mid-July, gliding around an airtight snake pit of sweating high schoolers and their smearing punk rock makeup. Not a single inch of my shirt is *not* sticking to my body, and I can't move without adhering to three other people. It smells like a farm and I don't have enough cash for a beer.

And yet, here I am, about to pass out from dehydration at a Jimmy Eat World concert at Emo's outdoor stage with a few hundred other troopers. Why? Because I've loved this band for years—long after those mysterious artistry watchdogs exposed them for "selling out." And if it meant hearing "Bleed American" live, I'd have put up with twice as

> Opening sets the scene, but only the title hints at what the issue may be.

> The argument assumes an audience reasonably familiar with the music of Jimmy Eat World.

Ehlers 2

many drunks and a few more degrees of heat. But, as it turned out, it didn't mean hearing "Bleed American"; it meant sweltering through an hour-long set of boring acoustic versions of songs off *Futures* and crappy filler off *Clarity.* "Bleed American" is one of Jimmy Eat World's big singles, written in a minor key with an unlikely upbeat chorus and the band's trademark curious lyrics; the confidence in Jimmy Eat World's music was first established in this single, breaking away from the fuzzy, wandering sound of prior work. While I already knew that the true gems were not concert material, the fact that "Bleed American" didn't land in the set list seemed—in the words of my roommate and fellow attendee—"f-cking lame." The urge to throw a preteenesque fit was almost uncontrollable, but I reminded myself that it's their show, their band, and their damn song, and they can do what they want.

But can they really? In our entertainment-loving, rockstar-glorifying culture, we have created an interesting debate: Who owes whom? Are musicians indebted to their fans for their livelihoods, or are fans indebted to musicians for their talent? Was I obligated to appreciate the trash Jimmy Eat World played that clammy evening, or should the band have sucked it up and played their hits for yet another worshipful crowd? Concerts fall into a funny gray area between art and commodity—and, admittedly, our free market economy seems to put emphasis on the latter.

Ehlers's argument is finally raised by the exploratory question, "But can they really?"

Ehlers 3

Musicians are largely granted the blameless freedom to do as they please because concerts are products; if consumers don't like them, they can stop buying them.

But there is a difference between putting out an album and putting on a show—the dynamics between musician and fan are altered. An album is a finite product, which musicians craft privately, release for profit, and hope will be successful. Do fans participate in the studio? No. Do they dictate what songs go on an album, demand subtle nuances, produce the general sound? No. They can buy it, steal it, or ignore it—but they certainly can't contribute to the album's production.

And whereas musicians undeniably possess full creative license over albums, concerts take on an element of customer service. In putting on shows, musicians assume two kinds of obligation to their fans: first, the professional obligation to make good on services *explicitly* promised (meaning that the band will show up and do something resembling a music performance); and second, the more important *ethical* obligation to make good on services *implicitly* promised (such as the understood assumption that a band will play its hits at the show). Musicians know what fans want to hear because they know what songs pay their Los Angeles mortgages—but the decision to actually perform their top-selling singles is the ethical prerogative of the musician.

Ehlers examines the relationship between artists and audiences to clarify the matter for herself and her readers.

She draws an important and impressive distinction between albums and live performances.

Ehlers 4

The details here help to establish Ehlers's ethos: She is reasonably knowledgeable about music and musicians, not just blowing off steam.

     Some musicians decide to completely scrap hits from their set lists—especially singles from previous albums. Radiohead periodically refuses to play their 1992 hit "Creep" off *Pablo Honey*, often for years at a stretch. In 2002, Beck announced to a Dallas crowd, "I just want to let you know now, I'm not going to play 'Loser.' It's not going to happen." Do Thome York and Beck know that "Creep" and "Loser" sold a significant portion of their tickets? Of course. But they've played those songs thousands of times—albums, practices, and especially those relentless tour schedules. And, as musicians, they have taken the liberty to shelve "Creep" and "Loser" until a time when playing them no longer causes physical pain. Yorke and Beck are under no explicit obligation to play their hits (or even to put on a quality show), and that's *why* it's a matter of ethics: the fact that musicians don't *have* to indulge fans with their implicit purchases, but still *should*.

     But it's not just a matter of musicians providing implicit services; more importantly, it's a matter of musicians fulfilling ethical obligations as *artists*, by gratefully responding to the patronage that their artistry receives. Musicians create art that becomes significant and personal to individuals—and ultimately, the personal attachment fans forge with music is what sells tickets. The majority of fans who go to concerts—particularly, those who go to concerts frequently—truly do show up as patrons and revere music as inseparable from life.

Ehlers 5

These are the people who find the discussion of favorite albums to be more sensitive than politics or religion. These are the people who will never part with their CD (or vinyl) collections, regardless of the digital technology available, and despite having several albums in all three forms. These are the people who lean on music to get through life: who depend on Beck when they'd rather die than clean their apartment, and who depend on Radiohead in the face of failure and loneliness.

I was at the Jimmy Eat World show because I'd listened to *Futures* three times in a row on a summer road trip with my dad. I skipped seventh period choir in high school to listen to *Bleed American* in a car parked behind the school, wondering about the future with my feet out the window. I listened to "My Sundown" on repeat for days after my mom passed away, and "She's Perfect" the entire first week of college when I found myself on a campus without friends or food money. I've made Jimmy Eat World's music a part of my life, and, in return, at the concert in Austin they played the music they weren't tired of playing yet.

Of course, musicians aren't contractually required to show gratitude for (or even acknowledge) the genuine relationship that fans develop with the band's music; in fact, it's easier and socially acceptable not to. The musicians' decision not to play the songs that they know people have fallen in love with—relying on them for comfort when things become unbearable,

Note how Ehlers makes playing songs fans want to hear an ethical, not a contractual, issue, upping the ante for artists.

The repetition in this paragraph gives the argument a powerful emotional turn, emphasizing the artists' obligations to fans.

Now the argument becomes personal.

There's a strategic nod here to the *other* side of the argument.

Ehlers 6

dancing to them on a coffee table with a sloshing wine glass in one hand—is neither a professional nor legal infraction. But again, this is what makes it an ethical matter: It's the musicians' *ethical* obligation to reciprocate fan support with equivalent appreciation, even though they simply don't have to. And yes, it means playing the songs that fans continue to yell for and buy tickets for and spend their last dollar on to see live—despite the dread it breathes into musicians the second they wake up, hung over on a multithousand-dollar tour bus, surrounded by vintage guitars and their per diem allowance of top-shelf liquor. Musicians owe at least half of their success to the people who gave their product a chance and who connected with their art. Putting on a killer show—and playing the songs that matter to their fans—is the least they can do.

But with all her evidence in place, Ehlers finally makes an unequivocal claim: "It's the musicians' *ethical* obligation to reciprocate fan support. . . ."

Hey, guys, play "Bleed American," why don't ya?

REFUTATION ARGUMENT   Cathy Young, a Russian immigrant and writer for the *Boston Globe* and the Libertarian magazine *Reason*, takes issue with new sexual harassment guidelines. In this argument, which appeared in the *Boston Globe*, she explains why she believes they are deeply flawed and insulting to women and men alike.

Duke's Sexist Sexual Misconduct Policy

Cathy Young

April 14, 2010

Four years ago, Duke University became the center of a national controversy about sexual assault, wrongful accusations, and campus politics when four lacrosse players were falsely accused of raping an exotic dancer at a party. Now, Duke is back in the news with a campus policy that ostensibly seeks to prevent sexual assault — but, in fact, infantilizes women, redefines much consensual sex as potentially criminal, and does a grave disservice to both sexes.

The policy, introduced last fall but recently challenged by the Foundation for Individual Rights in Education, co-founded by Boston attorney Harvey Silverglate, targets "sexual misconduct" — everything from improper touching to forced sex. Some of the examples given in the text of the policy, such as groping an unwilling woman's breasts, are clearly sexual offenses not just under university regulations but under the law.

But the policy's far-reaching definition of sex without "affirmative consent" covers much more. Unlike the notorious Antioch College rules of the 1990s that required verbal consent to every new level of intimacy, Duke's policy recognizes non-verbal expressions of consent. However, it stresses that "consent may not be inferred from silence [or] passivity" — even in an ongoing sexual relationship.

The thesis of the article comes at the end of the first paragraph, a common location.

Young acknowledges some good sense in the Duke harassment policy.

Then the article begins to enumerate flaws in the school's new rules — the meat of the article.

What's more, consent can be invalidated by various circumstances — not just obvious ones such as being threatened or unconscious, but also being intoxicated to any degree, or "psychologically pressured," or "coerced." The latter is an extremely broad term, particularly since the policy warns that "real or perceived power differentials . . . may create an unintentional atmosphere of coercion." As FIRE has noted, a popular varsity athlete may face a presumption of coercion in any relationship with a fellow student.

Meanwhile, women, the default victims in the Duke policy, are presumed passive and weak-minded: Goddess forbid they should take more than minimal responsibility for refusing unwanted sex. In one of the policy's hypothetical scenarios, a woman tells her long-term boyfriend she's not in the mood, but then "is silent" in response to his continued non-forcible advances; if he takes this as consent and they have sex, that is "sexual misconduct." Why she doesn't tell him to stop remains a mystery.

Supporting her thesis, Young explains why she believes that the policy demeans women.

The man's behavior may be inconsiderate. However, adult college students have no more of a right to be protected from such ordinary pressures in relationships than, say, from being cajoled into buying expensive gifts for their significant other.

The refutation requires that readers agree that the harassment policy goes too far. So Young uses specific, though hypothetical, examples.

Most insidiously, under the new Duke policy the "offender" may face sanctions even if the "victim" doesn't think she is one. If a woman has a sexual encounter she regrets and tells a friend who decides she was coerced, the friend's third-party report can trigger an investigation. And if she tells a dorm adviser or a women's center staffer, they are obligated to report the incident.

About 15 years ago, as an undergraduate, a friend of mine was talked into a one-night stand in a situation some would call coercive: the man was a graduate student, and she felt somewhat intimidated by his intellectual brilliance. She went to a campus counselor hoping for advice on developing her assertiveness skills — only to be told that she had been assaulted and should not blame herself. My friend was frustrated and angry: in her view, the counselor was not only being unhelpful but telling her how to interpret her own experience. Imagine how much

more betrayed she would have felt if the counselor had been compelled
to initiate proceedings on her behalf.

The policy has other questionable aspects. While such offenses as
theft or assault are judged by a panel of three students and two faculty/
staff members, sexual misconduct charges are to be heard by two
faculty/staff members and one student; perhaps a jury of one's peers
cannot be relied upon to enforce the party line.

Sexual violence and abuse is a real problem on college campuses;
so are attitudes that, sometimes, still condone such behavior. But a
pseudo-feminist sex police that turns a large percentage of students into
either criminals or victims — and, in the process, trivializes real sexual
violence — is hardly the solution.

Language
of the
conclusion
is tough
and heavily
connotative:
*pseudo-
feminist,
sex police,
criminals,
victims.*

Use of "the
party line"
aligns Duke's
policy with
that of
authoritarian
states.

VISUAL ARGUMENT   "Visualizing the BP Oil ~~Spill~~ Disaster" appeared on the Web site IfItWereMy-Home.com in the aftermath of the collapse of the *Deepwater Horizon* oil rig on April 20, 2010. A graphic on the site enabled viewers to visualize just how large the resulting oil spill was by entering their own location into a box on the site. In the screenshot here, the spill is centered over New York City and stretches from Philadelphia almost to Boston. Without offering any explicit claim (except perhaps the deliberate strike-through of the word "spill"), the IfItWereMyHome.com Web site makes a sobering argument about the extent of the crisis and those responsible for it.

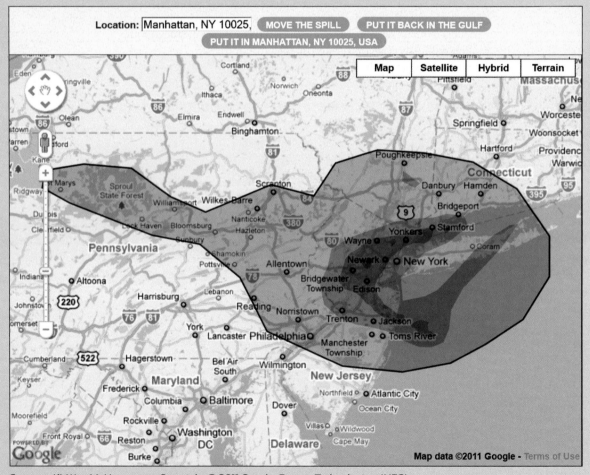

Courtesy IfItWereMyHome.com. Copyright © 2011 Google, Europa Technologies, INEGI.

1. **Argument to Advance a Thesis:** Review the way Scott Keyes supports a clearly stated thesis in "Stop Asking Me My Major" (p. 75). Then write an argument that similarly provides direct support for a controversial claim in the public sphere — one that has implications for other people. Like Keyes, take the time to explain the issue you are addressing and then try to offer multiple reasons to support your thesis.

2. **Exploratory Argument:** Write an argument that works its way toward a thesis rather than stating it outright in the opening section. Share with readers the process of your thinking the way Lynn Ehlers does in "Play 'Free Bird'!" (p. 95), encouraging them, perhaps, to come to the same conclusion, as you carefully lay out and explain your evidence. The paper will probably work best if you choose a topic about which you have strong feelings or opinions.

3. **Refutation Argument:** Find a text with which you strongly disagree and then systematically refute it, as Cathy Young does with the Duke University sexual harassment policy (p. 101). The text can be a position or policy promoted by a politician or public or corporate official, or it can be an argument in itself — a column, editorial, even a section in a textbook. Make your opposition clear, but also be fair to the position you are attempting to refute. It is especially important that your readers be able to understand whatever you are analyzing, even if they aren't familiar with it. That's a real challenge, so don't hesitate to summarize, paraphrase, or quote from the material.

4. **Visual Argument:** Although "Visualizing the BP Oil Spill Disaster" (p. 104) presents an issue dramatically and cleverly, the text allows readers to draw their own conclusions. But other visual arguments — such as advertisements or editorial cartoons — are typically more aggressive about stating a message, combining images and words to make a point. Create a visual argument of your own using whatever medium you believe will convey your message most successfully. Start with a clear point in mind. Then figure out how to present your claim powerfully and memorably.

5. **Your Choice:** These days, most serious arguments explode across interactive and networked environments, where they can take on a life of their own. Working with a group, design a media project (blog, Web site, mash-up, video, etc.) to focus on an issue that members of your group believe deserves more attention. Pool your talents to develop the site technically, rhetorically, and visually. Be sure your project introduces the subject, explains its purpose, encourages interaction, and includes relevant images and, if possible, links.

How to start

- Need a **topic**? See page 113.
- Need **criteria for your evaluation**? See page 117.
- Need to **organize your criteria and evidence**? See page 121.

4 Evaluations

make a claim about the merit of something

Evaluations and reviews are so much a part of our lives that you might notice them only when they are specifically assigned. Commentary and criticism of all sorts just happen.

PRODUCT REVIEW
Given your work experience at a camera store, you are invited to write a *product review* for a co-op newsletter about a new 15.1-megapixel digital SLR for photographers on tight budgets.

ARTS REVIEW
You're never shy about sharing your opinions of movies, films, and restaurants, but find it painful when you have to write an *arts review* of *Götter-dämmerung* for a music appreciation course. The opera lasts longer than a football game!

SOCIAL SATIRE
Tired of self-righteous cyclists who preach eco-fundamentalism and then clog traffic with monthly Critical Mass rides, you do what any irate citizen would — you mock them in a *social satire*.

VISUAL COMPARISON
You decide that the best way to document the work of a neighborhood group is to post *before* and *after* shots of the restorations it has done on several local buildings. Your *visual comparison* wins the group a grant from the city.

DECIDING TO WRITE AN EVALUATION   It's one thing to offer an opinion, an entirely different matter to back up a claim with reasons and evidence. Only when you do will readers (or listeners) take you seriously. But you'll also have to convince them that you know *how* to evaluate a book, a social policy, a cultural trend, or even a cup of coffee by reasonable criteria. It helps when you use objective standards to make judgments, counting and measuring the road to excellence. But evaluations frequently involve people debating matters of taste — which draws good sense and wit into the mix. Here's how to frame this kind of argument. ○

Make value judgments.   You'll either judge something as good, bad, or indifferent when you write an evaluation or challenge an opinion someone else has offered. Of course, fair judgments can be quite complex: Even movie critics who do thumbs-up-or-down routines don't offer those verdicts until after they first talk about their subjects in detail.

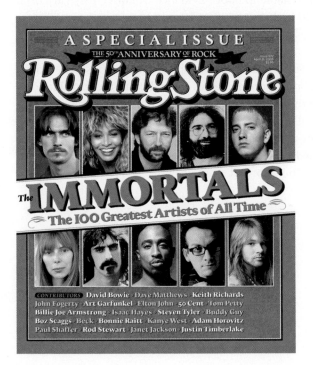

Popular magazines frequently evaluate or rank artists and celebrities, and their work.

(Cover photo from *Rolling Stone*, April 21, 2005. Copyright © Rolling Stone LLC 2005. All rights reserved. Reprinted by permission.)

○ choose a genre
p. 390

Establish and defend criteria.   *Criteria* are the standards by which objects are measured: *A good furnace should heat a home quickly and efficiently. Successful presidents leave office with the country in better shape than when they entered.* When readers will generally agree with your criteria, you need to explain little about them. When readers might disagree, you have to defend your criteria. ○ And sometimes you'll break new ground — as happened when critics first asked, *What is good Web design?* and *Which are the most significant social networks?* In such cases, new criteria of evaluation had to be invented and rationalized.

Offer convincing evidence.   Evidence in the form of facts, statistics, testimony, examples, good reasons, and keen observations provides the link between an evaluative claim and the criteria used to make it. If good furnaces heat homes quickly and efficiently, then you'd have to supply data to show that a product you judged faulty didn't meet those minimal standards. (It might be noisy and unreliable to boot.) Evidence will obviously vary from subject to subject; it could include anything from hard numbers to harrowing tales of personal woe. ○

Offer useful advice.   Some evaluations are just for fun: Consider all the hoopla that arguments about sports rankings generate. But most evaluations and reviews, when done right, also provide usable information, beneficial criticism, or even practical alternatives — sometimes offered in clever ways (charts, graphs, comparisons) to make it easy for readers to find and consult. So whether they examine humidifiers, restaurants, or candidates in a city council race, evaluations do important work.

develop ideas
p. 412

interview and
observe p. 478

In a world mesmerized by technology, product reviews like this one by David Pogue examining the just-released Apple iPad are both instructive and entertaining. What makes Pogue's review notable is his frank recognition that techies and ordinary consumers will judge the iPad by entirely different standards. Accordingly, he writes two reviews. The article appeared in the *New York Times*.

Looking at the iPad from Two Angles

David Pogue

March 31, 2010

In 10 years of reviewing tech products for the *New York Times*, I've never seen a product as polarizing as Apple's iPad, which arrives in stores on Saturday.

"This device is laughably absurd," goes a typical remark on a tech blog's comments board. "How can they expect anyone to get serious computer work done without a mouse?"

"This truly is a magical revolution," goes another. "I can't imagine why anyone will want to go back to using a mouse and keyboard once they've experienced Apple's visionary user interface!"

Those are some pretty confident critiques of the iPad — considering that their authors have never even tried it.

In any case, there's a pattern to these assessments.

The haters tend to be techies; the fans tend to be regular people. Therefore, no single write-up can serve both readerships adequately. There's but one solution: Write separate reviews for these two audiences.

Read the first one if you're a techie. (How do you know? Take this simple test. Do you use BitTorrent? Do you run Linux? Do you have more e-mail addresses than pants? You're a techie.)

Read the second review if you're anyone else.

> Think about the two quotations here: within them Pogue finds criteria of evaluation different enough to justify two reviews.

> Pogue's test is a "stipulative definition" of techies created just for this essay. Does it help you understand his use of the term?

fill the screen, a little blurry. Still, all the greats work this way: Dragon Dictation, Skype (even voice calls, through its speaker and microphone) and those gazillion games.

But the real fun begins when you try the apps that were specially designed for the iPad's bigger screen. (When the iPad section of the App Store opens Saturday, it will start with 1,000 of them.)

That Scrabble app shows the whole board without your zooming or panning: a free companion app for your iPhone or Touch is called Tile Rack; it lets you fiddle with your letters in private, then flick them wirelessly onto the iPad's screen. Newspaper apps will reproduce the layout, photos and colors of a real newspaper. The Marvel comic-book app is brilliant in its vividness and panel-by-panel navigation. (Oops, maybe that app belongs in the review for techies.)

Hulu.com, the Web's headquarters for free hit TV shows, won't confirm the talk that it's working on an iPad app, but wow—can you imagine? A thin, flat, cordless, bottomless source of free, great TV shows, in your bag or on the bedside table?

Speaking of video: Apple asserts that the iPad runs 10 hours on a charge of its nonremovable battery—but we all know you can't trust the manufacturer. And sure enough, in my own test, the iPad played movies continuously from 7:30 a.m. to 7:53 p.m.—more than 12 hours. That's four times as long as a typical laptop or portable DVD player.

The iPad is so fast and light, the multitouch screen so bright and responsive, the software so easy to navigate, that it really does qualify as a new category of gadget. Some have suggested that it might make a good goof-proof computer for technophobes, the aged and the young; they're absolutely right.

And the techies are right about another thing: the iPad is not a laptop. It's not nearly as good for creating stuff. On the other hand, it's infinitely more convenient for consuming it—books, music, video, photos, Web, e-mail and so on. For most people, manipulating these digital materials directly by touching them is a completely new experience—and a deeply satisfying one.

The bottom line is that the iPad has been designed and built by a bunch of perfectionists. If you like the concept, you'll love the machine.

The only question is: Do you like the concept?

An important insight: "Real fun" explains what many consumers want from their handheld devices.

Both reviews are detailed, providing useful information and advice.

The conclusion draws a thoughtful distinction between devices that create and consume stuff: Is it also a difference between the two audiences of the review?

Exploring purpose and topic

Most evaluations you're required to prepare for school or work come with assigned topics. But to choose an object to evaluate, follow different strategies, depending on what you hope to accomplish. ○

topic ◀

Evaluate a subject you know well.   This is the safest option, built on the assumption that everyone is an expert on something. Years of reading *Cooks Illustrated* magazine or playing tennis might make it natural for you to review restaurants or tennis rackets. You've accumulated not only basic facts but also lots of hands-on knowledge—the sort that gives you confidence when you make a claim. So go ahead and demonstrate your expertise.

Evaluate a subject you need to investigate.   Perhaps you are considering graduate schools to apply to, looking for family-friendly companies to work for, or thinking about purchasing an HDTV. To make such choices, you'll need more information. So kill two birds with a single assignment: Use the school project to explore the issues you face, find the necessary facts and data, and make a case for (or against) Michigan State, Whole Foods, or Sony.

Evaluate a subject you'd like to know more about.   How do wine connoisseurs tell one cabernet from another and rank them so confidently? How would a college football championship team from the fifties match up against more recent winning teams? Use an assignment to settle questions like these that you and your friends may have debated late into the evening.

Evaluate a subject that's been on your mind.   Not all evaluations are driven by a need to make particular decisions. Instead, you may feel an obligation to make a critical point about social, cultural, and political issues: You believe a particular piece of health-care or immigration legislation is bad policy or find yourself disturbed by political trends or changes in society. An evaluation is the appropriate genre for giving voice to those criticisms, whether you compose a conventional piece or venture into the realms of satire or parody.

find a topic
p. 356

Keep an open mind.   Whatever your topic, you probably shouldn't begin most academic evaluations already knowing the outcome — hating a book before you read it or dead set against any chilies not grown in Hatch, New Mexico. Follow your criteria and data to the reasonable choice — even if it's one you don't prefer. Obvious exceptions to these guidelines might include subjects of the kind described under the previous heading: social, cultural, or political issues already settled in your mind. But, even then, don't review what you can't treat fairly.

> **Your Turn**   Brainstorm to create a list of items or subjects that you know enough about, even without much research, to write a credible review. Some subjects will be obvious. If you make pottery, run track, or paint houses, you probably know enough about these subjects to judge pots, assess track shoes, or choose a good lacquer. But don't ignore other paths to expertise you may not even notice. Perhaps you have lived in several states long enough to write knowledgeably about their educational systems or arts communities. Or maybe you can write compellingly about local health-care facilities because of personal experiences with them. When you've compiled your list, compare it with ones that your classmates have drawn up. Their lists will probably suggest more topics for your own.

Understanding your audience

Your job as a reviewer is made easier when you can assume readers might be interested in your opinions. Fortunately, most people consult evaluations and reviews willingly, often hoping to find specific information: *Is the latest Stephen L. Carter novel up to snuff? Who's the most important American architect working today? Phillies or Braves in the NL East this year?* But you'll still have to gauge the level of potential readers and make appropriate adjustments — as David Pogue does explicitly in "Looking at the iPad from Two Angles" (p. 109).

Write for experts. Knowledgeable readers can be a tough audience because they may bring strong, maybe inflexible, opinions to a topic. But if you know your stuff, you can take on the experts because they know their stuff too: You don't have to provide tedious background information or discuss criteria of evaluation in detail. You can use the technical vocabulary experts share and make allusions to people and concepts they'd recognize. ○ Here are a few in-crowd sentences from a review of the football video game *Backbreaker* from an online gaming site:

> *Backbreaker* joins the sports design trend of placing emphasis on the right analog stick. It's everything from your swim/rip move on defense, to your bonecrunching hit or tackle, to juking, spinning, selecting receivers and passing. You use the right trigger as an action modifier ("aggressive mode") to go into other areas of your player's toolset. Everything is contextual to the type of player you control and it's pick-up-and-play intuitive after one trip through the tutorial.
>
> –Kotaku, "*Backbreaker* Review: The Challenger Crashes"

Write for a general audience. You have to explain more to general audiences than to specialists, clarifying your criteria of evaluation, providing background information, and defining key terms. But general readers usually are willing to learn more about a topic. Here's noted film critic Roger Ebert doing exactly that:

> *The Lake House* tells the story of a romance that spans years but involves only a few kisses. It succeeds despite being based on two paradoxes: time travel and the ability of two people to have conversations that are, under the terms established by the film, impossible. Neither one of these problems

Need help thinking about your audience? See "How to Revise Your Work" on pp. 456–57.

improve your
sentences p. 444

bothered me in the slightest. Take time travel: I used to get distracted by its logical flaws and contradictory time lines. Now in my wisdom I have decided to simply accept it as a premise, no questions asked. A time-travel story works on emotional, not temporal, logic.

—rogerebert.com, June 16, 2006

Write for novices.   You have a lot of explaining to do when readers are absolutely fresh to a subject and need lots of background information. For instance, because *Consumer Reports* reviews a range of products well beyond the expertise of any individual, the editors always take care to explain how they make their judgments, whether the subject is washing machines, waffles, or Web sites. Do the same yourself. Take special care to define technical terms for your readers.

For example, at Digital Photography Review, a Web site that examines photographic equipment in detail, you will find the following warning attached to all its camera reviews: "If you're new to digital photography you may wish to read the Digital Photography *Glossary* before diving into this article (it may help you understand some of the terms used)." Clicking the link leads to a fully illustrated dictionary of terms meant to help amateurs understand the qualities of a good digital camera.

Are buffalo dangerous?
For some audiences, you
have to explain everything.

Finding and developing materials

develop criteria ◄

When you are assigned to write a review, it makes sense to research your subject thoroughly, even one you think you know pretty well. Online research is inevitable: Do a quick Web search to see if your notions are still current in a world where opinions change rapidly. ○

For many subjects (and products especially), it's easy to discover what others have already had to offer, particularly when a topic has a distinctive name. Just type that name followed by the word *review* into an online search window and see what pops up. But don't merely parrot opinions you find in sources: Take issue with conventional views whenever you can offer smarter ones. (At one time, most critics thought good poetry should rhyme — until some poets and critics argued otherwise.) Make a fresh case of your own. To do that, focus on criteria and evidence.

Decide on your criteria.   Clarify your criteria, even if you're just evaluating pizza. Should the crust be hard or soft? Should the sauce be red and spicy, or white and creamy? How thick should the pizza be? How salty? And, for all these opinions — *why*?

Didn't expect the *why*? You really don't have a criterion until you attach a plausible reason to it. ○ The rationale should be clear in your own mind even if you don't expect to explain it in the review or evaluation itself: *Great pizza comes with a soft crust that wraps each bite and topping in a floury texture that merges the contrasting flavors*. More important, any criterion you use will have to make sense to readers either on its own (*Public art should be beautiful*) or after you've explained and defended it (*Public art should be scandalous because people need to be jolted out of conformist thinking*).

Look for hard criteria.   It helps when criteria are countable or observable. You'll seem objective when your criteria at least *seem* grounded in numbers. Think, for example, of how instructors set numerical standards for your performance in their courses, translating all sorts of activities, from papers to class participation, into numbers. Teachers aren't alone in deferring to numbers. CNET Reviews, for instance, uses a numerical rating system to evaluate televisions, as explained on its Web site:

refine your search
p. 472

develop a statement
p. 393

Design (30 percent of the total rating): We look at not only the overall aesthetics of the product but also its interface and included remote. An uninspiring but functional design will rate a 5. Higher scores will be given for a well-designed remote with backlit buttons, a clear onscreen navigation system, and particularly sleek cosmetics.

Features (30 percent of the total rating): The range of features is considered in determining this portion of the rating. From picture-in-picture (PIP) and 2:3 pull-down to the appropriate number of A/V inputs, we consider everything this product delivers to the consumer. A set that comes armed with a suitable number of inputs and basic features will earn a 5. Products with more inputs, individual input memories, or other extras will earn a better rating.

Performance (40 percent of the total rating): We consider picture quality to be the most important criteria for displays, so we give it the most weight. A score of 5 represents a television that can produce a serviceable picture with only a reasonable amount of adjustment. Sets with a particularly sharp picture; rich, accurate color; deep black levels; and good video processing will earn a higher score.

"Gentlemen, I've decided to retire. The new chairman will be the first one to throw a six."

Argue for criteria that can't be measured.   How do you measure the success or failure of something that can't be objectively calculated — a student dance recital, Jay-Z's latest recording, or the new abstract sculpture just hauled onto the campus? Do some research to find out how such topics are customarily evaluated and discussed. Get familiar with what sensible critics have to say about whatever you're evaluating — contemporary art, fine saddles, good teaching, effective foreign policy. If you read carefully, you'll find values and criteria embedded in all your sources. ○

In the following excerpt, for example, James Morris explains why he believes American television is often better than Hollywood films. Morris's criteria are highlighted.

> What I admire most about these shows, and most deplore about contemporary movies, is the quality of the scripts. The TV series are devised and written by smart people who seem to be allowed to let their intelligence show. Yes, the individual and ensemble performances on several of the series are superb, but would the actors be as good as they are if they were miming the action? TV shows are designed for the small screen and cannot rely, as movies do, on visual and aural effects to distract audiences. If what's being said on TV isn't interesting, why bother to watch? Television is rigorous, right down to the confinement of hour or half-hour time slots, further reduced by commercials. There's no room for the narrative bloat that inflates so many Hollywood movies from their natural party-balloon size to Thanksgiving-parade dimensions.
>
> —"My Favorite Wasteland," *Wilson Quarterly*, Autumn 2005

Stand by your values.   Make sure you define criteria that apply to more than just the individual case you are examining at the moment. Think about what makes socially conscious rap music, world-class sculpture, a great president. For instance, you may have a special fondness for Jimmy Carter, but should criteria for great presidents be measured by what they do *after* they leave office? Similarly, you might admire artists or actors who overcome great personal tragedies on their paths to stardom. But to make such heroics a *necessary* criterion for artistic achievement might look like special pleading.

read closely
p. 365

Gather your evidence.   Some of the evidence for your evaluation will come from secondary sources, especially if you are assessing something like a government program or historical event. Before offering an opinion on the merits of Social Security or the wisdom of Truman's decision to drop atomic bombs to end World War II, expect to do critical reading. Weigh the evidence and arguments you find in these sources before you offer your own judgment — and then cite some of these sources for evidence and support. ⓞ

Other evidence will come from careful observation. Sometimes, you'll just need to be attuned to the world around you — as Jordyn Brown is in cataloging the behavior of cell phone users (see p. 131). When reviewing a book, a movie, a restaurant, or a similar item, take careful notes not only of your initial impressions but also of the details that support or explain them. When appropriate, take the time to measure, weigh, photograph, or inter-view your subjects. If it makes sense to survey what others think about an issue (a campus political flap, for example), keep a record of such opinions. Finally, be willing to alter your opinion when the evidence you gather in support of a hypothesis heads in a direction you hadn't expected.

analyze claims and
evidence p. 487

Creating a structure

As with other arguments, evaluations have distinct parts that can be built into a pattern or structure.

organize criteria ◀

Choose a simple structure when your criteria and categories are predictable.   A basic review might announce a subject and make a claim, list the criteria of evaluation, present evidence to show whether the subject meets those standards, and draw conclusions. Here's one version of that pattern with the criteria discussed all at once, at the opening of the piece.

> **Introduction leading to an evaluative claim**
>
> **Criteria of evaluation stated and, if necessary, defended**
>
> **Subject measured by first criterion + evidence**
> **Subject measured by second criterion + evidence**
> **Subject measured by additional criteria + evidence**
>
> **Conclusion**

And here's a template with the criteria of evaluation introduced one at a time.

> **Introduction leading to an evaluative claim**
>
> **First criterion of evaluation stated and, if necessary, defended**
>
> **Subject measured by first criterion + evidence**
>
> **Second criterion stated/defended**
>
> **Subject measured by second criterion + evidence**
>
> **Additional criteria stated/defended**
>
> **Subject measured by additional criteria + evidence**
>
> **Conclusion**

You might find structures this tight and predictable, for instance, in job-performance reviews at work or in consumer magazines. Once a pattern is established for measuring TVs, computers, paint sprayers, or even teachers (consider those forms you fill in at the end of the term), it can be repeated for each new subject and results can be compared.

Yet what works for hardware and tech products is not quite so convincing when applied to music, books, political policies, or societal behaviors that are more than the sum of their parts. Imagine a film critic whose *every* review marched through the same predictable set of criteria: acting, directing, writing, cinematography, and special effects. When a subject can't (or shouldn't) be reviewed via simple categories, you will need to decide which of its many possible aspects deserve attention. ○

Choose a focal point.   Look for features that you and your readers will surely notice, that is, what makes you react strongly and intellectually to the subject. You could, in fact, organize an entire review around one or more shrewd insights, and many reviewers do. The trick is to make connections

Do political pundits like Chris Matthews and Michelle Malkin lose their clout when they become predictable? Maybe they're exceptions.

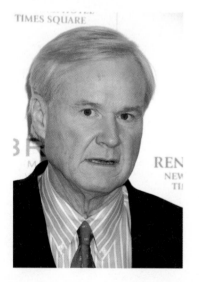

shape your work
p. 406

between key or controlling ideas and various aspects of your subject. Look carefully at Jordyn Brown's scathing satire of cell phone users (p. 131) and you'll discover that what holds it together is the complaint that people are missing important aspects of their life. Brown dramatizes that problem by beginning and ending the paper at a birthday party that she and a dozen friends are just barely attending:

> This dinner was supposed to be a festive gathering to celebrate our good friend Stacey's birthday. But no one mingled or celebrated, not even Stacey. Everyone seemed to be somewhere else. They had all wandered off to Google-town, Twitter-ville, and Texting-My-Boyfriend City; and I was left there alone at the Cheesecake Factory. . . . Twelve people preferred phone activities to talking to each other and *me* over three-tiered red velvet cheesecake. Seriously, people. Put those phones down. You're not thinking clearly.

Compare and contrast.   Another obvious way to organize an evaluation is to examine differences. ○ Strengths and weaknesses stand out especially well when similar subjects are examined critically, as in the following concluding paragraph of a road-test competition in *Popular Mechanics*:

> So was the Camaro worth the wait? Yes. The newest pony car delivers an undeniable mix of performance and value. It's the quickest and likely has the highest handling limits of the three coupes. The Mustang is the rough and tumble sports car. It's the most involving car to drive—it feels more organic than the other two. The Challenger R/T provides more comfort and practicality at the expense of all-out performance. Yet, to our eye, the Dodge just may be the best looking of the group. But these are muscle cars. And the Camaro's mix of power, poise and refinement just edges out the others—this time.
>
> —Ben Stewart, "Muscle Car Competition," March 23, 2009

use comparison and
contrast p. 404

Choosing a style and design

Depending on the aim of the review you are composing and your stance within it, evaluations can be written in any style, from high to low. ○ You should also look for opportunities to present evaluations visually.

Use a high or formal style.   Technical reviews tend to be the most formal and impersonal: They may be almost indistinguishable from reports, describing their findings in plain, unemotional language. Such a style gives the impression of scientific objectivity, even though the work may reflect someone's agenda. For instance, here's a paragraph in formal style from the National Assessment of Educational Progress summarizing the performance of American students in science.

> At grade 8, there was no overall improvement. In 2005, 59 percent of students scored at or above the *Basic* level. An example of the knowledge and skills at the *Basic* level is being able to compare changes in heart rate during and after exercise. Twenty-nine percent performed at or above the *Proficient* level. Identifying the energy conversions that occur in an electric fan is an example of the knowledge and skills at the *Proficient* level.
>
> —*Nation's Report Card*, 2005 Science Assessment (http://nationsreportcard.gov/science_2005)

Use a middle style.   When the writer has a more direct stake in the work — as is typical in restaurant or movie reviews, for example — the style moves more decisively toward the middle. Even though a reviewer may never use *I*, you still sense a person behind the writing, making judgments and offering opinions. That's certainly the case in these two paragraphs by Clive Crook, written shortly after the death of noted economist John Kenneth Galbraith: Words, phrases, even sentence fragments that humanize the assessment are highlighted, while a contrast to economist Milton Friedman also sharpens the portrait.

> Galbraith, despite the Harvard professorship, was never really an economist in the ordinary sense in the first place. In one of countless well-turned pronouncements, he said, "Economics is extremely useful as

define your style
p. 432

a form of employment for economists." He disdained the scientific pretensions and formal apparatus of modern economics—all that math and number crunching—believing that it missed the point. This view did not spring from mastery of the techniques: Galbraith disdained them from the outset, which saved time.

Friedman, in contrast, devoted his career to grinding out top-quality scholarly work, while publishing the occasional best seller as a sideline. He too was no math whiz, but he was painstakingly scientific in his methods (when engaged in scholarly research) and devoted to data. All that was rather beneath Galbraith. Brilliant, yes; productive, certainly. But he was a bureaucrat, a diplomat, a political pundit, and a popular economics writer of commanding presence more than a serious economic thinker, let alone a great one.

—"John Kenneth Galbraith, Revisited," *National Journal*, May 15, 2006

Use a low style.   Many reviews get personal with readers, and some get so chummy that they verge on rudeness. You probably want evaluations you write for academic or work assignments to be relatively polite and low-key in style, focused more on the subject than on you as the reviewer. But you do have an enormous range of options — especially when writing social and political commentary. Then, if your evaluations turn into satire, all the gloves come off. In such situations, humor or sarcasm can be powerful tools, but no style is more difficult to manage. Humor requires great precision and economy, or the jokes fall flat, which is a good reason to look at models of the kinds of evaluation you will be composing. Study the ones you admire for lessons in style.

Present evaluations visually.   Evaluations work especially well when claims can be supported by tables, charts, graphs, or other visual elements. Readers see relationships that could not be conveyed quite as efficiently in words alone. ○ And sometimes the images simply have more impact. Consider your response to images of real fast-food items posted on an offbeat

display data
p. 425

Web site called the West Virginia Surf Report. Here's the description of the feature that appeared on the site:

Fast Food: Ads vs. Reality   Each item was purchased, taken home, and photographed immediately. Nothing was tampered with, run over by a car, or anything of the sort. It is an accurate representation in every case. Shiny, neon-orange, liquefied pump-cheese, and all.

Here are several of the images the site presented of products purchased from well-known national chains:

All you need to do is recall the photographs of these items you've seen posted in the fast-food restaurants and you can draw your own conclusion: *Caveat emptor!*

Your Turn   Almost everyone reads at least one critic or type of review regularly—of restaurants, movies, TV shows, sports teams, gizmos, video games, and so on. Pick a review by your favorite critic or, alternatively, a review you have read recently and noted. Then examine its style closely. Is it formal, informal, or casual? Technical or general? Serious or humorous? Full of allusions to stuff regular readers would get? What features of the style do you like? Do you have any reservations about the style? In a detailed paragraph, evaluate only the style of the reviewer or review (not the substance), organizing your work to support a clear thesis.

Examining models

People rely on critics of every kind of art and entertainment to help them decide what to read, watch, see, or hear. Charles Isherwood is an influential critic of the theater. In "Stomping onto Broadway with a Punk Temper Tantrum," he reviews an unusual item for the *New York Times*: the punk rock album *American Idiot* turned into a Broadway musical.

Stomping onto Broadway with a Punk Temper Tantrum

Charles Isherwood

April 21, 2010

Opening sentence states a thesis: The musical is emotional, thrilling, and gorgeous.

Rage and love, those consuming emotions felt with a particularly acute pang in youth, all but burn up the stage in "American Idiot," the thrillingly raucous and gorgeously wrought Broadway musical adapted from the blockbuster pop-punk album by Green Day.

Pop on Broadway, sure. But punk? Yes, indeed, and served straight up, with each sneering lyric and snarling riff in place. A stately old pile steps from the tourist-clogged Times Square might seem a strange place for the music of Green Day, and for theater this blunt, bold and aggressive in its attitude. Not to mention loud. But from the moment the curtain rises on

American Idiot: John Gallagher Jr., left, as Johnny, and Tony Vincent as St. Jimmy in the musical *American Idiot* at the St. James Theater. (Sara Krulwich/*The New York Times*.)

127

Isherwood sets the scene: a punk musical by a young cast in a stately old theater.

a panorama of baleful youngsters at the venerable St. James Theater, where the show opened on Tuesday night, it's clear that these kids are going to make themselves at home, even if it means tearing up the place in the process.

Which they do, figuratively speaking. "American Idiot," directed by Michael Mayer and performed with galvanizing intensity by a terrific cast, detonates a fierce aesthetic charge in this ho-hum Broadway season. A pulsating portrait of wasted youth that invokes all the standard genre conventions—bring on the sex, drugs and rock 'n' roll, please!—only to transcend them through the power of its music and the artistry of its execution, the show is as invigorating and ultimately as moving as anything I've seen on Broadway this season. Or maybe for a few seasons past.

Formal style employs complex sentence structures and a spirited vocabulary to characterize the show: *galvanizing, pulsating, invigorating, moving.*

Burning with rage and love, and knowing how and when to express them, are two different things, of course. The young men we meet in the first minutes of "American Idiot" are too callow and sullen and restless—too young, basically—to channel their emotions construc-tively. The show opens with a glorious 20-minute temper tantrum kicked off by the title song.

Ample, almost lush, descriptions help readers imagine the show. Performers are carefully credited.

"Don't want to be an American idiot!" shouts one of the gang. The song's signature electric guitar riff slashes through the air, echoing the testy challenge of the cry. A sharp eight-piece band, led by the conductor Carmel Dean, is arrayed around the stage, providing a sonic frame for the action. The simple but spectacular set, designed by Christine Jones, suggests an epically scaled dive club, its looming walls papered in punk posters and pimpled by television screens, on which frenzied video collages flicker throughout the show. (They're the witty work of Darrel Maloney.)

Who's the American idiot being referred to? Well, as that curtain slowly rose, we heard the familiar voice of George W. Bush break through a haze of television chatter: "Either you are with us, or with the terrorists." That kind of talk could bring out the heedless rebel in any kid, particularly one who is already feeling itchy at the lack of prospects in his dreary suburban burg.

But while "American Idiot" is nominally a portrait of youthful malaise of a particular era—the album dates from 2004, the midpoint of the Bush years, and the show is set in "the recent past"—its depiction of the crisis of post-adolescence is essentially timeless. Teenagers eager for their lives to begin, desperate to slough off their old selves and escape boredom through

Isherwood here introduces an important criterion: timelessness.

pure sensation, will probably always be making the same kinds of mistakes, taking the same wrong turns on the road to self-discovery.

"American Idiot" is a true rock opera, almost exclusively using the music of Green Day and the lyrics of its kohl-eyed frontman, Billie Joe Armstrong, to tell its story. (The score comprises the whole of the title album as well as several songs from the band's most recent release, "21st Century Breakdown.") The book, by Mr. Armstrong and Mr. Mayer, consists only of a series of brief, snarky dispatches sent home by the central character, Johnny, played with squirmy intensity by the immensely gifted John Gallagher Jr. ("Spring Awakening," "Rabbit Hole").

"I held up my local convenience store to get a bus ticket," Johnny says with a smirk as he and a pal head out of town.

"Actually I stole the money from my mom's dresser."

Beat.

"Actually she lent me the cash."

Such is the sheepish fate of a would-be rebel today. But at least Johnny and his buddy Tunny (Stark Sands) do manage to escape deadly suburbia for the lively city, bringing along just their guitars and the anomie and apathy that are the bread and butter of teenage attitudinizing the world over. ("I don't care if you don't care," a telling lyric, could be their motto.)

The friend they meant to bring along, Will (Michael Esper), was forced to stay home when he discovered that his girlfriend (Mary Faber) was pregnant. Lost and lonely, and far from ready for the responsibilities of fatherhood, he sinks into the couch, beer in one hand and bong in the other, as his friends set off for adventure.

Beneath the swagger of indifference, of course, are anxiety, fear and insecurity, which Mr. Gallagher, Mr. Esper and Mr. Sands transmit with aching clarity in the show's more reflective songs, like the hit "Boulevard of Broken Dreams" or the lilting anthem "Are We the Waiting." The city turns out to be just a bigger version of the place Johnny and Tunny left behind, a "land of make believe that don't believe in me." The boys discover that while a fractious 21st-century America may not offer any easy paths to fulfillment, the deeper problem is that they don't know how to believe in themselves.

Johnny strolls the lonely streets with his guitar, vaguely yearning for love and achievement. He eventually hooks up with a girl (a vivid Rebecca

---

Rather than rehash the meager plot of the rock opera, Isherwood explains it through a string of telling incidents.

The style is given texture by song lyrics, characters' names, and crisp descriptions: "the swagger of indifference," "an androgynous goth drug pusher."

Naomi Jones) but falls more powerfully under the spell of an androgynous goth drug pusher, St. Jimmy, played with mesmerizing vitality and
piercing vocalism by Tony Vincent. Tunny mostly stays in bed, clicker
affixed to his right hand, dangerously susceptible to a pageant of propaganda about military heroism on the tube, set to the song "Favorite Son."
By the time the song's over, he's enlisted and off to Iraq.

In explaining
what
operas do,
Isherwood
offers
another
criterion of
evaluation.
Then he
applies it to
*American
Idiot.*

In both plotting and its emotional palette, "American Idiot" is drawn in
brash, primary-colored strokes, maybe too crudely for those looking for
specifics of character rather than cultural archetypes. But operas — rock
or classical — often trade in archetypes, and the actors flesh out their
characters' journeys through their heartfelt interpretations of the songs,
with the help of Mr. Mayer's poetic direction and the restless, convulsive
choreography of Steven Hoggett ("Black Watch"), which exults in both the
grace and the awkwardness of energy-generating young metabolisms.

Line by line, a skeptic could fault Mr. Armstrong's lyrics for their
occasional glibness or grandiosity. That's to be expected, too: rock
music exploits heightened emotion and truisms that can fit neatly
into a memorable chorus. The songs are precisely as articulate — and
inarticulate — as the characters are, reflecting the moment in youth
when many of us feel that pop music has more to say about us than we
have to say for ourselves. (And, really, have you ever worked your way
through a canonical Italian opera libretto, line by line?)

Predictably,
Isherwood
also evaluates
the show's
music by
standards
he defines
for rock/pop
music.

In any case the music is thrilling: charged with urgency, rich in
memorable melody and propulsive rhythms that sometimes evolve
midsong. The orchestrations by Tom Kitt (the composer of "Next to
Normal") move from lean and mean to lush, befitting the tone of each
number. Even if you are unfamiliar with Green Day's music, you are
more likely to emerge from this show humming one of the guitar riffs
than you are to find a tune from "The Addams Family" tickling your
memory.

Another
criterion? A
good musical
sends patrons
home
humming
a tune.

But the emotion charge that the show generates is as memorable as
the music. "American Idiot" jolts you right back to the dizzying roller
coaster of young adulthood, that turbulent time when ecstasy and
misery almost seem interchangeable states, flip sides of the coin of
exaltation. It captures with a piercing intensity that moment in life
when everything seems possible, and nothing seems worth doing, or
maybe it's the other way around.

The
conclusion
leaves no
doubt about
the reasons
for Isherwood's
rave review.

SOCIAL SATIRE   Satires, which poke fun at the foibles of society in order to correct them, often require writers to draw exaggerated but recognizable portraits of people and situations. That's what Jordyn Brown attempts to do in a paper aimed at getting her friends to shut off their cell phones and pay more attention to life. If readers laugh too, that's all to the good.

Brown 1

Jordyn Brown

Professor Ruszkiewicz

Rhetoric 325M

May 5, 20--

A Word from My Anti-Phone Soapbox

I sat for at least five minutes staring at the tops of the other dinner guests' heads. All twenty-four eyes (that's twelve pairs) were unwaveringly fixed on their respective laps. I didn't understand why my friends held their phones under the table. We weren't in class. Perhaps it was a subconscious admittance of shame for their inattentiveness. I sat at the dinner table confused. This dinner was supposed to be a festive gathering to celebrate our good friend Stacey's birthday. But no one mingled or celebrated, not even Stacey. Everyone seemed to be somewhere else. They had all wandered off to Google-town, Twitter-ville, and Texting-My-Boyfriend City; and I was left there alone at the Cheesecake Factory.

Bitter frustration grew inside me because (a) my party's behavior was ridiculous and (b) I'd left my own phone in the car. Luckily, my thoughts occupied me and kept me from mounting

> Opening paragraph, especially its final sentence, sets the scene and the tone.

Brown 2

my chair and giving my friends a stern and passionate tongue-lashing right in the middle of the restaurant. My peers disgusted me with their technological dependency. So I packaged the lecture I felt coming on at the dinner table neatly in my brain and will now recite it for you, minus the expletives.

Maybe I'm just bitter because my phone is only capable of Stone Age maneuvers like making calls and texting. But having the whole World Wide Web in your hands has ruined all of you tech fiends. Look at yourselves. You can't bear to face that terrible affliction people had to endure years ago called *boredom*. So you fill up your fancy little devices with applications, games, movies, and music to ensure that you'll never have an unoccupied moment. What a shame that would be! America's greatest pastime used to be baseball. The magic of a triple play or an out-of-the-park home run made the hours spent watching inning after inning well worth it. But now you need constant stimulation. You want to see a home run every at-bat. Your movies need to be 90 percent car chase. Your telephones are full-on pocket-sized entertainment centers. You've bastardized thrill and excitement; you can't be pleased. The movie you saw last night wasn't too slow; your world is just too fast.

Information just shouldn't be this readily available. You people can't handle it. You Urbanspoon one tasty restaurant

In classical terms, the paper is an invective.

First attack focuses on the obsessive need for stimulation: "your world is just too fast."

Brown 3

and think you're A. A. Gill, famous British food critic. This
constant tech stream has even ruined good arguments.
Before, you would argue fervently for hours.

> "*Top Gun* came out in '84!"

> "No man, it came out in '86!"

And then you'd go round and round and, at the end
of the night, no one really knew the right answer because
both debaters argued so well. But, oh no, these beautiful
moments are nearly extinct because some cocky know-it-all's
going to whip out his iPhone, always conveniently connected
to Google. And with a few strokes of his touch screen he'll
find a source, take the other guy down, and crush his spirit.
Braggarts today strut around like they know everything.
No, it's Google that knows everything; you just have a
cool phone.

And it's not just the search engines that give you
phone-tech junkies balloon heads. Twitter and Facebook have
you believing that people really want to know every minute
detail of your life. Now, I hate to be the bearer of bad news,
but unless you're Ashton Kutcher or Kim Kardashian, no one
is tracking your every move every second of the day. So cut
out all the Facebook statuses about your disposable-ware
crisis at Target. Don't waste the space on my news feed
with "Should I get paper or Styrofoam plates?" Annoying.

Second point is that technology makes us think we're smarter than we are.

Throughout, the casual style mimics speech: "what a shame that would be"; "but, oh no"; "pitiful."

Technology also makes us think we are the center of the universe.

Brown 4

And I don't care what you had for lunch. Don't TwitPic a picture of your meal, because it makes no sense. What if you'd done that ten years ago? If you had skipped into school with a picture you had gotten developed at the drugstore and gone around showing it to people, saying, "Hey guys, look what I had for dinner!" the whole fifth-grade class would have looked at you like you were insane. Twitter has made nonsense commonplace. No thought is too base to fill a tweet's 140 characters. Pitiful.

> The examples throughout work if readers recognize some truth under the exaggerations.

Sad to say, these handheld devices have turned you into technologically overindulged brats. You break into temper tantrums, stomping around, pouting, throwing your Blackberries at soft surfaces, and crossing your arms in agitation whenever you hit a dead zone and can't access your precious Internet. And you have even less patience for your friends when you text or call them. After all, everything you have to say—spoken or in text—is infinitely more important than anything else in their lives. The meaning of the word *urgent* has evolved since the earliest days of portable and instant communication devices. Once only physicians routinely received urgent messages: "Hurry, we need you, Dr. Cardiologist, to fix this man's horrible heart." But now *urgent* can mean, "911! What do you feel like eating for dinner? I'm at the grocery store now. Hurry and call me

> The paragraph shows how smartphones are leading to breakdowns in social relations.

Brown 5

back!!!" And I wouldn't dare let a text message from you sit in my in-box for more than an hour or I'd be in for a scolding the next time I see you.

So, Earth to you, the people who never part from their cell phones. I'm sure you've taken several breaks while reading this rant to check your e-mail and respond to a few texts. You probably missed most of the points of my argument too, much like you're missing what's going on in the world around you. Cell phones were initially meant to connect us, broadening the time frame during which people could communicate with one another. But with all the new apps being incorporated into these devices, isolation only grows, shrinking your world and perspective. You're all constantly talking and thinking about how *you* feel and what *you* think. You don't talk to Rachel or Stephen but to the "Twitter-verse" or to Facebook at large. You communicate without any idea of who's really listening.

Twelve people preferred phone activities to talking to each other and *me* over three-tiered red velvet cheesecake. Seriously, people. Put those phones down. You're not thinking clearly.

Like most satires, this one turns serious and offers a simple solution: Turn off the phone.

VISUAL COMPARISON   How might the Insurance Institute for Highway Safety memorably celebrate its fiftieth anniversary? By crashing two cars fifty years apart in age to show how much crash safety has improved, thanks in part to the efforts of the group. The visual evidence represents a startling and memorable evaluation of their work.

50 years
Insurance Institute for Highway Safety of research & communications

Crash Test

Insurance Institute for Highway Safety

Top photo testifies to the violence of the 40-mph crash.

Test compares crashworthiness then and now: 1959 Chevrolet Bel Air and 2009 Chevrolet Malibu in 40 mph frontal offset test (click on photos to see larger images).

Watch a video of the crash test

2009 Chevrolet Malibu   1959 Chevrolet Bel Air

The collision demolishes the front ends of both vehicles.

Malibu post-crash   Bel Air post-crash

But the passenger compartments tell a different story, providing clear evidence of fifty years of progress in structural design and safety.

In the 50 years since US insurers organized the Insurance Institute for Highway Safety, car crashworthiness has improved. Demonstrating this was a crash test conducted on Sept. 9 between a 1959 Chevrolet Bel Air and a 2009 Chevrolet Malibu. In a real-world collision similar to this test, occupants of the new model would fare much better than in the vintage Chevy.

"It was night and day, the difference in occupant protection," says Institute president Adrian Lund. "What this test shows is that automakers don't build cars like they used to. They build them better."

The crash test was conducted at an event to celebrate the contributions of auto insurers to highway safety progress over 50 years. Beginning with the Institute's 1959 founding, insurers have maintained the resolve, articulated in the 1950s, to "conduct, sponsor, and encourage programs designed to aid in the conservation and preservation of life and property from the hazards of highway accidents."

In the crash test involving the two Chevrolets, the 2009 Malibu's occupant compartment remained intact (above left) while the one in the 1959 Bel Air (right) collapsed.

Assignments

1. **Product Review:** Choose a product that you own or buy regularly, anything from a Coleman lantern to Dunkin' Donuts coffee. Then write a fully developed review modeled after David Pogue's "Looking at the iPad from Two Angles" (p. 109). Like Pogue, you should be attentive to your audience and specific about details, but you need not write separate reviews for different audiences. Use graphics if appropriate.

2. **Arts Review:** Drawing on your expertise as a consumer of popular culture (the way Charles Isherwood does in his *New York Times* review of *American Idiot*—see p. 127), explain why you admire a book, movie, television series, musical piece, artist, or performer that most people do not. For instance, you might argue that *Gilligan's Island* is as sophisticated a situation comedy as *Seinfeld*. Or, taking the opposite tack, explain why you don't share the public's enthusiasm for some widely admired artist or entertainment. Write a review strong enough to change someone's mind.

3. **Social Satire:** Using the techniques of social satire modeled in "A Word from My Anti-Phone Soapbox" (p. 131), assess a public policy, social movement, or cultural trend you believe deserves serious and detailed criticism. But don't write a paper simply describing your target as dangerous, pathetic, or unsuccessful. Instead, make people laugh at your target while also offering a plausible alternative.

4. **Visual Comparison or Review:** Construct an evaluation in which a visual comparison or some other sensory evidence plays a major role. You might use photographs the way the Insurance Institute for Highway Safety does (see p. 136). Or perhaps you can work in another medium to show, for example, how good or bad the instructions in a technical manual are, how much the brownies you baked differ from the ones on the box, or how ineffective the design of your school's Web site is. Be creative.

5. **Your Choice:** Evaluate a program or facility in some institution you know well (school, business, church, recreation center) that you believe works especially well or poorly. Prepare a presentation in the medium of your choice and imagine that your audience is an administrator with the power to reward or shut down the operation.

How to start ▶
- Need a **topic**? See page 144.
- Need to identify **possible causes**? See page 149.
- Need to **organize your analysis**? See page 152.

5 Causal Analyses

explain how, why, or what if something happens

We all analyze and explain things daily. Someone asks, "Why?" We reply, "Because . . ." and then offer reasons and rationales. Such a response comes naturally.

CAUSAL ANALYSIS
An instructor asks for a ten-page *causal analysis* examining the root causes of a major armed conflict during the twentieth century. You choose to write about the Korean War because you know almost nothing about it.

RESEARCH STUDY
You notice that most students now walk across campus chatting on cell phones or listening to music. You develop a *research study* to examine whether this phenomenon has any relationship to a recent drop in the numbers of students joining campus clubs and activities across the country.

EXPLORATORY ESSAY
To keep student enrollments from crashing, the provost of your school has proposed to tie future fee and tuition increases to the rate of inflation. In an *exploratory essay*, you respond that this move might actually have the opposite effect if student services and the development of new programs are curtailed.

CULTURAL ANALYSIS
Why, you wonder, in a fully illustrated *cultural analysis*, does the mullet survive, decade after decade? What explains its enduring popularity?

DECIDING TO WRITE A CAUSAL ANALYSIS   From climate change to childhood obesity to high school students performing poorly on standardized tests, the daily news is full of problems framed by *how*, *why*, and *what if* questions. These are often described as issues of *cause and effect*, terms we'll use frequently in this chapter. Take childhood obesity. The public wants to know why we have a generation of overweight kids. Too many cheeseburgers? Not enough dodgeball? People worry, too, about the consequences of the trend. Will these portly children grow into obese adults? Will they develop medical problems?

We're interested in such questions because they really do matter, and we're often simply curious to find answers. But successful analyses of this sort call for more than a passing interest. They demand persistence, precision, and research. ○ Even then, you'll have to deal with a world that seems complicated or contradictory. Not every problem or issue can—or should—be explained simply. ○

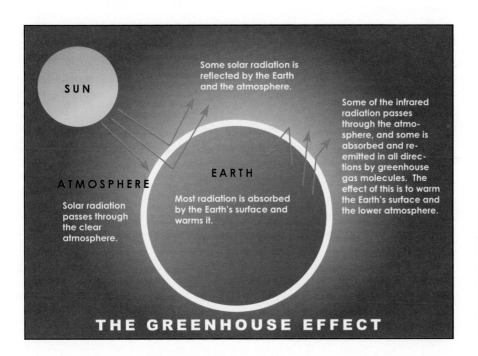

The Greenhouse Effect
Most scientists agree that the greenhouse effect, an increase in the concentration of certain atmospheric gases, is leading to climate change that will have dangerous consequences for us and our environment. (Other scientists have their doubts.)

choose a genre
p. 390

analyze claims and
evidence p. 487

Don't jump to conclusions. It's just plain hard to say precisely which factors, past or present, account for a particular event, activity, or behavior. And it is even tougher to project how events or actions occurring today might affect the future. So qualify your claims and explanations sensibly or offer them tentatively. ○

Trying to explain things to other people will quickly teach you humility—even if you *don't* jump to hasty conclusions. In fact, many explanations of cause and effect begin by undercutting or correcting someone else's prior claims, dutifully researched and sensibly presented.

Appreciate your limits. There are rarely easy answers when investigating why things happen the way they do. The space shuttle *Columbia* burned up on reentry in 2003 because a 1.67-pound piece of foam hit the wing of the 240,000-pound craft on liftoff. Who could have imagined such an unlikely sequence of events? Yet investigators had to follow the evidence relentlessly to its conclusion, in this case tracing backwards from effect to cause.

But even when you intend to find correct explanations, the fact remains that you'll often have to settle for answers that are merely plausible or probable. That's because explanations—especially outside the hard sciences—typically deal with imprecise and unpredictable forces (including *people*) and sometimes require a leap of imagination.

Offer sufficient evidence for claims. Your academic and professional analyses will be held to a high standard of proof—particularly in the sciences. ○ The evidence you provide may be a little looser when you write for popular media, where readers usually allow more anecdotal and casual examples. But even there, back up your claims with a preponderance of plausible evidence, not hearsay, and then be sure to qualify your conclusions carefully, making it clear when you are stepping into the realm of speculation.

develop a statement
p. 393

understand lab reports
p. 336

Causal Analysis

Whether the issue is the economy, health care, or climate change, public figures from presidents to pundits find themselves having to rely on expert opinion that is itself subject to interpretation. So do individual citizens. This short piece by Jonah Goldberg, a political commentator and global warming skeptic, typifies the dilemma. Not a scientist himself, Goldberg is in no position to make authoritative claims about the cause of global warming itself. But he can—and does—raise questions about how the studies are being reported to the public.

National Review Online

Posted: September 2, 2009
From: Jonah Goldberg

Global Warming and the Sun

The style of the analysis is colloquial, as might be expected in a blog.

On the last day of August, scientists spotted a teeny-weeny sun-spot, breaking a 51-day streak of blemish-free days for the sun. If it had gone just a bit longer, it would have broken a 96-year record of 53 days without any of the magnetic disruptions that cause solar flares. That record was nearly broken last year as well.

Wait, it gets even more exciting.

During what scientists call the Maunder Minimum — a period of solar inactivity from 1645 to 1715 — the world experienced the worst of the cold streak dubbed the Little Ice Age. At Christmas-time, Londoners ice-skated on the Thames, and New Yorkers (then New Amsterdamers) sometimes walked over the Hudson from Manhattan to Staten Island.

Identifies the "Maunder Minimum" and acknowl-edges that its relationship to the "Little Ice Age" is controversial.

Of course, it could have been a coincidence. The Little Ice Age began before the onset of the Maunder Minimum. Many scientists think volcanic activity was a more likely, or at least a more signifi-cant, culprit. Or perhaps the big chill was, in the words of scientist Alan Cutler, writing in the *Washington Post* in 1997, a "one-two punch from a dimmer sun and a dustier atmosphere."

Well, we just might find out. A new study in the American Geo-physical Union's journal, *Eos*, suggests that we may be heading into another quiet phase similar to the Maunder Minimum.

Goldberg is careful to cite what will look like credible sources: *Eos, Science*.

Meanwhile, the journal *Science* reports that a study led by the National Center for Atmospheric Research, or NCAR, has finally figured out why increased sunspots have a dramatic effect on the weather, increasing temperatures more than the increase in solar energy should explain. Apparently, sunspots heat the stratosphere, which in turn amplifies the warming of the climate.

Scientists have known for centuries that sunspots affect the climate; they just never understood how. Now, allegedly, the mystery has been solved.

Last month, in another study, also released in *Science*, Oregon State University researchers claimed to settle the debate over what caused and ended the last Ice Age. Increased solar radiation coming from slight changes in the Earth's rotation, not greenhouse-gas levels, were to blame.

What is the significance of all this? To say I have no idea is quite an understatement, but it will have to do.

Nonetheless, what I find interesting is the eagerness of the authors and the media to make it clear that this doesn't have any particular significance for the debate over climate change. "For those wondering how the (NCAR) study bears on global warming, Gerald Meehl, lead author on the study, says that it doesn't — at least not directly," writes Moises Velasquez-Manoff of the *Christian Science Monitor*. "Global warming is a long-term trend, Dr. Meehl says. . . . This study attempts to explain the processes behind a periodic occurrence."

This overlooks the fact that solar cycles are permanent "periodic occurrences," a.k.a. a very long-term trend. Yet Meehl insists the only significance for the debate is that his study proves climate modeling is steadily improving.

I applaud Meehl's reluctance to go beyond where the science takes him. For all I know, he's right. But such humility and skepticism seem to manifest themselves only when the data point to

Though not competent to critique the science itself, Goldberg is willing to comment on how scientific results are reported.

Goldberg complains that causal claims about climate are reported inconsistently.

something other than the mainstream narrative about global warming. For instance, when we have terribly hot weather, or bad hurricanes, the media see portentous proof of climate change. When we don't, it's a moment to teach the masses how weather and climate are very different things.

No, I'm not denying that man-made pollution and other activity have played a role in planetary warming since the Industrial Revolution.

But we live in a moment when we are told, nay lectured and harangued, that if we use the wrong toilet paper or eat the wrong cereal, we are frying the planet. But the sun? Well, that's a distraction. Don't you dare forget your reusable shopping bags, but pay no attention to that burning ball of gas in the sky — it's just the only thing that prevents the planet from being a lifeless ball of ice engulfed in darkness. Never mind that sunspot activity doubled during the 20th century, when the bulk of global warming has taken place.

What does it say that the modeling that guaranteed disastrous increases in global temperatures never predicted the halt in planetary warming since the late 1990s? (MIT's Richard Lindzen says that "there has been no warming since 1997 and no statistically significant warming since 1995.") What does it say that the modelers have only just now discovered how sunspots make the Earth warmer?

I don't know what it tells you, but it tells me that maybe we should study a bit more before we spend billions to "solve" a problem we don't understand so well.

The analysis grows highly rhetorical here to underscore what Goldberg sees as hypocrisy in climate change explanations.

Note that this analysis ends up with more questions than answers.

Exploring purpose and topic

▶ topic

To find a topic for an explanatory paper or causal analysis, begin a sentence with *why*, *how*, or *what if* and then finish it, drawing on what you may already know about an issue, trend, or problem. ○

This graph from *The Onion* (December 16, 2008) offers some explanations for the Great Recession.

(Reprinted with permission of THE ONION. Copyright © 2010, by ONION, INC. www.theonion.com.)

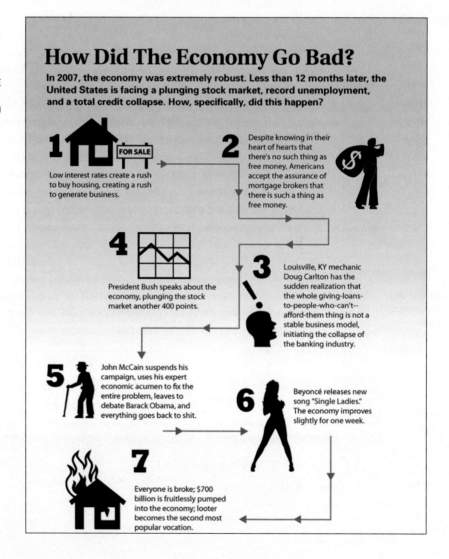

How Did The Economy Go Bad?

In 2007, the economy was extremely robust. Less than 12 months later, the United States is facing a plunging stock market, record unemployment, and a total credit collapse. How, specifically, did this happen?

1 Low interest rates create a rush to buy housing, creating a rush to generate business.

2 Despite knowing in their heart of hearts that there's no such thing as free money, Americans accept the assurance of mortgage brokers that there is such a thing as free money.

4 President Bush speaks about the economy, plunging the stock market another 400 points.

3 Louisville, KY mechanic Doug Carlton has the sudden realization that the whole giving-loans-to-people-who-can't--afford-them thing is not a stable business model, initiating the collapse of the banking industry.

5 John McCain suspends his campaign, uses his expert economic acumen to fix the entire problem, leaves to debate Barack Obama, and everything goes back to shit.

6 Beyoncé releases new song "Single Ladies." The economy improves slightly for one week.

7 Everyone is broke; $700 billion is fruitlessly pumped into the economy; looter becomes the second most popular vocation.

find a topic
p. 356

Why are American high schools producing fewer students interested in science?

Why is the occurrence of juvenile asthma spiking?

Why do so few men study nursing or so few women study petroleum engineering?

There are, of course, many other ways to phrase questions about cause and effect in order to attach important conditions and qualifications.

What if scientists figure out how to stop the human aging process—as now seems plausible within twenty years? What are the consequences for society?

How likely is it that a successful third political party might develop in the United States to end the deadlock between Republicans and Democrats?

As you can see, none of these topics would just drop from a tree—like the apocryphal apple that supposedly inspired Isaac Newton to ponder gravity. They require knowledge and thinking. So look for potential cause-and-effect issues in your academic courses or professional life. Or search for them in the culture and media—though you should probably shy away from worn-out subjects—college drinking, plagiarism, credit card debt—unless you can offer a fresh insight.

To find a subject, try the following approaches.

Look again at a subject you know well.   It may be one that has affected you personally or might in the future. Or a topic you think is ripe for rethinking because of insights you can offer. For instance, you may have experienced firsthand the effects of high-stakes testing in high school or have theories about why people your age still smoke despite the risks. Offer a hypothesis.

Look for an issue new to you.   Given a choice of topics for an academic paper, choose a subject you've always wanted to know more about (for example, the cultural effects of the Cold War). You probably won't be able to offer a thesis or hypothesis until after you've done some research, but that's the appeal of this strategy. The material is fresh and you are energized. O

find a topic
p. 356

Examine a local issue. Is there an issue you can explore or test with personal research or observation? ○ Look for recent changes and examine why these changes happened or what the consequences may be. With a community issue, talk to the people responsible or affected. Tuition raised? Admissions standards lowered? Speech code modified? Why, or what if?

Choose a subject with many dimensions. An issue that is complicated and challenging will simply push you harder and sharpen your thinking. Don't rush to judgment; remain open-minded about contrary evidence, conflicting motives, and different points of view.

Tackle an issue that seems settled. If you really have guts, look for a phenomenon that most people assume has been adequately explained. Tired of the way Republicans, feminists, Wall Street economists, vegans, fundamentalists, or the women on *The View* smugly explain the way things are? Pick one sore point and offer a different—and better—analysis.

> **Your Turn** After Richard Nixon won forty-nine states in the 1972 presidential election, the distinguished film critic Pauline Kael is reported to have said, "How can he have won? I don't know anyone who voted for him." Can you think of any times when you have similarly misread a situation because you did not have a perspective broad enough to understand all the forces in play? Identify such a situation and consider whether it might provide you with a topic for an explanatory paper. Alternatively, consider some of the times—maybe even beginning in childhood—when you have heard explanations for phenomena that you recognized as wildly implausible because they were superstitions, stereotypes, or simply errors. Again, consider whether you can turn one of these misconceptions into a topic for an explanatory paper.

interview and observe
p. 478

Understanding your audience

Audiences for cause-and-effect analyses and explanations are diverse, but it may help to distinguish between a readership you create by drawing attention to a subject and readers who come to your work because it deals with a topic they already care about.

Create an audience.   In some situations, you must set the stage for your causal analysis by telling readers why they should be concerned by the phenomenon you intend to explore. ○ Assume they are smart enough to become engaged by a topic once they appreciate its significance—and how it might affect them. But you first have to make that case. That's exactly what the editors of the *Wall Street Journal* do in an editorial noting the sustained *decrease* in traffic deaths that followed a congressional decision ten years earlier to do away with a national 55-mph speed limit.

> This may seem noncontroversial now, but at the time the debate was shrill and filled with predictions of doom. Ralph Nader claimed that "history will never forgive Congress for this assault on the sanctity of human life." Judith Stone, president of the Advocates for Highway and Auto Safety, predicted to Katie Couric on NBC's *Today Show* that there would be "6,400 added highway fatalities a year and millions of more injuries." Federico Peña, the Clinton administration's secretary of transportation, declared: "Allowing speed limits to rise above 55 simply means that more Americans will die and be injured on our highways."
>
> —"Safe at Any Speed," July 7, 2006

Anticipates readers who might ask, *Why does this issue matter?*

Write to an existing audience.   In many cases, you'll enter a cause-and-effect debate on topics already on the public agenda. You may intend to reaffirm what people now believe or, more controversially, ask them to rethink their positions. But in either case, you'll likely be dealing with readers as knowledgeable (and opinionated) as you are. In the following opening paragraphs, for example, from an article exploring the decline of sensuality in America, notice how culture critic Camille Paglia presumes an intelligent audience already engaged by her topic.

develop a statement
p. 393

Paglia guesses that readers understand the impetus for the new drug.

Will women soon have a Viagra of their own? Although a Food and Drug Administration advisory panel recently rejected an application to market the drug flibanserin in the United States for women with low libido, it endorsed the potential benefits and urged further research. Several pharmaceutical companies are reported to be well along in the search for such a drug.

Presumes readers who agree that "white upper middle class" means "anxious" and "overachieving."

The implication is that a new pill, despite its unforeseen side effects, is necessary to cure the sexual malaise that appears to have sunk over the country. But to what extent do these complaints about sexual apathy reflect a medical reality, and how much do they actually emanate from the anxious, overachieving, white upper middle class?

More concepts assumed: *1950s, frigidity, puritanism, media environment.*

In the 1950s, female "frigidity" was attributed to social conformism and religious puritanism. But since the sexual revolution of the 1960s, American society has become increasingly secular, with a media environment drenched in sex.

The real culprit, originating in the 19th century, is bourgeois propriety. As respectability became the central middle-class value, censorship and repression became the norm. Victorian prudery ended the humorous sexual candor of both men and women during the agrarian era, a ribaldry chroni-

Readers better know Western history too.

cled from Shakespeare's plays to the 18th-century novel. The priggish 1950s, which erased the liberated flappers of the Jazz Age from cultural memory, were simply a return to the norm.

– "No Sex Please, We're Middle Class," *New York Times*, June 25, 2010

In the same article, Paglia describes Lady Gaga as "a high-concept fabrication without an ounce of genuine eroticism."

Finding and developing materials

Expect to do as much research for a causal analysis as for any fact-based report or argument. Even when you speculate about popular culture, as Charles Paul Freund does in "The Politics of Pants" (see p. 170), you need to show that you have considered what others have written on the subject. ○

Be careful, however, not to ascribe the wrong cause to an event just because two actions might have occurred close in time or have some other fragile connection. Does job growth really grow following tax rebates? Do children in fact do better in school if they have participated in Head Start programs? Exposing faulty causality in situations like these can make for powerful arguments. ○ You can avoid faulty analyses by appreciating the various kinds of valid causal relationships outlined below.

Understand necessary causes. A *necessary cause* is any factor that must be in place for something to occur. For example, sunlight, chlorophyll, and water are all necessary for photosynthesis to happen. Remove one of these elements from the equation and the natural process simply doesn't take place. But since none of them could cause photosynthesis on their own, they are necessary causes, but not sufficient (see *sufficient cause* below).

consider causes ◄

On a less scientific level, necessary causes are those that seem so important that we can't imagine something happening without them. You might argue, for example, that a team could not win a World Series without a specific pitcher on the roster: Remove him and the team doesn't get to the play-offs. Or you might claim that, while fanaticism doesn't itself cause terrorism, terrorism doesn't exist without fanaticism. In any such analysis, it helps to separate necessary causes from those that may be merely *contributing* (see *contributing factors* on p. 151).

Understand sufficient causes. A *sufficient cause*, in itself, is enough to bring on a particular effect. Not being eighteen would be a sufficient cause for being arrested for drinking alcohol in the United States. But there are many other potential sufficient causes for getting arrested. In a causal argument, you might need to establish which of several possible sufficient causes is the one actually responsible for a specific event or phenomenon—assuming that a single explanation exists. A plane might have crashed because it was overloaded, ran out of fuel, had a structural failure, encountered severe wind shear, and so on.

Understand precipitating causes.   Think of a *precipitating cause* as the proverbial straw that finally breaks the camel's back. In itself, the factor may seem trivial. But it becomes the spark that sets a field gone dry for months ablaze. By refusing to give up her bus seat to a white passenger in Montgomery, Alabama, Rosa Parks triggered a civil rights movement in 1955, but she didn't actually cause it: The necessary conditions had been accumulating for generations.

Understand proximate causes.   A *proximate cause* is nearby and often easy to spot. A corporation declares bankruptcy when it can no longer meet its massive debt obligations; a minivan crashes because a front tire explodes; a student fails a course because she plagiarizes a paper. But in an analysis, getting the facts right about such proximate causes may just be your starting point as you work toward a deeper understanding of a situation. As you might guess, proximate causes may sometimes also be sufficient causes.

Need help assessing your own work? See "How to Use the Writing Center" on pp. 382–83.

Understand remote causes.   A *remote cause*, as the term suggests, may act at some distance from an event but is intimately related to it. That bankrupt corporation may have defaulted on its loans because of a decade of bad management decisions; the tire exploded because it was underinflated and its tread worn; the student resorted to plagiarism *because* she ran out of time *because* she was working two jobs to pay for a Hawaiian vacation *because* she wanted a memorable spring break to impress her friends—a string of remote causes. Remote causes—which are usually contributing factors as well (see p. 151)—are what make many causal analyses challenging and interesting: Figuring them out is like detective work.

Understand reciprocal causes.   You have a *reciprocal* situation when a cause leads to an effect which, in turn, strengthens the cause. Consider how creating science internships for college women might encourage more women to become scientists who then sponsor more internships, creating yet more female scientists. Many analyses of global warming describe reciprocal

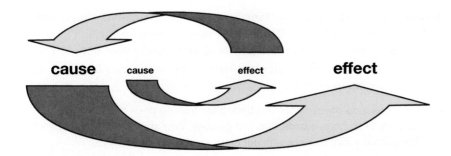

cause   cause   effect   **effect**

relationships, with CO_2 emissions supposedly leading to warming, which increases plant growth or alters ocean currents, which in turn releases more CO_2 or heat and so on.

Understand contributing factors.   When analyzing social or cultural issues, you'll often spend time assessing factors too general or ambiguous to be called necessary, sufficient, or even remote causes but which, nonetheless, might play a role in explaining an event. To account for an outbreak of high school violence in the late 1990s, social critics quickly identified a host of potential factors: divorce, guns, video games, goth culture, bullying, cliques, movies, psychosis, and so on. Though none of these explanations was entirely convincing, they couldn't simply be dismissed either. Many factors that might contribute to violence were (and remain) in play within the culture of American high schools.

Come to conclusions thoughtfully.   Explanations do often require some imagination: You are playing detective with the complexities of life, so you may need to think outside the box. But you also have to give your notions the same tough scrutiny that you would give any smart idea. Just because a causal explanation is clever or novel doesn't mean it's right. ○

Don't oversimplify situations or manipulate facts.   By acknowledging any weaknesses in your own explanations and analyses, you may actually enhance your credibility or lead a reader toward a better conclusion than what you've come up with. Sometimes, you may have to be content with solving only part of a problem.

think critically
p. 372

Creating a structure

▶ organize ideas

Take introductions seriously. In explanations, they are unusually important and often quite lengthy; you'll often need more than one paragraph to provide enough detail for readers to appreciate the significance of your subject. The following brief paragraph might seem like the opener of a causal essay on the failures of dog training. ○

> For thousands of years, humans have been training dogs to be hunters, herders, searchers, guards, and companions. Why are we doing so badly? The problem may lie more with our methods than with us.
>
> —Jon Katz, "Train in Vain," *Slate.com*, January 14, 2005

In fact, *seven* paragraphs precede this one to set up the causal claim. Those paragraphs help readers (especially dog owners) recognize a problem many will find familiar. The actual first paragraph has Katz narrating a dog owner's dilemma.

> Sam was distressed. His West Highland terrier, aptly named Lightning, was constantly darting out of doors and dashing into busy suburban Connecticut streets. Sam owned three acres behind his house, and he was afraid to let the dog roam any of it.

By paragraph seven, Katz has offered enough corroborating situations to provoke a crisis in dogdom, a problem that leaves readers hoping for an explanation.

> The results of this failure are everywhere: Neurotic and compulsive dog behaviors like barking, biting, chasing cars, and chewing furniture—sometimes severe enough to warrant antidepressants—are growing. Lesser training problems—an inability to sit, stop begging, come, or stay—are epidemic.

Like Katz, you'll want to take the time necessary to introduce your subject and get readers interested. Then you have a number of options for developing your explanation or causal analysis.

Explain why something happened. If you are simply offering plausible causes to explain a phenomenon, your structure will be quite simple. You'll move from an introduction that explains the phenomenon to a thesis

shape a beginning
p. 420

or hypothesis. Then you will work through your list of factors toward a conclusion. In a persuasive paper, you'd build toward the most convincing explanation supported by the best evidence.

> **Introduction leading to an explanatory or causal claim**
>
> **First cause explored + reasons/evidence**
> **Next cause explored + reasons/evidence . . .**
> **Best cause explored + reasons/evidence**
>
> **Conclusion**

Explain the consequences of a phenomenon. A structure similar to the one just given lends itself to exploring the effects that follow from some action, event, policy, or change in the status quo. Once again, begin with an introduction that fully describes a situation you believe will have consequences, and then work through those consequences, connecting them as you need to. The conclusion could then draw out the implications of your paper.

> **Introduction focusing on a change or cause**
>
> **First effect proposed + reasons**
> **Other effect(s) proposed + reasons . . .**
>
> **Assessment and conclusion**

Suggest an alternative view of cause and effect. A natural strategy is to open a causal analysis by refuting someone else's faulty claim and then offering a better one of your own. After all, we often think about causality when someone makes a claim we disagree with. It's a structure used in this chapter by Liza Mundy (p. 165).

> **Introduction questioning a causal claim**
>
> > **Reasons to doubt claim offered + evidence**
> > **Alternative cause(s) explored . . .**
> > **Best cause examined + reasons/evidence**
>
> **Conclusion**

Explain a chain of causes.   Quite often, causes occur simultaneously, so in presenting them you have to make judgments about their relative importance. But maybe just as often, you'll be describing causes that operate in sequence: A causes B, B leads to C, C trips D, and so on. In such a case, you might use a sequential pattern of organization, giving special attention to the links (or transitions) in the chain. ○

> **Introduction suggesting a chain of causes/consequences**
>
> > **First link presented + reasons/evidence**
> > **Next link(s) presented + reasons/evidence . . .**
> > **Final link presented + reasons/evidence**
>
> **Conclusion**

People have been writing causal analysis for centuries. Here is the title page of Edward Jenner's 1798 publication, *An Inquiry into the Causes and Effects of the Variolae Vaccinae.* Jenner's research led to a vaccine that protected human beings from smallpox.

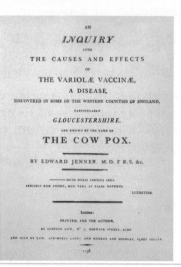

AN

INQUIRY

INTO

THE CAUSES AND EFFECTS

OF

THE VARIOLÆ VACCINÆ,

A DISEASE,

DISCOVERED IN SOME OF THE WESTERN COUNTIES OF ENGLAND,

PARTICULARLY

GLOUCESTERSHIRE,

AND KNOWN BY THE NAME OF

THE COW POX.

BY EDWARD JENNER, M.D. F.R.S. &c.

LONDON:

PRINTED, FOR THE AUTHOR,

1798

shape your work
p. 406

Choosing a style and design

When you analyze cause and effect, you'll often be offering an argument or exploring an idea for an audience you need to interest. You can do that through both style and design.

Consider a middle style.   Even causal analyses written for fairly academic audiences incline toward the middle style because of its flexibility: It can be both familiar and serious. ○ Here Robert Bruegmann, discussing the causes of urban sprawl, uses language that is simple, clear, and colloquial—and almost entirely free of technical jargon.

> When asked, most Americans declare themselves to be against sprawl, just as they say they are against pollution or the destruction of historic buildings. But the very development that one individual targets as sprawl is often another family's much-loved community. Very few people believe that they themselves live in sprawl or contribute to sprawl. Sprawl is where other people live, particularly people with less good taste. Much antisprawl activism is based on a desire to reform these other people's lives.
>
> – "How Sprawl Got a Bad Name," *American Enterprise,* June 2006

Adapt the style to the subject matter.   Friendly as it is, a middle style can still make demands of readers, as the following passage from an essay by Malcolm Gladwell demonstrates. To explain author Steve Johnson's theory that pop culture is making people smarter, Gladwell uses extremely intricate sentences filled with pop-culture allusions and cultural details. Yet he maintains a sense of voice too: Notice how he uses italics to signal how a word should be read. This is middle style at its complex best, making claims and proving them in a way that keeps readers interested.

> As Johnson points out, television is very different now from what it was thirty years ago. It's *harder.* A typical episode of *Starsky and Hutch*, in the 1970s, followed an essentially linear path: two characters, engaged in a single story line, moving toward a decisive conclusion. To watch an episode of *Dallas* today is to be stunned by its glacial pace – by the arduous attempts to establish social relationships, by the excruciating simplicity of the plotline, by how *obvious* it was. A single episode of *The Sopranos*, by contrast, might follow five narrative threads, involving a dozen characters

define your style
p. 432

who weave in and out of the plot. Modern television also requires the viewer to do a lot of what Johnson calls "filling in," as in a *Seinfeld* episode that subtly parodies the Kennedy assassination conspiracists, or a typical *Simpsons* episode, which may contain numerous allusions to politics or cinema or pop culture. The extraordinary amount of money now being made in the television aftermarket—DVD sales and syndication—means that the creators of television shows now have an incentive to make programming that can sustain two or three or four viewings.

—"Brain Candy," *The New Yorker*, May 16, 2005

Use appropriate supporting media.   Causal analyses have no special design features. But, like reports and arguments, they can employ charts that summarize information and graphics that illustrate ideas. *USA Today*, for instance, uses its daily "snapshots" to present causal data culled from surveys. Because causal analyses usually have distinct sections or parts (see "Creating a structure," p. 152), they do fit nicely into PowerPoint presentations. ○

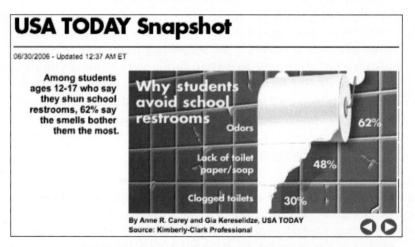

USA TODAY Snapshot

06/30/2006 - Updated 12:37 AM ET

Among students ages 12-17 who say they shun school restrooms, 62% say the smells bother them the most.

Why students avoid school restrooms

Odors   62%

Lack of toilet paper/soap   48%

Clogged toilets   30%

By Anne R. Carey and Gia Kereselidze, USA TODAY
Source: Kimberly-Clark Professional

A graphic like this one reflects a statistical approach to causality; its creators polled people to find out why they do what they do.

think visually
p. 592

Examining models

In a college paper, Kyu-heong Kim explains why the methods typically employed in writing centers to help students don't always work for some Asian students whose native language is not English. Like many causal analyses, his paper becomes an argument for change. But its most interesting parts are those that detail why best intentions sometimes go wrong.

Kim 1

Kyu-heong Kim

Professor Ruszkiewicz

English 300

April 26, 20--

Bending the Rules for ESL Writers

At most writing centers, the fundamental approaches and goals when tutoring ESL [English as a second language] students are essentially the same as those applied to native English writers. For example, at the University of Texas at Austin's Undergraduate Writing Center, writing consultants are trained to interact with ESL students just as they do "when working with native speakers, [being] nonevaluative, nondirective, and sensitive to writers' emotional investment in their writing" (Undergraduate 32). However, certain cultural barriers may prevent such nondirective and nonevaluative methods from being the most efficient or effective in improving the writing of ESL students from many backgrounds. Academic theorists fall on both sides of the issue regarding the merit of nondirectiveness and student empowerment, and this essay will examine both viewpoints.

> The opening paragraph explains the issue to be addressed and the methodology of the paper.

157

Kim 2

It also includes interviews with two foreign writers as they get help with their papers, experiencing both the strengths and shortcomings of the nondirective approach used in most writing centers.

Since writing centers first became common in the United States in the mid-twentieth century, much has changed in the landscape of university enrollment. Specifically, the number of international students entering American universities has risen dramatically. Since the National Center for Education Statistics (NCES) began to collect data, the number of international students in postsecondary institutions in the United States has steadily increased from around 135,000 in 1970 to the current level of more than 620,000 (Planty et al. 96). International students now make up nearly 2 percent of total undergraduate enrollment, and at many writing centers, roughly a quarter of all consultations involve students from foreign cultures. Is it prudent then to apply the same techniques of writing center mentorship to this growing class of international students as those used upon native English speakers? This paper will focus on international students from the relatively culturally homogeneous nations of the Far East—China, Korea, Japan, and Taiwan—from which nearly 35 percent of all international students hail (Planty et al. 96).

Current writing center doctrine promotes a nondirective approach to tutoring. Philosophically, this stance is intended

Background information and statistics explain why the issues the paper raises are important.

Style of the paper is academic: formal and impersonal.

Kim 3

to "help writers to move away from a passive position" to "an active position . . . making their own decisions about a piece of writing that is truly their own" (Undergraduate 20). When applied to ESL writers, however, there are legitimate questions about the efficacy of this nondirective process. One camp argues that, due to the fundamental linguistic shortcomings of foreign writers, the nondirective approach presents pressures and situations that do little to improve the writing of these students. According to Ferris and Hedgcock, "in empowering students to retain ownership of their writing, we force them into roles for which they are not prepared and with which they are not comfortable" (142).

A Korean student working on a research application paper for a human development and family science course reported exactly this kind of problem with the nondirective approach. "When I go to the writing center with my paper, I often don't get the specific help that I want," she said. "It depends on who my tutor is, but they often ask me a lot of questions that I don't know the answers for. So, a lot of times, I will just ask my friends to edit my papers for me" (Cho). This writer's experience may indicate the frustrations of many ESL writers during their consultations at writing centers—an obstacle perhaps attributable to an incompatibility between Eastern Asian education and the current nondirective philosophy at most centers.

Kim cites a critic who argues that nondirective tutoring may have unanticipated consequences for ESL students.

Kim 4

The overarching educational structure of East Asian nations is top-down, with instruction going from the teacher to the student. As William Cummings explains, "Whereas Western educators lean toward a cognitive reasoning approach to values education, Eastern Asian educators favor a directive approach involving explicit teaching and consistent reinforcement" (286). There tends to be very little feedback from the student to the instructor, and discussion is kept at a minimum in favor of conveying information. Some believe that the fundamental difference in learning style originates from "Confucius and other Eastern Chou dynasty philosophers [who] established scholarly traditions and sociopolitical patterns that are still significant culturally" (Lee 3). International students from such nations may feel an inherent need to "[balance] the hierarchical, social orientation of Confucian ethics, heavy on loyalty, obedience, and learnedness" (3). So students who come from this culture may naturally feel uncomfortable in situations where they are encouraged to respond to and even disagree with their tutors—who, in their eyes, are authority figures in the situation. Ferris and Hedgcock suggest that "a nondirective approach can be confusing, frustrating, and even threatening to some ESL students depending on their cultural expectations and language ability" (144).

Because writers view tutors as teachers, students may take suggestions offered during the session as truth—

> ESL students face problems because of their attitudes toward authority.

Kim 5

incorporating them word-for-word into their writing. In turn, Feuerbacher notes that "writing instructors and tutors alike are often tempted to change the writer's text so much that it no longer reflects the voice and linguistic abilities of the writer but rather that of the instructor or tutor." But perhaps this fear forces many tutors to overcompensate and become even more nondirective in their approach when working with ESL students.

ESL students also have difficulty describing the problems they wish to address.

      Many ESL sessions in writing centers also suffer from the effects of another common policy—student empowerment. Consultants at writing centers are usually trained to focus on issues the students want to work on. This approach may be beneficial when students enter the consultation clearly understanding the weaknesses of their papers, but may be insufficient if they do not. For example, ESL students from East Asia may hesitate to ask questions about higher-order concerns in their papers or be unable to formulate their concerns into questions. An ESL student who went to a writing center for help on his internal transfer application described this problem exactly:

> I always check the box for grammar [when I go to the
> writing center] because I don't know what else I should
> check. When the consultant asks me what I want to
> work on, I say "grammar" by default. That's what I
> did for this paper. (Chae)

The paper draws on printed sources as well as several interviews.

The student received plenty of grammatical feedback and was able to correct many of his mistakes; however, because of his

Kim 6

request to focus on grammar, several bigger problems in the paper were not addressed. As a result, the finished product lacked some key components of an internal transfer essay, such as a personal statement, a rationale for attending the school, and an explanation of the candidate's goals. "We didn't really talk about what makes a good transfer essay, because I told him [the tutor] I wanted to work on grammar," the writer said. "I didn't really know how to ask" (Chae).

The issue of formulating the right questions could indicate a greater cultural divide. According to Ki-joong Kim, a professor who has taught in both Korea and the United States, "Students in America often come with challenging questions regarding topics we have never covered, whereas Asian students' questions tend to be limited to the scope of material covered in classes" (Kim). Similarly, ESL expert Joy Reid attributes the inability of some foreign students to steer the consultation according to their concerns to inexperience, and offers expanded planning as a solution. "Because ESL student writers have probably had little or no experience with conferencing or with the responsibility of planning a conference, it is necessary to provide them with planning materials" (Reid 220).

Several solutions can be offered to address the issues stated above. When dealing with clarity and grammatical issues, it may be helpful if writing center tutors were given the freedom to be more directive with ESL students. ESL students would be

Kim makes it clear that cultural differences account for problems Asian students face in writing centers.

Kim 7

less discouraged if they saw progress in their papers through the session. To encourage ESL students to become more active in their consultations, steps might be taken to break down the perceived student-teacher barrier between the writer and the tutor. This might begin with an emphasis on peer tutoring, where writing center tutors introduce themselves as peers rather than as consultants. Before actual work begins on the paper, the consultant might take a few minutes to introduce himself or herself to help the writer feel more equal to the consultant. With a sense of equality, ESL writers might feel free to become a part of the discussion rather than remain listeners.

Similarly, consultants might also be given the freedom to go beyond addressing merely the concerns writers themselves identify and to address other problems that occur through the paper. Expanded pretutoring "planning materials" might also help ESL writers express thoughts and concerns they might find difficult to bring up during consultations (220).

The growing number of international students at American postsecondary institutions calls for adaptations in the methodology of writing centers. Understanding the differences in culture may enable providers of writing services at universities to better grasp techniques to service this growing clientele—techniques that often require modifications in traditional approaches.

> Kim offers specific suggestions to improve writing center services for ESL students.

Kim 8

Works Cited

Chae, Seung-jun. Personal interview. 8 Mar. 2010.

Cho, Eun-saem. Personal interview. 7 Mar. 2010.

Cummings, William K. "Human Resource Development: The
    J-Model." *The Challenge of Eastern Asian Education:*
    Implications for America. Ed. William K. Cummings and
    Philip G. Altbach. Albany: State U of New York P, 1997. Print.

Ferris, Dana, and John S. Hedgcock. *Teaching ESL Composition:*
    Purpose, Process, and Practice. Mahwah: Erlbaum, 1998.
    Print.

Feuerbacher, Kellie, et al. "The ESL Experience in the Writing
    Center." *Praxis: A Writing Center Journal* 2 (2005). Web.
    10 Mar. 2010.

Kim, Ki-joong. Personal communication. 14 Apr. 2010.

Lee, Albert H. *East Asian Higher Education: Traditions and*
    Transformations. Oxford: IAU P, 1995. Print.

Planty, M., et al. *The Condition of Education 2009*. National
    Center for Education Statistics, Institute of Education
    Sciences, U.S. Department of Education, June 2009.
    Web. 10 Mar. 2010.

Reid, Joy M. *Teaching ESL Writing*. Englewood Cliffs:
    Regents-Prentice Hall, 1993. Print.

Undergraduate Writing Center. *UWC Consultant Handbook*
    2009-2010. Austin: U of Texas at Austin. Dept. of
    Rhetoric and Writing, 2009. Print.

Documentation style used is MLA.

EXPLORATORY ESSAY   Liza Mundy, a writer for the *Washington Post,* offers a classic kind of causal analysis — one in which readers are asked to consider a subject from an entirely different point of view. That shift in perspective illuminates her subject and raises unexpected and scary consequences.

Slate.com

Posted: Wednesday, May 3, 2006, at 10:20 AM ET
From: Liza Mundy

What's Really behind the Plunge in Teen Pregnancy?

Identifies a trend that needs a causal explanation.

May 3 — in case you didn't know it — was "National Day to Prevent Teen Pregnancy." In the past decade, possibly no social program has been as dramatically effective as the effort to reduce teen pregnancy, and no results so uniformly celebrated. Between 1990 and 2000, the U.S. teen pregnancy rate plummeted by 28 percent, dropping from 117 to 84 pregnancies per 1,000 women aged 15–19. Births to teenagers are also down, as are teen abortion rates. It's an achievement so profound and so heartening that left and right are eager to take credit for it, and both can probably do so. Child-health advocates generally acknowledge that liberal sex education and conservative abstinence initiatives are both to thank for the fact that fewer teenagers are ending up in school bathroom stalls sobbing over the results of a home pregnancy test.

Poses a question about causality.

What, though, if the drop in teen pregnancy isn't a good thing, or not entirely? What if there's a third explanation, one that has nothing to do with just-say-no campaigns or safe-sex educational posters? What if teenagers are less fertile than they used to be?

Not the girls — the boys?

Offers a startling hypothesis.

It's a conversation that's taking place among a different and somewhat less vocal interest group: scientists who study human and animal reproduction. Like many scientific inquiries, this one is hotly contested and not likely to be resolved anytime soon. Still, the fact that it's going on provides a useful reminder that not every social trend is the sole result of partisan policy initiatives and think-tank-generated outreach efforts. It reminds us that a drop in something as profound as fertility, in human creatures of any age, might also have something to do with health, perhaps even the future of the species.

Reminds readers how contentious studies of causality can be.

The great sperm-count debate began in 1992, when a group of Danish scientists published a study suggesting that sperm counts declined globally by about 1 percent a year between 1938 and 1990. This study postulated that "environmental influences," particularly widely used chemical compounds with an impact like that of the female hormone estrogen, might be contributing to a drop in fertility among males. If true, this was obviously an alarming development, particularly given that human sperm counts are already strikingly low compared to almost any other species. "Humans have the worst sperm except for gorillas and ganders of any animal on the planet," points out Sherman Silber, a high-profile urologist who attributes this in part to short-term female monogamy. Since one man's sperm rarely has to race that of another man to the finish, things like speed and volume are less important in human sperm than in other animals, permitting a certain amount of atrophy among humans.

New causal factor is presented and explored.

The Danish study set an argument in motion. Other studies were published showing that sperm counts were staying the same; still others showed them going up. In the late 1990s, however, an American reproductive epidemiologist named Shanna Swan published work confirming the Danish findings. In a well-respected study published in *Environmental Health Perspectives*, Swan, now at the University of Rochester Medical Center, found that sperm counts are dropping by about 1.5 percent a year in the United States and 3 percent in Europe and Australia, though they do not

Detailed paragraphs present evidence that sperm counts are dropping.

appear to be falling in the less-developed world. This may not sound like a lot, but cumulatively — like compound interest — a drop of 1 percent has a big effect. Swan showed, further, that in the United States there appears to be a regional variation in sperm counts: They tend to be lower in rural sectors and higher in cities, suggesting the possible impact of chemicals (such as pesticides) particular to one locality.

Swan is part of a group of scientists whose work suggests that environmental changes are indeed having a reproductive impact. Under the auspices of a women's health group at Stanford University and an alliance called the Collaborative on Health and the Environment, some of these scientists met in February 2005 at a retreat in Menlo Park, California, to discuss their findings. Among the evidence presented are several trends that seem to point to a subtle feminization of male babies: a worldwide rise in hypospadias, a birth defect in which the urethral opening is located on the shaft of the penis rather than at the tip; a rise in crypt-orchidism, or undescended testicles; and experiments Swan has done showing that in male babies with high exposure to compounds called phthalates, something called the anogenital distance is decreasing. If you measure the distance from a baby's anus to the genitals, the distance in these males is shorter, more like that of . . . girls.

Wildlife biologists also talked about the fact that alligators living in one contaminated Florida lake were found to have small phalli and low testosterone levels, while females in the same lake had problems associated with abnormally high levels of estrogen. In 1980, the alligators' mothers had been exposed to a major pesticide dump, which, some believe, was working like an estrogen on their young, disrupting their natural hormones. A report later published by this group pointed out that similar disruptions have been found in a "wide range of species from seagulls to polar bears, seals to salmon, mollusks to frogs." As evidence that a parent's exposure to toxicants

Analysis assumes a knowledgeable, not expert, audience.

can powerfully affect the development of offspring, the example of DES, or diethylstilbestrol, was also, of course, offered. Widely given to pregnant women beginning in the late 1930s under the mistaken assumption that it would prevent miscarriage, DES left the women unaffected but profoundly affected their female fetuses, some of whom would die of cancer, others of whom would find their reproductive capacity compromised. The consensus was that the so-called chemical revolution may well be disrupting the development of reproductive organs in young males, among others. This research is controversial, certainly, but accepted enough, as a hypothesis, that it appears in developmental-biology textbooks.

Tellingly, the U.S. government is also taking this conversation seriously. Together, the National Institutes of Health and the U.S. Centers for Disease Control are sponsoring a longitudinal effort to study the effect of environment on fertility. This study will track couples living in Texas and Michigan, following their efforts to become pregnant. The aim is to determine whether toxicants are affecting the reproductive potential of female and male alike.

> Explains what other causal studies are needed.

It will be welcome information. In the United States, good statistics about infertility are strikingly hard to come by. There is no government-sponsored effort to track male fertility rates, even though male-factor problems account for half of all infertility. Even among women, who are regularly interrogated about reproductive details, it's difficult to get a good handle on developments. For years, government researchers included only married women in the category of "infertility," creating a real problem for demographers and epidemiologists looking for trends. The National Center for Health Statistics created a second category called "impaired fecundity," which includes any woman, of any marital category, who is trying to get pregnant and not having luck.

> Puts qualifications and limits on available statistics.

And the "impaired fecundity" category contains findings that may have a bearing on the are-young-men-more-infertile-than-their-fathers question. In the United States, "impaired fecundity" among women has seen, over several decades, a steady rise. And while much attention has focused on older women, the most striking rise between 1982 and 1995 took place among women under twenty-five. In that period, impaired fecundity in women under twenty-five rose by 42 percent, from 4.3 percent of women to 6.1 percent. Recently published data from 2002 show a continued rise in impaired fecundity among the youngest age cohort.

In a 1999 letter to *Family Planning Perspectives*, Swan sensibly proposed "that the role of the male be considered in this equation." If sperm counts drop each year, then the youngest men will be most acutely affected, and these will be the men who are having trouble impregnating their partners. In 2002, Danish researchers published an opinion piece in *Human Reproduction* noting that teen pregnancy rates (already much lower than in the United States) fell steadily in Denmark between 1985 and 1999. Unlike in the United States, in Denmark there have been no changes in outreach efforts to encourage responsible behavior in teens: no abstinence campaigns, no big new push for condom distribution. Wider social trends notwithstanding, they note that "it seems reasonable also to consider widespread poor semen quality among men as a potential contributing factor to low fertility rates among teenagers."

Among other things, the sperm-count debate reminds us that we should not be smug about the success of teen-pregnancy prevention efforts. We may not want today's teenagers to become pregnant now, but we certainly want them to become pregnant in the future, providing they want to be. If nothing else, the sperm-count hypothesis shows that when it comes to teenagers and sexual behavior, there's always something new to worry about.

Last paragraph warns against jumping to conclusions too quickly.

CULTURAL ANALYSIS   Charles Paul Freund's "The Politics of Pants," a summary of James Sullivan's book *Jeans: A Cultural History of an American Icon*, argues that consumers, not manufacturers or marketers, determine the cultural significance of products—such as jeans. In fact, Levi Strauss, the original manufacturer of blue jeans, had a hard time understanding why young people in the middle of the twentieth century adopted jeans as a symbol of freedom and protest. Maybe the pictures say it all?

The Politics of Pants

CHARLES PAUL FREUND

In the 1950s, Levi Strauss & Co. decided to update the image of its denim clothes. Until then, the company had been depending for sales on the romantic appeal of the gold rush and the rugged image of the cowboy. Hell, it was still calling its signature pants, the ones with the copper rivets, "waist overalls." It didn't want to abandon the evocative gold-rush connection, but the postwar world was filling with consumption-minded creatures called "teenagers," and it seemed time to rethink the company's pitch.

So in 1956 Levi Strauss tried an experiment, releasing a line of black denim pants it called Elvis Presley Jeans. It was the perfect endorsement. On the branding level, it was a successful marriage of an old product and its developing new character. People had long worn denim for work, or to "westernize" themselves; now a new set of customers was wearing it to identify themselves with the postwar scene of rebellious urban (and suburban) outliers. Upon the release of Elvis's 1956 hit movie *Jailhouse Rock*, writes James Sullivan in *Jeans: A Cultural History of an American Icon* (Gotham Books), "black jeans became the rage of the season." That transition would eventually make undreamed-of profits for Levi Strauss and its many competitors.

Elvis Presley made jeans hip, but he didn't like them.

Jeans were once for cowboys or actors who played them.

The endorsement was wonderfully revealing from within too. Elvis actually disliked denim. To him, as to most people from real working-class backgrounds, it was just a reminder of working hard and being poor. The less denim Elvis wore, the happier he was. As for the company suits at Levi Strauss, they had no idea where their new customers would take them. The company was a lot more comfortable dealing with a safe, midcult crooner like Bing Crosby. In 1951 Levi Strauss had presented Crosby with a custom-made denim tuxedo jacket, just the kind of empty PR stunt the company bosses understood. The eroticizing Presley was unknown territory to them, and they nearly fumbled the whole bad boy connection—one that had already emerged via Presley, Brando, James Dean, and even the Beats[1]—that would help put their product on nearly every pair of hips in the Western world (and on plenty of hips everywhere else too).

---

[1]**Brando, James Dean, and even the Beats:** In the early 1950s, actors Marlon Brando and James Dean were known for their roles in disaffected-youth films such as *The Wild One* and *Rebel Without a Cause*. The "Beat Generation" of young poets came to prominence in the late 1950s and early 1960s, subsequently affecting the wider youth culture.

The rest of Sullivan's book is addressed to the culture, the fashion, and of course the business of jeans. The last of these threads is the most valuable, since it is probably the least known and the most revealing. Who knew, for example, that leisure suits were introduced by Lee? (And what does *that* episode say about the marketers' conception, let alone control, of a product's meaning?) Sullivan's book is as comprehensive on its subject as you are likely to want, if not more so. Jeans and Jack Kerouac.[2] Jeans and the dude ranch. Jeans and the advent of the zipper. Jeans and punk. Jeans and disco. Jeans and the indigo trade. Thousand-dollar Jeans. Collectible jeans. Even pants (not jeans) and Brigham Young,[3] who in 1830 charged that trousers with buttons in front were "fornication pants."

There's even jeans and the color blue. Sullivan has penned an ode to blueness that goes on for four pages. ("The deeper blue becomes," he quotes the artist Wassily Kandinsky as saying, "the more urgently it summons man toward the infinite.") Best of all, though, is jeans and Vladimir Nabokov,[4] despite the fact that Nabokov has nothing much to say about jeans.

Sullivan uses Nabokov inventively, quoting from his 1955 novel, *Lolita*, to demonstrate how the narrator's "refined" sensibility is transformed by a whole world of low-end culture that has become — for him — eroticized. The novel's motels and shopping strips, writes Sullivan, "are the consummate low-culture backdrops for Lolita's jeans, sneakers, and lollipops." It's not just Lolita that Nabokov's intellectual narrator has fallen for. And if you don't see what eroticized low-end culture has to do with the triumph of American jeans, then Elvis really has left the building, and you've gone with him.

---

[2]**Jack Kerouac:** "Beat" writer; his novel *On the Road* was one of the best-known works to come out of the Beat Generation.

[3]**Brigham Young:** Influential nineteenth-century leader of the Church of Jesus Christ of Latter-day Saints (better known as the Mormon Church).

[4]**Vladimir Nabokov:** Russian writer of fiction; best known for his novel *Lolita*.

1. **Causal Analysis:** Like Jonah Goldberg in "Global Warming and the Sun" (p. 141), you've probably been curious about or even skeptical of some causal claims made routinely. It might just be college faculty complaining about why students browse the Web during their classes. Or, more seriously, maybe you belong to a group that has been the subject of causal analyses verging on prejudicial. If so, refute what you regard as some faulty analysis of cause and effect by offering a more plausible explanation.

2. **Research Study:** Using Kyu-heong Kim's research essay "Bending the Rules for ESL Writers" as a model (p. 157), write a paper based on sources that examines an issue or problem in your major or in some area of special concern to you. The issue should be one that involves questions of how, why, or what if. Base your analysis on a variety of academic or public sources, fully documented. Like Kim, you may also draw on interviews if appropriate to your subject.

3. **Exploratory Essay:** Liza Mundy's analysis of cause and effect in "What's Really behind the Plunge in Teen Pregnancy?" (p. 165) has both cultural and political implications. Locate a similarly challenging analysis in a national newspaper or news magazine. Then write a detailed response to the causal issues it raises, suggesting, for instance, why you find it convincing, or speculating about how society might respond to its conclusions. You'll find many analyses covering topics such as the environment, terrorism, education, sports, religion, culture, and so on.

4. **Cultural Analysis:** After examining the way Charles Paul Freund deals with jeans (p. 170), identify a comparable trend you have noticed or a change in society or culture that deserves scrutiny. It might relate to technology, entertainment, political preferences, fashion, popularity of careers, or other areas. Write an analysis of the phenomenon, considering either causes or potential consequences of this new mania. Then illustrate the trend with images that suggest its cultural reach or significance. Spend some time in the opening of your paper describing the trend and establishing that it is consequential.

5. **Your Choice:** Politicians and pundits alike are fond of offering predictions, some hopeful, but many dire. The economy, they might suggest, is about to boom or slide into depression; sports dynasties are destined to blossom or collapse; printed books to disappear; American teens to grow fond of musicals. Identify one such prediction about which you have some doubts and develop a cause-and-effect analysis to suggest why it is likely to go awry. Be sure to explain in detail what factors you expect will make the prediction go wrong. If you are brave, offer an alternative vision of the future.

How to start

- Need a **topic**? See page 182.
- Need to come up with a **solution**? See page 187.
- Need to **organize your ideas**? See page 189.

6 Proposals

define a
problem and
suggest a
solution

Proposals are written to try to solve problems. Typically, you'll make a proposal to initiate an action or change. At a minimum, you hope to alter someone's thinking—even if only to recommend leaving things as they are.

TRIAL BALLOON
Degree programs at your school have so many complicated requirements that most students take far more time to graduate than they expect—adding thousands of dollars to their loans. As a *trial balloon*, you suggest that the catalog include accurate "time-to-degree" estimates for all degree programs and certificates.

FORMAL PROPOSAL
Noticing the difficulty people with disabilities have navigating government offices, a member of the city council for whom you are interning asks you to look into the problem. You prepare a *formal proposal* that assesses the situation, offers three specific improvements, and estimates the costs of the improvements.

MANIFESTO
Packaging is getting out of hand, and you've had enough. People can barely open the products they buy because everything is zipped up, shrink-wrapped, blister-packed, containerized, or child-protected. So you write a *manifesto* calling for saner and more eco-friendly approaches to product protection.

VISUAL PROPOSAL
You create a PowerPoint so members of your co-op can visualize how much better your building's study area would look with a few inexpensive tweaks in furniture, paint, and lighting. Your *visual proposal* gets you the job of implementing the changes.

176

DECIDING TO WRITE A PROPOSAL   *Got an issue or a problem?*
Good—let's deal with it. That's the logic driving most proposals, both the
professional types that pursue grant money and the less formal propositions
that are part of everyday life, academic or otherwise. Like evaluations and
some explanations, proposals are another form of argument. ○

Although grant writing shares some of the elements of informal proposals, it is driven by rigid formulas set by foundations and government
agencies, usually covering things like budgets, personnel, evaluation,
outcomes, and so on. Informal proposals are much easier. Though they may
not funnel large sums of cash your way, they're still important tools for
addressing problems. A sensible proposal can make a difference in any
situation—be it academic, personal, or political.

You'll need to make the following moves in framing a proposal. Not
every proposal needs to do each of these things. In a first-round pitch, you
might launch a trial balloon to test whether an idea will work at all; a more
serious plan headed for public scrutiny would have to punch the ticket on
more of the items.

**Use Only What You
Need**   How do you
persuade people in a
community to save water?
Denver Water created an
innovative multimedia
ad campaign to sell its
proposal cleverly to its
community.

choose a genre
p. 390

Define a problem. Set the stage for a proposal by describing the specific situation, problem, or opportunity in enough detail that readers *get it*: They see a compelling need for action. In many cases, a proposal needs to explain what's wrong with the status quo.

Target the proposal. To make a difference, you have to reach people with the power to change a situation. That means first identifying such individuals (or groups) and then tailoring your proposal to their expectations. Use the Web or library, for example, to get the names and contact information of government or corporate officials. ○ When the people in power *are* the problem, go over their heads to more general audiences with clout of their own: voters, consumers, women, fellow citizens, the elderly, and so on.

Consider reasonable options. Your proposal won't be taken seriously unless you have weighed all the workable possibilities, explaining their advantages and downsides. Only then will you be prepared to make a case for your own ideas.

Make specific recommendations. Explain what you propose to do about the situation or problem; don't just complain that someone else has gotten it wrong. The more detailed your solution is, the better.

Make realistic recommendations. You need to address two related issues: *feasibility* and *implementation*. A proposal is feasible if it can be achieved with available resources and is acceptable to the parties involved. And, of course, a feasible plan still needs a plausible pathway to implementation: *First we do this; then we do this.*

plan a project
p. 466

Trial Balloon

The following proposal originally appeared in *Time* (August 21, 2005). Its author, Barrett Seaman, doesn't have the space to do much more than alert the general public (or, more likely, parents of college students) to the need for action to end alcohol abuse on campuses. Still, he does offer a surprising suggestion — a trial balloon for dealing with bingeing. Although many readers might reject his idea initially, the proposal does what it must: It makes a plausible case and gets people thinking.

How Bingeing Became the New College Sport

BARRETT SEAMAN

In the coming weeks, millions of students will begin their fall semester of college, with all the attendant rituals of campus life: freshman orientation, registering for classes, rushing by fraternities and sororities, and, in a more recent nocturnal college tradition, "pregaming" in their rooms.

Pregaming is probably unfamiliar to people who went to college before the 1990s. But it is now a common practice among eighteen-, nineteen- and twenty-year-old students who cannot legally buy or consume alcohol. It usually involves sitting in a dorm room or an off-campus apartment and drinking as much hard liquor as possible before heading out for the evening's parties. While reporting for my book *Binge*, I witnessed the hospitalization of several students for acute alcohol poisoning. Among them was a Hamilton College freshman who had consumed twenty-two shots of vodka while sitting in a dorm room with her friends. Such hospitalizations are routine on campuses across the nation. By the Thanksgiving break of the year I visited Harvard, the university's health center had admitted nearly seventy students for alcohol poisoning.

When students are hospitalized — or worse yet, die from alcohol poisoning, which happens about 300 times each year — college presidents tend to react by declaring their campuses dry or shutting down fraternity houses. But tighter enforcement of the minimum drinking age of twenty-one is not the solution. It's part of the problem.

Defines problem he intends to address: bingeing known as pregaming.

Proposal draws on research the author has done.

Points out that current solutions to college drinking don't work.

Over the past forty years, the United States has taken a confusing approach to the age-appropriateness of various rights, privileges, and behaviors. It used to be that twenty-one was the age that legally defined adulthood. On the heels of the student revolution of the late '60s, however, came sweeping changes: The voting age was reduced to eighteen; privacy laws were enacted that protected college students' academic, health, and disciplinary records from outsiders, including parents; and the drinking age, which had varied from state to state, was lowered to eighteen.

Then, thanks in large measure to intense lobbying by Mothers Against Drunk Driving, Congress in 1984 effectively blackmailed states into hiking the minimum drinking age to twenty-one by passing a law that tied compliance to the distribution of federal-aid highway funds — an amount that will average $690 million per state this year. There is no doubt that the law, which achieved full fifty-state compliance in 1988, saved lives, but it had the unintended consequence of creating a covert culture around alcohol as the young adult's forbidden fruit.

Drinking has been an aspect of college life since the first Western universities in the fourteenth century. My friends and I drank in college in the 1960s — sometimes a lot but not so much that we had to be hospitalized. Veteran college administrators cite a sea change in campus culture that began, not without coincidence, in the 1990s. It was marked by a shift from beer to hard liquor, consumed not in large social settings, since that is now illegal, but furtively and dangerously in students' residences.

In my reporting at colleges around the country, I did not meet any presidents or deans who felt that the twenty-one-year age minimum helps their efforts to curb the abuse of alcohol on their campuses. Quite the opposite. They thought the law impeded their efforts since it takes away the ability to monitor and supervise drinking activity.

What would happen if the drinking age was rolled back to eighteen or nineteen? Initially, there would be a surge in binge drinking as young adults savored their newfound freedom. But over time, I predict, U.S. college students would settle into the saner approach to alcohol I saw on the one

Explains factors responsible for the spike in alcohol abuse.

Points out that current law makes it harder to deal with bingeing.

Offers specific proposal tentatively, posed as question.

Proposal stands up to tests of feasibility, acceptability, and practicality.

campus I visited where the legal drinking age is eighteen: Montreal's McGill University, which enrolls about two thousand American undergraduates a year. Many, when they first arrive, go overboard, exploiting their ability to drink legally. But by midterms, when McGill's demanding academic standards must be met, the vast majority have put drinking into its practical place among their priorities.

A culture like that is achievable at U.S. colleges if Congress can muster the fortitude to reverse a bad policy. If lawmakers want to reduce drunk driving, they should do what the Norwegians do: Throw the book at offenders no matter what their age. Meanwhile, we should let the pregamers come out of their dorm rooms so that they can learn to handle alcohol like the adults we hope and expect them to be.

States his thesis and then offers precedents for students behaving more responsibly with lower drinking age.

Do current strict drinking laws in the United States actually encourage students to abuse alcohol? In 2008, a coalition of presidents from one hundred colleges recommended lowering the drinking age to eighteen.

Exploring purpose and topic

▶ topic

Most people will agree to a reasonable proposal—as long as it doesn't cost them anything. But moving audiences from *I agree* to *I'll actually do something about it* usually takes a powerful act of persuasion. And for that reason, proposals are typically structured as arguments, requiring all the strategies used in that genre. ○

Occasionally, you'll be asked to solve a particular problem in school or on the job. Having a topic assigned makes your task a little easier, but you can bet that any such problem will be complex and open to multiple solutions. Otherwise, there would be no challenge to it.

When choosing a proposal topic on your own, keep the following concerns in mind. ○

Look for a genuine issue.   Spend the first part of your project defining a problem readers will care about. You may think it's a shame no one retails Prada close to campus, but your classmates could plausibly be more concerned with outrageous student fees or the high price of gasoline. Go beyond your own concerns in settling on a problem.

Look for a challenging problem.   It helps if others have tried to fix it in the past, but failed—and for reasons you can identify. Times change, attitudes shift, technology improves: All of these can be factors that make what seemed like an insoluble problem in the past more manageable now. Choose a serious topic to which you can bring fresh perspectives.

Look for a soluble problem.   Challenges *are* good, but impossible dreams are for Broadway musicals. Parking on campus is the classic impasse—always present, always frustrating. Steer clear of problems no one has ever solved, unless you have a *really* good idea.

Look for a local issue.   It's best to leave "world peace" to celebrity activists like Bono. You can investigate a problem in your community more credibly, talking with people involved or searching local archives for material. ○ Doing so makes it easier to find an audience you can influence, including people potentially able to change the situation. It's more likely you'll get the attention of your dean of students than the secretary of state.

> Need help deciding what to write about? See "How to Browse for Ideas" on pp. 360–61.

understand argument
p. 72

find a topic
p. 356

interview and observe
p. 478

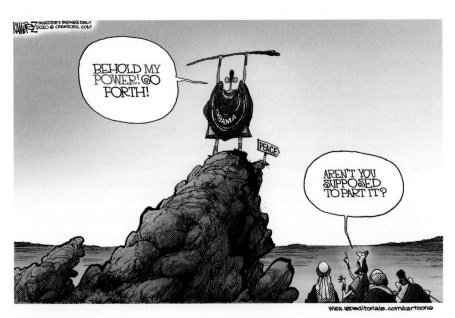

In an editorial cartoon, Michael Ramirez uses a familiar biblical story to suggest that President Obama may have made too challenging a proposal when he asked Israeli leaders to "take risks for peace" in the Middle East. This cartoon originally appeared in *Investor's Business Daily* on July 9, 2010. (By permission of Michael Ramirez and Creators Syndicate, Inc.)

Your Turn   In 46 BCE, Julius Caesar used his authority as dictator to impose a new calendar on Rome because the old one had fallen five months out of synch with the seasons. Play Caesar today by imagining what problems you would fix if you could simply impose your will. Make a list. Narrow your more grandiose schemes (world peace) to more plausible ones (less rowdiness in the student section at football games), and then consider which items on your roster could be argued rationally and compellingly in a short paper. Compare your list with those of other students and discuss workable proposal topics.

Understanding your audience

While preparing a proposal, keep two audiences in mind—one fairly narrow and the other more broad. The first group includes people who could possibly do something about a problem; the second consists of general readers who could influence those in the first group by bringing the weight of public opinion down on them. And public opinion makes a difference.

Writers adjust for audience all the time in offering proposals. Grant writers, especially, make it a point to learn what agencies and institutions expect in applications. Quite often, it takes two or three tries to figure out how to present a winning grant submission. You won't have that luxury with most academic or political pieces, but you can certainly study models of successful proposals, noting how the writers raise an issue with readers, provide them with information and options, and then argue for a particular solution.

Write to people who can make a difference. For example, a personal letter you might prepare for the dean of students to protest her policies against displaying political posters in university buildings (including offices and dormitories) would likely have a respectful and perhaps legalistic tone, pointing to case law on the subject and university policies on freedom of speech. You'd also want to assure the dean of your good sense and provide her with sound reasons to consider your case.

You'd be in good company adopting such a strategy. Listen to how matter-of-factly environmentalist David R. Brower argues—in a famous proposal—that the gates of the massive Glen Canyon Dam should be opened and the waters of Lake Powell drained. Radical stuff, but his strategy was sensible. For one thing, he argued, the artificial reservoir leaked.

> One of the strongest selling points [for removing the dam] comes from the Bureau of Reclamation itself. In 1996, the bureau found that almost a million acre-feet, or 8 percent of the river's flow, disappeared between the stations recording the reservoir's inflow and outflow. Almost 600,000 acre-feet were presumed lost to evaporation. Nobody knows for sure about the rest. The bureau said some of the loss was a gain – being stored in the

banks of the reservoir—but it has no idea how much of that gain it will ever get back. Some bank storage is recoverable, but all too likely the region's downward-slanting geological strata are leading some of Powell's waters into the dark unknown. It takes only one drain to empty a bathtub, and we don't know where, when, or how the Powell tub leaks. A million acre-feet could meet the annual domestic needs of 4 million people and at today's prices are worth $435 million in the Salt Lake City area—more than a billion on my hill in Berkeley, California.

—"Let the River Run Through It," *Sierra*, March/April 1997

Rally people who represent public opinion.

Imagine you've had no response from the dean of students on the political poster proposal you made. Time to take the issue to the public, perhaps via an op-ed or letter sent to the student paper. Though still keeping the dean firmly in mind, you'd now also write to stir up student and community opinion. Your new piece could be more emotional than your letter and less burdened by legal points—though still citing facts and presenting solid reasons for allowing students more leeway in expressing their political beliefs on campus. O

The fact is that people often need a spur to move them—that is, a persuasive strategy that helps them to imagine their role in solving a problem. Again, you'd be in good company in leading an audience to your position. As shown on page 186, when President John F. Kennedy proposed a mission to the moon in 1962, he did it in language that stirred a public reasonably skeptical about the cost and challenges of such an implausible undertaking.

refine your tone
p. 432

JFK Aims High In 1962, the president challenged Americans to go to the moon; today American astronauts ride to the International Space Station on a Russian *Soyuz*.

There is no strife, no prejudice, no national conflict in outer space as yet. Its hazards are hostile to us all. Its conquest deserves the best of all mankind, and its opportunity for peaceful cooperation may never come again. But why, some say, the moon? Why choose this as our goal? And they may well ask why climb the highest mountain? Why, thirty-five years ago, fly the Atlantic? Why does Rice play Texas?

We choose to go to the moon. We choose to go to the moon in this decade and do the other things, not because they are easy, but because they are hard, because that goal will serve to organize and measure the best of our energies and skills, because that challenge is one that we are willing to accept, one we are unwilling to postpone, and one which we intend to win, and the others, too.

–Rice Stadium "Moon Speech," September 12, 1962

Finding and developing materials

Proposals might begin with whining and complaining (*I want easier parking!*), but they can't stay in that mode for long. Like any serious work, proposals must be grounded in solid thinking and research.

consider solutions ◀

What makes them distinctive, however, is the sheer variety of strategies you might use in a single document. To write a convincing proposal, you may have to narrate, report, argue, evaluate, and explore cause and effect. A proposal can be a little like old-time TV variety shows, with one act following another, displaying a surprising range of talent. Here's how you might develop those various parts.

Define the problem.   First, research the existing problem fully enough to explain it to your readers. Run through the traditional journalist's questions—*Who? What? Where? When? Why? How?*—to be sure you've got the basics of your topic down cold. When appropriate, interview experts or people involved with an issue; for instance, in college communities, the best repositories of institutional memory will usually be staff. ○

Even when you think you know the topic well, spend time locating any documents that might provide hard facts to cite for skeptical readers. For instance, if you propose to change a long-standing policy, find out when it was imposed, by whom, and for what reasons.

Examine prior solutions.   If a problem is persistent, other people have certainly tried to solve it—or perhaps they caused it. In either case, do the research necessary to figure out, as best you can, what happened in these earlier efforts. But expect controversy. Your sources may provide different and contradictory accounts that you will have to sort out in a plausible narrative.

Once you know the history of an issue, shift into an evaluative mode to explain why earlier solutions or strategies did not work. ○ Provide reliable information so that readers can later make comparisons with your own proposal and appreciate its ingenuity.

Make a proposal.   Coming up with a proposal may take all the creativity you can muster, to the point where a strong case can be made for working collaboratively when that's an option. ○ You'll benefit from the additional

> The Journalist's Questions
>
> | Who? | What? |
> |------|-------|
> | Where? | When? |
> | Why? | How? |

interview and
observe p. 478

understand
evaluation p. 106

collaborate
p. 362

feedback. Be sure to write down your ideas as they emerge, so you can see what exactly you are recommending. Be specific about numbers and costs.

For instance, if you propose that high school students in your district take a course in practical economics (balancing a checkbook, credit card use, and so on) to better prepare them for adult responsibilities, do the research necessary to figure out who might teach such classes and how many new instructors the school district would have to hire. Your findings could preempt an implausibly expensive proposal or suggest more feasible alternatives for handling the problem that you see.

Defend the proposal.   Any ideas that threaten the status quo will surely provoke arguments. That's half the fun of offering proposals. So prove your position, using all the tools of argument available to you, from the logical and factual to the emotional. It is particularly important to anticipate objections, because readers invested in the status quo will have them in spades. Take time to define a successful solution to a problem, and point out every way your solution meets that definition. Above all, you've got to show that your idea will work.

Be prepared, too, to show that your plan is feasible—that is to say, that it can be achieved with existing or new resources. For example, you might actually solve your school's traffic problems by proposing a monorail linking the central campus to huge new parking garages. But who would pay for the multimillion-dollar system? Still, don't be put off too easily by the objection that *we can't possibly do that*. A little ingenuity goes a long way—it's part of the problem-solving process.

Figure out how to implement the proposal.   Readers will want assurances that your ideas can be implemented: Show them how. ○ Figure out what has to happen to meet your goals: where new resources will come from, how personnel can be recruited and hired, where brochures or manuals will be printed, and so on. Provide a timetable if you can.

think critically
p. 372

Creating a structure

Proposals follow the mental processes many people go through in dealing with issues and problems, and some of these problems have more history and complications than others. ○ Generally, the less formal the proposal, the fewer structural elements it will have. So you should adapt the proposal paradigm below to your purposes, using it as a checklist of *possible* issues to consider in your own project.

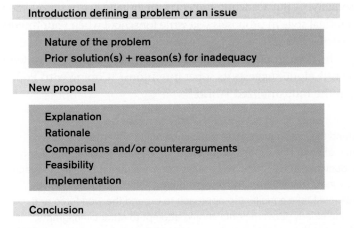

Introduction defining a problem or an issue

> **Nature of the problem**
> **Prior solution(s) + reason(s) for inadequacy**

New proposal

> **Explanation**
> **Rationale**
> **Comparisons and/or counterarguments**
> **Feasibility**
> **Implementation**

Conclusion

You might use a similar structure when you intend to explore the effects that follow from some action, event, policy, or change in the status quo. Once again, you'd begin with an introduction that fully describes the situation you believe will have consequences; then you would work through those consequences, connecting them as necessary. Your conclusion could then draw out the implications of your paper.

shape your work
p. 406

Choosing a style and design

Proposals do come in many forms and, occasionally, they may be frivolous or comic. But whenever you suggest upending the status quo or spending someone else's money, you probably need to show a little respect and humility.

Use a formal style.   Professional proposals—especially those seeking grant money—are typically written in a formal and impersonal high style, as if the project would be jeopardized by reviewers detecting the slightest hint of enthusiasm or personality. ○ But academic audiences are usually just as serious. So you might use a formal style in proposals you write for school when your intended readers are specific and official—a professor, a government agency, a dean.

Observe the no-nonsense tone Thao Tran adopts early in an academic essay whose title alone suggests its sober intentions: "Coping with Population Aging in the Industrialized World."

Point of view is impersonal: *This report* rather than *I.*

Purpose of proposal is clearly explained.

Premises and assumptions of proposal are offered in abstract language.

Leaders of industrialized nations and children of baby boomers must understand the consequences of population aging and minimize its economic effects. This report will recommend steps for coping with aging in the industrialized world and will assess counterarguments to those steps. With a dwindling workforce and rising elderly population, industrialized countries must take a multi-step approach to expand the workforce and support the elderly. Governments should attempt to attract immigrants, women, and elderly people into the workforce. Supporting an increasing elderly population will require reforming pension systems and raising indirect taxes. It will also require developing pronatalist policies, in which governments subsidize child rearing costs to encourage births. Many of these strategies will challenge traditional cultural notions and require a change in cultural attitudes. While change will not be easy, industrialized nations must recognize and address this trend quickly in order to reduce its effects.

Use a middle style, when appropriate.   You might shift toward a middle style whenever establishing a personal relationship could help your proposal or when you need to persuade a wider, more general audience.

It is possible, too, for styles to vary within a document. Your language might be coldly efficient as you scrutinize previous failures or tick off the advantages of your specific proposal. But as you near the end of the piece, you might decide another style would better reflect your vision for the future or your enthusiasm for an idea. Earlier in this chapter, environmentalist David R. Brower supplied an example of technical prose in explaining why

define your style
p. 432

draining Lake Powell would make commercial sense. Here is a far more emotional paragraph from the conclusion of his proposal:

The sooner we begin, the sooner lost paradises will begin to recover—Cathedral in the Desert, Music Temple, Hidden Passage, Dove Canyon, Little Arch, Dungeon, and a hundred others. Glen Canyon itself can probably lose its ugly white sidewalls in two or three decades. The tapestries can reemerge, along with the desert varnish, the exiled species of plants and animals, the pictographs and other mementos of people long gone. The canyon's music will be known again, and "the sudden poetry of springs," Wallace Stegner's beautiful phrase, will be revealed again below the sculptured walls of Navajo sandstone. The phrase, "as long as the rivers shall run and the grasses grow," will regain its meaning.

Place names listed have poetic effect.

Lush details add to emotional appeal of proposal.

Final quotation summarizes mission of proposal.

Pay attention to elements of design. Writers often incorporate images, charts, tables, graphs, and flowcharts to illustrate what is at stake in a proposal or to make comparisons easy. Images also help readers imagine solutions or proposals and make those ideas attractive. The SmartArt Graphics icon in the Microsoft Word Gallery opens up a range of templates you might use to help readers visualize a project.

form   structure   movement   color

You may have seen photographs of the new Dallas Cowboys Stadium that opened in Arlington, Texas, in 2009. But here's an early sketch of the HKS design, posted on the ArchDaily Web site, exploring various possibilities for the new building.

Your Turn The style of proposals varies dramatically, depending on audience and purpose. Review the proposals in this chapter offered as models—including the visual proposals. Then explain in some detail exactly how the language (or the visual details) of one item works to make its case. You can focus on a whole essay, but you may find it more interesting just to explicate a few sentences or paragraphs or one or two visual details. For example, when does Barrett Seaman (p. 179), Michael Ramirez (p. 183), or Katelyn Vincent (p. 198) score style points with you? Be ready to explain your observation orally.

think visually
p. 592

FORMAL PROPOSAL   If democracy is to thrive, Donald Lazere believes that Americans need to know more about citizenship. So writing for the academic audience of *The Chronicle Review*, he makes a specific proposal for course work in civic education. Lazere is a professor emeritus at California Polytechnic State University at San Luis Obispo.

A Core Curriculum for Civic Literacy

Donald Lazere

January 31, 2010

The past few years have seen an outpouring of books and reports deploring Americans' civic ignorance, with titles like *Just How Stupid Are We?, The Dumbest Generation, The Age of American Unreason,* and *Tuned Out: Why Americans Under 40 Don't Follow the News.* This is a problem that everyone seems to complain about but no one tries to solve through any coordinated, nationwide effort.

National organizations have recently been formed, including the Campaign for the Civic Mission of Schools, the Carnegie Foundation for the Advancement of Teaching's Political Engagement Project, and Campus Compact and its Research University Civic Engagement Network. These organizations have published important interdisciplinary books, such as *Educating for Democracy,* by Anne Colby et al. (Jossey-Bass, 2007), and *Civic Engagement in Higher Education,* by Barbara Jacoby et al. (Jossey-Bass, 2009).

Many campus programs have also been exemplary, as surveyed in Charles Muscatine's *Fixing College Education* (University of Virginia Press, 2009). In *The Assault on Reason* (Penguin Press, 2007), Al Gore praised the American Political Science Association for starting a Task Force on Civic Education. That should prompt similar task forces in the Modern Language Association (my discipline) and other professional associations, along with a unifying interdisciplinary organization for

Lazere defines a problem and surveys the ample literature on the subject.

The proposal argues for a commission to create "a core curriculum for civic literacy."

secondary and postsecondary education, a National Commission on Civic Education. Liberal and conservative educators and politicians should collaborate in hammering out their differences on what should constitute a core curriculum for civic literacy. We can hope for sponsorship in this effort by both conservative and liberal foundations, as well as for support from the U.S. Department of Education and National Endowment for the Humanities.

One way to prompt deliberation here is to spin E. D. Hirsch's much-debated agenda for what every American needs to know to be culturally literate: What does every American need to know to be a civically literate, critically conscious, responsible citizen? And, as a corollary, what role should the humanities play in a renewal of education for civic literacy?

Two questions help to focus on the civic literacy problem as Lazere sees it.

My agenda would give priority to the factual knowledge and analytic skills that students need to make reasoned judgments about the partisan screaming matches and special-interest propaganda that permeate political disputes. One source for such knowledge and skills can be the disciplines of critical thinking and argumentative rhetoric. Unfortunately, few high schools or colleges require courses with that focus, which was also shamefully ignored by No Child Left Behind.

We have all by necessity been thinking a lot lately about one particular branch of civic literacy: economic knowledge. How many among us understand how or why our personal economic fates—mortgages, retirement pensions, and our colleges' financing and endowments—are captive to booms and busts in the stock market and the occult realm of national and international high finance? In the prophetic words of the "corporate cosmology" revealed by the arch-capitalist Arthur Jensen in Paddy Chayefsky's 1976 film, *Network*, "The totality of life on this planet" is now determined by "one vast and immane, interwoven, interacting, multivariate, multinational dominion of dollars."

Lazere uses a current issue to dramatize the need for better civic education.

What a tragic gulf lies between most citizens' understanding of economic forces and their power over each of our daily lives and livelihoods. And what an enormous hole there is, in both K–12 and college curricula, in teaching about those forces as an integral part of general education. I am not talking about courses in formal economics, but in thinking critically about the rhetoric of economic issues at the everyday level of political debates and news and opinion—although those studies would identify oversimplifications at that level that could certainly be pursued in economics classes.

The term "core curriculum" has sadly become a culture-war wedge issue, with conservatives pre-empting it in the cause of Eurocentric tradition and American patriotism, thus provoking intransigent opposition from progressive champions of cultural pluralism and identity politics. Surely, however, we should urge the opposing sides to seek common ground in a core curriculum for critical citizenship that transcends—or encompasses—ideological partisanship.

To win wide support for civic education, the proposal stakes out a middle ground between warring political factions.

My own immodest proposal models a core curriculum that centrally includes critical thinking about, and analysis and practice of, public rhetoric, at the local, national, and international levels. Far from being a radical proposal, it is a conservative one in returning to something like the 18th-century rhetoric-based curriculum in American education.

Style here reflects the intended academic audience: formal and technical.

That curriculum, as the historian of rhetoric S. Michael Halloran describes it, "address[ed] students as political beings, as members of a body politic in which they have a responsibility to form judgments and influence the judgments of others on public issues." Halloran and other historians have lamented the modern diffusion of studies in forensics, literature, composition, and other humanistic fields, as a result of the hegemony of disciplines and departments oriented toward specialized faculty research, which have become the tail that wags the curricular dog. Those forces and a depressing array of others have caused the study of political rhetoric to fall between the cracks of most current curricula, almost to the disappearing point.

The ground-work laid, Lazere now offers detailed course recom-mendations.

So let's envision how a revived curriculum for civic literacy might be embodied in a sequence of undergraduate courses that would supplement, not supplant, basic courses in history, government, literature, and other humanist staples. These could be interdisciplinary offerings, with at least a partial component of English studies. Within English, they would follow, not replace, first-year writing—which in recent decades has focused on generating students' personal writing rather than critical analyses of readings or public rhetoric—and a second term in critical thinking and written and oral argumentative rhetoric.

The following headings correspond to chapters in my textbook for such a second-term course, but my own and other instructors' experience in using the book is that for any single course or textbook to "cover" what really demands a full curriculum is an impossible expectation. So I will break that material down, more appropriately, into four courses:

Course 1: Thinking Critically About Political and Economic Rhetoric

This would begin with a survey of semantic issues in defining terms like left wing, right wing, liberal, conservative, radical, moderate, freedom, democracy, patriotism, capitalism, socialism, communism, Marxism, fascism, and plutocracy. It would explore their denotative complexity and the ways in which they are oversimplified or connotatively slanted in public usage.

Study would then focus on defining ideological differences between and within the left and right, nationally and internationally, and on understanding the relativity of political viewpoints on the spectrum from left to right. For example, *The New York Times* is liberal in relation to Fox News but conservative in relation to *The Nation*; the Democratic Party is liberal in relation to the Republicans but conservative in relation to European social-democratic parties. Principles of argumentative rhetoric would then be applied to "reading the news" on political and economic issues in a range of journalistic and scholarly sources and from a variety of ideological viewpoints, with emphasis on identifying the predictable patterns of partisan rhetoric in opposing sources.

Course 2: Thinking Critically About Mass Media

Key questions would include: Do the media give people what they want, or condition what they want? Are news media objective and neutral, and should they be? The debate over liberal versus conservative bias in media would be approached through weighing the diverse influences of employees (editors, producers, writers, newscasters, performers); owners, executives, and advertisers; external pressure groups; and audiences. Research on the cognitive effects of mass culture would be applied to such issues as the impact of electronic media on reading, writing, and political consciousness. Implicit political ideology in news and entertainment media would be studied through images of corporations, workers, and unions; the rich, poor, and middle class; gender roles, ethnic minorities, and gays; military forces and war; and immigrants, foreigners, other parts of the world, and Americans' international presence. A final topic of study would be how the Internet has altered all of those issues.

Course 3: Propaganda Analysis and Deception Detection

Study here would begin with problems in defining and evaluating propaganda. A survey of its sources would include government and the military, political parties, lobbies, advertising, public relations, foundations, and sponsored research in think tanks and elsewhere. The role of special interests, conflicts of interest, and special pleading in political and economic rhetoric would be examined, along with propagators' frequent resort to deceptive modes of argument or outright lying—especially with statistics. This course (or another entire one) would include topics in critical consumer education: reading the fine print in contracts, like those for student loans, credit cards, rental agreements, and mortgages; examining health and environmental issues in consumer products; and seeking out the often hidden facts of the production and marketing of food and pharmaceuticals.

Course 4: Civic Literacy in Practice

This would connect these academic studies with service learning, community or national activism, or work in government or community organizations, journalism, and elsewhere.

Two possible objections:

"What you are proposing is that English and other humanities courses take on the impossible burden of remediation for the failures of the entire American education system in civic literacy."

You betcha. It's a dirty job, but someone has to do it, and I don't see any likelier disciplines jumping into the breach, especially ones with

The proposal concludes by addressing feasibility issues and anticipating potential objections.

courses that are conventionally general education and breadth requirements. (Some communication and speech departments are in schools of liberal arts, but others are not; many offer courses in political rhetoric and media criticism, but those are mostly advanced ones for majors.) An ideal solution would be for these to be offered as interdisciplinary core courses, in which humanities faculty members would collaborate with those in the social sciences, communication, and so on. If civic education at the secondary level ever picks up the slack that it should, the college humanities involvement in such instruction can be phased out.

"Mightn't your proposals just be a Trojan horse for dragging in the academic left's same old agenda and biases?"

The courses could be conceived in their specifics and taught by instructors with varying ideological viewpoints — or best of all, through team teaching by liberal and conservative instructors. In principle, this framework would "teach the conflicts," on Gerald Graff's model, not through advocacy or the monologic perspective of any teacher's own beliefs, but through enabling students to identify and compare a full range of opposing ideological perspectives (including those of the instructor and the students), their points of opposition, and the partisan patterns and biases of their rhetoric. I have found it easy to grade students on the basis of their skill in articulating those points, without regard to my political viewpoints or theirs.

To be sure, this conception runs up against the near impossibility of anyone's even defining terms and points of opposition between, say, the left and right with complete objectivity and without injecting value judgments. That problem itself, however, can become a subject of study within these courses and in advanced scholarly inquiry. Indeed, the courses could prompt a wealth of related research and theoretical explorations, creating a fruitful arena for bridging the gap between advanced scholarship and undergraduate teaching.

MANIFESTO   Proposals often arise from a critical look at contemporary culture. Here, Katelyn Vincent draws upon her own experiences to argue, finally, that technology is taking up too much of our lives. She draws attention to the issue by dramatizing her own struggle to survive for twelve hours without the Internet.

Vincent 1

Katelyn Vincent

Professor Ruszkiewicz

Composition 2

November 11, 20--

Technology Time-out

"Are you sure you want to shut down?" A gray box has popped up and is waiting for my answer. No, I think to myself, I'm really not—and it's true. I have become so reliant on my computer that the thought of willingly turning it off during the day feels strange, almost wrong. And these days, it seems that everyone else shares the same addiction. The other day, when my roommate's Internet was down for a few hours, she had a mild panic attack. I thought it was silly—until I realized I would have had the same reaction if something similar had happened to me. Now, I consider myself to be a reasonably independent person, and the thought of being so dependent on something—especially a *machine*—horrified me. So I made a resolution—to avoid the Internet for twelve hours.

The gray box still waits. A blue button flashes on the screen in front on me, and the words "Shut Down" pulsate

The problem of Web addiction is identified, connecting the essay to a wide audience.

Vincent 2

before my eyes, daring me to make my decision. Giving in to my curiosity, I click and watch as the luminous rectangle in front of me fades slowly to black. That was easy enough, I think to myself. Maybe I can handle this after all.

Looking for something to do now that my primary source of entertainment (and procrastination) has dissolved into nothingness, I realize that it is eight o'clock and I have not eaten anything since breakfast. In the kitchen, I reach for the Fruity Cheerios on the top shelf of the pantry — a food staple since I started college — and am this close to pouring when I realize that *making* dinner might actually be fun. Heck, I haven't made myself a real dinner in several weeks, and since I usually spend this time Facebook-stalking casual acquaintances from third grade and reading random health articles on a too-familiar 9 × 13 glowing screen, today I have the time to spare. Eagerly, I pull out the pasta box that has been sleeping on my shelf for the past four months and get to work. You know what would be great with this, I think — some chicken. Mmm, I know, they have an amazing chicken pasta recipe on Allrecipes.com, I'll just go and . . . dammit. Never mind, I'll improvise. Surprisingly, the chicken doesn't turn out horribly. My dinner is no "Nicole's Tailgate Party Chicken Salad," but an alarmingly strong lemon taste gives me a zesty kick in the mouth. And to be honest, the fact that dinner is warm and homemade makes it infinitely better than Fruity Cheerios.

Vincent shifts to present tense to intensify the action.

The details are homey and believable.

Vincent 3

After dinner I again find myself bored—and wondering how many people have commented on my Facebook status. Wait a minute—why am I so concerned about this? Am I really so lame that my happiness depends on what people comment on my Facebook posts? God, I hope not. Trying to distract myself from this disturbing thought, I pull out my textbook to study—and once again, something doesn't feel right. I realize it has been over an hour since I checked Hotmail, Facebook, or MSN. My hand itches to press the power button and start clicking and clacking away—my prestudy ritual. Who knows how many e-mails, Facebook notifications, and important articles are popping up without my knowledge? What if I am missing something hugely important? Still, determined to stick it out, I dig in my backpack and stare into *Corporate Finance*, Second Edition. After three minutes, all I can think about is how much I would love to put in my headphones and crank up Pandora.com and my Michael Bublé playlist. This is going to be a long night.

I guess, not surprisingly, I am more focused on *Corporate Finance* than I have ever been, which isn't saying much, but still—I'm impressed. I have turned off my cell phone and iPod as well, and before I know it I have read two whole sections of the book and done a chapter's worth of questions. Not bad for two hours of studying. Afterwards, I delve into marketing and manage to read an entire chapter from that book as well. I have to say, it feels good to accomplish something and not have to stress about it. And I actually think I learned

The strategy is to describe symptoms of Internet addiction that readers will recognize.

Without getting technical, a full paragraph examines the limits of multitasking and the potential consequences for college students.

Vincent 4

something—a feeling I don't always get from studying, which for me is usually marked more by frantic memorization than any real retention of information. I guess part of the reason for my inability to recall is that studying for me usually means multitasking between chapter skimming, shopping for new boots on Amazon.com, and watching online clips from the latest episode of *Glee*. I usually switch back and forth between book and computer, spending about five minutes (max) on the book before some arbitrary whim or want enters my head and I have to go online and check it out before I can resume studying. It's gratifying to do something well for a change.

> The paragraph ends with a clever but important insight, driving home a key theme of the paper.

It's also kind of nice not to be in continuous contact with the rest of the world, I think to myself. What with e-mail, Facebook, calling, and texting, I feel as if I am constantly communicating with everyone I know. I can text my mom, talk on the phone with my sister, Facebook-chat with my friend, and e-mail my professor—all at the same time! While establishing relationships with other people is fine, it is also enjoyable to spend some time alone once in a while: I feel as though I haven't been truly alone in ages. Even while studying finance, I realize I am calmer than I have been in weeks. For a change, I get the chance to recharge *my* batteries instead of just my Mac's.

The next morning I am back to Fruity Cheerios and instinctively reach for the power button on my Mac as soon as I wake up. Still moving around in the foggy space of sleepiness, it takes me a moment to realize that my self-imposed

Vincent 5

sentence is not up. So much for checking my e-mail and Weather.com before I head out. Then again, I realize, I go to bed so late that it doesn't really make sense that I would have gotten any new e-mails since the last time I checked— most normal people are in bed between the hours of 2 and 6 AM, after all. Why do I have to check everything in the morning again? I have done it for so long that I guess it's just habit by now. I could be using those twenty minutes to spend more time getting ready, or even better, sleeping. I guess the only Web site it really makes sense to check in the morning is Weather.com, and even that's not a complete necessity.

The extra moments give me more time to get ready, and those seemingly insignificant twenty minutes turn my usually hectic morning routine into a much calmer transition between sleep and class. For the first time this semester, I am *not* lathering myself into a frenzy, *not* frantically applying lip gloss on my way out, and *not* running to catch the bus that's about to leave (there goes my exercise). In fact, my entire morning is pretty mellow, and I don't even think about getting online again until lunchtime. By then, the twelve hours is up—but the only reason I get online is to register for classes. Why mess with a good thing?

As it turns out, the "hugely important" somethings I was missing during my online off-time consisted of one offer for a free colon cleanse, two "Take this quiz!" pop-ups on Facebook, a new MSN article on the latest *Dancing with the Stars*

Vincent realizes that technology has complicated her life and, by implication, the lives of her readers.

The humor here is yet another gesture to win over readers, who have likely received similar e-mails.

Vincent 6

results, and only one actual, legitimate e-mail—from my mother. Granted, I do get some important e-mails from time to time, but when I think about it, how many of them actually require that I respond immediately? Most likely, none.

So what did I learn from all this? That I *am* addicted to technology and our online world—and I have a feeling I am not too different from the rest of society. I couldn't go twelve hours Internet free without driving myself a little crazy. But at the same time, this addiction of ours is one that we, to some degree, have been forced into. While Amazon and Pandora are, admittedly, somewhat superfluous, the use of e-mail as the primary means of communication and Facebook as the major place of social interaction nowadays means that those who ignore them are left behind. We can't just decide to ignore technology completely; it has become a part of our world and something that we have to deal with daily, whether we want to or not.

But at the same time, it shouldn't be our *whole* world. After all, if our online world becomes our entire universe— what happens when the computer crashes? We crash with it. The only way to ensure that doesn't happen is to distance ourselves, when possible, from that which is slowly sucking us into dependency. We need to take some time to learn how to do things on our own, take time to do things well again, take time for ourselves, and, ultimately, just take time to learn that easier doesn't always mean better.

The essay concedes that most of us can't ignore technology: Turning off the Web entirely is not feasible.

In highly rhetorical language, Vincent makes a call for independence and change.

VISUAL PROPOSAL   Pallettruth.com is a site "dedicated to providing straight talk about wood pallets" in order to lobby for using plastic pallets to ship goods from country to country. In a graphic warning against bugs from wood pallets infesting trees in the New York City area, the group uses a poster to present alarming data from various government sites and to suggest how the trees might be saved.

Highly charged headline identifies a problem.

A map displays the growth of the beetle infestation.

Three specific solutions are offered.

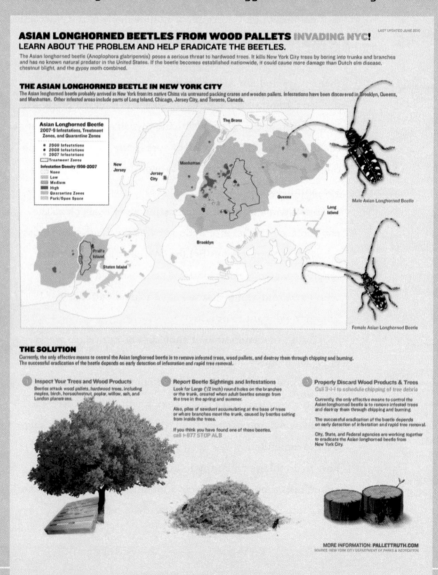

1. **Trial Balloon:** In calling for reducing the drinking age, Barrett Seaman's "How Bingeing Became the New College Sport" (p. 179) offers a solution to alcohol abuse that some might call "politically incorrect" — lowering the drinking age. Indeed, many politicians or school officials would likely be reluctant to support such a proposal — even if it might make people more responsible. Choose an issue that you think needs as radical a rethinking as college-age drinking, and write a research-based proposal of your own. Like Seaman, be sure to offer your ideas in language calm and persuasive enough to make responsible adults at least consider them.

2. **Formal Proposal:** Although Donald Lazere cites many studies to support his proposal for a formal curriculum in civic literacy, he likely was prompted to write "A Core Curriculum for Civic Literacy" (p. 192) by his experiences as a teacher for many years. Drawing on your own observations and experiences, identify a specific problem on your campus or in the local community. Research the issue thoroughly, using both human resources and materials such as college manuals and policies, campus newspapers, official records, reports, and so on. Come up with a plausible approach to the problem, and then write a proposal directed to a person or group with the power to deal with it. Use the formal, academic style of Lazere's essay as a model. Be sure to document your sources.

3. **Manifesto:** You likely identify with at least some of the issues Katelyn Vincent presents in "Technology Time-out" (p. 198) and with the manifesto she enunciates in her final paragraphs. Look for a problem that others might similarly recognize, describe the issue in enough detail to explain why adjustments may be necessary or desirable, and then make a compelling call for change.

4. **Visual Proposal:** The designers of "Asian Longhorned Beetles from Wood Pallets Invading NYC!" (p. 204) may have an agenda (selling plastic pallets), but their visual proposal provides useful information and a plan of action. Create a visual proposal of your own that does the same.

5. **Your Choice:** Proposals are usually practical documents, serving a specific need. Identify such a need in your life and address it through a clear, fact-based proposal. For example, you might write to your academic advisor or dean suggesting that a service-learning experience would be a better senior project for you than writing a traditional thesis — given your talents and interests. Or perhaps you might write to a banker (or wealthy relative) explaining why loaning you money to open a barbecue restaurant would make sound fiscal sense, especially since no one else in town serves decent brisket and ribs. In other words, write a paper to make your life better.

How to start
- Need to **find a text to analyze**? See page 217.
- Need to come up with **ideas**? See page 220.
- Need to **organize your ideas**? See page 226.

7 Literary Analyses

respond critically to cultural works

Unless you're an English major, the papers you write for Literature 101 may seem as mechanical as chemistry lab reports—something done just to get a degree. But hardly a day goes by when you don't respond strongly to some literary or cultural experience, sharing your insights and opinions about the books, music, and entertainment you love. It's worth learning to do this well.

LITERARY INTERPRETATION

After discussing Rudolfo Anaya's novel *Bless Me, Ultima* with classmates in a contemporary novels course, you write a *literary interpretation* of the work, arguing that it fits into the category of mythic coming-of-age story.

CLOSE READING

Unconvinced by a teacher's casual suggestion that the Anglo-Saxon author of "The Wanderer" (c. tenth century CE) was experiencing what we now call "alienation," you write a *close reading* of the poem to show why the modern concept doesn't suit the poem.

CULTURAL ANALYSIS

You've probably spent too many seasons watching the evolution of TV crime dramas that focus on detailed forensic analysis of victims—from *CSI* to *Bones*. But you use your knowledge to prepare a *cultural analysis* of these shows for a rhetoric class, suggesting that the programs subtly reinforce the public's faith in technology and science.

PHOTOGRAPHS AS LITERARY TEXTS

Rather than roll your eyes like your companions, you take abstract art seriously. So you study Kayla Mohammadi's painting (on p. 207), and then write a *visual analysis* to explain what you see in the work to someone who "doesn't get it."

DECIDING TO WRITE A LITERARY ANALYSIS   In a traditional
literary analysis, you respond to a poem, novel, play, or short story. That
response can be analytical, looking at theme, plot, structure, characters,
genre, style, and so on. Or it can be critical, theoretical, or evaluative—
locating works within their social, political, historic, and even philosophic
neighborhoods. Or you might approach a literary work expressively, describing
how you connect with it intellectually and emotionally. Or you can combine
these approaches or imagine alternative ones—perhaps reflecting new attitudes
and assumptions about media.

Other potential genres for analysis include films, TV offerings, popular
music, comic books, and games. ○ Distinctions between high and popular
culture have not so much dissolved as ceased to be interesting. After all,
you can say dumb things about *Hamlet* and smart things about *Mad Men*.
Moreover, every genre of artistic expression—from sonnets to opera to
graphic novels—at some point struggled for respectability. What matters
is the quality of a literary analysis and whether you help readers appreciate

Red Tide — Maine by Kayla Mohammadi
The artist explains that "the intention is not
literal portrayal, but rather a visual translation.
A translation based on color, value, and space."

choose a genre
p. 390

the novel *Pride and Prejudice* or, maybe, the video game *Red Dead Redemption*. Expect your literary or cultural analyses to do *some* of the following.

Begin with a close reading.   In an analysis, you slow the pace at which people in a 24/7 world typically operate to look deliberately and closely at a text. You might study the way individual words and images connect in a poem, how plot evolves in a novel, or how complex editing defines the character of a movie. In short, you think about the *calculated* choices writers and artists make in creating their work. ○

Make a claim or an observation.   Your encounter with a text will ordinarily lead to a thesis. The claim won't always be argumentative or controversial: You may be amazed at the simplicity of Wordsworth's Lucy poems or blown away by Jimi Hendrix's take on "All Along the Watchtower." But more typically, you'll make a statement or an observation that you believe is worth proving either by research or, just as often in college papers, by evidence from within the work itself.

Present works in context.   Works of art exist in our real world; that's what we like about them and why they sometimes change our lives. Your analysis can explore these relationships among texts, people, and society.

Draw on previous research.   Your response to a work need not agree with what others have written. But you should be willing to learn from previous scholarship and criticism—readily available in libraries or online. ○

Use texts for evidence.   A compelling analysis unwraps the complexities of a book, movie, poem, drama, or song, explaining it so that readers might better appreciate what they did not notice before. In short, direct them to the neat stuff. For that reason, the well-chosen quotation is the mighty tool of successful literary papers. In your reading, mark any passages that strike you as memorable or important and keep track of them for later use.

read closely
p. 365

plan a project
p. 466

In "Authentic Beauty in Morrison's *The Bluest Eye*," Kelsi Stayart assembles ample evidence both from the text of a novel and from library research to show that the book affirms a new definition of beauty for African American women. Notice, too, that she places Toni Morrison's first novel within the context of its time — an era of important social change.

Stayart 1

Kelsi Stayart

Professor Samuels

E314L Reading Women Writers

May 8, 20--

Authentic Beauty in Morrison's *The Bluest Eye*

In *The Bluest Eye* (1970), novelist Toni Morrison critiques the ideals of beauty that cause racial self-loathing and, in the case of lead-character Pecola Breedlove, mental ruin. Beauty, as Morrison states, is "Probably the most destructive [of] ideas in the history of human thought" (122). However, within Morrison's scathing denunciation of conventional ideals of beauty is a subtle counterdiscourse; she suggests a new concept of beauty that goes beyond white skin, straight hair, and blue eyes. Through her diction, Toni Morrison embraces an authentically African American aesthetic in *The Bluest Eye* by creating a positive connotation for traditionally negative black characteristics.[1]

Morrison suggests an authentic and natural notion of beauty through her word choice in the description of her own

> In a clear thesis sentence, Stayart makes the claim that the rest of the paper will develop.

[1] I use the term "black" interchangeably with "African American" throughout this paper. However, my use of the term "black" reflects its usage in my historical research on the Black Power movement of the 1960s, as well as the text.

Stayart 2

body given by Claudia MacTeer, who narrates parts of the story. When Claudia remarks, "We felt comfortable in our skins, enjoyed the news that our senses released to us, admired our dirt, cultivated our scars," the reader notices Claudia's contentment with her natural, African American characteristics (Morrison 74). Words like "dirt" and "cultivated" carry an earthy, natural connotation that stresses Claudia's real and authentic beauty. The verbs in this passage give a positive tone to characteristics usually considered unappealing: "admired our dirt" and "cultivated our scars." Critic Mermann-Jozwiak comments that "Claudia experiences pleasure in her body," as is evident in words like "comfortable" and "admired" (199). Claudia's contentment with her body exemplifies an appreciation of black physical attributes; this attitude reflects that of the Black Power movement of the 1960s, in which African Americans were attempting to "embrace their African heritage and challenge white domination by reversing notions of beauty" (Spencer 970). This cultural return to an authentic black aesthetic resembles Claudia's pride in her natural characteristics. Morrison expands on this idea of appreciating the natural by her depictions of dirtiness as a desirable and down-to-earth characteristic.

In *The Bluest Eye*, Morrison embraces *dirtiness* as authentic and natural by altering the standard connotation of *cleanliness*. After establishing the typical associations between

Important characters are identified, even though the audience for the paper would be familiar with the novel.

Sources are cited to add more evidence and back up claims.

Transition at the end of this paragraph introduces the theme of the paragraph that follows.

Stayart 3

African Americans and dirt, she portrays cleanliness as synthetic and dirtiness as natural. For example, when Geraldine, a socially self-conscious black woman, encounters Pecola, she criticizes the girl's dirty appearance, "the dirty torn dress . . . the muddy shoes . . . the soiled socks . . . hair uncombed . . . shoes untied and caked with dirt" (Morrison 91-92). The reader understands that this idea of dirtiness is associated with African Americans when Geraldine thinks, "She had seen this girl all her life. . . . They were everywhere" (91-92). The word choice of this passage emphasizes dirtiness as a physical characteristic of Pecola and, by extension, African Americans. However, Morrison combats this derogatory stereotype by embracing dirtiness and devaluing cleanliness as sterile and undesirable. For example, Claudia describes, "a hateful bath in a galvanized zinc tub . . . the scratchy towels and the dreadful and humiliating absence of dirt. The irritable, unimaginative cleanliness. Gone the ink marks from legs and face, all my creations and accumulations of the day gone" (22). Morrison's diction here is ironic because she criticizes cleanliness as "scratchy," "hateful," "irritable," and "unimaginative" and the lack of dirt as "humiliating." Claudia describes her dirtiness as "creations and accumulations," which emphasizes the relationship of dirtiness to real life. Moreover, the use of "irritable" directly contrasts with the earlier phrase, "comfortable in our skins."

Throughout the paper, Stayart supports her claims with quotations from the novel.

The paper carefully examines the diction of the novel.

Stayart 4

Morrison embraces dirtiness as a natural physical attribute to uplift a stereotypically negative black characteristic. By devaluing cleanliness, Morrison portrays this supposed ideal as sterile and artificial. Similarly, she negatively depicts a white baby doll given to Claudia as synthetic and lifeless to reflect her preference for the authentic.

By describing the blue-eyed baby doll as synthetic and artificial, Morrison is also able to devalue the ideal and uplift the real, living child of Pecola. Claudia imagines Pecola's baby with a "flared nose, kissing-thick lips, and the living, breathing silk of black skin" (Morrison 190). Racist exaggerations of African American features are countered here by the adjective "kissing-thick," which embraces the beauty of "black lips" (Spencer 969). "Living" and "breathing" similarly emphasize the lifelike authenticity of the black baby's skin. The positive connotations of "silk" reclaim the dark skin tone ordinarily used to subjugate and oppress African Americans. Claudia's description of Pecola's baby directly contrasts to her earlier, positive thoughts about her white doll. Comparing Pecola's infant to the doll, she notes, "No synthetic yellow bangs suspended over marble-blue eyes" (Morrison 190). She also notes that the doll's "hard unyielding limbs resisted my flesh . . . irritated any embrace" (20). Her depiction of the doll stresses that the blonde-haired, blue-eyed ideal of beauty is actually sterile, lifeless, and cold. In contrast, the black baby is a living body.

> A second major point contrasts synthetic and real beauty in the novel.

Stayart 5

A third major point follows carefully from the preceding one, helping to connect the argument.

Morrison extends this idea of a lifelike aesthetic by her sensual descriptions in the novel of African American females, showing appreciation for a realistic beauty that incorporates more than just the visual. Likewise, Mermann-Jozwiak notes that Morrison argues for a sensual beauty by "dislodging vision from its dominant position and emphasizing the role of the whole sensorium" (199-200). Morrison develops the idea of sensual beauty with her description of the youth of Cholly's elderly aunts:

> The odor of their armpits and haunches had mingled into a lovely musk; their eyes had been furtive, their lips relaxed, and the delicate turn of their heads on those slim black necks had been like nothing other than a doe's. Their laughter had been more touch than sound. (138)

In MLA style, quotations longer than three lines are indented.

The description of their odor as "a lovely musk" exemplifies an appreciation for physical characteristics that are natural, authentic, and atypically used to describe beauty. The comparison to a doe allows Morrison to highlight the grace and beauty in the women's mannerisms. Moreover, her description of their laughter as a "touch" builds upon this idea of defining beauty beyond visual terms. In this passage, Morrison creates an idea of beauty that stresses pride in black attributes that sets them apart from the "European standard of beauty" (Spencer 969).

Stayart 6

In the novel, Morrison also harshly critiques those who, like her character Geraldine, have denied their black authenticity and conformed to white standards. In Geraldine, Morrison creates a woman who represents the antisensual, her diction emphasizing the sterility of those who reject the authentic. The characterization of Geraldine moves from the general to the specific, stressing what she fears about her racial character:

> Wherever it erupts, this Funk, they wipe it away; where it crusts, they dissolve it; where it drips, flowers or clings, they find it and fight it until it dies. They fight this battle all the way to the grave. The laugh that is a little too loud; the enunciation a little too round; the gesture a little too generous. They hold their behind in for fear of a sway too free; when they wear lipstick, they never cover the entire mouth for fear of lips too thick, and they worry, worry, worry about the edges of their hair. (Morrison 83)

The words "wipe it away" and "dissolve" emphasize the cleansing of racial characteristics. The laugh, gestures, and lips of women like Geraldine are carefully controlled to avoid any hint of racial authenticity; in "worry, worry, worry" about their hair, Morrison references the practice of hair relaxation to mimic the standard white straight hair (Spencer 970). Morrison's move

The focus shifts to a character who resists the standard of beauty Morrison has defined in the novel. By undercutting Geraldine, Morrison also undercuts the ideas the character represents.

Stayart 7

against conforming to white standards again reflects the Black Power movement of the time, which called for racial pride and embraced "black culture as something unique, different and compelling" (Kuryla 115). During the 1960s, black models began to sport natural hairstyles and women were urged to "reject all white-oriented styles and to appreciate that 'black is beautiful'" (Wilson). Stokely Carmichael, a Black Power activist, stated, "We have to stop being ashamed of being black. A broad nose, a thick lip and nappy hair is us, and we are going to call that beautiful . . . we are not going to fry our hair anymore" (Spencer 971). Clearly, Morrison's criticism in *The Bluest Eye* reflects a general discourse during the 1960s that focused on a newfound appreciation for uniquely black qualities. Morrison's condemnation of Geraldine reflects the movement that called for African American women to "throw away their straightening combs" (Wilson). Through Geraldine, Morrison argues for black women to stop taming their natural appearances and appreciate the features that make them unique.

In *The Bluest Eye*, Morrison critiques white ideals of beauty by her celebration of African American features that had long been condemned as ugly. Her language and diction carefully argue for ethnic authenticity and an appreciation for one's natural characteristics. Morrison dares to imagine, in her novel, an authentic beauty that embraces the unique, distinctive, and genuine aspects of a woman.

Stayart sets her observations about the novel into a historical context.

The concluding paragraph efficiently summarizes the theme of the paper.

Stayart 8

Works Cited

Kuryla, Peter. "Black Consciousness." *Encyclopedia of African
American Society*. Ed. Gerald D. Jaynes. Vol. 1. Thousand
Oaks: Sage, 2005. 114-16. *Gale Virtual Reference Library*.
Gale. Web. 23 Apr. 2009.

Mermann-Jozwiak, Elisabeth. "Re-Membering the Body:
Body Politics in Toni Morrison's *The Bluest Eye*." *Lit:
Literature Interpretation Theory* 12.2 (June 2001):
189-203. *MLA International Bibliography*. EBSCO. Web.
22 Apr. 2009.

Morrison, Toni. *The Bluest Eye*. New York: Vintage, 2007.
Print.

Spencer, Robyn. "Hair and Beauty Culture in the United
States." *Encyclopedia of African-American Culture and
History*. Ed. Colin A. Palmer. 2nd ed. Vol. 3. Detroit:
Macmillan, 2006. 969-73. *Gale Virtual Reference Library*.
Gale. Web. 27 Apr. 2009.

Wilson, Jean Sprain. "Negro Models Capitalize on Their
African Heritage." *Los Angeles Times (1886-Current File)*.
20 Aug. 1968, f4. *ProQuest Historical Newspapers Los
Angeles Times (1881-1986)*.ProQuest. Web. 27 Apr. 2009.

Exploring purpose and topic

In most cases, you write a literary analysis to meet a course requirement, a paper usually designed to improve your skills as a reader of literature and art. Such a lofty goal, however, doesn't mean you can't enjoy the project or put your own spin on it.

find a text ◀

Your first priority is to read any assignment sheet closely to find out exactly what you are supposed to do. Underline any key words in the project description and take them seriously. Typically you will see terms such as *compare and contrast, classify, analyze,* or *interpret.* They mean different things.

Once you know your purpose in writing an analysis, you may have to choose a subject. ○ It's not unusual to have a work assigned (*Three pages on The House on Mango Street by Friday*), but more typically, you'll be able to select works to study from within a range defined by a course title or unit: British sci-fi; Puritan sermons; Native American literature since 1920. Which should you choose?

Choose a text you connect with. It makes sense to spend time writing about works that move you, perhaps by touching on an aspect of your life or identity. You may feel more confident commenting on them because of who you are and what you've experienced.

Choose a text you want to learn more about. In the back of their minds, most people have lists of works and artists they've always wanted to read or explore. So use an assignment as an opportunity to sample one of them: *Beowulf; The Chronicles of Narnia;* or the work of William Gibson, Leslie Marmon Silko, or the Clash. Or use an assignment to venture beyond works within your comfort zone: Examine writers and artists from different cultures and with challenging points of view.

Choose a text that you don't understand. Most writers tend to write about works that are immediately accessible and relatively new: Why struggle with a hoary epic poem when you can just watch *The Lord of the Rings* on DVD? One obvious reason may be to figure out how works from different eras can still be powerfully connected to our own; the very strangeness of older and more difficult texts may even prompt you to ask more provocative questions. In short, you'll pay more attention to literary texts that place demands on you.

Stills from *Smoke Signals* (1998) and *Bury My Heart at Wounded Knee* (2007) How much do you know about Native American fiction or film? Use an assignment as an opportunity to learn more.

get an idea
p. 356

Understanding your audience

Unless you write book reviews or essays for a campus literary magazine, the people reading your analyses of works of art and culture are likely a professor and other students in your course. But in either situation, assume a degree of expertise among your readers. Moreover, many people will examine a literary analysis simply because they're interested—a tremendous advantage. So be sure to respect the needs of your audience.

Clearly identify the author and works you are analyzing.   Seems like common sense, but this courtesy is often neglected in academic papers precisely because writers assume that *the teacher must know what I'm doing.* Don't make this mistake. Also briefly recap what happens in the works you are analyzing—especially with texts not everyone has read recently. ○ Follow the model of good reviewers, who typically summarize key elements before commenting on them. Such summaries give readers their bearings at the beginning of a paper. Here's James Wood introducing a novel by Marilynne Robinson that he will be reviewing for the *New York Times.*

> *Gilead* is set in 1956 in the small town of Gilead, Iowa, and is narrated by a seventy-six-year-old pastor named John Ames, who has recently been told he has angina pectoris and believes he is facing imminent death. In this terminal spirit, he decides to write a long letter to his seven-year-old son, the fruit of a recent marriage to a much younger woman. This novel is that letter, set down in the easy, discontinuous form of a diary, mixing long and short entries, reminiscences, moral advice, and so on.

Define key terms.   Many specialized and technical expressions are used in a literary analysis. Your instructor will know what an *epithet, peripeteia,* or *rondel* might be, but you may still have to define terms like these for a wider audience—your classmates, for instance. Alternatively, you can look for more familiar synonyms and expressions.

sum up ideas
p. 491

Don't aim to please professional critics.   Are you tempted to imitate the style of serious academic theorists you've encountered while researching your paper? No need—your instructor probably won't expect you to write in that way, at least not until graduate school.

Your Turn   In "Authentic Beauty in Morrison's *The Bluest Eye*" (p. 209), Kelsi Stayart summarizes the novel only minimally. What issues of audience might explain the exclusion of plot details from her paper, written for a college course in a sophomore-level class? Would *you* have appreciated more details about story and character—as a member of an audience Stayart could *not* have anticipated when she wrote her piece? Why or why not? Use your analysis of her paper and her original audience to guide your own choices in writing a literary analysis.

Finding and developing materials

▶ develop ideas

With an assignment in hand and works to analyze, the next step—and it's a necessary one—is to establish that you have a reliable "text" of whatever you'll be studying. In a course, a professor may assign a particular edition or literary anthology for you to use, making your job easier.

This Bedford/St. Martin's edition of *Frankenstein* provides important textual information and background. Look for texts with such material when studying classic novels, poems, and plays.

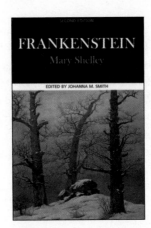

Be aware that many texts are available in multiple editions. (For instance, the novel *Frankenstein* first appeared in 1818, but the revised third edition of 1831 is the one most widely read today.) For classical works, such as the plays of Shakespeare, choose an edition from a major publisher, preferably one that includes thorough notes and perhaps some essays and criticism. When in doubt, ask your professor which texts to use. Don't just browse the library shelves.

Other kinds of media pose interesting problems as well. For instance, you may have to decide which version of a movie to study—the one seen by audiences in theaters or the "director's cut" on a DVD. Similarly, you might find multiple recordings of musical works: Look for widely respected performances. Even popular music may come in several versions: studio (*American Idiot*), live (*Bullet in a Bible*), alternative recording (*American Idiot: The Original Broadway Cast Recording*). Then there is the question of drama: Do you read a play on the page, watch a video when one is available, or see it in a theater? Perhaps you do all three. But whatever versions of a text you choose for study, be sure to identify them in your project, either in the text itself or on the works cited page. ○

220

understand citation
styles p. 501

Establishing a text is the easy part. How then do you find something specific to write about, an angle on the subject? ○ Try the following strategies and approaches.

Examine the text closely.   Guided by your assignment, begin your project by closely reading, watching, or examining the selected work(s) and taking notes. Obviously, you'll treat some works differently than others. You can read a Seamus Heaney sonnet a dozen times to absorb its nuances, but it's unlikely you'd push through Rudolfo Anaya's novel *Bless Me, Ultima* more than once or twice for a paper. But, in either case, you'll need a suitable way to take notes or to annotate what you're analyzing.

Honestly, you should count on a minimum of two readings or viewings of any text, the first to get familiar with the work and find a potential approach, the second and subsequent readings to confirm your thesis and to find supporting evidence for it.

Focus on the text itself.   Your earliest literature papers probably tackled basic questions about plot, character, setting, theme, and language. But these are not simple matters—just the kinds of issues that fascinate most readers. You might, for example, look for moments when the plot of the novel you're examining reinforces its theme or study how characters change in response to specific events. Even the setting of a short story or film might be worth writing about when it becomes a factor in the story: Can you imagine the film *Casablanca* taking place in any other location? In how many books, TV shows, and films is New York City a virtual character?

Questions about language loom large in many analyses. How does word choice work with or against the subject of a poem? Does the style of a novel reinforce its story? How does a writer create irony through diction or dialogue? Indeed, any feature of a work might be researched and studied, from the narrators in novels to the rhyme schemes in poetry.

Focus on its meanings, themes, and interpretations.   Although finding themes or meanings in literary works seems like an occupation mostly for English majors, the tendency is actually universal and irresistible. If you take any work seriously, you'll discover angles and ideas worth sharing with readers.

find a topic
p. 356

Maybe *Seinfeld* is a modern version of *Everyman*, or *O Brother, Where Art Thou?* is a retelling of the *Odyssey* by Homer, or maybe not. Open your mind to possible connections: What have you seen like this before? What patterns do you detect? What images recur in the text or what ideas are supported or undercut?

Focus on its authorship and history.   Some artists stand apart from their creations, while others cannot be separated from them. So you might explore in what ways a work reflects the life, education, and attitudes of its author. What psychological forces or religious perspectives might be detected in particular characters or themes? Is the author writing to represent his or her gender, race, ethnicity, or class? Or does the work repudiate its author's identity, class, or religion?

Similarly, consider how a text embodies the assumptions, attitudes, politics, fashions, and even technology of the times during which it was composed. A work as familiar as Jonathan Swift's "A Modest Proposal" still requires readers to know at least a *little* about Irish and English politics in the eighteenth century. How does Swift's satire open up when you learn even more about its world?

Focus on its genre.   Literary genres are formulas. Take a noble hero, give him a catastrophic flaw, have him make a bad choice, and then kill him off: That's tragedy—or, in the wrong hands, melodrama. With a little brainstorming, you could identify dozens of genres and subcategories: epics, sonnets, historical novels, superhero comics, grand opera, soap opera, and so on. Artists' works often fall between genres, sometimes creating new ones. Readers, too, bring clear-cut expectations to a text: Try to turn a 007 action-spy thriller into a three-hankie chick flick, and you've got trouble in River City.

You can analyze genre in various ways. For instance, track a text backward to discover its literary forebears—the works that influenced its author. Even texts that revolt against previous genres bear traces of what they have rejected. It's also possible to study the way artists combine different genres or play with or against the expectations of audiences. Needless to say, you can also explore the relationships of works within a genre. In fact, it's often a shared genre that makes comparisons interesting or provocative. For example, what do twentieth-century coming-of-age stories such as *A Separate Peace, The Catcher in the Rye,* and *Lord of the Flies* have in common?

Focus on its influence.   Some works have an obvious impact on life or society, changing how people think or behave: *Uncle Tom's Cabin*, *To Kill a Mockingbird*, *Roots*, *Schindler's List*. TV shows have broadened people's notions of family; musical genres such as jazz and gospel have created and sustained entire communities.

But impact doesn't always occur on such a grand scale or express itself through social movements. Books influence other books, films other films, and so on—with not a few texts crossing genres. Who could have foreseen all the ties between comic books in the 1930s, TV shows in the 1950s, superhero films in the 1980s, and video games in the new century? And, for better or worse, books, movies, and other cultural productions influence styles, fashions, and even the way people speak. Consider *Clueless*, *High School Musical*, or *Glee*. You may have to think outside the box, but projects that trace and study influence can shake things up.

Focus on its social connections.   In recent decades, many texts have been studied for what they reveal about relationships between genders, races, ethnicities, and social classes. Works by new writers are now more widely read in schools, and hard questions are asked about texts traditionally taught: What do they reveal about the treatment of women or minorities? Whose lives have been ignored in dominant texts, or how are minorities or working classes represented? What responsibility do cultural texts have for maintaining repressive political or social arrangements? These critical approaches have changed how many people view literature and art, and you can follow up on such studies and extend them to texts you think deserve more attention. Such inquiries themselves, however, are as driven by political and social agendas as other kinds of analysis and so should also be subjected to the same critical scrutiny.

Find good sources.   Developing a literary paper provides you with many opportunities and choices. Fortunately, you needn't make all your decisions on your own. Ample commentary and research is available on almost any literary subject or method, both in print and online. ○ Your instructor and local librarians can help you focus on the best resources for your project, but the following boxes list some possibilities.

refine your search
p. 472

Literary Resources in Print

Abrams, M. H., and Geoffrey Harpham. *A Glossary of Literary Terms*. 9th ed. New York: Wadsworth, 2008.

Beacham, Walton, ed. *Research Guide to Biography and Criticism*. Washington: Research, 1986.

Birch, Dinah, ed. *The Oxford Companion to English Literature*. 7th ed. Oxford: Oxford UP, 2009.

Crystal, David. *The Cambridge Encyclopedia of Language*. 3rd ed. New York: Cambridge UP, 2010.

Encyclopedia of World Literature in the 20th Century. 3rd ed. Farmington Hills: St. James, 1999.

Gates, Henry Louis, Jr., et al. *The Norton Anthology of African American Literature*. 2nd ed. New York: Norton, 2003.

Gilbert, Sandra M., and Susan Gubar. *The Norton Anthology of Literature by Women: The Traditions in English*. 3rd ed. New York: Norton, 2007.

Harmon, William, and Hugh Holman. *A Handbook to Literature*. 11th ed. New York: Prentice, 2008.

Harner, James L. *Literary Research Guide: A Guide to Reference Sources for the Study of Literature in English and Related Topics*. 5th ed. New York: MLA, 2008.

Hart, James D. *The Oxford Companion to American Literature*. 6th ed. New York: Oxford UP, 1995.

Howatson, M. C. *The Oxford Companion to Classical Literature*. 2nd ed. New York: Oxford UP, 2006.

Leitch, Vincent, et al. *The Norton Anthology of Theory and Criticism*. 2nd ed. New York: Norton, 2010.

Preminger, Alex, and T. V. F. Brogan, eds. *The New Princeton Encyclopedia of Poetry and Poetics*. Princeton: Princeton UP, 1993.

Sage, Lorna. *The Cambridge Guide to Women's Writing in English*. Cambridge: Cambridge UP, 1999.

Literary Resources Online

Annual Bibliography of English Language and Literature (ABELL) (subscription)

Atlantic Unbound (http://www.theatlantic.com) (for culture and reviews)

Browne Popular Culture Library (http://www.bgsu.edu/colleges/library/pcl)

The Complete Works of William Shakespeare (http://thetech.mit.edu/Shakespeare)

Eserver.org: Accessible Writing (http://eserver.org)

A Handbook of Rhetorical Devices (http://www.virtualsalt.com/rhetoric.htm)

Images: A Journal of Film and Popular Culture (http://www.imagesjournal.com/)

Internet Public Library: Literary Criticism (http://www.ipl.org/div/litcrit/)

Literary Resources on the Net (http://andromeda.rutgers.edu/~jlynch/Lit)

Literature Resource Center (Gale Group – subscription)

MIT Libraries: Literature Resources (http://libraries.mit.edu/guides/subjects/literature/)

MLA on the Web (http://www.mla.org)

New York Review of Books (http://www.nybooks.com/)

New York Times Book Review (http://www.nytimes.com/pages/books)

The Online Books Page (http://onlinebooks.library.upenn.edu)

VoS: Voice of the Shuttle (http://vos.ucsb.edu/)

Yahoo! Arts: Humanities: Literature (http://dir.yahoo.com/arts/humanities/literature/)

Creating a structure

organize ideas

The shape of your literary analysis evolves as you learn more about your topic and decide how to treat it. Your project takes on the character of a report if you're interested in sharing information or demonstrating a case. Or it becomes an argument if your thesis veers toward a controversial position. ○ Whatever its trajectory, give attention to certain features.

Focus on a particular observation, claim, or point. Always have a point firmly in mind as you draft a project, whether you work with individual literary texts or more general cultural questions. Consider the following examples of claims or points that literary analyses might explore.

STUDY OF THEME

In *Bless Me, Ultima*, the youngster Antonio has to find a way to reconcile his traditional values and mystical beliefs with Ultima's prediction that he will become a "man of learning."

CONTRAST OF GENRES

The movie version of Annie Proulx's short story "Brokeback Mountain" actually improves on the original work, making it more powerful, specific, and believable.

CULTURAL ANALYSIS

One likely impact of digital technology will be to eliminate the barriers between art, entertainment, and commerce—with books becoming films, films morphing into games, and games inspiring graphic art.

Imagine a structure. Here are three simple forms a literary analysis might take, the first developing from a thesis stated early on, the second comparing two works to make a point, and the third building toward a conclusion rather than opening with a thesis. ○

Introduction leading to a claim

First supporting reason + textual evidence
Second supporting reason + textual evidence
Additional supporting reasons + textual evidence

Conclusion

understand argument
p. 72

develop a statement
p. 393

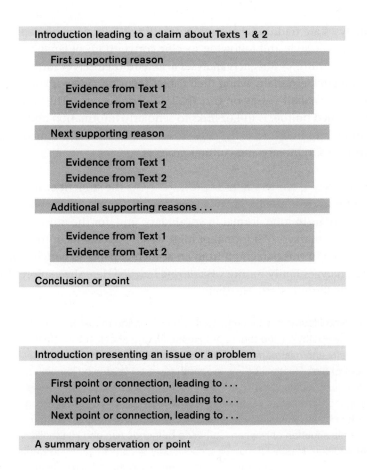

Introduction leading to a claim about Texts 1 & 2

   First supporting reason

      Evidence from Text 1
      Evidence from Text 2

   Next supporting reason

      Evidence from Text 1
      Evidence from Text 2

   Additional supporting reasons . . .

      Evidence from Text 1
      Evidence from Text 2

Conclusion or point

Introduction presenting an issue or a problem

   First point or connection, leading to . . .
   Next point or connection, leading to . . .
   Next point or connection, leading to . . .

A summary observation or point

Work on your opening.   Be certain that your introductory sections provide background for your analysis and identify what works you may be examining, and what you hope to accomplish. ⃝ Provide enough context so that the project stands on its own and would make sense to someone other than the instructor who assigned it.

shape a beginning
p. 420

Choosing a style and design

Literary analyses are traditional assignments still typically done on paper using an academic style and following specific conventions of language and MLA documentation. ○ But such analyses also lend themselves surprisingly well to new media, especially when their topics focus on video or aural texts—as Kelli Marshall's essay on *Glee* (p. 238) demonstrates. The original version, published online, is full of links to scholarly information and, probably more important, to video clips from the show. Style and media can be relevant issues in literary and cultural projects.

Use a formal style for most assignments. As the student examples in this chapter suggest, the literary analyses you write for courses will typically be serious in tone, formal in vocabulary, and, for the most part, impersonal—all markers of a formal or high style. ○ Elements of that style can be identified in this paragraph from an academic paper in which Manasi Deshpande analyzes Emily Brontë's *Wuthering Heights*. Here she explores the character of its Byronic hero, Heathcliff:

Examines Heathcliff from the perspective of a potential reader, not from her own.

Complex sentences smoothly incorporate quotations and documentation.

Related points are expressed in parallel clauses.

Vocabulary throughout is accessible, but formal. No contractions are used.

In witnessing Heathcliff's blatantly violent behavior, the reader is caught between sympathy for the tormented Heathcliff and shock at the intensity of his cruelty and mistreatment of others. Intent on avenging Hindley's treatment of him, Heathcliff turns his wrath toward Hareton by keeping him in such an uneducated and dependent state that young Cathy becomes "upset at the bare notion of relationship with such a clown" (193). Living first under Hindley's neglect and later under Heathcliff's wrath, Hareton escapes his situation only when Catherine befriends him and Heathcliff dies. In addition, Heathcliff marries Isabella only because Catherine wants to "'torture [him] to death for [her] amusement'" and must "'allow [him] to amuse [himself] a little in the same style'" (111). Heathcliff's sole objective in seducing and running away with Isabella is to take revenge on Catherine for abandoning him. Heathcliff's sadism is so strong that he is willing to harm innocent third parties in order to punish those who have caused his misery. He even forces young Cathy and Linton to marry by locking them in Wuthering Heights and keeping Cathy from her dying father until she has married Linton, further illustrating his willingness to torture others out of spite and vengeance.

cite in MLA
p. 503

define your style
p. 432

Use a middle style for informal or personal papers.   Occasionally, for example, you may be asked to write brief essays called *position papers*, in which you record your immediate reactions to poems, short stories, or other readings. In these assignments, an instructor may expect to hear your voice and even encourage exploratory responses. Here is Cheryl Lovelady responding somewhat personally to a cultural text in a proposal to revive the Broadway musical *Fiddler on the Roof*:

> How can a play set in a small, tradition-bound Jewish village during the Russian Revolution be modernized? I would argue that *Fiddler on the Roof* is actually an apt portrayal of our own time. Throughout the show, the conflicted main character, Tevye, is on the brink of pivotal decisions. Perplexed by his daughters' increasingly modern choices, Tevye prays aloud, "Where do they think they are, America?" Tevye identifies America as a symbol of personal freedom—the antithesis of the tradition which keeps his life from being "as shaky as a fiddler on the roof." Forty years after the play's debut, America has become startlingly more like the Anatevka Tevye knows than the America he envisions. Post-9/11 America parallels Anatevka in a multitude of ways: political agendas ideologically separate the United States from most of the world; public safety and conventional wisdom are valued over individual freedoms; Americans have felt the shock of violence brought onto their own soil; minority groups are isolated or isolate themselves in closed communities; and societal taboos dictate whom people may marry.

Question focuses paragraph. Reply suggests strong personal opinion.

Basic style remains serious and quite formal: Note series of roughly parallel clauses that follow colon.

Describe action in the present tense.   Literary papers usually follow any number of stylistic conventions. In writing literary analyses, for example, you'll be doing plenty of summarizing and paraphrasing. In most cases, when you narrate the events in a story or poem, set the action in the present tense.

Provide dates for authors and literary works.   The first time you name authors or artists in a paper, give their dates of birth and death in parentheses. Similarly, provide a year of publication or release date for any major work you mention in your analysis.

> Joan Didion (b. 1934) is the author of *Play It as It Lays* (1970), *Slouching Towards Bethlehem* (1968), and *The Year of Magical Thinking* (2005).

A 1964 production of the musical *Fiddler on the Roof*.

Use appropriate abbreviations.   An English or rhetoric major may want to own a copy of the *MLA Handbook for Writers of Research Papers* if for nothing more than its full chapter on abbreviations common in literary papers. Some of the abbreviations appear chiefly in notes and documentation; others make it easier to refer to very familiar texts; still others identify various parts and sections of literary works.

Follow conventions for quotations.   In a literary paper, you'll be frequently citing passages from novels, short stories, and poems as well as quoting the comments of critics. All of these items need to be appropriately introduced and, if necessary, modified to fit smoothly into your sentences and paragraphs. ○

Cite plays correctly.   Plays are cited by act, scene, and line number. In the past, passages from Shakespeare were routinely identified using a combination of roman and arabic numerals. But more recently, MLA recommends arabic numerals only for such references.

FORMER STYLE

Hamlet's final words are "The rest is silence" (*Ham.* V.ii.358).

CURRENT STYLE

Hamlet's final words are "The rest is silence" (*Ham.* 5.2.358).

Explore alternative media.   You can be creative with literary and cultural projects, depending on the tools and media available to you. ○ An oral presentation on a literary text can be handled impressively using presentation software such as PowerPoint or Prezi. When you want to show complex relationships between plot and character, you may find mind-mapping software of various kinds useful. And students have even used Google Maps to trace the physical locations or journeys in literary works as different as *The Aeneid* of Virgil and Cormac McCarthy's *The Road*. If your project is to be submitted in electronic form, you can, of course, incorporate photographs, images, or the spoken word into your project, as appropriate. "Appropriate" means that the media elements genuinely enrich your analysis.

use quotations
p. 497

go multimodal
p. 568

Examining models

CLOSE READING In "Insanity: Two Women," Kanaka Sathasivan examines a poem (Emily Dickinson's "I felt a Funeral, in my Brain") and a short story (Charlotte Perkins Gilman's "The Yellow Wallpaper") to discover a disturbing common theme in the work of these two American women writers. The essay, written in a formal academic style, uses a structure that examines the works individually, drawing comparisons in a final paragraph. Note, in particular, how Sathasivan manages the close reading of the poem by Emily Dickinson, moving through it almost line by line to draw out its themes and meanings. Here's the text of "I felt a Funeral, in my Brain."

I felt a Funeral, in my Brain,
And Mourners to and fro
Kept treading – treading – till it seemed
That Sense was breaking through –

And when they all were seated,
A Service, like a Drum –
Kept beating – beating – till I thought
My Mind was going numb –

And then I heard them lift a Box
And creak across my Soul
With those same Boots of Lead, again,
Then Space – began to toll,

As all the Heavens were a Bell,
And Being, but an Ear,
And I, and Silence, some strange Race
Wrecked, solitary, here –

And then a Plank in Reason, broke,
And I dropped down, and down –
And hit a World, at every plunge,
And Finished knowing – then –

You can find the full text of "The Yellow Wallpaper" by searching online by the title. One such text is available at the University of Virginia Library Electronic Text Center: http://etext.virginia.edu/toc/modeng/public/GilYell.html.

Sathasivan 1

Kanaka Sathasivan

Professor Glotzer

English 102

March 3, 20--

Insanity: Two Women

The societal expectations of women in the late nineteenth century served to keep women demure, submissive, and dumb. Although women's rights had begun to improve as more people rejected these stereotypes, many women remained trapped in their roles because of the pressures placed on them by men. Their suppression had deep impacts not only on their lives but also on their art. At a time when women writers often published under male aliases to gain respect, two of America's well-known authors, Emily Dickinson (1830-1886) and Charlotte Perkins Gilman (1860-1935), both wrote disturbing pieces describing the spiritual and mental imprisonment of women. In verse, Dickinson uses a funeral as a metaphor for the silencing of women and the insanity it subsequently causes. Gilman's prose piece "The Yellow Wallpaper" (1899) gives us a firsthand look into the mental degradation of a suppressed woman. These two works use vivid sensory images and rhythmic narration to describe sequential declines into madness.

Marginal notes:

Works to be analyzed are set in context: late nineteenth century.

Identifies authors and sets works in thematic relationship.

States thesis for the comparison.

Sathasivan 2

In "I felt a Funeral, in my Brain" (first published in 1896), Dickinson outlines the stages of a burial ceremony, using them as metaphors for a silenced woman's departure from sanity. The first verse, the arrival of Mourners, symbolizes the imposition of men and society on her mind. They are "treading" "to and fro," breaking down her thoughts and principles, until even she is convinced of their ideas (Dickinson 3, 2). The Service comes next, representing the closure—the acceptance of fate. Her "Mind was going numb" as the sounds of the service force her to stop thinking and begin accepting her doomed life. These first two verses use repetition at parallel points as they describe the Mourners as "treading—treading" and the service as a drum "beating—beating" (Dickinson 3, 7). The repetition emphasizes the incessant insistence of men; they try to control threatening women with such vigor and persistence that eventually even the women themselves begin to believe men's ideas and allow their minds to be silenced.

As the funeral progresses, the Mourners carry her casket from the service. Here Dickinson describes how they scar her very Soul using the "same Boots of Lead" which destroyed her mind (Dickinson 11). From the rest of the poem, one can infer that the service took place inside a church, and the act of parting from a house of God places another level of finality on the loss of her spirituality. While the figures in the poem transport her, the church's chimes begin to ring, and, as if

> Offers close reading of Dickinson's poem.

Sathasivan 3

"all the Heavens were a Bell / And Being, but an Ear," the noise consumes her (Dickinson 13). In this tremendous sound, her voice finally dissolves forever; her race with Silence has ended, "Wrecked," and Silence has won (Dickinson 16). Finally, after the loss of her mind, her soul, and her voice, she loses her sanity as they lower her casket into the grave and bury her. She "hit a World, at every plunge, / And Finished knowing" (Dickinson 20). The worlds she hits represent further stages of psychosis, and she plunges deeper until she hits the bottom, completely broken.

Like Dickinson, Gilman in "The Yellow Wallpaper" also segments her character's descent into madness. The narrator of the story expresses her thoughts in a diary written while she takes a vacation for her health. Each journal entry represents another step toward insanity, and Gilman reveals the woman's psychosis with subtle hints and clues placed discreetly within the entries. These often take the form of new information about the yellow room the woman has been confined to, such as the peeled wallpaper or bite marks on the bedpost. The inconspicuous presentation of such details leads the reader to think that these artifacts have long existed, created by someone else, and only now does the narrator share them with us. "I wonder how it was done and who did it, and what they did it for," she says, speaking of a groove that follows the perimeter of the walls. Here, Gilman reuses specific words at

With simple transition, turns to Gilman's short story.

Sathasivan 4

crucial points in the narration to allude to the state of her
character's mental health. In this particular example, both the
narrator and the maid use the word "smooch" to describe,
respectively, the groove in the wall and yellow smudges on the
narrator's clothes. This repetition indicates that she created the
groove in the room, a fact affirmed at the end of the story.

Gilman's narrator not only seems to believe other people
have caused the damage she sees but also imagines a woman
lives trapped within the paper, shaking the pattern in her
attempts to escape. "I think that woman gets out in the
daytime!" the narrator exclaims, recounting her memories of a
woman "creeping" about the garden (Gilman 400, 401). Again,
Gilman uses repetition to make associations for the reader as
the narrator uses "creeping" to describe her own exploits. As
in the previous example, the end of the story reveals that the
woman in the paper is none other than the narrator, tricked by
her insanity. This connection also symbolizes the narrator's
oppression. The design of the wallpaper trapping the woman
represents the spiritual bars placed on the narrator by her
husband and doctor, who prescribes mental rest, forbidding
her from working or thinking. Even the description of the room
lends itself to the image of a dungeon or cell, with "barred"
windows and "rings and things in the walls" (Gilman 392).
Just as the woman escapes during the daytime, so too does
the narrator, giving in to her sickness and disobeying her

> Uses present
> tense to
> describe
> action in
> "The Yellow
> Wallpaper."

Sathasivan 5

husband by writing. Finally, like the woman in the paper breaking free, the narrator succumbs to her insanity.

Both Dickinson's and Gilman's works explore society's influence on a woman's mental health. Like Dickinson's character, Gilman's narrator has also been compelled into silence by a man. Although she knows she is sick, her husband insists it isn't so and that she, a fragile woman, simply needs to avoid intellectual stimulation. Like a Mourner, "treading—treading," he continually assures her he knows best and that she shouldn't socialize or work. This advice, however, only leads to further degradation as her solitude allows her to indulge her mental delusions. When the narrator attempts to argue with her husband, she is silenced, losing the same race as Dickinson's character.

In both these pieces, the characters remain mildly aware of their declining mental health, but neither tries to fight it. In Dickinson's poem, the woman passively observes her funeral, commenting objectively on her suppression and burial. Dickinson uses sound to describe every step, creating the feel of secondary sensory images—images that cannot create a picture alone and require interpretation to do so. Gilman's narrator also talks of her sickness passively, showing her decline only by describing mental fatigue. In these moments she often comments that her husband "loves [her] very dearly" and she usually accepts the advice he offers (Gilman

(margin note) Draws attention to common themes and strategies in the two works.

(margin note) Notes difference in technique between authors.

Sathasivan 6

396). Even on those rare occasions when she disagrees, she remains submissive and allows her suppression to continue. In contrast to Dickinson, Gilman uses visual images to create this portrait, describing most of all how the narrator sees the yellow wallpaper, an approach that allows insight into the narrator's mental state.

Concludes that writers use similar techniques to explore a common theme in two very different works.

Both Dickinson and Gilman used their writing to make profound statements about the painful lives led by many women in the nineteenth century. Through repetition, metaphor, symbolism, and sensory images, both "I felt a Funeral, in my Brain" and "The Yellow Wallpaper" describe a woman's mental breakdown, as caused by societal expectations and oppression. The poetry and prose parallel one another and together give insight into a horrific picture of insanity.

Sathasivan 7

MLA documentation style used for in-text notes and works cited.

Works Cited

Dickinson, Emily. "I felt a Funeral, in my Brain." *Concise Anthology of American Literature.* 5th ed. Ed. George McMichael. Upper Saddle River: Prentice, 2001. 1129. Print.

Gilman, Charlotte Perkins. "The Yellow Wallpaper." *The American Short Story and Its Writer, An Anthology.* Ed. Ann Charters. Boston: Bedford, 2000. 391-403. Print.

CULTURAL ANALYSIS   In "Show Musical Good, Paired Segments Better: *Glee*'s Unevenness Explained," Kelli Marshall uses the online academic forum FlowTV to present a detailed analysis of a problem she identifies in a popular television series. Her article includes traditional academic footnotes and documentation as well as images and charts in color and fully functioning links. Someone reading the item online can immediately access the various episodes of *Glee* that Marshall discusses in her argument.

FlowTV

Posted: January 16, 2010
From: Kelli Marshall, University of Toledo

Show Musical Good, Paired Segments Better: *Glee*'s Unevenness Explained

Opening paragraph provides background information on *Glee* necessary to understand its musical structure.

Before I explain why Fox's musical comedy-drama *Glee* often feels uneven, I'd like to point out what the show gets right. Principally, *Glee*'s creator, Ryan Murphy (*Nip/Tuck*), has adopted the most suitable musical subgenre for his project: the show musical.[1] Of the subgenres — fairy tale, folk, and show — the show musical, whose

Hey kids, let's put on a show (musical)!

numbers typically perform a purpose (e.g., auditions, rehearsals, performances), best caters to Murphy's objective that the cast doesn't "suddenly burst into song."[2] When the characters sing, Murphy claims, they will do so only when they are on stage practicing or performing, in the rehearsal classroom, or in a fantasy state (i.e., a performance in their head). Limiting the numbers to these situations, he believes, will make *Glee* "more accessible to people."[3]

Glee may have assumed the best musical subgenre for its purpose, but the show doesn't always thrive within said subgenre. And people notice. For example, reviews of the first season swing frantically back and forth, from the show is "so funny, so bulging with vibrant characters" and "these performances are wonderful, . . . shaping a fully realized world" to this is "wildly incoherent" and "simply a mess." Much of this unevenness, I believe, boils down to Murphy's refusal to implement consistently one of the most important structural conventions of the musical genre: paired segments, evenly spaced thematic and/or sexual comparisons/oppositions underscored via setting, shot selection, music, dance, and personal style.[4] As Rick Altman explains, with musicals the viewer must "forget familiar notions of plot, psychological motivation, and causal relationships" and surrender instead to "simultaneity and similarity" (e.g., male/female, talented/inept, teacher/student, gay/straight, popular/ostracized).[5]

At least three episodes of *Glee* feature uniform parallel segments: "Pilot," "Wheels," and "Journey." Significantly, these episodes are also the most highly praised of the season.[6] Unlike those which critics have panned or are divided over (e.g., "Hairography," "Once Upon A Mattress," "Home," "Funk"), these three carefully and consistently juxtapose individual characters and groups. For example, "Wheels" begins and ends with Artie (Kevin McHale) dancing in the school's auditorium, first by himself and then with his friends in

Marshall makes a clear and specific claim about the show to explain its perceived "unevenness."

A footnote directs readers to evidence that critics prefer episodes of *Glee* with the structure that Marshall examines in this paper.

The first chart helps readers visualize the "paired segments" discussed in the previous paragraph.

Episodes with Paired Segments

<u>"Pilot"</u>

Rachel	"On My Own"	10m
Finn	"I Can't Fight This Feeling" / "Lovin', Touchin', Squeezin'"	20m
Rachel (et al)	"You're the One That I Want"	30m
Finn (et al)	"You're the One That I Want"	30m
Vocal Adrenaline	"Rehab"	40m
New Directions	"Don't Stop Believin'"	50m

<u>"Wheels"</u>

Artie	"Dancin' with Myself"	5m
Kurt	"Defying Gravity"	30m
Rachel	"Defying Gravity"	30m
Artie (et al)	"Proud Mary"	55m

<u>"Journey"</u>

New Directions	"Journey Mash-up"	12m
Vocal Adrenaline	"Bohemian Rhapsody"	20m
New Directions	"To Sir with Love" [to Schuester]	35m
Schuester	"Somewhere Over the Rainbow" [to New Directions]	55m

Not all that colorful, but at least consistent.

the glee club. Likewise, "Journey" contrasts the vocal and dance abilities of New Directions with that of its show-choir nemesis, Vocal Adrenaline, and then closes with another parallel segment: New Directions singing to their teacher/mentor, Mr. Schuester (Matthew Morrison) and Schuester returning the favor to his students (see table above). Through these parallel numbers, the characters develop and the viewer understands their growth.[7]

What's more, the musical numbers in these three episodes are limited (unlike those in "The Power of Madonna," for instance) and spread evenly throughout. For example, like its show-musical predecessors *Singin' in the Rain* (Stanley Donen and Gene Kelly, 1952) and *The Band Wagon* (Vincente Minnelli, 1953), *Glee's* "Pilot" features a song about every 10 minutes; moreover, "Wheels" positions its songs in a nearly perfect arc: one at the beginning, middle, and end. Finally, each of the numbers in these episodes serves a convincing purpose. For instance, in "Pilot," Rachel (Lea Michele) auditions for glee club with "On My Own," effectively informing the viewer she is both passionate about Broadway musicals and isolated in high school. Echoing this number, Finn (Cory Monteith) sings REO Speedwagon's "I Can't Fight This Feeling," conveying to us that although glee club isn't traditionally for football players, he won't be able to "fight the feeling" to join.

While "Pilot," "Wheels," and "Journey" achieve narrative and stylistic continuity via paired segments and purposeful performances, a large number of *Glee's* episodes do not. As a result, the entire series can feel unbalanced, schizophrenic even. For example, the majority of the musical numbers in "Showmance," "Acafellas," "The Power of Madonna," and "Funk" may individually charm and/or entertain the viewer, but because they are detached from one another, they fail to form a coherent whole (see table p. 242). Admittedly, Sue Sylvester's (Jane Lynch) copycat performance of Madonna's "Vogue" is interesting and ambitious, but it has no corresponding number; hence, we do not fully understand what purpose it serves. The same goes for Schuester's weird flirtation with Sue ("Tell Me Something Good"), Rachel's cries over her love for Finn ("Take a Bow"), and Mercedes's (Amber Riley) fiery reaction to Kurt's (Chris Colfer) rejection of her ("Bust Your Windows"). Had Ryan Murphy et al. created musical numbers through which Sue, Finn, and Kurt

Marshall presents examples to explain why unpaired musical numbers don't work well.

Episodes without Paired Segments

<u>"Showmance"</u>

New Directions	"Gold Digger"
New Directions	"Push It"
Quinn (et al)	"Say a Little Prayer for Me"
Rachel	"It's Over Now"

<u>"Acafellas"</u>

Schuester (et al)	"Poison"
Vocal Adrenaline	"Mercy"
Mercedes	"Bust Your Windows"
Schuester (et al)	"I Wanna Sex You Up"

<u>"The Power of Madonna"</u>

Cheerios	"Ray of Light"
New Directions (girls)	"Express Yourself"
Rachel/Finn	"Borderline"/"Open Your Heart"
Sue Sylvester	"Vogue"
Couples (3)	"Like a Virgin"
Cheerios (Kurt/Mercedes)	"4 Minutes"
New Directions (guys)	"What It Feels Like for a Girl"
New Directions	"Like a Prayer"

<u>"Funk"</u>

Vocal Adrenaline	"Another One Bites the Dust"
Quinn	"It's a Man's Man's Man's World"
Puck/Mercedes	"Good Vibrations"
Will Schuester	"Tell Me Something Good"
Puck (et al)	"Loser"
New Directions	"Give Up the Funk"

More colors, more erratic.

The second chart helps readers visualize the contrast between *Glee* episodes with and without paired musical segments.

could reciprocate their feelings, rather than using snippets of dialogue or in some cases silence, these episodes would likely feel more complete. In this genre, reacting to such emotional performances via dialogue alone generally doesn't cut it.[8]

In interviews, Murphy claims that with *Glee* he is creating a "post-modern musical" in the vein of *Chicago* (Rob Marshall, 2002) or *Moulin Rouge* (Baz Luhrmann, 2001). But what he ostensibly fails to realize is that these two films — while perhaps modern in look, themes, and style (editing in particular) — still conform to the structure of classical musicals, operating almost exclusively through doubling or paired segments.[9] Furthermore, Murphy admits that he bases *Glee*'s musical numbers on "stuff that I like and that I think fits the characters and moves the story along." On its surface this is perhaps fine, but since musical narratives — like all genres, television shows included — necessitate structure, that "stuff that Murphy likes" needs to be framed more consistently within matched scenes and sequences. Perhaps then *Glee* wouldn't feel so uneven.

Marshall points to other successful musicals to reinforce her claim that *Glee* succeeds when it uses a traditional structure.

Notes

These are explanatory notes, with books and articles documented per the *Chicago Manual of Style*.

1. The show musical is also known as the backstage musical and the self-reflective musical. On the latter, see Jane Feuer, "The Self-reflective Musical and the Myth of Entertainment," *Genre: The Musical*. Ed. Rick Altman (London: Routledge, 1981), 159-74.

2. Well-known examples of the fairy tale musical are *Top Hat* (Mark Sandrich, 1935) and *An American in Paris* (Vincent Minnelli, 1951), of the folk musical, *Oklahoma!* (Fred Zinnemann, 1955) and *Meet Me in St. Louis* (Vincent Minnelli, 1944), and of the show musical, *Singin' in the Rain* (Stanley Donen and Gene Kelly, 1952) and *Cabaret* (Bob Fosse, 1972). For a detailed explanation of the three musical subgenres, see Rick Altman, *The American Film Musical* (Bloomington: Indiana University Press, 1987).

3. There are other reasons the show musical is the best option for *Glee* and Murphy's aims: first, it is the subgenre most closely tied to the music industry (Altman 271); second, its performances (like those in the folk musical) emphasize "the integration of the individual into a community or group" (Feuer 166); and third, it employs clichéd stereotypical characters but mainly to "restore meaning to the atmosphere that seems devoid of it" (Altman 252).

4. Altman, 33-45. While I'm arguing that *Glee* feels uneven because it consistently rejects paired segments, I'm also aware that the show likely feels this way because it juxtaposes ridiculous storylines (e.g., Terri Schuester's fake pregnancy, Sue Sylvester's outlandish attempts to sabotage Schuester and the glee club) with rather poignant ones (e.g., Kurt's conversations with his father, Quinn's parents disowning her). Moreover, as Todd VanDerWerff points out, some of *Glee*'s unpredictability may also have to do with its three-writer problem, i.e., *Glee*'s three writers — Ryan Murphy, Brad Falchuk, and Ian Brennan — "seem to have wildly different ideas of what the show is."

5. Altman, 28. In his work, Altman mostly considers hetero-sexual romantic couples; however, musicals also create parallel segments for groups of characters like those found in *Glee,* for instance, Sharks/Jets in *West Side Story* (Robert Wise and Jerome Robbins, 1961), Pink Ladies/T-Birds in *Grease!* (Randal Kleiser, 1978), and children/parents in *Mary Poppins* (Robert Stevenson, 1964), *The Sound of Music* (Robert Wise, 1965), and *Annie* (John Huston, 1982).

6. For critical reception, see *The Onion*'s AV Club, *Time*'s Tuned In, Metacritic, as well as *Wikipedia*'s summaries of "Pilot," "Wheels," and "Journey." I should note, however, that while "Wheels" was widely praised, it was not without controversy; some performers

with disabilities claimed it was inappropriate to cast an able-bodied actor (Kevin McHale) as a disabled student. Still, this criticism, while perhaps warranted, has little to do with the show's narrative structure.

7. One of the other relatively highly praised episodes, "Dream On," also includes paired segments. First, Schuester and his old show-choir nemesis, Bryan Ryan (Neil Patrick Harris), reunite by singing "Piano Man" and then compete with "Dream On." Second, Rachel and her mother, Shelby (Idina Menzel), pair up for "I Dreamed a Dream" (this also recalls Rachel's *Les Miserables* song from the "Pilot"). Third, an idealistic Artie performs "Safety Dance," and then later, a more rational Artie leads New Directions in "Dream a Little Dream of Me."

8. Musical numbers in these "unpaired-segment" episodes are also unevenly timed. For example, "Showmance" features songs at 10m, 35m, 50m, and 55m; "Acafellas" at 17m, 22m, 40m, and 50m; and "The Power of Madonna" at 10m, 14m, 22m, 38m, 41m, 52m, 58m, and 62m. Moreover, unlike "On My Own," "I Can't Fight This Feeling," and "To Sir with Love," many songs in these episodes fail to serve a convincing purpose. For instance, Finn and Rachel's "Borderline"/"Open Your Heart" duet takes the characters nowhere; at the end of the episode, neither character's heart is truly opened to the other. Likewise, "Gold Digger" does little more than showcase Mr. Schuester's rap/dance abilities.

9. Marsha Kinder, "Moulin Rouge," *Film Quarterly* (55.3): 52-59; Karen Perlman, "Cutting Rhythms in Chicago and Cabaret," *Cineaste* (Spring 2009): 28-32.

PHOTOGRAPHS AS LITERARY TEXTS   Photography attained its status as art in the twentieth century. Even documentary photographs not originally conceived as works of art became prized for their striking depictions of the human condition. Three artists recognized for such work are Dorothea Lange (1895–1965), Walker Evans (1903–1975), and Gordon Parks (1912–2006). During the Great Depression and subsequent years, they produced photographs for the Farm Security Administration (FSA) intended to record all aspects of American life. But their best portraits of people and places often reach beyond the immediate historical context, as the three images below and on pages 247–48 demonstrate. Note how these photographs present and frame their subjects, encouraging viewers to expand and interpret their meanings.

Dorothea Lange, "Jobless on Edge of Pea Field, Imperial Valley, California" (1937)

Walker Evans, "Burroughs Family Cabin, Hale County, Alabama" (1936)

Gordon Parks, "American Gothic" (1942)

Assignments

1. **Literary Interpretation:** Review Kelsi Stayart's "Authentic Beauty in Morrison's *The Bluest Eye*" (p. 209). Then examine how a favorite author or filmmaker treats a specific gender, ethnic, religious, political, sexual, or age group in a short story, novel, or film. Look in particular for themes or patterns that most readers (or you) may not have noticed before and which you can help readers better appreciate — reverse sexism in a summer superhero film, bigotry by exclusion in a children's novel, and so on. When readers would benefit, put these ideas in their specific cultural or historical contexts, as Stayart does with Toni Morrison's novel. If you can (as with poems or episodes of TV shows), consider examining several works by a single artist.

2. **Close Reading:** In "Insanity: Two Women" (p. 231), Kanaka Sathasivan does a close, almost line-by-line analysis of Emily Dickinson's "I felt a Funeral, in my Brain"; then she compares the themes and strategies of the poem to those she finds in Charlotte Gilman's "The Yellow Wallpaper." For a project of your own, do *either* a close reading of a favorite short poem or song *or* a comparison of two works from different genres or media.

   For the close reading, tease out all the meanings and strategies you can uncover and show readers how the text works. For the comparison, be sure to begin with works that interest you because of some important similarity: They may share a theme or plot, or even be the *same* work in two different media — *The Prince of Persia* video game and movie, for instance.

3. **Cultural Analysis:** In "Show Musical Good, Paired Segments Better: *Glee*'s Unevenness Explained" (p. 238), Kelli Marshall writes about the structure of a TV show that became a cultural phenomenon. Examine any work of literature, art, or popular culture that similarly reflects what you find to be an important trend or attitude in society. You may write about that trend itself or, like Marshall, examine some aspect of the work in detail: its meaning, theme, authorship, genre, and so on.

4. **Photographs as Literary Texts:** Photographers Dorothea Lange, Walker Evans, and Gordon Parks (pp. 246–48) recorded images documenting the long-term effects of the Great Depression. In a short paper, describe the specific scenes you would photograph today if you hoped to leave as important a documentary legacy as Lange, Evans, and Parks. To make the project manageable, focus on your local community. Showcase your own images in a photo-essay.

5. **Your Choice:** Write a paper about any work of poetry or fiction that you wish more people would read. Use your essay to explain (or, if necessary, defend) the qualities of the work that make it worth someone's serious attention.

How to start
- Need to **find a text to analyze**? See page 256.
- Need to come up with **ideas**? See page 259.
- Need to **organize your ideas**? See page 262.

Rhetorical Analyses

examine in detail the way texts work

Rhetorical analyses foster the kind of close reading that makes writers better thinkers. Moreover, they're everywhere in daily life, especially in politics and law. In fact, they're hard to avoid, especially if you spend much time reading new media.

ANALYSIS OF AN ADVERTISEMENT

You've seen too many slick TV spots touting smart phones that do everything but wash dishes. Your own new phone doesn't work quite so well. You consider writing an *analysis of an advertisement* as an op-ed piece for a local paper that would explore why consumers fall so readily for questionable claims.

ANALYSIS OF AN ARGUMENT

You find yourself impressed by a politician's authority and good sense, so you choose one of his speeches as the subject of an *analysis of an argument* you must write for a composition course. You want to discover exactly how and why he manages to sound so much more persuasive than most Washington pols.

CULTURAL ANALYSIS

You hear your great-grandmother reminiscing about an old neighborhood where every house had a front porch and swing where friends gathered in the evening. You realize that the porch embodies a great many lost values to her and could easily be the subject of a *cultural analysis* for a history class.

ANALYSIS OF A VISUAL TEXT

When your boss at a clothing store reports that upper management isn't happy with the company's online sales, you offer to do an *analysis of a visual text*: the retailer's Web site. Out-of-focus photographs and cluttered graphics make the site look downscale. You argue for a new look and masthead for the store's site.

DECIDING TO WRITE A RHETORICAL ANALYSIS You react to what others say or write all the time. Sometimes an advertisement, speech, or maybe a cultural image grabs you so hard that you want to take it apart to see how it works. Put those discoveries into words and you've composed a *rhetorical analysis.* ○

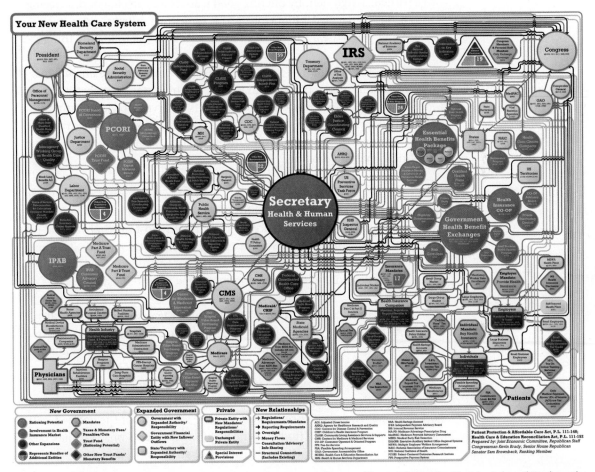

"Your New Health Care System" At first glance, this item might seem like an informative flowchart describing how the health-care system works in the United States. But a rhetorical analysis of its details, especially its headings (for example, *New Government, Expanded Government, Special Interest Provisions*) and its authorship, might lead you to read it as a political argument.

○ choose a genre
p. 390

Rhetoric is the art of using language and media to achieve particular goals. A rhetorical analysis is an argument that takes a close look at the strategies of persuasion within a text; it lists and describes specific techniques that a writer, speaker, editor, artist, or advertiser has employed and then assesses their effectiveness. ○ You can take a rhetorical analysis one step further and respond to a particular argument by offering good reasons for agreeing or disagreeing with it. Such a detailed critique of a text is sometimes called a *critical analysis*.

When you write a rhetorical analysis, you'll do the following things.

Take words and images seriously.   When you compose an analysis, whether admiring or critical, hold writers to a high standard because their ideas may have consequences. Good notions deserve to be identified and applauded. And bad ones should be ferreted out, exposed, and sent packing. Learning to discern one from the other takes practice — which is what rhetorical analyses provide.

Make strong claims about texts.   Of course, you cannot make claims about texts until you know them inside out. The need for close examination may seem self-evident, but we blow through most of what we read (and see) without much thought. Serious critical or rhetorical analysis does just the opposite: It makes texts move like bullets in the movie *The Matrix*, their trajectories slowed and every motion magnified for careful study. ○

Pay attention to audience.   When doing a rhetorical analysis, understanding for *whom* a text is written can be as important as *what* it says. In fact, audiences drive the content, shape, and language of most arguments.

Mine texts for evidence.   Not only should you read texts closely in preparing a rhetorical analysis, but you should also use their words (and any other elements) as evidence for your claims. That's one of the goals of critical work of this kind: to find and cite what other readers of a text may have missed. Expect to quote often in a rhetorical analysis. ○

understand
argument p. 72

read closely
p. 365

use quotations
p. 497

Analysis of an Advertisement

This polished and highly entertaining rhetorical analysis is from the "Ad Report Card" series on *Slate.com*. Frequent contributor Seth Stevenson finds a highly suggestive TV ad for Hall's Refresh cough drops so puzzling that he does an in-depth examination of its potential target audiences to figure out what may be going on. His essay demonstrates the importance of audience analysis in understanding a rhetorical situation.

Slate.com

Posted: Monday, November 9, 2009, at 3:11 PM ET
From: Seth Stevenson

Ad Report Card: Can Cougars Sell Cough Drops?

Articles in this series always open with a description of the ad for readers who haven't seen it.

The Spot: *It's move-in day at a college dorm. A student asks his new roommate's mom whether she'd care for a Halls Refresh. The young man and the middle-aged mom suck on their lozenges, staring lasciviously into each other's eyes. We hear their thoughts. "So juicy!" thinks the mom. "Yeah, she likes it," thinks the student. The woman's husband and son walk in on this intimate moment. "Mom!" shouts the horrified son as the dad recoils. "New Halls Refresh with moisture action," says the announcer. "Surprisingly mouthwatering."*

This ad has been catching flak for its mildly disturbing visual of a frumpy mom making bedroom eyes at a college-age nerd. The American Decency Association posted a breathless, run-on rant on its Web site, sounding particularly distressed about the fact that the ad shows "mouths moving in sexually suggestive ways." A *Slate* colleague is also grossed out by the ad's use of the evocative phrase "moisture action."

A personal and informal style works well in an online magazine like *Slate.com*.

True, the ad is a wee bit icky. But I'm having trouble working up much outrage. I'm more interested in a fundamental marketing question: Who, exactly, is this ad supposed to reach?

Stevenson uses a key question to focus and structure his analysis.

I generally expect ads to use actors matching the product's target audience. Thus ads for Viagra feature older men, while ads for Barbie dolls star little girls. But in this ad, the characters shown enjoying Halls Refresh represent two different demographic categories with starkly different buying habits. Is Halls hoping to tempt fortysomething women with this new line of lozenges? Or college-age guys?

Let's first examine the evidence suggesting that the ad is meant to charm young dudes:

Cadbury, which owns Halls, is for the most part a candy company. Its offerings include Bubblicious, Sour Patch Kids, Swedish Fish, and countless chocolaty goodies. Unlike other Halls products, Halls Refresh is being pitched on the basis of its "mouthwatering," candylike qualities — not as a medicinal remedy for a sore throat.

Candy ads these days tend to rely on surreal, absurdist humor. There's the Starburst ad in which a guy communes with a llama and the Skittles ad that shows a man with a prehensile beard. Cadbury actually owns another confectionary brand that uses nonsensical, dude-focused advertising: Check out the Stride gum spot in which a team of lederhosen-clad dancers assaults a young man in a parking garage.

This Halls Refresh spot seems like a close cousin to those crazy candy ads. It's easy to imagine the mom and the student chewing on Skittles instead of sucking on Halls. And, through prior reporting, I happen to know that the target demographic for Skittles is 15-17 year-olds. Because that's who buys candy. Young guys — not middle-aged women.

Case closed, yes? Not quite. Let's consider the evidence on the other side of the ledger:

First, Halls Refresh is sugarless. This is an attribute not traditionally prized by young fellas, who like to guzzle down sugary colas and munch on 500-calorie burgers. The young man shown in the ad surely wouldn't be watching his weight. But the mom might be.

Looking up Halls Refresh on a search engine, I found a bunch of blogs that had been given samples of the lozenge to review. These samples were handed out by people trying to promote Halls Refresh. What sort of blogs were the samples given to? Almost exclusively blogs written by professional women and stay-at-home moms.

A press release introducing Halls Refresh also suggests that the product was designed to meet the needs not of carefree young

First part of the analysis looks in detail at the case for "dudes" as the target audience.

Second part presents evidence that older women may be the intended audience.

men but of harried adults. Its first paragraph declares that Halls Refresh is the perfect antidote whenever you get "the feeling that your mouth needs a refresher just as your presentation begins, when meeting the in-laws, when running errands under a tight schedule . . ." Not a lot of 18-year-old guys spend their time worrying about meeting in-laws. Or running errands, for that matter.

The clincher? Cadbury aired this ad during the premiere episode of *Cougar Town*, the Courteney-Cox-starring ABC show about an older woman who is forever scheming to date younger men. Referring back to my cast-your-target-demographic rule, I have to assume that a show with Courteney Cox in the lead role is meant to appeal to Courteney-Cox-age women. Though it's not totally clear to me why portrayals of cougardom are fun for middle-age women to watch. Is it an affirmation that they are still sexual beings? Or do they relate to Cox's foibles and take comfort in the show's sympathetic humor?

I have similar questions about the Halls Refresh spot, if it is, indeed, aimed at middle-age ladies. Do women fantasize about sharing a naughty moment over a lozenge with a scrawny dweeb? Being caught by their husband and child mid-suck?

Perhaps Cadbury — which has for the past several years been diversifying out of chocolate and into sugar-free chewing gum and cough drops — wants to reach a new category of consumer but doesn't yet know how to market effectively to anyone over 19. Or perhaps it hopes to split the difference, by pitching Halls Refresh to young men as a candy while telling grown-up women it's a functional cure for dry-mouthed moments.

Grade: C–. The ad's goals seem muddled. Worse, it's not funny. Cadbury didn't respond to my inquiries by press time, so I can't be sure about their intentions. But what do you think? Who, if anyone, does this ad appeal to?

> Best evidence comes last, but it raises more questions.

> The conclusion and C– grade suggest that Stevenson finds the ad ineffective in reaching *any* viewers.

Exploring purpose and topic

▶ find a text

Make a difference. Done right, rhetorical analyses can be as important as the texts they examine. They may change readers' opinions, open their eyes to new ideas, or keep an important argument going. They may also draw attention to rhetorical strategies and techniques worth imitating or avoiding.

When you write an angry letter to the editor complaining about bias in the news coverage, you won't fret much about defining your purpose or topic—they are given. But when responding to a course assignment, particularly when you can choose a text on your own to analyze rhetorically, you've got to establish the boundaries. Given a choice, select a text to analyze with the following characteristics.

Choose a text you can work with. Find a gutsy piece that makes a claim you or someone else might actually disagree with. It helps if you have a stake in the issue and already know something about it. The text should also be of a manageable length that you can explore coherently within the limits of the assignment.

Need help deciding what to write about? See "How to Browse for Ideas" on pp. 360–61.

Choose a text you can learn more about. Some items won't make much sense out of context. So choose a text or series of texts that you can study and research. ○ It will obviously help to know when it was written, presented or produced, by whom, and where it first appeared. This information is as important for visual texts, such as advertisements, posters, and films, as for traditional speeches or articles.

Choose a text with handles. Investigate arguments that do interesting things. Maybe a speech uses lots of anecdotes or repetition to generate emotional appeals; perhaps a photo-essay's commentary is more provocative than the images; a print ad may arrest attention by its simplicity but still be full of cultural significance. You've got to write about the piece. Make sure it offers you interesting things to say.

find a topic
p. 356

Choose a text you know how to analyze.   Stick to printed texts if you aren't sure how to write about ads or films or even speeches. But don't sell yourself short. You can pick up the necessary vocabulary by reading models of rhetorical and critical analysis. Moreover, you don't always need highly technical terms to describe poor logic, inept design, or offensive strate- gies, wherever they appear. Nor do you need special expertise to describe cultural trends or detect political implications.

Your Turn   You don't need a highbrow or sophisticated topic for a success- ful rhetorical analysis, as Stevenson's essay on cough drops demonstrates (p. 253). It's a much better strategy to dissect a text that genuinely intrigues you and then make an audience as intrigued by it as you are. If you take an item seriously (zombies, for example: see p. 264), chances are that your readers will too. So begin an open-ended assignment by listing the sorts of texts you engage with regularly. Even text messages and tweets can be studied rhetorically if you find an angle on them.

Some published rhetorical analyses are written for ready-made audiences already inclined to agree with the authors. Riled up by an offensive editorial or a political campaign, people these days may even seek out and enjoy mean-spirited, over-the-top criticism, especially on the Web. But the rhetorical and critical analyses you write for class should be relatively restrained because you can't predict how your readers might feel about the arguments you are critiquing. So assume that you are writing for a diverse and thoughtful audience, full of readers who prefer reflective analysis to clever put-downs. You don't have to be dull or passionless. Just avoid the easy slide into rudeness. O

"got milk?" Advertisements in this famous series lend themselves to rhetorical analysis because they are so carefully designed for specific audiences, in this case fans of country singer Miranda Lambert.

respect your readers
p. 440

Finding and developing materials

Before you analyze a text of any kind, do some background research. ideas ◄ Discover what you can about its author, creator, publisher, sponsor, and so on. For example, it may be important to know that the TV commercial you want to understand better has aired only on sports networks or lifestyle programs on cable. Become familiar, too, with the contexts in which an argument occurs. If you reply to a *Wall Street Journal* editorial, know what news or events sparked that item and investigate the paper's editorial slant.

Read the piece carefully just for information first, highlighting names or allusions you don't recognize. Then look them up: There's very little you can't uncover quickly these days via a Web search. When you think you understand the basics, you are prepared to approach the text rhetorically. Pay attention to any standout aspects of the text you're analyzing—perhaps how it wins over wary readers through conciliatory language or draws on the life experiences of its author to frame its subject. ○ You might look at any of the following elements.

Consider the topic or subject matter of the text.   What is novel or striking about the topic? How well defined is it? Could it be clearer? Is it important? Relevant? Controversial? Is the subject covered comprehensively or selectively? What is the level of detail? Does the piece make a point?

Consider the audiences of the text.   To whom is the piece addressed? How is the text adapted to its audience? Who is excluded from the audience and how can you tell? What does the text offer its audience: information, controversy, entertainment? What does it expect from its audience?

Consider its author.   What is the author's relationship to the material? Is the writer or creator personally invested or distant? Is the author an expert, a knowledgeable amateur, or something else? What does the author hope to accomplish?

Consider its medium or language.   What is the medium or genre of the text: essay, article, editorial, advertisement, book excerpt, poster, video, podcast, or other format? How well does the medium suit the subject? How might the material look different in another medium? What is the level of the language: formal, informal, colloquial? ○ What is the tone of the

find reliable
resources p. 482

read closely
p. 365

define your style
p. 432

text—logical, sarcastic, humorous, angry, condescending? How do the various elements of design—such as arrangement, color, fonts, images, white space, audio, video, and so on—work in the text?

Consider its occasion.   Why was the text created? To what circumstances or situations does it respond, and what might the reactions to it be? What problems does it solve or create? What pleasure might it give? Who benefits from the text?

This poster appears on the Web site of the Navy Environmental Health Center. Does that fact about its context change its message in any way?

Consider its contexts.   What purposes do texts of this type serve? Do texts of this sort have a history? Do they serve the interests of specific groups or classes? Have they evolved over time? Does the text represent a new genre?

Consider its use of rhetorical appeals.   Persuasive texts are often analyzed according to how they use three types of rhetorical appeal. Typically, a text may establish the character and credibility of its author (*ethos*), generate emotions in order to move audiences (*pathos*), and use evidence and logic to make its case (*logos*).

  Ethos—the appeal to character—may be the toughest argumentative strategy to understand. Every text and argument is presented by someone or something, whether an individual, a group, or an institution. Audiences are usually influenced and swayed by writers or speakers who present themselves as knowledgeable, honest, fair-minded, and believable. Here Michael Ruse describes a witness whose frank words established his ethos at a 1981 court case dealing with requiring creation science in Arkansas schools.

> The assistant attorney general was trying to tie him into knots over some technical point in evolutionary biology. Finally, the man blurted out, "Mr. Williams, I'm not a scientist. . . . I am an educator, and I have my pride and professional responsibilities. And I just can't teach that stuff [meaning creationism] to my kids."
>
> —"Science for Science Teachers," *The Chronicle of Higher Education*, January 13, 2010

  Pathos—the emotional appeal—is usually easy to detect. Look for ways that a text generates strong feelings to support its points, win over readers, or influence them in other ways. The strategy is legitimate so long as an emotion fits the situation and doesn't manipulate audiences. For example, columnist Peggy Noonan routinely uses emotions to make her political points.

> We fought a war to free slaves. We sent millions of white men to battle and destroyed a portion of our nation to free millions of black men. What kind of nation does this? We went to Europe, fought, died, and won, and then taxed ourselves to save our enemies with the Marshall Plan. What kind of nation does this? Soviet communism stalked the world and we were the ones who steeled ourselves and taxed ourselves to stop it. Again: What kind of nation does this?
>
> Only a very great one.
>
> —"Patriots, Then and Now," *Wall Street Journal*, March 30, 2006

Logos—the appeal to reason and evidence—is most favored in academic texts. Look carefully at the claims a text offers and whether they are supported by facts, data, testimony, and good reasons. What assumptions lie beneath the argument? Ask questions about evidence too. Does it come from reliable sources or valid research? Is it up-to-date? Has it been reported accurately and fully? Has due attention been given to alternative points of view and explanations? Has enough evidence been offered to make a valid point? You might ask such questions, for example, when a political commentator like George Will runs the numbers to prove a point, as in this excerpt from a column that appeared after Michelle and Barack Obama failed to win the 2016 Olympics for the city of Chicago.

> Both Obamas gave heartfelt speeches about . . . themselves. Although the working of the [International Olympic] committee's mind is murky, it could reasonably have rejected Chicago's bid for the 2016 Games on aesthetic grounds—unless narcissism has suddenly become an Olympic sport.
>
> In the 41 sentences of her remarks, Michelle Obama used some form of the personal pronouns "I" or "me" 44 times. Her husband was, comparatively, a shrinking violet, using those pronouns only 26 times in 48 sentences. Still, 70 times in 89 sentences conveyed the message that somehow their fascinating selves were what made, or should have made, Chicago's case compelling.
>
> —"An Olympic Ego Trip," *Washington Post*, October 6, 2009

Creating a structure

▶ organize ideas

In a rhetorical analysis, you'll make a statement about how well the argumentative strategy of a piece works. Don't expect to come up with a thesis immediately or easily: You need to study a text closely to figure out how it works and then think about its strengths and weaknesses. Draft a tentative thesis (or hypothesis) and then refine your words throughout the process of writing until they assert a claim you can prove. ○

Look for a complex thesis. Don't just list some rhetorical features: *This ad has good logical arguments and uses emotions and rhetorical questions.* Why would someone want to read (or write) a paper with such an empty claim? The following thesis yields a far more interesting rhetorical analysis:

> The latest government antidrug posters offer good reasons for avoiding steroids but do it in a visual style so closely resembling bland health posters that most students will just ignore them.

Develop a structure. Once you have a thesis or hypothesis, try sketching a design based on a thesis/supporting reason/evidence plan. Focus on those features of the text that illustrate the points you wish to make. You don't have to discuss every facet of the text.

> **Introduction leading to a claim**
>
> **First supporting reason + textual evidence**
> **Second supporting reason + textual evidence**
> **Additional supporting reasons + textual evidence**
>
> **Conclusion**

In some cases, you might perform a line-by-line or paragraph-by-paragraph deconstruction of a text. This structure shows up frequently online. Such analyses practically organize themselves, but your commentary must be smart, accurate, and stylish to keep readers onboard.

> **Introduction leading to a claim**
>
> **First section/paragraph + detailed analysis**
> **Next section/paragraph + detailed analysis**
> **Additional section/paragraph + detailed analysis**
>
> **Conclusion**

develop a statement
p. 393

Choosing a style and design

The style of your textual analyses will vary depending on audience, but you always face one problem that can sometimes be helped by design: making the text you are analyzing more accessible to readers.

Consider a high style.   Rhetorical and critical analyses you write in school will usually be formal and use a "high" style. ○ Your tone should be respectful, your vocabulary as technical as the material requires, and your perspective impersonal—avoiding *I* and *you*. Such a style gives the impression of objectivity and seriousness. Unless an instructor gives you more leeway, use a formal style for critical analyses.

Consider a middle style.   Oddly, rhetorical and critical analyses appearing in the public arena—rather than in the classroom—will usually be less formal and exploit the connection with readers that a middle style encourages. While still serious, such a style gives writers more options for expressing strong opinions and feelings (sometimes including anger, outrage, and contempt). In much public writing, you can detect a personal voice offering an opinion or advancing an agenda.

Make the text accessible to readers.   A special challenge in any rhetorical analysis is to help readers understand the texts you are scrutinizing. When possible with printed texts, attach a photocopy of the material directly to your analysis or include a link to it if you are working online. Also be sure to provide basic information about the author, title, place of publication, and date, and briefly explain the context of the work. With other types of subjects—such as movies, advertising campaigns, and so on—your task is more complicated. You'll often have to describe or summarize what you are describing in considerable detail.

As you can see, your rhetorical analysis should typically be written *as if readers do not have that text in hand or in front of them*. One way to achieve that clarity is to summarize and quote selectively from the text as you examine it, or to provide visual images. You can see examples of this technique in Matthew James Nance's essay on pages 264–69 and in J. Reagan Tankersley's analysis on pages 270–78.

Annotate the text.   When analyzing an image or a text available in digital form, consider attaching your comments directly to the item. Do this by simply inserting a copy of the image or article directly into your project and then using the design tools of your word processor to create annotations.

define your style
p. 432

Examining models

For a class assignment on rhetorical analysis, Matthew James Nance chose as his subject the award-winning feature article "Can't Die for Trying" by journalist Laura Miller — who later would serve as mayor of Dallas. In the essay, Nance explains in detail how Miller manages to present the story of a convicted killer who wants to be executed to readers who might have contrary views about capital punishment. Nance's analysis is both technical and objective. He does an especially good job of helping readers follow the argument of "Can't Die for Trying," a fairly long and complicated article.

Nance 1

Matthew James Nance

Professor Norcia

English 2

June 14, 20--

A Mockery of Justice

In 1987, David Martin Long was convicted of double homicide and sentenced to death. He made no attempt to appeal this sentence, and surprisingly, did everything he could to expedite his execution. Nonetheless, due to an automatic appeals process, Long remained on Texas's Death Row for twelve years before he was finally executed. For various reasons, including investigations into whether he was mentally ill, the state of Texas had continued to postpone his execution date. In 1994, when David Long was still in the middle of his appeals process, *Dallas Observer* columnist Laura Miller took up his case in the award-winning article "Can't Die for Trying." In this article, Miller explores the enigma of a legal

> Sets scene carefully and provides necessary background information.

Nance 2

system in which a sociopath willing to die continues to be mired in the legal process. The article is no typical plea on behalf of a death-row inmate, and Miller manages to avoid a facile political stance on capital punishment. Instead, Miller uses an effective combination of logical reasoning and emotional appeal to evoke from readers a sense of frustration at the system's absurdity.

Miller defies expectations and Nance explains why in his thesis.

Long paragraph furnishes detailed evidence for Miller's two premises.

To show that David Martin Long's execution should be carried out as soon as possible, Miller offers a reasoned argument based on two premises: that he wants death and that he deserves it. Miller cites Long's statement from the day he was arrested: "I realize what I did was wrong. I don't belong in this society. I never have. . . . I'd just wish they'd hurry up and get this over with" (5). She emphasizes that this desire has not changed, by quoting Long's correspondence from 1988, 1991, and 1992. In this way, Miller makes Long's argument seem reasoned and well thought out, not simply a temporary gesture of desperation. "Yes, there are innocent men here, retarded men, insane men, and men who just plain deserve another chance," Long wrote [State District Judge Larry] Baraka in April 1992, "But I am none of these!" (5). Miller also points out his guilty plea, and the jury's remarkably short deliberation: "The jury took only an hour to find Long guilty of capital murder—and 45 minutes to give him the death penalty" (5). Miller does not stop there, however. She

Nance 3

gives a grisly description of the murders themselves, followed by Long's calculated behavior in the aftermath:

> He hacked away at Laura twenty-one times before going back inside where he gave Donna fourteen chops. The blind woman, who lay in bed screaming while he savaged Donna, got five chops. Long washed the hatchet, stuck it in the kitchen sink, and headed out of town in Donna's brown station wagon. (5)

Miller's juxtaposition of reasoned deliberation with the bloody narrative of the murders allows her to show that Long, in refusing to appeal, is reacting justly to his own sociopathy. Not only is it right that he die; it is also right that he does not object to his death.

In the midst of this reasoned argument, Miller expresses frustration at the bureaucratic inefficiency that is at odds with her logic. She offers a pragmatic, resource-based view of the situation:

> Of course, in the handful of instances where a person is wrongly accused . . . this [death-penalty activism] is noble, important work. But I would argue that in others—David Martin Long in particular—it is a sheer waste of taxpayer dollars. And a mockery of justice. (6)

Miller portrays the system as being practically incompatible with her brand of pragmatism. The figures involved in Long's case are painted as invisible, equivocal, or

Provides both summaries and quotations from article so that readers can follow Miller's argument.

To clarify Miller's point, Nance adds a phrase in brackets to the quotation.

Nance 4

both. For instance, in spite of Long's plea, Judge Baraka was forced to appoint one of Long's attorneys to start the appeals process. "The judge didn't have a choice. Texas law requires that a death-penalty verdict be automatically appealed. . . . [This] is supposed to expedite the process. But the court sat on Long's case for four long years" (5). Miller also mentions Danny Burn, a Fort Worth lawyer in association with the Texas Resource Center, one of the "do-good . . . organizations whose sole feverish purpose is to get people off Death Row. . . . No matter how airtight the cases" (6). Burn filed on Long's behalf, though he never met Long in person. This fact underscores Miller's notion of the death-row bureaucracy as being inaccessible, and by extension, incomprehensible.

> Notice how smoothly quotations merge into Nance's sentences.

This parade of equivocal incompetence culminates in Miller's interview with John Blume, another activist who argued on Long's behalf. Miller paints Blume as so equivocal that he comes across as a straw man. "As a general rule," says Blume, "I tend to think most people who are telling you that are telling you something else, and that's their way of expressing it. There's something else they're depressed or upset about" (6). The article ends with Miller's rejoinder: "Well, I'd wager, Mr. Blume, that something is a lawyer like you" (6). Whereas the article up to this point has maintained a balance between reason and frustration, here Miller seems to let gradually building frustration get the best of her. She

> Nance makes a clear judgment about Miller's objectivity — then offers evidence for his claim.

Nance 5

does not adequately address whether Blume might be correct in implying that Long is insane, mentally ill, or otherwise misguided. She attempts to dismiss this idea by repeatedly pointing out Long's consistency in his stance and his own statements that he is not retarded, but her fallacy is obvious: Consistency does not imply sanity. Clearly, Miller would have benefited from citing Long's medical history and comparing his case with those of other death-row inmates, both mentally ill and well. Then her frustrated attack on Blume would seem more justified.

Miller also evokes frustration through her empathetic portrayal of Long. Although the article is essentially a plea for Long to get what he wants, this fact itself prevents Miller from portraying Long sympathetically. Miller is stuck in a rhetorical bind; if her readers become sympathetic toward Long, they won't want him to die. However, the audience needs an emotional connection with Long to accept the argument on his behalf. Miller gets around this problem by abandoning sympathy altogether, portraying Long as a cold-blooded killer. The quotation "I've never seen a more cold-blooded, steel-eyed sociopath ever" (5) is set apart from the text in a large font, and Miller notes, "This is a case of a really bad dude, plain and simple. . . . Use any cliché you want. It fits" (5). Miller here opts for a weak appeal, evoking from the audience the same negative emotion that Long feels. She gives voice to Long's

Nance examines the way Miller deals with the problem she has portraying a cold-blooded killer to readers.

frustration over his interminable appeals: "Long stewed. . . . Long steamed. . . . Long fumes. . . ." (6). She also points out Long's fear of himself: "I fear I'll kill again" (6). Clearly, the audience is meant to echo these feelings of frustration and fear. This may seem like a weak emotional connection with Long, but perhaps it is the best Miller could do, given that a primary goal of hers was to show that Long deserves death.

Laura Miller won the H. L. Mencken Award for this article, which raises important questions about the legal process. Part of its appeal is that it approaches capital punishment without taking a simplistic position. It can appeal to people on both sides of the capital punishment debate. The argument is logically valid, and for the most part, the emotional appeal is effective. Its deficiencies, including the weak emotional appeal for Long, are ultimately outweighed by Miller's overarching rationale, which calls for pragmatism in the face of absurdity.

Work Cited

Miller, Laura. "Can't Die for Trying." *Dallas Observer*
    12 Jan. 1994: 5-6. Print.

J. Reagan Tankersley argues that zombies in movies and TV represent what people fear most at any given time. They become the image of our fears.

Tankersley 1

J. Reagan Tankersley

Professor Wilkes

Composition 1

November 24, 20--

Humankind's Ouroboros

Arguably, what we fear is perhaps the greatest indicator of how we behave as human animals. Fear is the emotion with the greatest impact on our fight or flight instincts; our animal brain is exposed when we decide to cover our eyes or keep on watching. It is why both lanes of traffic slow when there's been an accident: One lane brakes due to the obstruction; drivers in the other lane linger because everyone wants to see what happened, knowing it could've been us.

Horror films act in the same way. The monster movie of the Golden Age of Hollywood was the first sign that people can't always look away from what scares them. And it was lucrative. The horror genre remains one of the most prolific and profitable of the eleven classic genres of film, beginning with such titles as *Frankenstein* and *Dracula*. Within this body of works, none seems more prevalent today than the zombie movie, with the possible exception of highly sexualized vampire and werewolf dramas. Yet, despite a singular ability

Tankersley 2

to scare audiences, the zombie movie has never been a solid form in itself. The zombies of classical Hollywood are strikingly different from those seen in the summer blockbusters of the past few years. More than any other monster, the zombie is able to evolve according to what will scare us the most, depending on where we stand in our own history. So the ever-evolving design of the zombie is an arguably strong tether to our fears, to how we react as humans.

The first film considered to be a zombie movie was released in 1932, in the heart of the Classical Hollywood era, and starred the master of the monster film, Bela Lugosi. While *White Zombie* is a long stretch from the zombie films of today, it broke ground on the very concept of "zombification." The plot involves a plantation owner from Haiti who, using

A scene from *Dracula*.

Tankersley introduces his thesis: that zombies in films embody the current fears of our society.

Tankersley 3

witchcraft to win his love interest, accidentally turns her into a zombie obeying his every command. This plot hints at the roots of the zombie concept, which lie in voodoo legends, the word *zombie* originating in West Africa. The film was also the first to present on screen something akin to our modern image of the zombie: After she becomes a zombie, the love interest of the film is pale white, with the look of a corpse.

The film of that era that best predicted the future of the zombie film was the aptly named *Things to Come*, released in 1936. This adaptation of H. G. Wells's novel of the same name does not directly focus on zombies; however, its epic storyline includes a viral plague, which causes the infected to wander aimlessly, spreading the contagion on contact—an essential plot point in the large-scale zombie films to come. Both of these films reflect the concerns of the horror audience of the 1930s: fear of the mystical and fear of the future. *White Zombie* played to an uneasiness with voodoo magic, which some people associated with post-slavery African American culture. *Things to Come* captured the signature pessimism of H. G. Wells during an era of economic recession in the troubled period between two great wars.

Zombies took a backseat in the horror genre following the fall of Classical Hollywood. Moreover, the new medium of television did not allow for such sensational and scary subject matter. Things changed, however, with the rise of the New American Cinema in the 1960s, a school of filmmaking

The analysis explores the historical roots of today's zombie films.

Tankersley 4

that promoted noncontinuous editing and deliberately explicit images. George A. Romero, considered the father of the modern zombie, released *Night of the Living Dead* to horrify audiences in 1968. Romero is given this lofty title simply because he introduced what is considered the paradigmatic zombie, that is, the walking corpse who exists only to eat the flesh of the living. The film broke many cinematic taboos of the time, especially with a sequence involving a zombified child eating her parents. The shocking imagery from this scene sent tremors through the film community. This reimagining of the zombie played to an audience perhaps changed by the televised violence of the Vietnam War era; certainly, the explicit images of cannibalistic corpses brought the horror genre to a much higher level than the monster films of the previous age.

Romero's cult masterpiece was followed by a slew of mediocre-to-downright-horrible zombie films, all produced in the wake of *Night*'s success. These cheap imitations were quelled only briefly by Romero's next project, *Dawn of the Dead*, which debuted in 1978. Although it was released just ten years after the original, the film altered the nature of the zombie to again depict the current fears of the audience. With the demoralizing end of the Vietnam War, Americans adopted a more critical view of their national values. Romero's film, which takes place primarily in a shopping mall, became a direct commentary on growing levels of consumerism in

Tankersley focuses on the visual imagery of modern zombie films.

Tankersley 5

A scene from *Night of the Living Dead.*

America. Romero heightened his societal critique by increasing the scale of the zombie outbreak, presenting images of zombies—once people themselves—mindlessly consuming other people in a shopping mall, of all places. This level of rebuke represents a paradigm shift in the zombie film: It shows that the fear we experience from zombies comes not just from the gore and frightening images. Rather, it is from the fact that zombies *are* society, without its rules or adornments. Zombies became mindless consumers, a description increasingly given to society itself.

Romero's cinematic shift to a larger-scale zombie drama with social commentary failed to have much impact until recently. Between the original *Dawn of the Dead* and Zack Snyder's remake in 2004, there was again a very long train of awful zombie films. It wasn't until 2002, with the release of *28 Days Later*, that the zombie film again became a genre to be

Presents the post–Vietnam War zombie as a metaphor for consumerism.

Tankersley 6

reckoned with. Danny Boyle's foray into the zombie film is most notable for its sweeping views of an abandoned London, providing a postmortem view of society destroyed by an infection. Not only did Boyle manage to make the catastrophe seem brutally real through such heart-wrenching images as a notice board plastered with missing persons reports, he also revolutionized the zombie as a species. His ghouls—the result of animal testing gone horribly wrong—were more realistic and more frightening, leaving their infected victims with something similar to rabies. The defining differences between Boyle's zombies and those of the past, however, were their ability to run and their virus's aggressive capacity to infect on contact, transforming a victim into the undead in a matter of seconds. This gave the zombie genre a much-needed boost, especially since previous films were often criticized for featuring antagonists who could barely walk. Boyle's new zombies could sprint for longer periods than normal humans, due to a lack of physical pain, leaving the protagonists with no safe place to hide for long.

Tankersley analyzes the physical details of *28 Days Later*.

Boyle's film made another point: that zombie films can be constructed around more than just spooky lighting, token characters, cheap scares, and nauseating images. He achieved this goal by focusing on the living characters: Their personal fears and their realization that all the people they loved were gone, raising the question of what there was to survive for. This approach made the fear of zombies

Tankersley 7

A scene from *28 Days Later*.

as much internal as external; the fear becomes personal to each individual audience member. A scene in which the protagonist finds his parents — who committed suicide before the infection spread to them — is all one needs to understand the real terror that an event as widespread as a zombie infection would create.

Numerous films after *28 Days Later* have approached the human dimension of the zombie film similarly, ensuring

Tankersley 8

that audiences would effectively place themselves in dire emotional situations. Of course, there remain the blood-filled blockbusters, such as the *Resident Evil* franchise, but Boyle's film, and some that followed, gave a film buff something to appreciate in a zombie movie. This greater sophistication is evident in what is currently the zombie production to see, *The Walking Dead*, a television series on AMC (American Movie Classics). The story has its origin in a popular comic book series, but the television show, directed by Frank Darabont (*The Shawshank Redemption*), follows in Boyle's footsteps, exploring the internal dramas of the characters as much as the physical threat of the zombies. The series, still in release, has so far been lauded by zombie enthusiasts, primarily because it pulls back to the traditional zombies of Romero's age, the aimlessly hobbling, sunken-eyed corpses. Thus far, the show appears to have found a place in the zombie canon.

The zombie began as a mysterious creature of mystical origin, with no will of its own. It quickly evolved into the flesh-eating monster that many associate with the term today. And, although it has recently become the product of viral testing and chemical warfare, the textbook zombie remains unwavering in its basic mission—to scare people. At the beginning of the twentieth century, audiences feared the unknown, whether that was mysticism or troubling

Tankersley explains how zombie films are currently evolving.

Tankersley 9

political events. In the post-Vietnam War era, they began to question themselves, doubting their values and wondering if they were still the good guys that American leaders made them out to be. And finally, with the increasing threat of terrorism, people have returned to fearing the possibilities the future might bring. Now, *The Walking Dead* has moved beyond even this horror, with the source of its zombie infection completely unnamed. In the zombie films of the past ten years, it is clear that what we fear most is ourselves. We fear what people next to us may be capable of if their reason is taken from them by some man-made virus, unknown pathogen, or something else entirely. We all know that deep down, people are capable of heinous acts, and it is only reason that can stop them. But when reason is lost, human society has every faculty to consume itself.

> The conclusion finally explains the visual image offered in the title of the paper: the serpent that devours itself.

Tankersley 10

Works Consulted

The Internet Movie Database (IMDb). Web. 15 Nov. 2010.

"List of Zombie Films." *Wikipedia*. Wikimedia Foundation, 13 Nov. 2010. Web. 15 Nov. 2010.

"Main Film Genres." *Greatest Films—The Best Movies in Cinematic History*. Ed. Tim Dirks. 2010. Web. 15 Nov. 2010.

ANALYSIS OF A VISUAL TEXT   Can a jacket be read rhetorically? Beth Teitell gives it a try in this Web report posted on *Boston.com* after Republican candidate Scott Brown won the U.S. Senate seat held for decades by Ted Kennedy. A folksy, man-of-the-people image helped Brown to upset the much-favored Democratic candidate. But, as Teitell discovers, sometimes a jacket is just a jacket. Or is it?

Boston.com

Posted: January 28, 2010
From: Beth Teitell, *Globe* Correspondent

A Jacket of the People

Scott Brown's pickup truck got almost as much attention as the Senate candidate, but somehow his equally ubiquitous, equally everyman barn jacket cruised below the pundits' radar.

And yet, there it was, starring in his now-famous truck ad. There it was again, waving to motorists. And voting in the election.

But what do we know about that brown jacket, really? We spent more time talking about what Brown *wasn't* wearing than what he was. Is the slightly worn leather jacket what it appears to be — just something Brown had lying around the house? Or did the campaign hire a stylist to find Brown a jacket that said "Joe the Plumber," but cost $850, like the Burberry canvas barn jacket Saks is selling this season?

With the Senator-elect poised to start making national policy, a call to one of his campaign masterminds was in order. "It was made by an American company Golden Bear Sportswear," Brown senior adviser Eric Fehrnstrom told us. "He loves it because it fits and his daughter bought it for him, and he only has two jackets." (The other is a blue puffer snow jacket.)

Beyond providing warmth, Fehrnstrom said, the jacket did indeed send a message, just like the truck: Brown's a regular guy. "Scott is the Rocky Balboa of Massachusetts politics, and his barn coat may be as famous as Rocky's leather jacket. Maybe someday it will hang in the Smithsonian next to the *Spirit of St. Louis*."

Longtime Democratic consultant Michael Goldman, a senior consultant with the Government Insight Group, had a slightly different take. "There is no question that jacket was supposed to say, I'm not some wealthy lawyer from the suburbs, I'm just like you, a plain old truck-driving guy."

Teitell intends to probe how deliberately Brown's jacket was used as a symbol in his campaign.

Teitell first establishes the facts: The made-in-the-USA jacket was a gift.

Two political professionals read the jacket as symbolic.

Mary Lou Andre, a Needham-based wardrobe and corporate image consultant, says the jacket sent a rugged message that an "elitist" trench coat would not have.

"Most politicians, when you see them, don't have outerwear on," Andre said. "That jacket signified that he was out and about meeting people, that he was on the road, not in secret meetings trying to be made over."

Sadly, there's no exit polling showing how the election would have gone had he not worn the barn jacket, but history shows that garments as billboards don't always work. And John Kerry's barn jacket couldn't erase his man-of-only-certain-people image in 2004.

So what kind of guy wears a Golden Bear Sportswear leather barn jacket?

"We sell to everyone," said Everett LaRose, a salesman at the Andover Shop's Andover location, where a similar-looking Golden Bear Sportswear barn jacket goes for $675. Guess that depends on what your definition of "everyone" is.

Brown himself didn't buy the jacket, it turns out. It was a gift from Arianna (the daughter who's "definitely not available"). Taking a break from studying pre-calculus over the weekend at Syracuse University, she reported that she bought it at the Wrentham Village Premium Outlets as a birthday present about five years ago.

"I like to make him look nice," Arianna said, adding that she also bought him a pea coat for Christmas, which he wore a few times on the campaign trail before "reverting" back to the barn jacket.

"I like buying clothes for him," she said. That's in contrast to her sister and her mother, she added, who are afraid to buy him clothes. "He never really wears them." But he does wear clothes from his own mother, she said, including that blue snow jacket.

"She seems to know what he likes to wear, which is good I guess," she said.

Arianna doesn't recall the barn jacket's price, but she says she can't imagine she spent more than $200 on the gift. What she does know is this: Before the campaign, the jacket didn't get quite as much use. "Until this election he probably only wore it to nice things. It's funny to see it all the time."

Margin notes:

So does a fashion consultant, who offers a useful contrast.

Teitell confirms that the jacket was a gift from the candidate's daughter.

While the jacket may not have been purchased with prior intentions, it could still have become part of a deliberate campaign strategy.

Assignments

1. **Analysis of an Advertisement:** Using Seth Stevenson's "Ad Report Card: Can Cougars Sell Cough Drops?" on p. 253 as a model, write your own critical analysis of a single ad or full ad campaign you find worthy of attention. Choose a fresh campaign, one that hasn't yet received much commentary.

2. **Analysis of an Argument:** Browse recent news or popular-interest magazines (such as *Time, The Atlantic, GQ, The New Yorker,* and so on) to locate a serious article you find especially well argued and persuasive. Like Matthew James Nance in "A Mockery of Justice" (p. 264), study the piece carefully enough to understand the techniques it uses to influence readers. Then write a rhetorical analysis in which you make and support a specific claim about the rhetorical strategies of the piece.

3. **Cultural Analysis:** Identify a cultural phenomenon (TV talent shows), theme (men who won't grow up), trend (divorce parties) or image (disaster photos) and examine the way it either influences society or reflects the way that people are thinking or behaving. Make the analysis rhetorical by focusing on questions related to audience, social context, techniques of persuasion, or language. Help readers to see your subject in a new light or from a fresh perspective. Use J. Reagan Tankersley's "Humankind's Ouroboros" (p. 270) as a starting point.

4. **Analysis of a Visual Text:** Identify a physical object that has taken on a special symbolic or persuasive value not connected with its original purpose or use. Then examine it the way Beth Teitell looks into Scott Brown's jacket in "A Jacket of the People" (p. 279)—though your paper might move beyond reporting facts to become an argument with a specific claim. The trick will be to find an iconic object to write about: They can become so deeply embedded in our culture that we cease to notice their symbolic importance. Consider Mickey Mouse, Air Force One, a Yankee's baseball cap, the Starbucks logo, throwaway plastic shopping bags, Darth Vader's mask, the Duke's Dodge Charger, and so on.

    Alternatively, study the home page of an important institutional Web site to determine what signals its design sends to users. Examine all of its elements carefully, from the content on the page to its structure, design elements, images, colors, links, usability, and so on. Decide upon the qualities the site conveys, such as authority, credibility, power, competence, friendliness, danger, welcome, or warning. Then compose a piece in which you support a thesis about the rhetoric of the site design.

5. **Your Choice:** Fed up by the blustering of a talk-show host, political figure, op-ed columnist, local editorialist, or stupid advertiser? Try an item-by-item or paragraph-by-paragraph refutation of such a target, taking on his or her poorly reasoned claims, inadequate evidence, emotional excesses, or lack of credibility. Try to find a transcript or reproduction of the text you want to refute so that you can work from the facts just as they have been offered. If you are examining a visual text you can reproduce electronically, experiment with using callouts to annotate the problems as you find them.

Special Assignments

2

Need a form you don't see here? Try "Genres," p. 2.

How to start
● **Got a test tomorrow?**
Read exam questions carefully. See page 285.

9

Essay Examinations

require
answers
written
within a
time limit

Essay examinations test not only your knowledge of a subject but also your ability to write about it coherently and professionally.

● For a class in nursing, you must write a short essay about the role health-care providers play in dealing with patients who have been victims of domestic abuse.

● For an examination in a literature class, you must offer a close reading of a sonnet, explicating its argument and poetic images line by line.

● For a standardized test, you must read a passage by a critic of globalization and respond to the case made and evidence presented.

● For a psychology exam, you must explore the ethical issues raised by two research articles on brain research and the nature of consciousness.

UNDERSTANDING ESSAY EXAMS   You've probably taken enough essay exams to know that there are no magic bullets to slay this dragon, and that the best approach is to know your material well enough to make several credible points in an hour or so. You must also write—*under pressure*—coherent sentences and paragraphs. ○ Here are some specific strategies to increase your odds of doing well.

got a test ◀ tomorrow?

Anticipate the types of questions you might be asked.   What happens in class—the concepts presented, the issues raised, the assignments given—is like a coming-attractions trailer for an exam. If you attend class regularly and do the required readings, you'll figure out at least some of an instructor's habitual moves and learn something to boot. Review any sample essay exams too—they may even be available on a course Web site.

Read exam questions carefully.   Underscore key words such as *divide*, *classify*, *evaluate*, *compare*, *compare and contrast*, and *analyze* and then respect the differences between these strategies. ○ Exam questions may be short essays themselves, setting out background information or offering a passage to read before the actual query appears. Respond to that specific question and not to your own take on any preliminary materials.

Sketch out a plan for your essay(s).   The first part of the plan should deal with *time*. Read all the exam questions carefully and then estimate how many minutes to spend on each—understanding that some will take more effort than others. (Pay attention to point totals too: Focus on essay questions that count more, but don't ignore any. Five points is five points.) Allow time for planning and editing each answer. Sketch outlines and come up with a thesis for each question. ○ Then stick to your time limits.

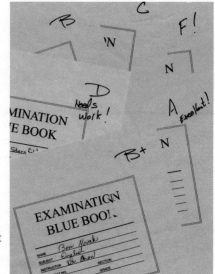

Organize your answer strategically.   If any form of writing benefits from a pattern of development worn like an exoskeleton, it's a response to an essay question. In your first paragraph, state your main point and preview the structure of the whole essay. That way, even if you cannot finish, a reader will know where you were heading and possibly give you partial credit for incomplete work.

improve your
sentences p. 444

develop a draft
p. 398

develop a statement
p. 393

Offer strong evidence for your claims.   The overall structure of the essay should convey your grasp of concepts—your ability to see the big picture. Within that structure, arrange details and evidence to show your command of the subject. Use memorable examples culled from class reading to make your points: Cite important names, concepts, and dates; mention critical issues and terms; rattle off the accurate titles of books and articles.

Come to a conclusion.   Even if you run short on time, find a moment to write a paragraph that brings your ideas together. Don't just repeat the topic sentences of your paragraphs. A reader will already have those ideas firmly in mind as he or she judges your work. So add something new—an implication or extrapolation—to chew on. ○

Keep the tone serious.   Write essay examinations in a high or middle style. ○ Avoid a personal point of view unless the question invites you to enter your opinion on a controversy. Given the press of time, you can probably get away with contractions and some standard abbreviations. But make sure the essay reads like prose, not a text message.

Don't panic.   Keep your eye on the clock, but *don't panic*. Everyone else is working under the same constraints and will be able to produce only so much prose in an hour or two. If you've prepared for the exam and start with a plan, you may find first-rate ideas materializing in the process of writing. Even if they don't, keep writing. You'll get no credit for blank pages.

Your Turn   Preparing for an examination now? Take a moment to list *from memory* as many of the key names, titles, and concepts likely to appear on that exam as you can—terms you are certain to need when you compose your essays. Then check these terms as you have written them down against the way they appear in your notes or textbooks, or on the course Web site. Have you gotten the names and titles right? Have you phrased the concepts correctly, and can you explain what they mean? Just as important, as you review your course materials, do you notice any important ideas that should have made your list, but didn't?

---

shape an ending
p. 425

refine your tone
p. 432

Wade Lamb offered the following response to this essay question on a midterm essay examination in a course entitled Classical to Modern Rhetoric:

> The structure of Plato's *Phaedrus* is dominated by three speeches about the lover and non-lover—one by Lysias and two by Socrates. How do these speeches differ in their themes and strategies, and what point do they make about rhetoric and truth?

Lamb 1

Wade Lamb

Professor Karishky

Rhetoric 101

September 19, 20--

    Plato's *Phaedrus* is unique among Platonic dialogues because it takes place in a rural setting between only two characters—Socrates and the youth Phaedrus. It is, however, like Plato's *Gorgias* in that it is "based on a distinction between knowledge and belief" and focuses on some of the ways we can use rhetoric to seek the truth.

    The first speech presented in *Phaedrus*, written by Lysias and read aloud by Phaedrus, is the simplest of the three. Composed by Lysias to demonstrate the power of rhetoric to persuade an audience, it claims perversely that it is better to have a sexual relationship with someone who doesn't love you than someone who does.

    Socrates responds with a speech of his own making the same point, which he composes on the spot, but which he describes as "a greater lie than Lysias's." Unlike Lysias,

---

Opening focuses directly on issues posed in question.

Short quotation functions as piece of evidence.

Sensibly organized around three speeches to be examined: one paragraph per speech.

Lamb 2

however, Socrates begins by carefully defining his terms and organizes his speech more effectively. He does so to teach Phaedrus that in order to persuade an audience, an orator must first understand the subject and divide it into its appropriate parts. However, Socrates delivers this speech with a veil over his head because he knows that what he and Lysias have claimed about love is false.

The third speech—again composed by Socrates—is the most important. In it, Socrates demonstrates that persuasion that leads merely to belief (not truth) damages both the orator and the audience. He compares rhetoric such as that used by Lysias to the unconcerned and harmful lust of a non-lover. Good rhetoric, on the other hand—which Socrates says is persuasion that leads to knowledge—is like the true lover who seeks to lead his beloved to transcendent truth. Socrates shows that he believes good rhetoric should ultimately be concerned with finding and teaching truth, not just with making a clever argument someone might falsely believe, as Lysias's speech does.

By comparing the three speeches in *Phaedrus*, Plato shows that he gives some value to rhetoric, but not in the form practiced by orators such as Lysias. Plato emphasizes the importance of the distinction between belief and knowledge and argues that rhetoric should search for and communicate the truth.

Most important speech gets lengthiest and most detailed treatment.

Conclusion states Lamb's thesis, describing the point he believes Plato wished to make about rhetoric in *Phaedrus*.

Getting the details right

Allow a few minutes near the end of the exam period to reread what you have written and insert corrections and emendations. You won't have time to fix large-scale issues: If you've confused the Spanish Armada with Torquemada, you're toast. But a quick edit may catch embarrassing gaffes or omissions. When you write quickly, you probably leave out or transpose some words or simply use the wrong expression. Take a moment to edit these fixable errors. In the process, you may also amplify or repair an idea or two. Here are some other useful strategies to follow.

Use transition words and phrases.   Essay examinations are the perfect place to employ such transparent transitional devices as *first, second*, and *third*, or *next, even more important, nonetheless, in summary, in conclusion*, and so on. Don't be subtle: The transitions guide you as you write and help keep your instructor on track later. ○ You will seem to be in control of your material.

Do a quick check of grammar, mechanics, and spelling.   Some instructors take great offense at mechanical slips, even minor ones. At a minimum, avoid the common errors covered in Part 9 of this book. Also be sure to spell correctly any names and concepts that you've been reviewing in preparation for the examination. ○ It's *Macbeth*, not *McBeth*.

Write legibly or print.   Few people do much handwriting anymore. But essay examinations still often use paper or blue books. If you are out of practice or your handwriting is just flat-out illegible, print. Printing takes more time, but instructors appreciate the effort. Write in ink, as pencil can be faint and hard to read. Also consider double-spacing your essay to allow room for corrections and additions. But be careful not to spread your words too far apart. A blue book with just a few sentences per page undermines your ethos: It looks juvenile.

revise and edit
p. 452

help with common
errors p. 600

How to start ● **Confused?**

Read the assignment carefully. See page 292.

10 Position Papers

require a
brief critical
response

A course instructor may ask you to respond to an assigned reading, lecture, film, or other activity with a position paper in which you record your reactions to the material—such as your impressions or observations. Such a paper is usually brief—often not much longer than a page or two—and due the next class session. Typically, you won't have time for more than a draft and quick revision.

● You summarize and assess the findings of a journal article studying the relationship between a full night's sleep and student success on college exams.

● You speculate about how a feminist philosopher of science, whose work you have read for a class, might react to recent developments in genetics.

● You respond to ideas raised by a panel of your classmates discussing a proposition to restore the military draft or require an alternative form of national service.

● You offer a gut reaction to your first-ever viewing of *Triumph of the Will*, a notorious propaganda film made by director Leni Riefenstahl for Germany's National Socialist (Nazi) Party in 1935.

UNDERSTANDING POSITION PAPERS   Instructors usually have several goals in assigning position papers: to focus your attention on a particular reading or class presentation; to measure how well you've understood course materials; to push you to connect one concept or reading with another. Because they may want you to take some risks, instructors often mark position papers less completely than full essays and grade them by different standards.

You might be tempted to blow off these assignments because they can seem like quick, low-stakes items. That would be an error. Position papers give you practice in writing about a subject and so prepare you for other papers and exams. The assignments *may* even preview the types of essay questions an instructor favors. Position papers also help to establish your ethos in a course, marking you as a careful reader and thinker or, alternatively, someone just along for the ride.

Use a few simple strategies to write a strong position paper.

Protesters Taking a Position   While some feel that security cameras ensure safety, others believe them to be an invasion of privacy.

▶ confused?

Read the assignment carefully.   Understand exactly what your instructor wants: Look for key words such as *summarize, describe, classify, evaluate, compare, compare and contrast,* and *analyze* and then respect the differences between them. ○

Review assigned material carefully.   Consider photocopying readings so that you can annotate their margins or underscore key claims and evidence. Practice smart reading: Always look for conflicts, points of difference, or issues raised in class or in the public arena—what some writers call *hooks*. Then use the most provocative material to jump-start your own thinking, using whatever brainstorming techniques work best for you. ○

Mine the texts for evidence.   Identify key passages worth quoting or features worth describing in detail. ○ Anchor your position paper around such strong passages. For instance, you may find some facts in the piece startling enough to mention, a claim or two you resist fiercely and want to dispute, or concise summaries of complicated positions you admire. Be sure, too, you know how to merge quoted material smoothly with your own writing.

Organize the paper sensibly.   Unless the assignment specifically states otherwise, don't write the position paper off the top of your head. Take the time to offer a thesis or to set up a comparison, an evaluation, or another structure of organization. Give a position paper the same structural integrity you would a longer and more consequential assignment.

Here's a position paper written by Heidi Rogers as an early assignment in a lower-level course on visual rhetoric. Rogers's assignment was to offer an honest response to director Leni Riefenstahl's infamous documentary, *Triumph of the Will*, which showcases the National Socialist Party rallies in Munich in 1934. In the film, we see the German people embracing Hitler and his Nazi regime as they consolidate their power.

develop a draft
p. 398

get an idea
p. 356

use quotations
p. 497

Rogers 1

Heidi Rogers

Professor Wachtel

Writing 203

September 22, 20--

Triumph of the Lens

The 1935 film *Triumph of the Will*, directed by Leni Riefenstahl, masterfully shows how visuals can be a powerful form of rhetoric. In the documentary we see Adolf Hitler, one of the greatest mass murderers in history, portrayed as an inspirational leader who could be the savior of Germany. Watching the film, I was taken aback. I am supposed to detest Hitler for his brutal crimes against humanity, and yet I found myself liking him, even smiling as he greets his fellow Germans on the streets of Munich. How did Riefenstahl accomplish this, drawing viewers into her film and giving Germans such pride in their leader?

Riefenstahl's technique is to layer selected visuals so as to evoke the emotions she wants her audience to feel toward Hitler and his regime. Her first step is to introduce images of nature and locations that are peaceful and soothing. Next, she inserts images of the German people themselves: children playing, women blowing kisses to Hitler, men in uniform proudly united under the Nazi flag. The next step is to weave images of Hitler himself among these German people, so that even when he isn't smiling or showing any emotions, it seems as if he is conveying the happiness, pride, or strength evoked

Offers a thesis to explain how film makes Hitler attractive.

To explain how film works, describes pattern she sees in Riefenstahl's editing technique.

Triumph of the Will features numerous imposing shots of crowds cheering for Hitler.

Rogers 2

by the images edited around him. The final piece of the puzzle is always to put Hitler front and center, usually giving a rousing speech, which makes him seem larger than life.

A good example of this technique comes during the youth rally sequence. First, Riefenstahl presents peaceful images of the area around the Munich stadium, including beautiful trees with the sun streaming between the branches. We then see the vastness of the city stadium, designed by Hitler himself. Then we watch thousands of young boys and girls smiling and cheering in the stands. These masses erupt when Hitler enters the arena and Riefenstahl artfully juxtaposes images of him, usually with a cold, emotionless face, with enthusiastic youth looking up to him as if he were a god. Hitler then delivers an intoxicating speech about the future of Germany and the greatness that the people will achieve under his leadership. The crowd goes wild as he leaves the stage and we see an audience filled with awe and purpose.

What Riefenstahl did in *Triumph of the Will* is a common technique in film editing. When you have to reach a massive audience, you want to cover all of your bases and appeal to all of them at once. Therefore, the more kinds of *ethos*, *pathos*, and *logos* you can layer onto a piece of film, the better your chances will be of convincing the greatest number of people of your cause. As hard as this is to admit, if I had lived in a devastated 1935 Germany and I had seen this film, I might have wanted this guy to lead my country too.

Provides extended example to support claim about how *Triumph of the Will* was edited.

Explores implications of claim — that clever editing enabled Riefenstahl to reach many audiences.

Getting the details right

Edit the final version. Edit and proofread your text carefully before you turn it in. ○ Think of a position paper as a trial run for a longer paper. As such, it should follow the conventions of any given field or major. Even when an instructor seems casual about the assignment, don't ease up.

Identify key terms and concepts and use them correctly and often. The instructor may be checking to see how carefully you read. So, in your paper, make a point of referring to the new concepts or terms you've found in your reading, as Rogers does with *ethos*, *pathos*, and *logos* in her essay.

Treat your sources appropriately. Either identify them by author and title within the paper or list them at the end in the correct documentation form (e.g., MLA or APA). Make sure quotations are set up accurately, properly introduced, and documented. Offer page numbers for any direct quotations. ○

Spell names and concepts correctly. You lose credibility if you misspell technical terms or proper nouns that appear throughout the course readings. In literary papers especially, get characters' names and book titles right.

Respond to your colleagues' work. Position papers are often posted to electronic discussion boards to jump-start conversations. So take the opportunity to reply substantively to what your classmates have written. Don't just say "I agree" or "You're kidding!" Add good reasons and evidence to your remarks. Remember, too, that your instructor may review these comments, looking for evidence of engagement with the course material. ○

Your Turn Many blogs encourage readers to comment on their postings. You can use such sites to practice your skill at responding to what you read. On a news or cultural blog you scan regularly, locate a fairly lengthy and serious article to which some readers have already offered substantive responses, more than a line or two. After reading the article, think about what you might post in response. Then read through the actual postings. How does your brief response compare with what others have said? What strategies have they used that you admire? How did the best responders establish their credibility? And which responders did you take less seriously *and why?*

Chances are you'll be disappointed in much of what you read in online commentary. People may respond from prejudiced positions, focus on irrelevant points, or take personal potshots at the original author. But from such respondents, you may learn what *not* to do in a serious academic paper.

---

revise and edit
p. 452

understand citation
styles p. 501

comment
p. 458

11

Annotated Bibliographies

summarize
and assess
sources

When preparing a term paper, senior thesis, or other lengthy research project, an instructor may expect you to submit an annotated bibliography. The bibliography may be due weeks before you turn in the paper, or it may be turned in with the finished project.

● A sociology instructor asks that your topic proposal for a midterm paper on rural poverty include an annotated bibliography that demonstrates a range of perspectives in your reading.

● Your senior history thesis is based upon letters and archival materials found only in a local museum. So you attach an annotated bibliography to your completed project to give readers a clearer sense of what some of the handwritten documents cover.

● In writing a term paper on the cultural roots and connections of gangsta/reality rap, you decide to annotate your works cited items to let readers know what sources you found most authoritative and useful for future research.

UNDERSTANDING ANNOTATED BIBLIOGRAPHIES   An annotated bibliography is an alphabetical list of the sources and documents you have used in developing a research project, with each item in the list summarized and, very often, evaluated.

Instructors usually ask you to attach an annotated bibliography to the final version of a project, enabling them to determine at a glance how well you've researched your subject. But some may ask you to submit an annotated bibliography earlier in the writing process—sometimes even as part of the topic proposal—to be sure you're on track, poring over good materials, and getting the most out of them. ○

Begin with an accurate bibliography of research materials.   Items in the alphabetical list should follow the guidelines of some documentation system, typically MLA or APA. In a paper using MLA documentation, the list is labeled "Works Cited" and includes only books, articles, and other materials actually mentioned in the project; it is labeled "Works Consulted" if you also want to include works you've read, but not actually cited. In APA-style projects, the list is called "References." ○

need to write ◀
a summary?

Describe or summarize the content of each item in the bibliography.   These summaries should be *very* brief, often just one or two sentences. Begin with a brief description of the work if it isn't self-evident (*a review of; an interview with; a CIA report on*). Then, in your own words, describe its contents, scope, audience, perspective, or other features relevant to your project. Your language should be descriptive and neutral. Be sure to follow any special guidelines offered by your instructor. For more about summarizing, see Chapter 45, "Summarizing Sources." ○

plan a project
p. 466

cite in APA
p. 540

understand citation
styles p. 501

Assess the quality or importance of the work.   Immediately follow-ing the summary, offer a brief appraisal of the item, responding to its quality, authority, thoroughness, length, relevance, usefulness, age (e.g., *up-to-date/ dated*), reputation in field (if known), and so on. Your remarks should be professional and academic: You aren't writing a movie review.

Explain the role the work plays in your research.   When an anno-tated bibliography is part of a topic proposal, assess the preliminary materi-als you have found and describe how you expect to use them in your project. Highlight works that seem to provide creative or fresh ideas, authoritative coverage, up-to-date research, diverse perspectives, or ample bibliographies.

The following three items are from an annotated bibliography offered as part of a topic proposal on the cultural impact of the iPod.

Full bibliographical citation in MLA style.

Summary of Stephenson's argument.

Potential role source might play in paper.

Stephenson, Seth. "You and Your Shadow." *Slate.com* 2 Mar. 2004. Web. 3 Mar. 2007. This article from *Slate.com*'s "Ad Report Card" series argues that the original iPod ads featuring silhouetted dancers may alienate viewers by suggesting that the product is cooler than the people who buy it. Stephenson explains why some people may resent the advertisements. The piece may be useful for explaining early reactions to the iPod as a cultural phenomenon.

Evaluation of Sullivan's opinion piece.

Sullivan, Andrew. "Society Is Dead: We Have Retreated into the iWorld." *Sunday Times* 20 Feb. 2005. Web. 27 Feb. 2007. In this opinion piece, Sullivan examines how people in cities use iPods to isolate themselves from their surroundings. The author makes a highly personal, but plausible case for turning off the machines. The column demonstrates how quickly the iPod has changed society and culture.

Citation demonstrates how to cite an article from a database — in this case, *OneFile.*

Walker, Rob. "The Guts of a New Machine." *New York Times Magazine* 30 Nov. 2003. *OneFile.* Web. 1 Mar. 2007. This lengthy report describes in detail how Apple developed the concept and technology of the iPod. Walker not only provides a detailed early look at the product, but also shows how badly Apple's competitors underestimated its market strength. May help to explain Apple's later dominance in smartphones as well.

Getting the details right

Annotated bibliographies can be informative and time-saving documents, as you'll discover if you happen to find a reliable one that covers a subject you are researching. As you prepare such a list, think about how your work might benefit other readers.

Get the information on your sources right.   As you format the items in your list, be sure that the titles, authors, page numbers, and dates are correct so that users can quickly locate the materials you have used.

Follow correct documentation style.   Documentation systems like MLA and APA can seem fussy, but they make life easier for researchers by standardizing the way all the identifying features of a source are treated. So if you get an entry right in your annotated bibliography, you make life easier for the next person who needs to cite that source. ○

Keep your summaries and assessments brief.   Don't get carried away. In most cases, instructors and other readers will want an annotated bibliography that they can scan. They'll appreciate writing that is both precise and succinct.

Follow directions carefully.   Some instructors may provide specific directions for annotated bibliographies, depending on the field or subject of your research. For example, they may ask you to supply the volume numbers, locations, and physical dimensions of books; describe illustrations; and so on.

> **Your Turn**   For a quick exercise in preparing an annotated bibliography, choose a film that has opened very recently, locate five or six reviews or news articles about it, and then prepare an annotated bibliography using these items. Imagine that you'll be writing a research paper about the public and critical reception the film received when it debuted. (Public and critical reaction may be quite different.) Be sure to choose a documentation system for your bibliography and to use it appropriately.

understand citation
styles p. 501

How to start ▶ ● **Need to write a synthesis paper?**
Summarize and paraphrase what you have read.
See page 301.

12 Synthesis Papers

require a response to multiple sources

In some classes, you may be asked to write a synthesis paper—in which you summarize, compare, or assess the views offered by different sources covering a specific topic. (This assignment is sometimes called a "literature review," but here "literature" is used as a general term to describe scholarship in a field; it does not mean you will work only with fiction, poetry, or drama.) A synthesis exercise or literature review prepares you to write on a topic by requiring you to stake out the claims already made by reputable writers, thus enabling you to move the argument forward. It also gives you important practice in using sources.

● In an English class, you review several new claims by writers challenging the authorship of the plays generally ascribed to William Shakespeare.

● For an engineering course, you are asked to prepare a literature review covering the most recently published research on lithium-ion polymer batteries.

● For a first-year writing course, you write a detailed synthesis examining the positions of authors who both support and challenge your view that we must learn to adapt to new media.

● In preparing a prospectus for a senior thesis, you prove your topic is viable by including a section in which you summarize the sources you expect to use and explain the different positions they represent.

UNDERSTANDING SYNTHESIS PAPERS   In a synthesis, you weigh and consider the full range of responsible, fact-based opinion on a subject. For an assignment designed to teach how to use sources, you will ordinarily summarize and analyze a range of reputable authorities. In doing such an exercise, note what types of sources you must review, how to document them, ○ whether you may quote from them, and whether you are expected to develop a thesis derived from the materials you have read.

Need to write a ◄ synthesis paper?

If your assignment is to prepare a review of literature, you will identify and report on the most important books and articles on a subject, usually over a specified period of time: *currently, from the last five years, over the past three decades.* The topic of the review may be assigned to you or be one you are considering for a thesis, term paper, or capstone project. Check whether your synthesis must follow a specific pattern of organization: Most literature reviews are chronological, though some are thematic, and still others are arranged by comparison and contrast. ○

Read reputable sources on your subject.   Synthesis papers almost always involve examining multiple articles, books, and research studies and then describing the relationships between them: *similarity, difference, congruence, divergence, consistency, inconsistency,* and so on. Consult with your instructor or a research librarian to separate mainstream and essential works on your topic from outliers, which may or may not deserve a closer look. Don't offer a thesis until you have carefully weighed the claims, reasons, and evidence in the sources you have examined. ○

In 1993, artists Tibor Kalman and Scott Stowell erected this yellow billboard in New York City's heavily trafficked Times Square perhaps to suggest a world of limitless choices. Exploring a new topic, you face similar possibilities and need to sort them out.

Summarize and paraphrase what you have read.   A typical synthesis assignment moves one step beyond summaries and paraphrases, but you will still need them to provide material for the judgments you make about various sources. (Review these skills, as necessary, in Chapters 45–46.) Summarize the sources you expect to mention briefly and paraphrase those materials you will refer to more extensively or quote from directly.

understand citation
styles p. 501

develop a draft
p. 398

read closely
p. 365

Examine the connections between your sources.   Read the sources you have collected *in relationship to each other* to determine precisely where they stand on a subject or how they affect the development of your own thesis. In particular, identify any sources that help readers understand how an issue is defined or how your own claims and reasons develop logically from ideas and information reported by other writers. Introduce such materials with verbs of attribution such as *describes, reports, points out, asserts, argues, claims, agrees, concurs.*

Acknowledge disagreements and rebuttals.   Your synthesis should summarize and paraphrase any reputable sources that challenge your thesis or, in a review of literature, represent a full range of opinions. Describe all the opinions you encounter accurately, introducing them with verbs of attribution such as *questions, denies, disagrees, contradicts, undermines, disputes, calls into question, takes issue with.*

If you have done an effective synthesis, your review of sources should enrich and complicate your understanding of a subject and prepare you to join an academic discussion already in progress. To give you an idea of how to bring sources into a conversation, we'll build a brief essay from a set of paragraphs drawn from sources focusing on one topic: whether new media technologies like the Web pose a threat to literacy and culture. Ideas that play a role in the essay are highlighted. The sources are presented alphabetically by author:

> I ask my students about their reading habits, and though I'm not surprised to find that few read newspapers or print magazines, many check in with online news sources, aggregate sites, incessantly. They are seldom away from their screens for long, but that's true of us, their parents, as well.
>
> – Sven Birkerts, "Reading in a Digital Age"

> The picture emerging from the research is deeply troubling, at least to anyone who values the depth, rather than just the velocity, of human thought. People who read text studded with links, the studies show, comprehend less than those who read traditional linear text. People who watch busy multimedia presentations remember less than those who take in information in a more sedate and focused manner. People who are continually distracted by emails, alerts and other messages understand less than those who are able to

restate ideas
p. 494

concentrate. And people who juggle many tasks are less creative and less productive than those who do one thing at a time.

It is this control, this mental discipline, that we are at risk of losing as we spend ever more time scanning and skimming online. If the slow progression of words across printed pages damped our craving to be inundated by mental stimulation, the Internet indulges it. It returns us to our native state of distractedness, while presenting us with far more distractions than our ancestors ever had to contend with.

— Nicholas Carr, "Does the Internet Make You Dumber?"

Today some 4.5 billion digital screens illuminate our lives. Words have migrated from wood pulp to pixels on computers, phones, laptops, game consoles, televisions, billboards and tablets. Letters are no longer fixed in black ink on paper, but flitter on a glass surface in a rainbow of colors as fast as our eyes can blink. Screens fill our pockets, briefcases, dashboards, living room walls and the sides of buildings. They sit in front of us when we work — regardless of what we do. We are now people of the screen. And of course, these newly ubiquitous screens have changed how we read and write.

— Kevin Kelly, "Reading in a Whole New Way"

I have been reading a lot on my iPad recently, and I have some complaints — not about the iPad but about the state of digital reading generally. Reading is a subtle thing, and its subtleties are artifacts of a venerable medium: words printed in ink on paper. Glass and pixels aren't the same.

— Verlyn Klinkenborg, "Further Thoughts of a Novice E-Reader"

The new media have caught on for a reason. Knowledge is increasing exponentially; human brainpower and waking hours are not. Fortunately, the Internet and information technologies are helping us manage, search and retrieve our collective intellectual output at different scales, from Twitter and previews to e-books and online encyclopedias. Far from making us stupid, these technologies are the only things that will keep us smart.

— Steven Pinker, "Mind over Mass Media"

No teenager that I know of regularly reads a newspaper, as most do not have the time and cannot be bothered to read pages and pages of text while they could watch the news summarized on the Internet or on TV.

— Matthew Robson, "How Teenagers Consume Media"

Then again, perhaps we will simply adjust and come to accept what James called "acquired inattention." E-mails pouring in, cell phones ringing, televisions blaring, podcasts streaming—all this may become background noise, like the "din of a foundry or factory" that James observed workers could scarcely avoid at first, but which eventually became just another part of their daily routine. For the younger generation of multitaskers, the great electronic din is an expected part of everyday life. And given what neuroscience and anecdotal evidence have shown us, this state of constant intentional self-distraction could well be of profound detriment to individual and cultural well-being. When people do their work only in the "interstices of their mind-wandering," with crumbs of attention rationed out among many competing tasks, their culture may gain in information, but it will surely weaken in wisdom.

—Christine Rosen, "The Myth of Multitasking"

The past was not as golden, nor is the present as tawdry, as the pessimists suggest, but the only thing really worth arguing about is the future. It is our misfortune, as a historical generation, to live through the largest expansion in expressive capability in human history, a misfortune because abundance breaks more things than scarcity. We are now witnessing the rapid stress of older institutions accompanied by the slow and fitful development of cultural alternatives. Just as required education was a response to print, using the Internet well will require new cultural institutions as well, not just new technologies.

—Clay Shirky, "Does the Internet Make You Smarter?"

Both Carr and Rosen are right about one thing: The changeover to digital reading brings challenges and changes, requiring a reconsideration of what books are and what they're supposed to do. That doesn't mean the shift won't be worth it. The change will also bring innovations impossible on Gutenberg's printed page, from text mixed with multimedia to components that allow readers to interact with the author and fellow consumers.

—Peter Suderman, "Don't Fear the E-Reader"

Here is a brief paper that synthesizes the positions represented in the preceding sources, quoting extensively from them and leading up to a thesis. We have boldfaced the authors' names the first time they appear, to emphasize the number of sources used in this short example.

Chiu 1

Lauren Chiu

Professor Larondo

Writing 203

March 19, 20--

Time to Adapt?

There is considerable agreement that the Internet and other electronic media are changing the way people read, write, think, and behave. Scholars such as **Sven Birkerts** report that their students do not seem to read printed materials anymore, a fact confirmed by fifteen-year-old intern **Matthew Robson**, when asked by his employer Morgan Stanley to describe the media habits of teenagers in England: "No teenager that I know of regularly reads a newspaper, as most do not have the time and cannot be bothered to read pages and pages of text."

But the changes we are experiencing may be more significant than just students abandoning the printed word. Working with an iPad, for instance, makes **Verlyn Klinkenborg** wonder whether reading on a screen may actually be a different and less perceptive experience than reading on paper. More worrisome, **Nicholas Carr** points to a growing body of research suggesting that the cognitive abilities of those who use media frequently may actually be degraded, weakening their comprehension and concentration. Yet, according to **Clay Shirky**, the Internet is increasing our ability to communicate immeasurably, and so we simply have to deal with whatever consequences follow from such a major shift in technology.

Two sources are cited to support a general claim about the media.

Other authorities amplify and complicate the issue.

Carr and Shirky are well-known authors with opposing views of the Web.

Chiu 2

Thinkers like Shirky argue that we do not, in fact, have any choice but to adapt to such changes.

Even **Christine Rosen**, a critic of technology, acknowledges that people will likely have to adjust to their diminished attention spans (110). After all, are there really any alternatives to the speed, convenience, and power of the new technologies when we have become what **Kevin Kelly** describes as "people of the screen" and are no more likely to return to paper for reading than we are to vinyl for music recordings? Fears of the Internet may be overblown too. **Peter Suderman** observes that changes in media allow us to do vastly more than we can with print alone. Moreover, because the sheer amount of knowledge is increasing so quickly, **Steven Pinker** argues that we absolutely need the new ways of communicating: "these technologies are the only things that will keep us smart."

We cannot, however, ignore voices of caution. The differences Carr describes between habits of deep reading and skimming are especially troubling because so many users of the Web have experienced them. And who can doubt the loss of seriousness in our public and political discussions these days? Maybe Rosen *is* right when she worries that our culture is trading wisdom for a glut of information. But it seems more likely that society will be better off trying to fix the problems electronic media are causing than imagining that we can return to simpler technologies that have already just about vanished.

In a full-length essay, this section would be much longer and quote more sources.

Concerns about the Web are portrayed as reasonable.

The writer states a thesis that might guide a longer analysis.

Chiu 3

Works Cited

Birkerts, Sven. "Reading in a Digital Age." *The American Scholar*. Phi Beta Kappa, Spring 2010. Web. 10 Sept. 2010.

Carr, Nicholas. "Does the Internet Make You Dumber?" *Wall Street Journal*. Wall Street Journal, 5 June 2010. Web. 9 Sept. 2010.

Kelly, Kevin. "Reading in a Whole New Way." *Smithsonian .com*. Smithsonian, Aug. 2010. Web. 13 Sept. 2010.

Klinkenborg, Verlyn. "Further Thoughts of a Novice E-Reader." *New York Times*. New York Times, 28 May 2010. Web. 12 Sept. 2010.

Pinker, Steven. "Mind over Mass Media." *New York Times*. New York Times, 10 June 2010. Web. 12 Sept. 2010.

Robson, Matthew. "How Teenagers Consume Media." *Guardian .co.uk*. Guardian News and Media, 13 July 2009. Web. 14 Sept. 2010.

Rosen, Christine. "The Myth of Multitasking." *The New Atlantis* 20 (Spring 2008): 105–110. Print.

Shirky, Clay. "Does the Internet Make You Smarter?" *Wall Street Journal*. Wall Street Journal, 4 June 2010. Web. 9 Sept. 2010.

Suderman, Peter. "Don't Fear the E-Reader." *Reason.com*. Reason Magazine, 23 Mar. 2010. Web. 11 Sept. 2010.

Getting the details right

Although synthesis assignments vary enormously, certain fine points are worth remembering.

Introduce materials that provide a context for your topic.   Open a synthesis paper by mentioning sources that help to shape your topic, place the subject in its historical or cultural contexts, and provide a rationale for your project. Look for authors or materials that help readers understand why an issue is important.

Cite materials that explain or complicate your thesis.   Introduce any writers whose ideas amplify or expand an issue you want to explore. In particular, look for authors who grab your attention or get cited as authorities in other materials. Summarize these materials adequately, yet concisely. In the preceding example, we are limited to only a sentence or two of discussion, but in a full essay your presentation would offer much more detail.

Don't rush to judgment.   In synthesizing, writers sometimes divide their sources too conveniently between those that support a claim and those that oppose it, ignoring complications and subtleties. Quite often, the most interesting relationships are to be found in places where belligerent authors unexpectedly agree or orthodox research generates unexpected results. When synthesizing sources for an assignment or a research project, don't precook the results or try to fit your materials into an existing framework.

Tell a story.   Whether your synthesis merely summarizes varying points of view or defends a thesis statement, create a narrative readers can follow. ○ Help them to understand the issues as you have come to appreciate them yourself. Separate major issues from minor ones, and use transitions as necessary to establish connections (*consequently*), highlight contrasts (*on the other hand*), show parallels (*similarly*), and so on.

Cite materials that support your thesis.   If you've done your job well, any thesis you derive from reading sources should do more than just echo opinions you have found in your research. But be sure to cite those writers who support or amplify your ideas.

understand narratives
p. 4

Acknowledge materials that run counter to your thesis.   The voices hardest to bring into your work may be those that disagree with you. Yet in academic and professional writing, you must not only acknowledge these dissenters, but also outline their ideas objectively and introduce any quotations from them fairly (Rosen *says*, not Rosen *whines*). ○

Pay attention to language.   Remember that the summaries of materials you cite should be in your own words; some synthesis assignments may even preclude direct quotations. If you do quote from sources, choose statements that cogently represent the positions of your sources.
    Keep the style of your synthesis objective, neutral, and fairly formal. In most cases, avoid *I* when summarizing and paraphrasing. ○

Be sure to document your sources.   Keep track of all the materials you consult and be prepared to document them fully in an academic paper.

> **Your Turn**   All the sources from which the paragraphs in this section come are available online. Choose two or three of them and write a detailed synthesis of their full positions, being sure to highlight the similarities and/or differences. For this exercise, you need not state a position of your own, nor should you criticize or slant your presentation of the source material. Keep your analysis as neutral and objective as you can, *especially* if you find yourself taking sides. When you are done, a reader should have some sense of the overall media controversy that these pieces address, but have no idea where you might stand.

use quotations
p. 497

refine your tone
p. 432

E-mails

communicate
electronically

E-mail has quickly become the preferred method for most business (and personal) communication because it is quick, efficient, easy to archive, and easy to search.

- You write to the coordinator of the writing center to apply for a job as a tutor, courtesy copying the message to a professor who has agreed to serve as a reference.

- You send an e-mail to classmates in a writing class, looking for someone to collaborate on a Web project.

- You e-mail the entire College of Liberal Arts faculty to invite them to attend a student production of Chekhov's *Uncle Vanya*.

- You e-mail a complaint to your cable supplier because a premium sports channel you subscribe to has been unavailable for a week.

UNDERSTANDING E-MAIL   E-mail is now so common and informal that writers take it for granted, forgetting the role e-mail can play when transacting business. Though usually composed quickly, e-mails have a long shelf life once they're archived. They can also spread well beyond their original audiences. Remember, too, that e-mails can be printed and filed as hard copy.

You probably know how to handle personal e-mails well enough. But you may not be as savvy about the more specialized messages you send to organizations, businesses, professors, groups of classmates, and so on. The following strategies will help.

Explain your purpose clearly and logically.   Use both the subject line and first paragraph of an e-mail to explain your reason for writing: Be specific about names, titles, dates, places, and so on, especially when your message opens a discussion. Write your message so that it will still make sense a year or more later, specifying references and pronouns (*we, it, them*). ○

Tell readers what you want them to do.   Lay out a clear agenda for accomplishing one task: Ask for a document, a response, or a reply by a specific date. If you have multiple requests to make of a single person or group, consider writing separate e-mails. It's easier to track short, single-purpose e-mails than to deal with complex documents requiring several different actions.

help with common
errors p. 600

Write for intended and unintended audiences.   The specific audience in the "To" line is usually the only audience for your message. But e-mail is more public than traditional surface mail, easily duplicated and sent to whole networks of recipients with just a click. So compose your business e-mails as if they *might* be read by everyone in a unit or even published in a local paper. Assume that nothing in business e-mail is private.

Minimize the clutter.   When e-mails run through a series of replies, they grow so thick with headers, copied messages, and signatures that any new message can be hard to find. Make the latest message stand out, perhaps separating it slightly from the headers and transmission data.

Keep your messages brief.   Lengthy blocks of e-mail prose without paragraph breaks irritate readers. Indeed, meandering or chatty e-mails in business situations can make a writer seem disorganized and out of control. Try to limit your e-mail messages to what fits on a single screen. If you can't, use headings, spacing, and color to create visual pauses—but remember that many people now view e-mail on mobile devices. Keep messages simple. O

Distribute your messages sensibly.   Send a copy of an e-mail to any-one directly involved in the message, as well as to those who might need to be informed. For example, if filing a grade complaint with an instructor, you may also copy the chair of his or her academic department or the dean of students. But don't let the copy (Cc) and blind copy (Bcc) lines in the e-mail header tempt you to send messages beyond the essential audience.

Here's a fairly informal e-mail announcing a weekend trip, written to members of a department. Despite the relaxed event it describes, the e-mail still provides clear and direct information, gets to the point quickly, and offers an agenda for action.

think visually
p. 592

Sent: September 7, 2011
To: DRW Faculty
From: John Ruszkiewicz
Subject: Annual Big Bend Trip
Cc: Alumni in Rhetoric
Bcc:
Attachments:

> Clear, specific subject line
> makes message easy to
> find and search: Key search
> term would be "Big Bend."

Dear Colleagues–

> Business letters use colon
> after greeting, but e-mails
> are often less formal.

The Division of Rhetoric and Writing's eighth annual Big Bend trip is scheduled for October 7–10, 2011, at Big Bend National Park in West Texas. If you are considering making the trip this year, please let me know by e-mail and I will put you on the mailing list.

> Opening paragraph
> explains point of e-mail and
> what colleagues should do.

You should know that the trip is neither an official DRW event, nor highly organized – just a group of colleagues enjoying the best natural environment Texas has to offer for a few days. If you've been to Big Bend, you know what to expect. If you haven't, see <http://www.nps.gov/bibe/index.htm>.

> Second paragraph provides
> background information for
> readers who haven't been
> on trip before—including
> helpful Web link.

The weather at Big Bend in October is usually splendid. I say "usually" because we had heavy rains a few years ago and even an ice storm once. But such precipitation is rare: It is a desert park.

> Tone is professional, but
> casual, and language
> is tight and correct. No
> emoticons.

In the past, most people have camped at the campground, which is first come, first serve. Lodging may be available in the park itself, but rooms are hard to get throughout the fall season. Also available are hotels in nearby Study Butte, Terlingua, and Lajitas.

I'll contact those interested in the trip in a few weeks. We can begin then to plan sharing rides and equipment. And please let other friends of the DRW know about the trip.

> Final paragraph outlines
> subsequent actions, letting
> readers know what to
> expect.

Best,
JR

John Ruszkiewicz, Professor
The University of Texas at Austin
Department of Rhetoric and Writing
Austin, TX
Phone: (512) 555-1234

> Signature is complete,
> opening various routes for
> communication.

Getting the details right

▶ want to get the
reader's attention?

Because most people receive e-mail messages frequently, make any you send easy to process.

Choose a sensible subject line.   The subject line should clearly identify the topic and include helpful keywords that might later be searched. If your e-mail is specifically about a grading policy, your student loan, or mold in your gym locker, make sure a word you'll recall afterward—like *policy, loan,* or *mold*—gets in the subject line. In professional e-mails, subjects such as *A question, Hi!* or *Meeting* are useless.

Arrange your text sensibly.   You can do almost as much visually in e-mail as you can in a word-processing program, including choosing fonts, inserting lines, and adding color, images, and videos. But because so many people now read their messages on mobile devices, a simple block style with spaces between single-spaced paragraphs probably works best for most messages.

Check the recipient list before you hit send.   Routinely double-check all the recipient fields—especially when you're replying to a message. The original writer **may** have copied the message widely: Do you want to send your reply to that entire group or just to the original writer?

Include an appropriate signature.   Professional e-mail of any kind should include a signature that identifies you and provides contact information readers need. Your e-mail address alone may not be clear enough to identify who you are, especially if you are writing to your instructor. Be sure to set up a signature for your laptop, desktop, or mobile device.

But be careful: You may not want to provide readers with a *home* phone number or address since you don't know precisely who may see your e-mail message. When you send e-mail, the recipient can reach you simply by replying.

Consider, too, that a list of incoming e-mails on a cell phone typically previews just the first few lines of a message. If you want a reader's attention, make your point quickly.

Use standard grammar. Professional e-mails should be almost as polished as business letters: At least give readers the courtesy of a quick review to catch humiliating gaffes or misspellings. ○ Emoticons and smiley faces have also disappeared from most professional communications.

Have a sensible e-mail address. You might enjoy communicating with friends as HorribleHagar or DaisyGirl, but such an e-mail signature will undermine your credibility with a professor or potential employer. Save the oddball name for a private e-mail account.

Don't be a pain. You just add to the daily clutter if you send unnecessary replies to e-mails—a pointless *thanks* or *Yes!* or *WooHoo!* Just as bad is CCing everyone on a list when you've received a query that needs to go to one person only: For example, when someone trying to arrange a meeting asks members of a group for available times and those members carbon copy their replies to all other members.

Your Turn Take a quick look at the formatting of the e-mails that appear on your mobile device. Many phones now have no problem displaying images, complex pages, or other textual features within e-mail. But note the limitations too. Images clutter a message on a small screen, so place them after your text. And you might not want to put any links you include too close together because they can be hard to select if they are side-by-side or beneath each other.

---

revise and edit
p. 452

● **Want to get a response?**
Explain your purpose clearly and logically.
See page 317.

14 Business Letters

**communicate
formally**

The formal business letter remains an important instrument for sending information in professional situations. Though business letters can be transmitted electronically these days, legal letters or decisions about admissions to schools or programs often still arrive on paper, complete with a real signature.

● Responding to a summer internship opportunity, you outline your credentials for the position in a cover letter and attach your résumé.

● You send a brief letter to the director of admissions of a law school, graciously declining your acceptance into the program.

● You send a letter of complaint to an auto company, documenting the list of problems you've had with your SUV and indicating your intention to seek redress under your state's "lemon law."

● You write to a management company to accept the terms of a lease, enclosing a check for the security deposit on your future apartment.

UNDERSTANDING BUSINESS LETTERS　As you would expect, business letters are generally formal in structure and tone, and follow a number of specific conventions, designed to make the document a suitable record or to support additional communication. Yet the principles for composing a business or job letter are not much different from those for a business e-mail. ○

want to get a ◀
response?

Explain your purpose clearly and logically.　Don't assume a reader will understand why you are writing. Use the first paragraph to announce your concern and explain your purpose, anticipating familiar *who, what, where, when, how,* and *why* questions. Be specific about names, titles, dates, and places. If you're applying for a job, scholarship, or admission to a program, name the specific position or program and mention that your résumé is attached. Remember that your letter may have a long life in a file cabinet: Write your document so that it will make sense months or years later.

Tell your readers what you want them to do.　Don't leave them guessing about how they should respond to your message. Lay out a clear agenda for accomplishing one task: Apply for a job, request information, or make an inquiry or complaint. Don't hesitate to ask for a reply, even by a specific date when that is necessary.

understand e-mail
p. 310

Write for your audience.   Quite often, you won't know the people to whom you are sending a business letter. So you have to construct your letter considering how an executive, employer, admissions officer, or complaints manager might be most effectively persuaded. Courtesy and goodwill go a long way—though you may have to be firm and impersonal in some situations. Avoid phony emotions or tributes.

A job application or cover letter (with your résumé attached) poses special challenges. You need to present your work and credentials in the best possible light without seeming full of yourself. Be succinct and specific, letting achievements speak mostly for themselves—though you can explain details that a reader might not appreciate. Focus on recent events and credentials and explain what skills and strengths you bring to the job. Speak in your own voice, clipped slightly by a formal style. O

Keep the letter focused and brief.   Like e-mails, business letters become hard to read when they extend beyond a page or two. A busy administrator or employee prefers a concise message, handsomely laid out on good stationery. Even a job-application letter should be relatively short, highlighting just your strongest credentials: Leave it to the accompanying résumé or dossier to flesh out the details.

Use a conventional form.   All business letters should include your address (called the *return address*), the date of the message, the address of the person to whom you are writing (called the *inside address*), a formal salutation or greeting, a closing, a signature in ink (when possible), and information about copies or enclosures.

Both *block format* and *modified-block format* are acceptable in business communication. In block forms, all elements are aligned against the left-hand margin (with the exception of the letterhead address at the top). In modified-block form, the return address, date, closing, and signature are aligned with the center of the page. In both cases, paragraphs in the body of the letter are set as single-spaced blocks of type, their first lines not indented, and with an extra line space between paragraphs.

define your style
p. 432

In indented form (not shown), the elements of the letter are arranged as in modified-block form, but the first lines of body paragraphs are indented five spaces, with no line spaces between the single-spaced paragraphs.

Distribute copies of your letter sensibly.   Copy anyone involved in a message, as well as anyone who might have a legitimate interest in your action. For example, in filing a product complaint with a company, you may also want to send your letter to the state office of consumer affairs. Copies are noted and listed at the bottom of the letter, introduced by the abbreviation *Cc* (for *courtesy copy*).

The following are two business letters: the first is a cover letter written by a student sending a résumé in a quest for a summer internship; the second is a concise letter of complaint.

Cover letter

In modified-block form, return address, date, closing, and signature are centered.

1001 Harold Circle #10
Austin, TX 78712
June 28, 20--

Mr. Josh Greenwood
ABC Corporate Advisors, Inc.
9034 Brae Rd., Suite 1111
Austin, TX 78731

Dear Mr. Greenwood:

Opening paragraph clearly states thesis of letter: Nancy Linn wants this job.

Rita Weeks, a prelaw advisor at the University of Texas at Austin, e-mailed me about an internship opportunity at your firm. Working at ABC Corporate Advisors sounds like an excellent chance for me to further my interests in finance and corporate law. I would like to apply for the position.

Letter highlights key accomplishments succinctly and specifically.

As my attached résumé demonstrates, I have already interned at an estate-planning law firm, where I have learned to serve the needs of an office of professionals and clients. I also have a record of achievement on campus: I have used my skills as a writer and speaker to obtain funding for the Honors Business Association at UT-Austin, for which I serve as vice president and financial director. By e-mailing and speaking with corporate recruiters, I raised $5,500 from Microsoft, ExxonMobil, Deloitte, and other companies and secured $2,400 from the University Co-op through written proposals.

Candidate repeatedly explains how internship fits career goals.

I am ready now for a job that more closely relates to my academic training and career goal: becoming a certified financial and/or valuation analyst and corporate lawyer.

Additional contact information provided.

Please contact me at 210-555-0000 or NLINN@abcd.com to schedule an interview. Thank you for considering me as a potential intern. I look forward to meeting you.

                              Sincerely,

                              N. Linn
                              Nancy Linn

Courtesy copy of letter sent to advisor mentioned in first paragraph; can be contacted as reference.

Enclosure: Résumé
CC: Rita Weeks

Complaint letter

John Humbert
95 Primrose Lane
Columbus, OH 43209

September 23, 2011

Home Design Magazine
3652 Delmar Drive
Prince, NY 10012

Dear *Home Design* Magazine:

I am a subscriber to your magazine, but I never received my July 2011 or August 2011 issues. When my subscription expires at the end of this year, please extend it two more months at no charge to make up for this error. Originally, my last issue would have been the December 2011 magazine. Since I have missed two issues and since my subscription was paid in full almost a year ago, please send me the January and February 2012 issues of *Home Design* at no additional charge.

Thank you for your attention.

Sincerely,

J. Humbert
John Humbert

Letterhead is preprinted stationery carrying the return address of the writer or institution. It may also include a corporate logo.

Allow two or three spaces between the date and address.

Allow one line space above and below the salutation. A colon follows the greeting.

The letter is in block form, with all major elements aligned with the left margin.

Getting the details right

Perhaps the most important detail in a business letter is keeping the format you use consistent and correct. Be sure to print your letter on good-quality paper or letterhead and to send it in a proper business envelope, one large enough to accommodate a page $8\frac{1}{2}$ inches wide.

Use consistent margins and spacing. Generally, 1-inch margins all around work well, but you can use larger margins (up to $1\frac{1}{2}$ inches) when your message is short. The top margin can also be adjusted if you want to balance the letter on the page, though the body need not be centered.

Finesse the greeting. Write to a particular person at a firm or institution. Address him or her as *Mr.* or *Ms.*—unless you actually know that a woman prefers *Mrs.* You may also address people by their full names: *Dear Margaret Hitchens*. When you don't have a name, fall back on *Dear Sir or Madam* or *To Whom It May Concern*, though these forms of address (especially *madam*) are increasingly dated. When it doesn't sound absurd, you can address the institution or entity: *Dear Exxon* or *Dear IRS*—again, this is not a preferred form.

Spell everything right. Be scrupulous about the grammar and mechanics too—especially in a job-application letter. Until you get an interview, that piece of paper represents you to a potential client or employer. Would you hire someone who misspelled your company's name or made noticeable errors? O

Photocopy the letter as a record. An important business letter needs a paper copy, even when you have an electronic version archived: The photocopied signature may mean something.

Don't forget the promised enclosures. A résumé should routinely accompany a job-application letter. O

help with common errors p. 600

understand résumés p. 324

Fold the letter correctly and send it in a suitable envelope. Business letters always go on $8\frac{1}{2} \times 11$-inch paper and are sent in standard business envelopes, generally $4\frac{1}{8} \times 9\frac{1}{2}$ inches. Fold the letter in three sections, trying to put the creases through white space in the letter so that the body of the message remains readable.

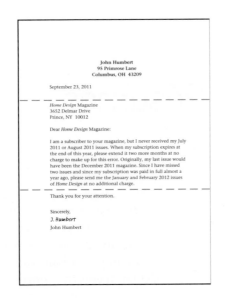

John Humbert
95 Primrose Lane
Columbus, OH 43209

September 23, 2011

Home Design Magazine
3652 Delmar Drive
Prince, NY 10012

Dear *Home Design* Magazine:

I am a subscriber to your magazine, but I never received my July 2011 or August 2011 issues. When my subscription expires at the end of this year, please extend it two more months at no charge to make up for this error. Originally, my last issue would have been the December 2011 magazine. Since I have missed two issues and since my subscription was paid in full almost a year ago, please send me the January and February 2012 issues of *Home Design* at no additional charge.

Thank you for your attention.

Sincerely,

J. Humbert

John Humbert

Your Turn   Have you received a business letter recently? If so, pull it out and take a minute to note the specific features described in this chapter. They are easy to overlook: letterhead, date, inside address, greeting, closing, attachments, spacing. Are their functions obvious and do they make sense? Now take a look at a recent e-mail you may have received from an institution or business (rather than a friend or colleague). What features does the business e-mail have in common with a business letter? In what ways are they different?

How to start

● **Want to get a job?**
Design pages that are easy to read. See page 327.

Résumés

record
professional
achievements

A one-page résumé usually accompanies any letter of application you send for a position or job. The résumé gathers and organizes details about your experiences at school, on the job, and in the community. In some careers, you may recap years of work and achievements in a longer, but similarly organized, document called a CV (curriculum vitae).

- Applying for a part-time position at a local day-care center, you assemble a résumé that chronicles your relevant experience.

- For an application to graduate school, you prepare a résumé that gives first priority to your accomplishments as a dean's list dual major in government and English.

- You modify your résumé slightly to highlight your internships with several law firms because you are applying for a paralegal clerk position at Baker Botts LLP.

- For a campus service scholarship, you tweak your résumé to emphasize activities more likely to interest college administrators than potential employers.

UNDERSTANDING RÉSUMÉS   The point of a résumé is to provide a quick, easy-to-scan summary of your accomplishments to someone interested in hiring you. The document must be readable at a glance, meticulously accurate, and reasonably handsome. Think of it this way: A résumé is your one- or two-page chance to make a memorable first impression.

Contrary to what you may think, there's no standard form for résumés, but they do usually contain some mix of the following information:

- Basic contact data: your name, address, phone number, and e-mail address

- Educational attainments (usually college and above, once you have a BA, BS, or other postsecondary credential): degrees earned, where, and when

- Work experience: job titles, companies, dates of employment, with a brief list of the skills you used in specific jobs (such as customer service, sales, software programs, language proficiencies, and so on)

- Other accomplishments: extracurricular activities, community service, volunteer work, honors, awards, and so on. These may be broken into subcategories.

A strong résumé can be your ticket to the job or position you want.

Depending on the situation, you might also include the following elements:

- A brief statement of your career goals
- A list of people willing to serve as references (with their contact information)

You can add additional categories to your résumé too, whenever they might improve your chances at a job. The résumé you'll compile as your career evolves, for instance, may eventually include items such as administrative appointments, committee service, awards, patents, publications, lectures, participation in business organizations, community service, and so on. But keep the document brief. Ordinarily, a first résumé shouldn't exceed one page—though it may have to run longer if you are asked to provide references.

Résumés, which often resemble outlines without the numbers or letters, vary enormously in design. You have to decide on everything from fonts and headings to alignments and paper. You can choose to pay companies to fashion your résumé or buy special software to produce these documents. But your word processor has all the power you need to create a competent résumé on your own. Here's some advice.

Gather the necessary information.   You'll have to assemble this career data sooner or later. It's much simpler if you start in college and gradually build a full résumé over the years.

Don't guess or rely on memory for résumé information: Take the time necessary to get the data right. Verify your job titles and your months or years of employment; identify your major as it is named in your college catalog; make an accurate list of your achievements and activities without embellishing them. Don't turn an afternoon at a sandlot into "coaching high school baseball." Focus on attainments during your college years and beyond. Grade school and high school achievements don't mean much, unless you're LeBron James.

Decide on appropriate categories.   In most cases, right out of college or postsecondary school training, you'll use the résumé categories noted above. But you may vary their order and emphasis, depending on the job or career you pursue. In the past, one expensively printed résumé served all occasions; today you can—and should—tailor your electronically crafted résumé to individual job searches.

Arrange the information within categories in reverse chronological order. The most recent attainments come first in each of your categories. If such a list threatens to bury your most significant items, you have several options: Cut the lesser achievements from the list, break out special achievements in some consistent way, or highlight those special achievements in the cover letter that should always accompany a résumé. ○

Design pages that are easy to read. Basic design principles aren't rocket science: Headings and key information should stand out and individual items should be clearly separated. The pages should look substantive but not cluttered. White space makes any document friendly, but too much in a résumé can suggest a lack of achievement. ○

In general, treat the résumé as a conservative document. This is not the time to experiment with fonts and flash or curlicues. Don't include a photograph either, even a good one.

want to get ◀
a job?

Proofread every line in the résumé several times. Careful editing isn't a "detail" when it comes to résumés: It can be the whole ball game. When employers have more job candidates than they can handle, they may look for reasons to dismiss weak cases. Misspelled words, poor design of headings and text, and incomplete or confusing chronology are the kinds of mistakes that can terminate your job quest. ○

The following résumé, by Andrea Palladino, is arranged in reverse chronological order. Palladino uses a simple design that aligns the major headings and dates in a column down the left-hand margin and indents the detailed accomplishments to separate them, making them highly readable.

Applying for a job need not be as dreary as it once was—or as sexist.

understand business
letters p. 316

think visually
p. 592

help with common
errors p. 600

Contact information centered at top of page for quick reference. If necessary, give both school and permanent addresses.

Optional "career objective" functions like thesis.

Alignments further empha-size headings and dates.

Ample, but not excessive, white space enhances readability.

Andrea Palladino
600 Oak St.
Austin, TX 78705
(281) 555-1234

CAREER OBJECTIVE   Soon-to-be college graduate seeking full-time position that allows for regular interpersonal communication and continued professional growth.

EDUCATION
8/07–5/11   University of Texas at Austin – Psychology, BA

EXPERIENCE
3/10–Present   Writing Consultant
University of Texas at Austin Undergraduate Writing Center – Austin, TX
Tutor students at various stages of the writing process. Work with a variety of assignments. Attend professional development workshops.

5/10–Present   Child Care Provider
CoCare Children's Services – Austin, TX
Care for infants through children aged ten, including children with physical and mental disabilities. Change diapers, give food and comfort, engage children in stimulating play, and clean/disinfect toys after child care. Work on standby and substitute for coworkers when needed.

5/09–12/10   Salesperson/Stockperson
Eloise's Collectibles – Katy, TX
Unpacked new shipments, prepared outgoing shipments, and kept inventory. Interacted with customers and performed the duties of a cashier.

ACCOMPLISHMENTS
2009– Present   College Scholar for three years – acknowledgment of in-residence GPA of at least 3.50

10/11–Present   Big Brothers Big Sisters of Central Texas

Fall 2009   University of Texas at Austin Children's Research Lab – Research Assistant

Getting the details right

With its fussy dates, headings, columns, and margins, a résumé is all about the details. Fortunately, it is brief enough to make a thorough going-over easy. Here are some important considerations.

Don't leave unexplained gaps in your education or work career.
Readers will wonder about blanks in your history (Are you a spy? Slacker? Felon?) and so may dismiss your application in favor of candidates whose career chronology raises no red flags. Simply account for any long periods (a year or so) you may have spent wandering the capitals of Europe or flipping burgers. Do so either in the résumé or in the job-application/cover letter—especially if the experiences contributed to your skills.

Be consistent. Keep the headings and alignments the same throughout the document. Express all dates in the same form: For example, if you abbreviate months and seasons, do so everywhere. Use hyphens between dates.

Protect your personal data. You don't have to volunteer information about your race, gender, age, or sexual orientation on a job application or résumé. Neither should you provide financial data, Social Security or credit card numbers, or other information you don't want in the public domain and that is not pertinent to your job search. However, you do need to be accurate and honest about the relevant job information: Any disparity about what you state on a résumé and your actual accomplishments may be a firing offense down the road.

Consider having your résumés designed and printed professionally.
You may save time by letting someone else design and print your document, if you aren't computer savvy. If you do produce your own résumé, be sure to print it on high-quality paper. Ordinary printer paper won't cut it.

> **Your Turn** If you already have a résumé, open it up and check its features against the suggestions offered in this chapter. Consider how you might modify it for the different kinds of positions you may be applying for over the next several years. And if you don't yet have a résumé, now is an excellent time to draft one. You will more likely need it sooner than later.

16 Personal Statements

explain a person's experiences and goals

Preparing a short personal statement has become almost a ritual among people applying for admission to college, professional school, or graduate school, or for jobs, promotions, scholarships, internships, and even elective office.

- An application for an internship asks for an essay in which you explain how your career goals will contribute to a more tolerant and diverse society.

- All candidates for the student government offices you're interested in must file a personal statement explaining their positions. Your statement, limited to three hundred words, will be printed in the campus newspaper and posted online.

- You dust off the personal statement you wrote to apply to college to see what portions you can use in an essay required for admission to upper-division courses in the College of Communication.

UNDERSTANDING PERSONAL STATEMENTS Institutions that ask for personal statements are rarely interested in who you are. Rather, they want to see whether you can *represent* yourself as a person with whom they might want to be affiliated. That may seem harsh, but consider the personal statements you have already written. At best, they are a slice of your life—the verbal equivalent of you in full-dress mode.

TURNING A 20-FOOT WALL INTO A CANVAS TAKES VISION. SO DOES GETTING INTO COLLEGE.

Get started at
KnowHow2GO.org
You've got what it takes.

Lumina Ad Council ACE

If you want a sense of what a school, business, or other institution expects in the essays they request from applicants, read whatever passes for that group's core values or mission statement, often available online. If their words sound a little stiff, inflated, and unrealistic, you've got it—except that you shouldn't actually sound as pretentious as an institution. A little blood has to flow through the veins of your personal statement, just not so much that someone in an office gets nervous about your emotional shape.

Hitting the right balance between displaying overwhelming competence and admitting human foibles in a personal statement is tough. Here's some advice for composing a successful essay.

Read the essay prompt carefully. Essay topics are often deliberately open-ended to give you some freedom in pursuing a topic, but only answer the question actually posed, not one you'd prefer to deal with. Ideally, the question will focus on a specific aspect of your work or education; try to write about this even if the question is more general.

Be realistic about your audience. Your personal statements are read by strangers. That's scary, but you can usually count on them to be reasonable people and well-disposed to give you a fair hearing. They measure you against other applicants—not unreachable standards of perfection.

Gather your material. Don't repeat in your personal statement what's already on record in an application letter or résumé. Instead, look for incidents that will bring your résumé lines to life. Talk about the experiences that prepared you for the work you want to do or, perhaps, determined the direction of your life. If the prompt encourages personal reminiscences (e.g., *the person who influenced you the most*), think hard about how to convey those experiences to a stranger.

feeling lost?

Decide on a focus or theme.   Personal statements are short, so make the best use of a reader's time. Don't ramble about summer jobs or vague educational opportunities. Instead, find a theme that focuses on the strongest aspects of your application. If you're driven by a passion for research, arrange the elements of your life to illustrate this. If your best work is extracurricular, explain in a scholarship application how your commitment to people and activities makes you a more well-rounded student. In other words, turn your life into a thesis statement and make a clear point about yourself. ○

Organize the piece conventionally.   Many personal statements take a narrative form, though they may also borrow some elements of reports and even proposals. Whatever structures you adopt for the essay, pay attention to the introduction, conclusion, and transitions: You cannot risk readers getting confused or lost. ○

Try a high or middle style.   You don't want to be breezy or casual in an essay for law school or medical school, but a *personal* statement does invite a human voice. So a style that marries the correctness and formal vocabulary of a high style with the occasional untailored feel of the middle style might be perfect for many personal statements. ○

The Academic Service Partnership Foundation asked candidates for an internship to prepare an essay addressing a series of questions. The prompt and one response to it follows.

ASPF NATIONAL INTERNSHIP PROGRAM

Please submit a 250- to 500-word typed essay answering the following three questions:

Specific questions limit reply, but also help to organize it.

1. Why do you want an internship with the ASPF?
2. What do you hope to accomplish in your academic and professional career goals?
3. What are your strengths and skills, and how would you use these in your internship?

---

develop a statement
p. 393

connect ideas
p. 416

define your style
p. 432

Michael Villaverde

April 14, 20--

The opportunity to work within a health-related government agency alongside top-notch professionals initially attracted me to the Academic Service Partnership Foundation (ASPF) National Internship Program. Participating in the ASPF's internship program would enable me to augment the health-services research skills I've gained working at the VERDICT Research Center in San Antonio and the M.D. Anderson Cancer Center in Houston. This internship could also help me gain experience in health policy and administration.

I support the ASPF's mission to foster closer relations between formal education and public service and believe that I could contribute to this mission. If selected as an ASPF intern, I will become an active alumnus of the program. I would love to do my part by advising younger students and recruiting future ASPF interns. Most important, I make it a point to improve the operations of programs from which I benefit. Any opportunities provided to me by the ASPF will be repaid in kind.

Other strengths I bring to the ASPF's National Internship Program are my broad educational background and dedication. My undergraduate studies will culminate in two honors degrees (finance and liberal arts) with additional premed course work. Afterward, I wish to enroll in a combined MD/PhD program in health-services research. Following my formal

Opening sentence states writer's thesis or intent; first two paragraphs address first question.

Essay uses first person (*I, me*) but is fairly formal in tone and vocabulary, between high and middle style.

Personal note slips through in enthusiasm author shows for internship opportunity.

This statement transitions smoothly into second issue raised in prompt.

Formidable and specific
goals speak for themselves
in straightforward
language.

Another transition
introduces third issue
raised by prompt.

Qualifications offered are
numerous and detailed.

Special interest/concern
is noted and is likely to
impress reviewers of
statement.

Final sentence affirms
enthusiasm for technical
internship.

education, I will devote my career to seeing patients in a primary-care setting, researching health-care issues as a university faculty member, teaching bioethics, and developing public policy at a health-related government agency.

The course work at my undergraduate institution has provided me with basic laboratory and computer experience, but my strengths lie in oral and written communication. Comparing digital and film-screen mammography equipment for a project at M.D. Anderson honed my technical-writing skills and comprehension of statistical analysis. The qualitative analysis methods I learned at VERDICT while evaluating strategies used by the Veterans Health Administration in implementing clinical practice guidelines will be a significant resource to any prospective employer. By the end of this semester, I will also possess basic knowledge of Statistical Package for the Social Sciences (SPSS) software.

During my internship I would like to research one of the following topics: health-care finance, health policy, or ethnic disparities in access to high-quality health care. I have read much about the Patient Protection and Affordable Care Act of 2010 and anticipate studying its implications. I would learn a great deal from working with officials responsible for the operation and strategic planning of a program like Medicare (or a nonprofit hospital system). The greater the prospects for multiple responsibilities, the more excited I will be to show up at work each day.

Getting the details right

As with résumés, there's no room for errors or slips in personal statements. ○ They are a test of your writing skills, plain and simple, so you need to get the spelling, mechanics, and usage right. In addition, consider the following advice.

Don't get too artsy.   A striking image or two may work well in the statement, as may the occasional metaphor or simile. But don't build your essay around a running theme, an extended analogy, or a pop-culture allusion that a reader might dismiss as hokey or simply not get. If a phrase or feature stands out too noticeably, change it, even though *you* may like it.

Use common sense.   You probably already have the good grace not to offend gender, racial, religious, and ethnic groups in your personal statement. You should also take the time to read your essay from the point of view of people from less protected groups who may take umbrage at your dismissal of *old folks, fundamentalists,* or even *Republicans.* You don't know who may be reading your essay.

Write the essay yourself.   It's the ethical thing to do. If you don't and you're caught, you're toast. You might ask someone to review your statement or take a draft to a writing center for a consultation. ○ This review or consult by a parent or English-major roommate should not purge your *self* from the essay. Remember, too, that wherever you arrive, you'll need to write at the level you display in the statement that got you there.

Your Turn   Amused by the thought of your life as a thesis statement? Give it a try. Compose *three* thesis sentences that might be plausibly used to organize three different personal statements, emphasizing varying aspects of your life and career. Which statement do you think describes you best? Would it always be the best thesis for a personal statement? Why or why not?

How to start ● **First time writing a lab report?**
Look at model reports. See page 338.

17 Lab Reports

**record a
scientific
experiment**

In most courses in the natural or social sciences, you are expected to learn how to describe experiments systematically and report information accurately. It goes with the territory. The vehicle for such work is the familiar lab report.

● For a physics course, you describe an experiment that uses a series of collisions to demonstrate the conservation of energy.

● In an organic chemistry lab, you try to produce chemical luminescence and report your results.

● For a psychology class, you describe the results of an experiment you created to determine whether students taking examinations benefit from a good night's sleep the night before the test.

UNDERSTANDING LAB REPORTS   Formal scientific papers published in academic journals have conventional features designed to convey information to readers professionally interested in the results of studies and experiments. The key elements of such a scientific paper are the following:

- Title page with the title clearly describing the contents of the paper; includes names of authors and their institutional affiliations
- Abstract (not always required) summarizing the main points in the paper
- Introduction explaining the purpose of the study or experiment and reviewing previous work on the subject (called a literature review)
- Description of materials and methods, explaining the factual and procedural details of the experiment
- Results section, tabulating and reporting the data
- Discussion of the results, interpreting the data
- References list or bibliography, documenting articles and books cited in the paper
- Figures, tables, and other supporting materials (if any)

For details about composing full scientific papers, consult the handbooks used in your particular field (and recommended by your instructor), such as *The CSE Manual for Authors, Editors, and Publishers* (7th edition, 2006) or the *Publication Manual of the American Psychological Association* (6th edition, 2009).

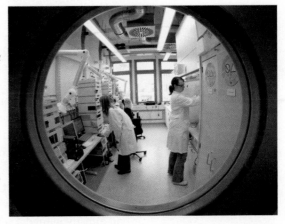

Lab reports borrow many of the features of the scientific papers published in academic journals, but are generally much shorter and tailored to specific situations. Typically, you prepare lab reports to describe the results of experiments you're assigned to perform in science courses. But you may also write lab reports to document original research done with colleagues or professors.

▶ first time writing
   a lab report?

Follow instructions to the letter.   In a course with a lab, you typically receive precise instructions on how to compile a lab notebook or prepare and submit reports. Read these guidelines carefully and ask the instructor or teaching assistant questions about any specifications you do not understand. Each section of a lab report provides a specific kind of information that helps a reader understand and, possibly, repeat a procedure or an experiment.

Look at model reports.   Lab report requirements may vary not only from subject to subject but also from course to course. So ask the instructor whether sample reports might be available for a particular lab section. If so, study them closely. The best way to understand what your work should look like is to see a successful model.

Be efficient.   If an abstract is required, keep it brief. Use charts, tables, and graphs (as required) to report information and don't repeat that data elsewhere. Keep your reporting of results separate from the discussion and commentary.

Edit the final version.   In a lab report, editing means not only proofreading your language but also reviewing the structure of equations or formulas, assessing the clarity of methods or procedures sections, and checking any numbers, calculations, equations, or formulas. ○ Be sure to label all sections and items accurately, numbering any figures, tables, and charts. Use these numbers to refer to these items in the body of your report.

The following lab report was produced for a course in organic chemistry. It follows a structure defined in a full page of instructions. Some sections— such as "Main Reactions and Mechanisms"—are clearly tied to the specific subject matter of the chemistry class. Other sections—such as "Data and Results"—would be found in lab reports in many disciplines.

   Like any lab report, this one is mostly business. But there are informal moments ("Did it glow? Yes!"), probably reflecting the fact that the writer had already gained a sense of what was acceptable in this course: This was the seventh of more than a dozen required reports.

revise and edit
p. 452

Shane McNamee

Professor Lyman

Chemistry 300

March 22, 20--

Synthesis of Luminol

CH 300 Syllabus, Supplement I

INTRODUCTION

The purpose of this lab is to synthesize a chemiluminescent product and observe chemiluminescence.

Almost all lab reports use headings for their structure. "Introduction" functions as thesis.

MAIN REACTIONS AND MECHANISMS

"Materials and Methods" section starts here. (Assignment instructions specified different language for these headings.)

a.

Luciferin Decarboxyketoluciferin

b.

3- Nitrophthalic Acid Hydrazine 5- Nitrophthalhydrazide Luminol

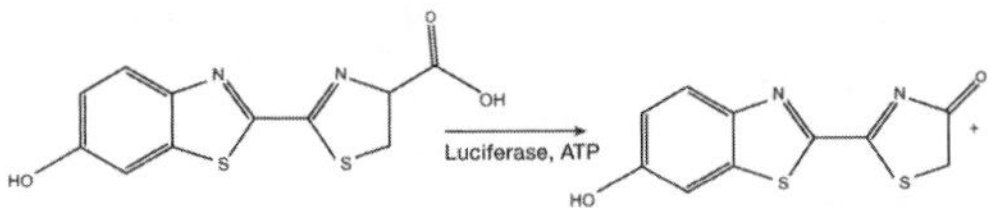

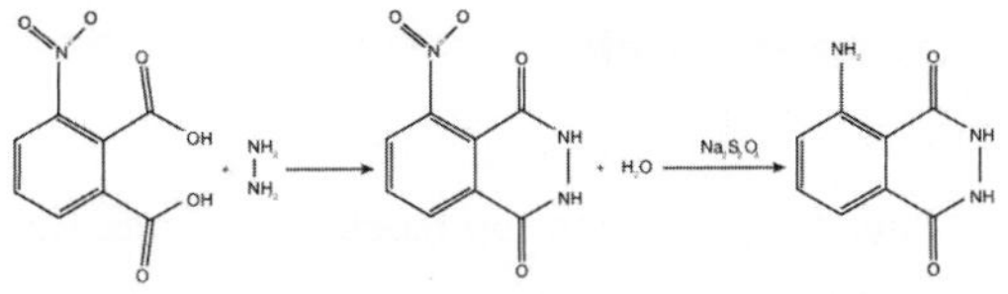

Synthesis of Luminol 2

c.

3- aminophthalate
Singlet state

3- aminophthalate
Triplet state

Proposed peroxide

3- aminophthalate
Ground state

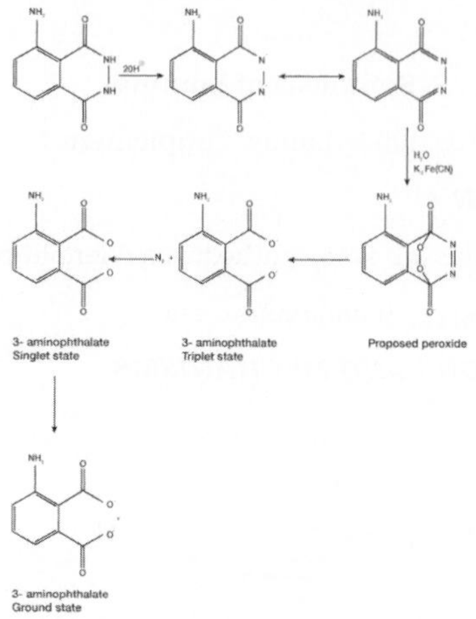

TABLE OF REACTANTS AND PRODUCTS

Included 3-nitrophthalic acid, hydrazine solution, triethylene glycol, NaOH, sodium hydrosulfite dihydrate, acetic acid, luminol, potassium ferricyanide, hydrogen peroxide

SYNOPSIS OF PROCEDURE

APPARATUS:

5 ml conical vial, hot plate, heating block, spin vane, Hirsch funnel, 250 ml Erlenmeyer flask, and thermometer

SYNTHESIS OF LUMINOL:

1. Heated 5 ml vial containing 200 mg 3-nitrophthalic acid and 0.4 ml aq 8% hydrazine solution until solid dissolved.

Abbreviations are not followed by periods.

Synthesis of Luminol 3

2. Once dissolved, added 0.6 ml triethylene glycol and clamped vial in vertical position. Added spin vane and inserted thermometer into vial.

3. Brought solution to vigorous boil to boil away excess water. During this time, temperature should be around 110°C.

4. Once water boiled off, temperature rose to 215°C in a 3-4 minute period. Maintained the 215-220°C temperature for 2 minutes.

5. Removed the vial and cooled it to 100°C. While cooling, placed 10 ml water in Erlenmeyer flask and heated to boiling.

6. Once sample cooled to 100°C, added 3 ml boiling water.

7. Collected yellow crystals by vacuum filtration using a Hirsch funnel.

8. Transferred solid back to vial and added 1 ml of 3.0 M NaOH and stirred with a stirring rod until the solid was dissolved. Then added 0.6 g of fresh sodium hydrosulfite dihydrate to the deep brown-red solution.

9. Heated solution slightly under boiling for 5 minutes, taking care not to cause bumping. Then added 0.4 ml acetic acid.

10. Cooled tube in beaker of cool water, and collected solid luminol by vacuum filtration using Hirsch funnel.

Chapter 17   Lab Reports

Synthesis of Luminol 4

LIGHT-PRODUCING REACTION:

1. Combined two samples of luminol. Dissolved them in 2 ml of 3 M NaOH and 18 ml water (solution A).

2. Next, prepared a solution of 4 ml 3% aqueous potassium ferricyanide, 4 ml 3% H_2O_2, and 32 ml H_2O (solution B).

3. Then, diluted 5 ml solution A with 35 ml water. In a dark place, poured diluted solution and solution B simultaneously into an Erlenmeyer flask. Swirled flask; looking for blue-green light.

Standard notation is used to describe chemical reactions.

DATA AND RESULTS

Did it glow? Yes!

Data sections are rarely this simple. Most would require tables, charts, and so on.

DISCUSSION AND CONCLUSION

When a chemical reaction generates light, chemiluminescence has occurred. The product of such a reaction is in an excited electronic state and emits a photon. One example of chemiluminescence is the luciferase-catalyzed reaction of luciferin with molecular oxygen in the male firefly. Chemiluminescence occurring through biochemical processes is also called bioluminescence.

Luminol is synthesized through two steps. Hydrazine and 4-nitrophthalic acid react to produce 5-nitrophthalhydrazide, which is reduced by sodium dithionite to form luminol. In alkaline solution, luminol emits blue-green light when mixed with H_2O_2 and potassium ferricyanide.

Synthesis of Luminol 5

Although the mechanism of this reaction isn't fully understood, chemists believe that a peroxide decays to form 3-diaminophthalate in an excited triplet state (two unpaired electrons with the same spin). Slowly, the 3-diaminophthalate converts to a singlet state (two unpaired electrons now have different spins), which then decays to the ground state, emitting light through fluorescence. In contrast, phosphorescence occurs in reactions where a triplet state emits photons while converting to a singlet state.

Blue-green light glowed for a fraction of a second when solutions A and B were mixed. This indicates that enough luminol was successfully synthesized to run the chemiluminescent reaction. Only a small amount of dissolved luminol was required, so a high yield was not necessary.

Getting the details right

Even the conventions of scientists vary, so it helps to know what sorts of issues may come up in preparing a lab report for a given course. Again, ask questions when you aren't sure what conventions to follow.

Keep the lab report impersonal.   Keep yourself and any lab partners out of the work. In fact, most instructors will *require* that you use the third person and passive voice throughout: *The beaker was heated* rather than *We heated the beaker.* Though some instructors do allow the use of first-person pronouns in undergraduate work—preferring the clarity of active sentences—always check before using *I* or *we.* ○

Keep the style clear.   Written for knowledgeable readers, lab reports needn't apologize for using technical terms, jargon, and scientific notation. However, sentences still need to be coherent and grammatical in structure and free of clutter. Avoid contractions, however, as well as any trendy or slang terms.

Follow the conventions.   Learn the rules as they apply in particular fields. In general, however, you should italicize scientific names expressed in Latin, write out formulas and equations on separate lines, use only metric quantities and measures, use standard abbreviations, and narrate the materials and methods section in the past tense.

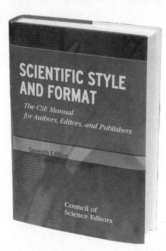

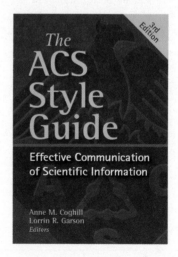

344

define your style
p. 432

Label charts, tables, and graphs carefully. Any data you present graphically should make sense at a glance if your design is sensible and the labels are thorough and accurate. Don't leave readers wondering what the numbers in a column represent or what the scale of a drawing might be. ○

Document the report correctly. Most lab reports won't require documentation or a list of references. But a scientific paper will. Determine the documentation style manual used in the subject area and follow its guidelines closely. ○

> **Your Turn**   As a highly "formulaic" genre of writing, lab reports have well-defined elements that follow a predictable structure and precise guidelines. Can you identify other kinds of writing that are this conventional? Could the structure of the lab report, moving clearly from an introduction and methods to results and discussion, work in any writing situations outside of the laboratory?

display data
p. 584

understand citation
styles p. 501

How to start ▶ ● **Adapting material?**
Organize your presentation. See page 347.

18 Oral Reports

present
information
to a live
audience

In an oral report, you present material you have researched to an audience listening and watching rather than reading. So you must organize information clearly and find ways to convey your points powerfully, memorably, and sometimes graphically.

● For a psychology course, you use presentation software to review the results of an experiment you and several classmates designed to test which types of music were most conducive to studying for examinations.

● In a Shakespeare class, you use slides to give an oral report on Elizabethan theaters that draws upon research you are doing for your end-of-semester term paper.

● Prepping a crowd for a protest march, you use a bullhorn and a little humor to review the very serious ground rules for staging a peaceful demonstration on the grounds of the state capitol.

UNDERSTANDING ORAL REPORTS   Oral reports can be deceptive. When watching someone give an effective five-minute talk, you may assume the speaker spent less time preparing it than he or she would a ten-page paper. But be warned: Oral presentations require all the research, analysis, and drafting of any other type of assignment, and then some. After all the background work is done, the material needs to be distilled into its most important points and sold to an audience. Here is some advice for preparing effective oral reports.

Know your stuff.   Having a firm grasp on your subject will make your presentation more effective—which is why you should base reports on serious research. Knowledge brings you confidence that will ease some anxieties about public speaking. You'll appear believable and persuasive to an audience. And you'll feel more comfortable when improvising or taking questions. If you are in command of your subject, you'll survive even if equipment fails or you misplace a note card.

Organize your presentation.   If your report is based on material you've already written, reduce the text to an outline, memorize its key points (or put them on cards), and then practice speaking about each one. ○ If it helps, connect the main ideas to one or two strong examples listeners might later remember. Make the report *seem* spontaneous, but plan every detail.

adapting ◀
material?

The best equipment can't save a poorly prepared report.

The process is similar for an oral report built from scratch. First, study your subject. Then list the points you want to cover and arrange them in a way that will engage listeners—choosing a pattern of organization that fits your topic. Use note cards or the outlining tools in programs like Word or PowerPoint to explore options for structuring your talk.

Cover only a limited number of points. It's better to leave your listeners with two or three good ideas than to bore them with a string of underdeveloped concepts.

At the beginning of your report, tell your audience briefly what you intend to cover and in what order. Then at critical transitions in the report, remind listeners where you are by simply stating what comes next: *The second issue I wish to discuss . . . ; Now that we've examined the phenomenon, let's look at its consequences.* Don't be shy about making your main points this directly or worry about repetition. In an oral report, strategic repetition is your friend.

order ideas p. 408

Stay connected to your listeners.   For about thirty seconds, you'll probably have the spontaneous goodwill of an audience. After that, you've got to earn every minute of their continued attention. Begin by introducing yourself and your subject, if there is no one to perform that task. For longer reports, consider easing into your material with an anecdote that connects you, your subject, and your listeners. Self-deprecating humor usually works. (Short, in-class presentations won't need much, if any, warm-up material.)

Once the oral presentation begins, maintain eye contact with members of the audience. Watch their reactions. When it's clear you've made a point, move on. If you see puzzled looks, explain more. No speaker charms everyone, so don't let a random yawn or frown throw you. But if the whole crowd starts to snooze, you *are* the problem. Connect or lose 'em: pick up your pace; move on to the next point; skip to your best material. ○

Be sure to speak *to* your listeners, not to your notes or text. Arrange your materials and print them large enough so that you can read them easily from a distance and not lose your place. If you look downward too often, you'll lose eye contact and your voice may be muffled, even with a microphone.

Use your voice and body.   Speak clearly and deliberately, and be sure people in the back of the room can hear you. Nervous speakers unconsciously speed up until they're racing to their conclusions. If you get skittish, calm yourself by taking a deep breath and smiling.

If the room is large and a fixed microphone doesn't confine you, move around on the stage to address more of the audience. Use gestures too. They are a natural part of public speaking, especially for arguments and personal narratives. If you get stuck behind a podium, be sure to scan the entire audience (not just speak to the middle of the room) and modulate your voice. Keep your body steady too: Don't rock as you speak.

Adapt your material to the time available.   If you know your subject well, don't worry about running out of things to say. Once they get rolling, most speakers have the opposite problem: They talk too much. So be realistic about how much you can cover within the assigned limit, especially if you have to take questions at the end. Tie your key ideas to fixed points on a

○

connect ideas
p. 416

clock or watch. Know where you need to be at a quarter, half, and three-quarters of the way through the available time.

When you finally get near the end, signal your conclusion and wrap up the report shortly thereafter, as promised. If you're taking questions after your presentation, follow up with *Any questions?*

Practice your presentation. Any oral report needs several dry runs to increase your confidence and alert you to potential problems. Speak any material aloud *exactly* as you intend to deliver it and go through all the motions, especially if you will use media such as slides or video clips. Have one or more friends or classmates watch you practice and give you feedback.

Use the practice session to time the presentation too. If you practice only in your head, you will greatly underestimate the length of the report.

If your presentation is collaborative, choreograph the report with the full group, agreeing on the introductions, handoffs, and interactions with the audience. Who runs the computer? Who distributes the handouts and when? Who handles the question-and-answer session? Handoffs like these seem minor until they are fumbled on game day.

Prepare for the occasion. Before the report, check out the locale and any equipment you will need. Be sure your laptop will connect to the multi-media projector in the room; know how to dim the lights; be sure a screen or electrical outlets are available.

Then dress up. A little spit and polish earns you the goodwill of most audiences. Your classmates may razz you about the tie or skirt, but it just proves they're paying attention. And that's a good thing.

The following PowerPoint presentation was created by Terri Sagastume, a resident of a small Florida town who opposes a proposed real-estate development, Edenlawn Estates, on property near his home. J&M Investments, the real-estate developer that recently purchased the property, hopes to create a new multistory condominium complex in place of the property's existing single-family homes. Sagastume's goal is to inform the public of the damage such a development would do to the surrounding area, and he is trying to convince his audience to sign a petition, which he will present to the local government in an effort to shut the project down.

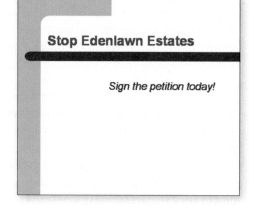

Edenlawn Estates

- What the developers want
- Why we should fight
- How we can win

What Developers Want

- Zoning variance
- Concrete seawall
- Four new traffic lights
- Height restriction exemption

Why We Should Fight

- Will cost taxpayers money
- Will harm environment
- Will increase traffic
- Will detract from quality of life

Stop Edenlawn Estates

Sign the petition today!

     The slides themselves are extremely simple and brief: They are merely the bullet points that Sagastume uses to ground his presentation.

     With the first slide as his backdrop, Sagastume provides a preview of his speech in three broad sections. First, he explains to his audience that the real-estate developer—a Miami-based conglomerate with no personal ties to the area—wants to change the existing building codes and zoning laws in order to maximize profits. Second, he reminds his audience of the reason those codes and laws are there, and that much could be lost if exceptions are made. And finally, he convinces his audience that, together, they can fight the big developer and win.

Getting the details right

There's nothing wrong with a report that relies on the spoken word alone. Still, audiences appreciate supporting material, including flip charts, hand-outs, slides, and visual or audio samplings. All such materials, clearly labeled and handsomely reproduced, should also be genuinely relevant to the report. Resist the temptation to show something just because it's cool.

Most oral reports use presentation software such as the dominant player in this field, PowerPoint. With presentation software, you create a sequence of slides to accompany an oral report, building the slides yourself or picking them from a gallery of ready-made designs and color schemes that fit different occasions. You can also choose individual layouts for slides to accommodate text only, text and photos, text and charts, images only, and so on.

Presentation software offers so many bells and whistles that novices tend to overdo it, allowing the software to dominate the report. Here's how to make PowerPoint or Keynote work for you.

Be certain you need presentation software. A short talk that makes only one or two points probably works better if viewers focus on you, not on a screen. Use presentation software to keep audiences on track through more complicated material, to highlight major issues or points, or to display images viewers really need to see. A little humor or eye candy is fine once in a while, but don't expect audiences to be impressed by glitz. What matters is the content of the report. ○

For presentations, PowerPoint offers design templates such as this one.

Use slides to introduce points, not cover them. If you find yourself reading your slides, you've put too much material on them. And you'll bore your audience to distraction. Put material on-screen that audiences need to see: main points, charts, and images directly relevant to the report (see the "Edenlawn Estates" slides on p. 350). It's fine, too, for a slide to outline your presentation at the beginning and to summarize your points at the end. In fact, it's helpful to have a slide that obviously signals a conclusion.

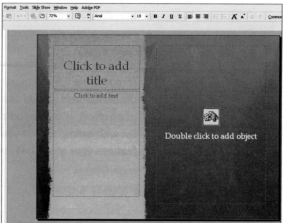

reference

Ideas

Need help organizing or drafting? See page 388.

19 Brainstorming

find a topic/
get an idea

A great deal of thinking occurs at the beginning of a project or assignment. How exactly will you fill ten or twenty pages with your thoughts on Incan architecture, the life cycle of dung beetles, or what you did last summer? What hasn't already been written about religion in America, cattle in Africa, or the cultural hegemony of Google? What do you do when you find yourself clueless or stuck or just overwhelmed by the possibilities—or lack thereof? Simple answer: Brainstorm.

Put a notion on the table and see where it goes—and what you might do with it or learn about it. Toy with an idea like a kitten with a catnip mouse. Push yourself to think through, around, over, and under a proposition. Dare to be politically incorrect or, alternatively, so conventional that your good behavior might scare even your elders.

But don't think of brainstorming as disordered and muddled. Consider the metaphor itself: Storms are awesomely organized events. They generate power by physical processes so complex that we're just beginning to understand them. Similarly, a first-rate brainstorming session spins ideas from the most complex chemistry in our bodies, the tumult of the human brain.

Naturally, you'll match brainstorming techniques to the type of writing you hope to produce. Beginning a personal tale about a trip to Wrigley Field, you might make a list of sensory details to jog your memory—the smell of hot dogs, the catcalls of fans, the green

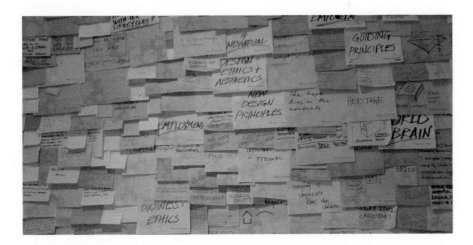

Chalkboards, flip charts, and even sticky notes can help you rapidly record your ideas.

grass of the outfield. ○ But for an assigned report on DNA fingerprinting, your brainstorming might itemize things you still must learn about the subject: what DNA fingerprinting is, how it is done, when it can be used, how reliable it is, and so on. ○

Find routines that support thinking.　Use whatever brainstorming techniques get you invested in a project. Jogging, swimming, knitting, or sipping brew at the coffeehouse may be your stimulus of choice. Such routine activities keep the body occupied, allowing insights to mature. Your thoughts do need to be captured and recorded, either in notes or, perhaps, voice memos.

One warning: Brainstorming activities of this kind can become simple procrastination. That comfortable chair in Starbucks might evolve into a spot too social for much thinking or writing. Recognize when your productivity has been compromised and change tactics.

Build lists.　Brainstorm to list potential topics or, if you already have a subject, to explore the major points you might cover. Add all items that come to mind: If you're too picky or detailed at the start, you defeat the power of brainstorming—in which one idea, written on paper or on a screen, suggests another, then another. Even grocery lists work this way.

understand
narratives p. 4

understand
reports p. 44

> Ideas won't keep; something must be done about them.

—Alfred North Whitehead

Lists work especially well when you already know something about a subject. For instance, preparing a letter to the editor in defense of collegiate sports, you can first inventory the arguments you've heard from friends or have made yourself. Then list the counterarguments you come up with as well. Write down everything that bubbles up, both reasonable and off-the-wall. Finally, winnow out the better items based on their quality or plausibility, and arrange them tentatively, perhaps pairing arguments and counterarguments. Even when you don't know much about a potential topic, assemble a list of basic questions that might lead to greater knowledge, to stimulate your ideas and thinking.

Map your ideas.   If you find a list too static as a prompt for writing, another way may be to explore the relationships between your ideas *visually*. Some writers use logic trees to represent their thinking, starting with a single general concept and breaking it into smaller and smaller parts. You can find examples of "tree diagrams" from many fields by using a search engine to investigate a keyword and then clicking the Image option.

Try freewriting.   Freewriting is a brainstorming technique of nonstop composing designed to loosen the bonds we sometimes use to clamp down on our own thinking. Typically, freewriting sessions begin slowly, with disconnected phrases and words. Suddenly, there's a spark and words stream onto the paper—but slow or fast, you must still keep writing. The moment you settle back in your chair, you break the circuit that makes freewriting work. By forcing yourself to write, you push yourself to think and, perhaps, to discover what really matters in a subject.

Like other brainstorming techniques, freewriting works best when you already have some knowledge of your subject. You might freewrite successfully about standardized testing or working at fast-food restaurants if you've experienced both; you'll stumble trying to freewrite on subjects you know next to nothing about, such as, perhaps, thermodynamics, ergonomics, or the career of Maria Callas. Freewriting tends to work best for personal narratives, personal statements, arguments, ○ and proposals, ○ and less well for reports and technical projects.

understand
argument p. 72

understand
proposals p. 176

Although freewriting comes in many forms, the basic formula is simple.

STAGE ONE

- Start with a blank screen or sheet of paper.
- Put your subject or title at the top of the page.
- Write on that subject nonstop for ten minutes.
- Don't stop typing or lift your pen from the paper during that time.
- Write nonsense if you must, but keep writing.

STAGE TWO

- Stop at ten minutes and review what you have written.
- Underscore or highlight the most intriguing idea, phrase, or sentence.
- Put the highlighted idea at the top of a new screen or sheet.
- Freewrite for another ten minutes on the new, more focused topic.

Use memory prompts.   When writing personal narratives, institutional histories, or even résumés, you might trigger ideas with photographs, yearbooks, diaries, or personal memorabilia. An image from a vacation may bring events worth writing about flooding back to you. Even checkbooks or credit card statements may help you reconstruct past events or see patterns in your life worth exploring in writing.

Search online for your ideas.   You can get lots of ideas by simply exploring most topics online through keywords. Indeed, determining those initial keywords and then following up with new terms you discover while browsing is in itself a potent form of brainstorming.

A photo album is a great place to look for writing ideas, because we tend to document meaningful moments.

Your Turn   If you have never used freewriting as a brainstorming activity, give it a try. Pick a general topic from among courses you are currently studying, news events that interest you, or activities you are deeply involved in: for example, the Japanese concept of Bushido, immigration reform, or unpaid internships. (You want a topic about which you have *some* knowledge or opinions.) Then follow the preceding directions. See what happens.

How to... *Browse for ideas*

Uncle Bob, who's a cop, complains about the "*CSI* effect." What is that?

I found a study by professors of law and psychology. What do they think?

 Google CSI effect

About 20,600,000 results (0.15 secon

▶ **Scholarly articles for CSI effect**
CSI Effect: Popular Fiction about Forensic S
... Concerning Scientific Evidence: Does the
The **CSI effect**: fact or fiction - Thomas - Cit

CSI effect - Wikipedia, the free encyclope
en.wikipedia.org/wiki/**CSI**_**effect** - Cached
The **CSI effect**, also known as the CSI syndrome a
in which the exaggerated portrayal of forensic scien
Background - Manifestations - Trials - References

The '**CSI Effect**': Does It Really Exist? | N
www.nij.gov/journals/259/**csi-effect**.htm - Cached
by DE Shelton - Cited by 12 - Related articles
Mar 17, 2008 — Do law-related television shows like
influence juror expectations and demands for forens

/archive/csieffect.pdf

108% — Find

ARTICLE

THE *CSI* EFFECT: POPULAR FICTION ABOUT FORENSIC SCIENCE AFFECTS THE PUBLIC'S EXPECTATIONS ABOUT REAL FORENSIC SCIENCE

N.J. Schweitzer
Michael J. Saks*

ABSTRACT: Two of a number of hypotheses loosely referred to as the CSI Effect suggest that the television program and its spin-offs, which wildly exaggerate and glorify forensic science, affect the public, and in turn affect trials either by (a) burdening the prosecution by creating greater expectations about forensic science than can be delivered or (b) burdening the defense by creating exaggerated faith in the capabilities and reliability of the forensic sciences. The present study tested these hypotheses by presenting to mock jurors a simulated trial transcript that included the testimony of a forensic scientist. The case for conviction was relatively weak, unless the expert testimony could carry the case across the threshold of reasonable doubt. In addition to reacting to the trial evidence, respondents were asked about their television viewing habits. Compared to non-CSI viewers, CSI viewers were more critical of the forensic evidence presented at the trial, finding it less believable. Regarding their verdicts, 29% of non-CSI viewers said they would convict, compared to 18% of CSI viewers (not a statistically significant difference). Forensic science viewers expressed more confidence in their verdicts than did non-viewers. Viewers of general crime programs, however, did not differ significantly from their non-viewing counterparts on any of the other dependent measures, suggesting that skepticism toward the forensic science testimony was specific to those whose diet consisted of heavy doses of forensic science television programs.

1 Find reliable sources.

> Wikipedia isn't an academic source, but it will help me get a sense of the big picture.

> This article comes from a government publication—does that automatically mean it's not biased?

Article Discussion

CSI effect

From Wikipedia, the free encyclopedia

The **CSI effect**, also known as the **CSI syndrome**[1] and the **CSI** public perception. The term most often refers to the belief that jur American legal professionals, several studies have shown that cr

There are several other manifestations of the CSI effect. Greater and popularity of forensic science programs at the university leve forensic science shows teach criminals how to conceal evidence

Contents [hide]

1 Background
2 Manifestations
  2.1 Trials
  2.2 Academia
  2.3 Crimes
  2.4 Police investigations
3 References

Background

The CSI effect is named for *CSI: Crime Scene Investigation*, a tel discovery of a dead body leads to a criminal investigation by men which debuted in 2002, and *CSI: NY*, first aired in 2004. The *CSI Bones, Cold Case, Cold Case Files, Cold Squad, Criminal Minds*

WIKIPEDIA
The Free Encyclopedia

Main page
Contents
Featured content
Current events
Random article
Donate to Wikipedia

▼ Interaction
  Help
  About Wikipedia
  Community portal
  Recent changes
  Contact Wikipedia
▶ Toolbox
▶ Print/export
▼ Languages
  Česky
  Deutsch
  Español
  Français
  Italiano

2

Stay alert to differing perspectives.

OFFICE OF JUSTICE PROGRAMS

NATIONAL INSTITUTE OF JUSTICE
Research • Development • Evaluation

HOME | FUNDING | PUBLICATIONS & MULTIMEDIA | EVENTS | TRAINING |

NIJ Home Page > NIJ Journal > NIJ Journal No. 259

NIJ JOURNAL NO. 259

Director's Message

The 'CSI Effect': Does It Really Exist?

Voice Stress Analysis: Only 15 Percent of Lies About Drug Use Detected in Field Test

Shopping Malls: Are They Prepared to Prevent and Respond to Attack?

Software Defined Radios Help Agencies Communicate

The 'CSI Effect': Does It Really Exist?

by Honorable Donald E. Shelton

Crime and courtroom proceedings have long been fodder f scriptwriters. In recent years, however, the media's use o for drama has not only proliferated, it has changed focus. our criminal justice process, many of today's courtroom dr cases. *Court TV* offers live gavel-to-gavel coverage of trial month. Now, that's "reality television"!

Reality and fiction have begun to blur with crime magazine *Hours Mystery, American Justice,* and even, on occasion, portray actual cases, but only after extensively editing the narration for dramatic effect. Presenting one 35-year-old *Hours Mystery* filmed for months to capture all pretrial hea trial; the program, however, was ultimately edited to a 1- the crime remained a "mystery" . . . notwithstanding the j

3

Question claims.

Brainstorming with Others

collaborate

You've probably seen films or TV series that mock groupthink in corporations—wherein cowering yes-men and yes-women gather around a table to rubber-stamp the dumb ideas of a domineering CEO. Real group brainstorming is just the opposite. It encourages a freewheeling discovery and sharing of ideas among people with a stake in the outcome.

Group brainstorming comes in several varieties. The notorious college dorm-room bull session is a famous example, though with obvious defects. Such boozy late-night talk is likely to be frank, open-ended, wide-ranging, and passionate. But it typically doesn't lead anywhere or produce an agenda for action.

In academic or professional situations, formal brainstorming within a group requires specific strategies to produce solid results.

In academic and professional situations, formal brainstorming within a group requires specific strategies to produce solid results.

Choose a leader.   Leaders should be strong enough to keep discussions moving, cordial enough to encourage everyone to participate, and modest enough to draw out a range of opinions without pursuing agendas of their own. The leader probably shouldn't be the person with the most power in the group—not the CEO, chair of the department, or president of the student government. In fact, in serious brainstorming sessions, an outsider or trained facilitator might be the best choice.

Begin with a goal and set an agenda.   Most groups don't brainstorm for the pleasure of it. Some need or concern brings participants to the table—for instance, an assignment that requires a committee's response or a project that involves more work than one person can handle. The leader should get the group to agree on a goal and a simple agenda. Even if that goal is open-ended, it will help keep discussions on track. And both the goal and agenda can be written on a board or flip chart to keep the group on task. Without an agenda, brainstorming activity can dissolve into a bull session.

As the session evolves, a leader should help the group understand what it is accomplishing by stating and restating positions as they develop from discussion, posing important questions, and recording ideas as they emerge.

Set time limits.   Groups are most productive when working against reasonable time restraints. Given open-ended sessions (such as those dorm-room all-nighters), nothing productive may ever occur. But with only an hour or two for brainstorming, a group serious about its work will focus mightily. Time restraints also give a leader leverage to stifle the chatterers.

Encourage everyone to participate.   A leader or facilitator can call on the quiet types, but other participants can help, too, just by asking a colleague, "What do you think?" In a group setting, a reluctant participant's first contribution is usually the toughest to elicit, but it's worth any prodding: The silent observer in a group may come up with the sharpest insight.

Avoid premature criticism.   Leaders and participants alike need to encourage outside-the-box thinking and avoid a tendency to cut off contributions at the knees. No sneering, guffawing, or eye rolling—even when ideas *are* stupid. Early on, get every scheme, suggestion, and proposal on the blackboard or flip chart. Criticism and commentary can come later.

It might even help to open the session with everyone freewriting on a key idea for five or ten minutes as a warm-up, then reading their best ideas aloud. O

Test all ideas.   Sometimes, a group agrees too readily when a sudden good idea gains momentum. Such a notion should be challenged hard—even if it means someone has to play devil's advocate, that is, raise arguments or objections just to test the leading idea or claim. Even good ideas need to have their mettle proved.

Keep good records.   Many brainstorming sessions fail not because the ideas didn't emerge, but because no one bothered to catch them. Someone competent should take notes detailed enough to make sense a month later, when memories start to fade. Here again, a flip chart may be useful, since points written on it don't get erased. The facilitator should follow up on the session by seeing that the notes get organized, written up, and promptly distributed to the group.

Agree on an end product.   Effective brainstorming sessions should lead to action of some kind or, at least, a clear agenda for further discussion. Keeping an eye on the clock, the leader of the group should wind up general discussion early enough to push the group toward conclusions and plans for action. Not every brainstorming session reaches its goals, but participants will want closure on their work.

Your Turn   Can you describe a time when a group brainstorming activity either generated great ideas or failed miserably? If so, briefly describe that incident and try to account for its success or failure. Be open-minded about the definition of "group activity." Your moment may have occurred among campers stranded by a flat tire or campus activists gathered to spread a political message.

---

get an idea
p. 356

Smart Reading

There's probably no better strategy for generating ideas than reading. Reading can deepen your impressions of a subject you are studying, enrich your awareness, sharpen your critical acumen, and introduce you to alternative views. Reading also places you within a community of writers who have already thought about a subject.

Of course, not all reading serves the same purposes.

- You check out a dozen scholarly books to do research for a paper and then look for journal articles online.

- You consult stock market quotes and baseball box scores because you need info. *now.*

- You study an organization chart to figure out who actually controls the student government budget.

- You read an old diary to discover what life was like before photocopiers, air conditioning, and (*gulp!*) cell phones.

- You pack a *Twilight Saga* novel for pleasure reading on the Jersey shore.

read closely

Yet any of these reading experiences, as well as thousands of others, might lead to ideas for projects.

You've probably been thoroughly schooled in basic techniques of academic reading: Survey the table of contents, preread to get a sense of the whole, look up terms or concepts you don't know, summarize what you've read, and so on. Such suggestions are practical, especially for difficult scholarly or professional texts. Following is advice about reading to sharpen your college-level writing.

> If you don't have the time to read, you don't have the time or tools to write.

— Stephen King

Read to deepen what you already know.   Whatever your interests or experiences in life, you're not alone. Others have explored similar paths and probably written about them. Reading such work may give you confidence to bring your own thoughts to public attention. Whether your passion is tintype photography, skateboarding, or film fashions of the 1930s, you'll find excellent books on the subject by browsing library catalogs or even just checking Amazon.com. ○

For example, if you have worked at a fast-food franchise and know what goes on there, you might find a book like Eric Schlosser's *Fast Food Nation: The Dark Side of the All-American Meal* engrossing. You'll be drawn in because your experience makes you an informed critic. You can agree and disagree intelligently with Schlosser and, perhaps, see how his arguments might be extended or amended. At a minimum, you'll walk away from the book understanding even more about the fast-food industry and knowing the titles of dozens of additional sources, should you want to learn more.

Read above your level of knowledge.   It's comfortable to connect with people online who share your interests, but you'll often be chatting with people who don't know much more than you do. To find new ideas, push your reading to a higher and more demanding level. Spend some time with books and articles you can't blow right through. You'll know you are there when you find yourself looking up names, adding terms to your vocabulary, and feeling humbled at what you still need to learn about a subject. That's when thinking occurs and ideas germinate.

Read what makes you uncomfortable.   Most of us today have access to technologies that connect us to endless paths of information. But all those channels also mean that we can choose to read (or watch) only materials that confirm our existing beliefs and prejudices—and many people do. Yet such narrowness will be quickly exposed whenever you write on a controversial subject and find readers pushing back with facts and ideas you never considered before. Surprise! The world is more complicated than you thought. The solution is simple: Get out of the echo chamber and read more broadly, engaging with those who see the world differently.

refine your search
p. 472

> **Your Turn** Working with a small group, make a list of the newspapers, Web sites, magazines, TV shows or networks, or other resources that members of the group use to gather their news and information about politics, society, and culture. Then try to locate these media resources along a ribbon that moves from the political far left to the political far right. Be prepared for considerable disagreement. When you are done, compare your placements with those of other groups working on the same project. What may account for your differences?
>
> Far left _____ Left _____ Center _____ Right _____ Far right

Read against the grain. Skeptics and naysayers may be no fun at parties, but their habits may be worth emulating whenever you are reading. It makes sense to read with an open mind, giving reputable writers and their ideas a fair hearing. But you always want to raise questions about the assumptions writers make, the logic they use, the evidence they present, and the authorities and sources upon which they build their arguments.

Reading against the grain does not mean finding fault with everything, but rather letting nothing slip by without scrutiny. Treat the world around you as a text to be read and analyzed. ○ Ask questions. Why do so few men take liberal-arts courses? What topics does your campus paper avoid and why? Have your friendships changed now that you deal with people mostly online? Notice such phenomena, ponder their meaning, and write about them.

Read slowly. Browsing online has made many of us superficial readers. For serious texts, forget speed-reading and your own Web habits. Settle in for the duration. Find the thesis; look up unfamiliar words and names; don't jump to another article until you've finished the one in hand.

Annotate what you read. Find some way to record your reactions to whatever you read. If you own the text and don't mind marking it, highlighting pens and

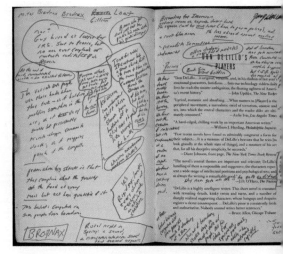

The late writer David Foster Wallace took copious notes when he read—in this case, the Don DeLillo novel *Players*.

think critically
p. 372

comments in the margin remain great tools for drawing your attention to weighty ideas. Electronic media and e-readers offer a range of built-in commenting tools. Even Post-it notes work in some circumstances. What's key is to interact with your reading.

Read visually.   Much information comes to us today not in words only but in visual formats that expand the way data can be presented. Whether in print or on screen, visual texts are inherently appealing, but don't assume they are simplistic or easy to interpret.

Consider how much information the humble campus map conveys, relying on nothing more than drawings, colors, symbols, and various legends or keys. When enhanced by sound and motion, as they routinely are in electronic environments, visual texts can become complex multimedia experiences.

When reading or using the following types of images and graphics, try the strategies suggested here.

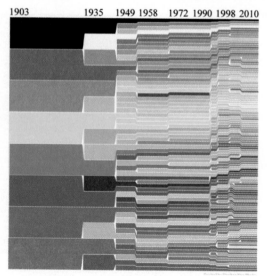

"Velo's Crayola Color Chart, 1903–2010"

- **Read an image showing a sequence.** Like a narrative, an image can break information into stages or steps. So study a graphic for its structural pattern: the way it gives order to its components. Elements may be arranged alphabetically, chronologically, or by degree or magnitude (for example, greater to lesser, cheaper to more expensive)—whatever works for the material. Begin your interpretation by paying attention to headings and navigation devices (especially for electronic images); then study any legends and keys, which will explain the meaning of symbols, colors, and other devices used in the graphic. An elegant chronological graphic like Stephen Von Worley's "Velo's Crayola Color Chart, 1903–2010" leaves some of the work of interpretation to you.

- **Read an image demonstrating a process.** Sequences grow more complicated when they begin to offer choices and alternative pathways. Flowcharts, for example, may display complicated options and feedback loops that you must navigate to reach a goal or conclusion. Look carefully at such diagrams to be sure you understand the meaning of intersections, lines and line graphics, and colors. For an excellent example of a complex flowchart, see "How Our Laws Are Made" on page 70.

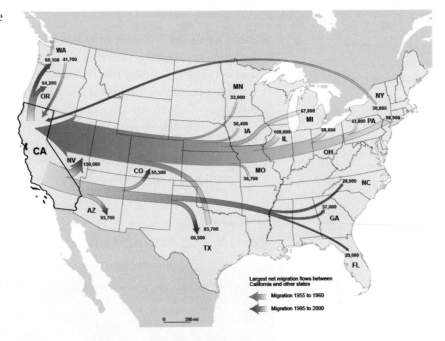

- **Read an image displaying relationships and differences.** Many graphics use boundaries —lines, boxes, columns, contrasting colors, and so on—to highlight divisions. A seating guide to an auditorium might mimic its floor plan to guide you to your box and use colors to show the price difference between the loge and the mezzanine sections. More complicated are the charts, graphs, and tables you'll encounter in natural and social science courses. These items use visual elements to array information or to plot relationships between variables. So you have to carefully examine their labels, column titles, interpretive keys, and other devices to be certain that you understand them. You may also need to know the sources of the data they present, the scales used to express changes over time, and so on. For good reason, we talk about "studying" charts and graphs. In recent years, much attention has been paid to designing informative graphics to convey data memorably. The United States Census Bureau's data visualization above (available at http://www.census.gov/dataviz) is an example of such an infographic.

● **Read an image showing how items are connected.** Quite often, information needs to be presented in diagrams that show hierarchies and other ties. A family tree illustrates the genealogical connections among a person's ancestors. A site map displays the main pages and subpages of a Web site. An organizational chart (or "org. chart," as it is commonly called) lets you know who reports to whom within an organization. You may struggle with some diagrams of this sort, but that's usually a flaw in their design. These types of visuals should be self-explanatory and clear.

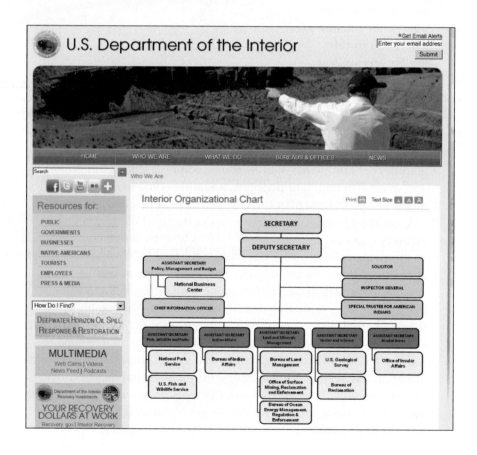

- **Read a map.** Surveys indicate that as many as one-third of drivers can't read a street map; weather maps may be just as puzzling. The problem is that while maps seem simple, they ask you to imagine the complications of real life reduced to symbols. On a map you must contend with direction, scale, geography, terrain, distance, boundaries, road symbols and names, place names, speed, and time. Hold the map wrong and you already have a problem. Weather maps introduce other variables. Yet the genius of a good map is the enormous amount of information it will offer once you master its symbols, keys, and scale. That's where to begin.

- **Read an image imitating three dimensions.** Many images, particularly in the fields of science and engineering, attempt to convey three-dimensional information in two dimensions, enabling viewers to understand how objects work, how parts mesh, or how the natural world functions (see "Geologic Hazards at Volcanoes"). Such cutaway or "exploded" drawings enable viewers to see relationships that would be very difficult to explain in words alone. And yet they require you to imagine how the various layers fit together when you see the parts either cut away or pulled apart. You may have to study such images to figure them out; not surprisingly, some 3-D information is better conveyed on video. **O**

≋USGS
science for a changing world

Geologic Hazards at Volcanoes

Prevailing Wind

Eruption Cloud

Tephra (Ash) Fall

Acid Rain

Bombs

Lava Dome

Lava Dome Collapse

Pyroclastic Flow

Lava Flow

Lahar (Mud or Debris Flow)

Eruption Column

Debris Avalanche (Landslide)

Pyroclastic Flow

Vent

Fumaroles

Conduit   Ground Water

Crack

Magma

Most volcano hazards are associated with eruptions. However, some hazards, such as lahars and debris avalanches, can occur even when a volcano is not erupting.

By Bobbie Myers and Carolyn Driedger 2008

U.S. Department of the Interior
U.S. Geological Survey

General Information Product 64

go multimodal
p. 568

22 Critical Thinking

We all get antsy when our written work is criticized (or even edited) because the ideas we put on a page or screen emerge from our own thinking—writing is *us*. Granted, our words rarely express *exactly* who we are or what we've been imagining, but such distinctions get lost quickly when someone points to our work and says, "That's stupid" or "What nonsense!" The criticism cuts deep; it feels personal.

Fortunately, the surest way to avoid embarrassing criticism is also the best way to come up with ideas that look plausible when they find their way into print: *critical thinking*. Critical thinking is a term that describes mental habits that bolster logical reasoning and analysis. There are lots of ways to foster critical thinking, from following the general strategies of smart reading described in Chapter 21 to using the specific rhetorical tactics presented throughout the "Guide" section of this book. To report, argue, explain, or analyze well is, in effect, to practice critical thinking.

Here we focus on several aspects of critical thinking that you will find useful in college writing.

Think in terms of claims and reasons. When you read reports, arguments, or analyses, chances are you begin by examining the claims writers make and the good reasons they have for offering them. Logically, then, when you write in these genres, you should expect the same scrutiny.

Claims are the passages in a text where you make an assertion, offer an argument, or present a hypothesis for which you intend to provide evidence.

Using a cell phone while driving is dangerous.

Playing video games can improve intelligence.

Worrying about childhood obesity is futile.

Early in a work, you may state a *thesis* or goal for a project, but that's only one type of claim. ○ Sentences that make a specific point may occur just about anywhere in an article, report, or book. You'll need to offer clear claims as the topic sentences in many paragraphs, in transitional sentences, and in summary materials at various points in the work, especially at the conclusion. (The exception may be formal scientific writing, in which the hypothesis, results, and discussion will occur in specific sections of an article.) ○

Critical thinking really begins when you make sure that all such major claims in a text are accompanied by plausible supporting *reasons* either in the same sentence or in adjoining material. These reasons may be announced by expressions as straightforward as *because, if, to,* and *so.* Once you attach reasons to a claim, you have made a deeper commitment to it. You must then do the hard work of providing readers with convincing evidence, logic, or conditions for accepting your claim. Seeing your ideas fully stated on paper early in a project may even persuade you to abandon an implausible claim—one you cannot or do not want to defend.

Using a cell phone while driving is dangerous *because* distractions are a proven cause of auto accidents.

Playing video games can improve intelligence *if* they teach young gamers to make logical decisions quickly.

~~Worrying about childhood obesity is futile because there's nothing we can do about it.~~

Think in terms of premises and assumptions.   Underlying all important claims and reasons are the core principles and values upon which researchers and writers operate: These are called *premises* or *assumptions.*

develop a statement
p. 393

understand lab
reports p. 336

△

In oral arguments, when people say *I understand where you're coming from,* they signal that they get your assumptions. You want similar clarity and connection when writing reports and arguments, especially when your claims may be regarded as controversial or argumentative. Your assumptions can be specific or general, conventional or highly controversial, as in the following examples.

> We should discourage behaviors that contribute to traffic accidents. [specific]
>
> Improving intelligence is a desirable goal. [general]
>
> The physical world is organized by coherent and predictable principles. [conventional]
>
> Freedom is better than tyranny. [conventional]
>
> Exploiting the environment is better than preserving it. [controversial]

With some audiences, you may be able to assume that most readers agree with your underlying values. In such cases, your premises may simply be implied. But when your arguments are more controversial, you will need to take the time to explain and defend your assumptions. Naturally—and here's where the critical thinking comes in—you need to be aware of the premises upon which your arguments are built. Do they make sense? Can you defend your assumptions?

Your Turn   Working in a group, find an example of a short argument that impresses most of you. (Your instructor might suggest a particular article.) Carefully locate the claims within the piece that all of you regard as its most important, impressive, or controversial statements. Then see if you can formulate the premises or values upon which these claims rest. Try to state these premises as clearly as you can in a complete, declarative sentence. Are the assumptions you have uncovered statements that you agree with? If the assumptions are controversial, does the piece explain or defend them? Be prepared to present your group's analysis and conclusions in class.

Think in terms of evidence.   As you write, be sure that all your major claims as well as your assumptions (when they are controversial) are supported by *evidence*. A claim without evidence attached is just that—a barefaced assertion no better than a child's "Oh, yeah?" You should choose supporting material attentively, always weighing whether it is sufficient, complete, reliable, and unbiased. ○ Has an author you want to cite done original research and drawn on respectable sources or, instead, relied on evidence that seems flimsy or anecdotal? And can you offer enough evidence to make a convincing case? How much evidence might be too much? These are questions to ask routinely and persistently.

Anticipate objections.   Critical thinkers understand that serious issues have many dimensions—and rarely just two sides. That's because they have done their homework, which means trying to understand even those positions with which they strongly disagree. When you start writing with this kind of knowledgeable perspective, you'll hear voices of the loyal opposition in your head and can address objections even before potential readers make them. At a minimum, you will enhance your credibility. But more important, you'll have done the kind of thinking that makes you smarter.

Avoid logical fallacies.   Honest, fair-minded writers have nothing to hide. They name names, identify sources, and generate appropriate emotions. They acknowledge weakness in their arguments and concede readily when the opposition has a point. These are qualities you want to display in your serious academic and professional work.

One way to enhance your reputation as a writer and critical thinker is to avoid logical fallacies. *Fallacies* are rhetorical moves that corrupt solid reasoning—the verbal equivalent of sleight of hand. The following classic, but all too common, fallacies can undermine the integrity of your writing.

● **Appeals to false authority.** Be sure that any experts or authorities you cite on a topic have real credentials in the field and that their claims can be verified. Similarly, don't claim or imply knowledge, authority, or credentials yourself that you don't have. Be frank about your level of expertise. Framing yourself as an honest, if amateur, broker on a subject can even raise your credibility.

refine your search
p. 472

- *Ad hominem* **attacks.** In arguments of all kinds, you may be tempted to bolster your position by attacking the personal integrity of your opponents when character really isn't an issue. It's easy to resort to name-calling (*socialist, racist*) or character assassination, but it usually signals that your own case is weak.

- **Dogmatism.** Writers fall back on dogmatism whenever they want to give the impression, usually false, that they control the party line on an issue and have all the right answers. You are likely indulging in dogmatism when you begin a paragraph, *No serious person would disagree* or *How can anyone argue. . . .*

- **Either/or choices.** A shortcut to winning arguments, which even Socrates abused, is to reduce complex situations to simplistic choices: good/bad,

"Either you left the TV on downstairs or we have whales again."

right/wrong, liberty/tyranny, smart/dumb, and so on. If you find yourself inclined to use some version of the *either/or* strategy, think again. Capable readers will see right through your tactic.

- **Scare tactics**. Avoid them. Arguments that make their appeals chiefly by raising fears—usually of the unknown—are automatically suspect. When fears are legitimate, provide evidence for the threat and don't overstate it.

- **Sentimental or emotional appeals**. Maybe it's okay for the Humane Society to decorate its pleas for cash with pictures of sad puppies, but you can see how the tactic might be abused. In your own work, be wary of using language that pushes buttons the same way, *oohing* and *aahing* readers out of their best judgment.

- **Hasty generalizations**. It is remarkably tempting to draw conclusions from just one or two poignant examples that fit your preconceived notions—or those of your intended audiences. But avoid the temptation to hang a claim on such scant evidence. Your integrity is at stake.

- **Faulty causality**. Just because two events or phenomena occur close together in time doesn't mean that one caused the other. (The Red Sox didn't start winning *because* you put on the lucky boxers.) People are fond of leaping to such easy conclusions, and many pundits and politicians do routinely exploit this weakness, particularly in situations involving economics, science, health, crime, and culture. Causal

relationships are almost always complicated, and you will get credit for dealing with them honestly. ○

● **Equivocations, evasions, and misstatements.** *Equivocations* are lies that look like truths; *evasions* simply avoid the truth entirely. Skilled readers know when a writer is using these devices, so avoid them.

● **Straw men.** *Straw men* are easy or habitual targets that writers aim at to win an argument. Often the issue in such an attack has long been defused or discredited: for example, welfare recipients driving Cadillacs, immigrants taking jobs from hard-working citizens, the rich not paying a fair share of taxes. When you resort to straw-man arguments, you signal to your readers that you may not have much else in your arsenal.

● **Slippery-slope arguments.** Take one wrong step off the righteous path and you'll slide all the way down the hill: That's the warning that slippery-slope arguments make. They aren't always inaccurate, but they are easy to overstate. Will using plastic bags really doom the planet? Maybe or maybe not. If you create a causal chain, be sure that you offer adequate support for every step and don't push beyond what's plausible.

● **Bandwagon appeals.** You haven't made an argument when you simply tell people it's time to cease debate and get with popular opinion. Too many bad decisions and policies get enacted that way. If you order readers to jump aboard a bandwagon, expect them to resist.

● **Faulty analogies.** Similes and analogies are worth applauding when they illuminate ideas or make them comprehensible or memorable. But seriously analyze the implications of any analogies you use. Calling a military action either "another Vietnam" or a "crusade" might raise serious issues, as does comparing one's opponents to "Commies" or the KKK. Readers have a right to be skeptical of writers who use such ploys.

understand causal
analysis p. 138

Experts 23

Forget about *expert* as an intimidating word. When you need help with your writing, seek advice from people who either know more about your subject than you do or have more experience developing such a project. Advice may come from different people, but that's not a problem: The more people you talk to, the better.

Knowledgeable people can get you on track quickly, confirming the merit of your topic ideas, cutting through issues irrelevant to your work, and directing you to the best resources.

ask for help

Talk with your instructor. Don't be timid. Instructors hold office hours to answer your questions, especially about assignments. Save yourself time and, perhaps, much grief by getting early feedback on your ideas and topic. It's better to learn that your thesis is hopeless *before* you compose a first draft.

Just as important, your instructor might help you see aspects of a topic you hadn't noticed or direct you to indispensable sources. Don't write a paper only to please instructors, but you'd be foolish to ignore their counsel.

Take your ideas to the writing center. Many student writers think the only time to use a campus writing center is when their teacher returns a draft on life support. Most writing center tutors prefer not to be seen as EMTs. So they are eager to assist at the start of a project, when you're still developing ideas. Tutors may not be experts on your subject, but they have seen enough bad papers to offer sensible advice for focusing a topic, shaping a thesis, or adapting a subject to an audience. ○ They also recognize when you're so clueless that you need to talk with your instructor pronto.

Find local experts.   Don't bother an expert for information you could find easily yourself in the library or online: Save human contacts for when you need serious help on a major writing project—a senior thesis, an important story for a campus periodical, a public presentation on a controversial subject. But, then, do take advantage of the human resources you have. Campuses are teeming with knowledgeable people and that doesn't just include faculty in their various disciplines. Staff and administrative personnel at your school can advise you on everything from trends in college admissions to local crime statistics.

Look to the local community for expertise and advice as well. Is there a paper to be written about declining audiences for foreign films? You couldn't call Pedro Almodóvar and get through, but you could chat with a few local theater owners or managers to learn what they think about the business. Their perceptions might change the direction of your project.

Check with librarians.   Campus librarians have lots of experience helping writers find information, steering them toward fertile topics and away from ideas that may not have much intellectual standing. Librarians can't be as specific or directive as, for example, your instructor, but they have just as firm a grasp on the resources available for a project and what sorts of topic ideas the library's resources will and will not support.

Chat with peers.   Peers aren't really experts, but an honest classroom conversation among fellow students can be an eye-opening experience. You'll likely see a wide spectrum of opinions (if the discussion is frank) and even be surprised by objections to your ideas that you hadn't anticipated. Peers often have a surprising range of knowledge and, if the group is diverse, your friends will bring a breadth of life experiences to the conversation. You might be eager to champion advances in medical technology, but someone

develop a statement
p. 393

from a community where hospitals can't afford high-tech gear might add a
wrinkle to your thinking.

Colleges and universities
often provide lists of faculty and staff with special
expertise in their fields.

Your Turn   If you were asked to identify yourself as an expert on a subject,
what would it be? Don't consider academic subjects only. Think about *any*
areas or activities about which you could confidently offer authoritative and
reliable advice. Make a list, and share it with your classmates. Do their lists
give you additional ideas?

1 Bring materials with you, including the assignment, previous drafts or outlines, comments from your instructor if you have any, a pen, and a notebook.

2 Be actively involved during the session, and arrive with specific goals in mind. Your tutor may ask questions about your writing process and your paper. Be prepared to think about and respond to your tutor's suggestions.

3 Keep revising. While the tutor may be able to help you with some aspects of your writing, you are ultimately responsible for the finished paper — and your grade.

24 Writer's Block

tackle hard
stuff

Waiting until the last minute to write a paper hasn't been defined as a medical problem yet. But give it time. Already a condition called *executive dysfunction* describes the inability of some children and adults to plan, organize, pace, and complete tasks. No doubt we've all experienced some of its symptoms, describing the state as *procrastination* when it comes to doing the laundry and *writer's block* when it applies to finishing papers on time.

Getting writing done isn't hard because the process is painful, but rather because it is so fragile and vulnerable to ridiculous excuses and distractions. Who hasn't vacuumed a floor or washed a car rather than compose a paragraph? Writing also comes with no guarantees, no necessary connection between labor put in and satisfactory pages churned out. Like baseball, writing is a game without time limits. When a paper isn't going well, you can stretch into fruitless twelfth and thirteenth innings with no end in sight. And if you do finish, readers may not like what you have done — even when you know the work is solid, based on honest reading, observation, and research. Such concerns are enough to give anyone writer's block.

So what do you do when you'd rather crack walnuts with your teeth than write a term paper?

Break the project into parts. Getting started is usually the hard part for writers simply because the project taken as a whole seems overwhelming. Even a simple one-page position paper can ruin a whole weekend, and a term paper—with its multiple drafts, abstract, notes, bibliography, tables, and graphs—stretches beyond the pale.

But what if, instead of thinking about how much time and energy the whole project will take, you divide it into manageable stages? Then you can do the work in chunks and celebrate the success that comes from completing each part. That position paper might be broken down into two, maybe three, less daunting steps: doing the assigned reading; brainstorming the paper; writing the page required. The same procedure makes a research paper less intimidating: You have more parts to manage, but you also have a strategy to finish them.

Set manageable goals.   Unless you are very disciplined, writing projects absorb all the time available for them. Worse, you'll likely expend more energy fretting than working. To gain control, set reasonable goals for completing the project and stick to them. In other words, don't dedicate a whole Saturday to preparing your résumé or working up a lab report; instead, commit yourself to the full and uninterrupted two hours the task will really take if you sit down and concentrate.

If you have trouble estimating how much time a project may require, consider that it is better to set a goal than to face an open-ended commitment. That's one good reason both teachers and publishers set deadlines.

Create a calendar.   For complicated assignments that extend over weeks or even months, create a calendar or timeline and stick with it. ○ First break the task into parts and estimate how much time each stage of the paper or other project will take. Knowing your own work habits, you can draw on past experience with similar assignments to construct a levelheaded plan. You'll feel better once you've got a road map leading to completion.

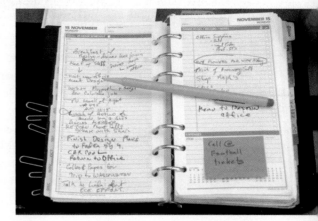

plan a project
p. 466

Don't draw up a schedule so elaborate that you build in failure by trying to manage too many events. Assume that some stages, especially research or drafting, may take more time than you originally expect. But do stick to your schedule, even if it means starting a draft with research still remaining or cutting off the drafting process to allow time for thorough revision.

Limit distractions.   Put yourself in a place that encourages writing and minimizes any temptations that might pull you away from your work. Schedule a specific time for writing and give it priority over all other activities, from paying your bills to feeding the dog. (On second thought, feed that dog to stop the barking.) Shut down your Facebook and e-mail accounts, turn off your cell phone, shuffle from the Killers to Bill Frisell on your iPod, start writing, and don't stop for an hour.

Do the parts you like first.   Movies aren't filmed in sequence and papers don't have to be written that way either. Compose those parts of a project that feel ready to go or interest you most. You can work on the transitions later to make the paper feel seamless, the way editors cut disparate scenes into coherent films. Once you have portions of a paper already composed you'll be more inclined to continue working on it: The project suddenly seems manageable.

Write a zero draft.   When you are *really* blocked, try a zero draft—that is, a version of the paper composed in one sitting, virtually nonstop. The process may resemble freewriting, but this time you aren't trawling for ideas. You're ready to write, having done the necessary brainstorming, reading, and research. You might even have a thesis and an outline. What you lack is the confidence to turn this preparation into coherent sentences. So repress your inhibitions by writing relentlessly, without pausing to reread and review your stuff. Keep at it for several hours if need be. Imagine you're writing an essay exam. O

> Inspiration is wonderful when it happens, but the writer must develop an approach for the rest of the time. . . . The wait is simply too long.

—Leonard Bernstein

understand essay
exams p. 284

The draft you produce won't be elegant (though you might surprise yourself), and some spots might be rough indeed. But keep pushing until you've finished a full text, from introduction to conclusion. Put this version aside, delaying any revision for a few hours or even days. Then, instead of facing an empty tablet or screen, you have full pages of prose to work with.

Reward yourself.   People respond remarkably well to incentives, so promise yourself some prize correlated to the writing task you face. Finishing a position paper is probably worth a personal-size pizza. A term paper might earn you dinner and a movie. A dissertation is worth a used Honda Civic.

> **Your Turn**   Do you have a good writer's block story to share? You might describe an odd thing you have done rather than start a paper — especially one that might seem far more arduous than putting words down on a page. Or maybe you have figured out an infallible method for overcoming writer's block. Or you have endured a roommate's endless excuses for failing to complete a writing assignment. Tell your story in a paragraph or two, which you will start writing *NOW*.

Shaping & Drafting

Need help developing your ideas? See page 412. / Need style help? See page 432.

25 Genre

choose a
genre

What's a *genre*? You already know. You use the concept of genre whenever you identify movies by type: *sci-fi films, westerns, action/ adventure films, romances* (a.k.a. "chick flicks"), *horror movies,* and so on. You surely recognize that movies have distinct *subgenres* too. Horror movies, for example, can be broken down into slasher pics, monster films, psychological thrillers, and more—all with well-established features and characteristics that audiences expect to encounter in a darkened theater.

Genre is also a term used to describe important categories of writing such as novels, short stories, poems, or nonfiction. Each of these genres can be clearly defined, described by their features, and taught by using formulas or templates.

But now consider a more dynamic view of *genre,* one that treats genres of writing not as fixed categories but as real-life responses to ever-changing situations. Simply put, writers have to figure out what they must do to achieve a goal and to reach particular readers. So they adapt a familiar form of writing to a specific moment, context, reader, and purpose. That's how genres are presented in this book.

For instance, in recent years, as more and more organizations and businesses have required potential job candidates to describe their lives and qualifications, the genre of the "personal statement" has evolved. Today, people recognize and expect such a task whenever they apply for internships, jobs, or scholarships. As a result, it's now possible to describe the strategies and conventional features of successful personal statements—and explain how writers can compose them successfully. You can find such information in Chapter 16.

But because genres respond to real-world situations, they change to fit the times. So when you learn a new genre, you don't necessarily acquire a hard-and-fast set of rules for writing; instead, you gain control over that genre's possibilities. That enables you to adapt its moves to your specific needs. So genres don't complicate your life; instead, they enable you to address widely varying writing situations.

> **Your Turn**   Generate a list of all the genres of writing or communication that you produce in a typical week in all aspects of your life, not just in school. How did you learn to produce those genres? Which did you learn on your own and which required formal instruction? Which have you yet to master? Compare your list of genres with those produced by classmates, noting in particular any types of writing they use that you don't.

Recognize the variety of genres.   Some genres of writing are broad and open-ended, such those presented in Part 1 of this book: personal narratives, reports, arguments, analyses, and so on. When you study genres like these, you encounter the basic strategies people use in school and the professional world. But when you actually write, you will usually produce a narrower version of these genres—one of those subgenres discussed earlier. So you won't compose a nonspecific report; you'll write a history term paper or sports column about college recruiting. You won't produce a generic evaluation; ○ you'll write a movie or restaurant review or job assessment. In effect, you'll adapt a genre to your needs.

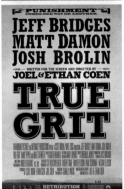

Part 2, "Special Assignments," covers a range of subgenres especially important to people studying in school or entering the job market—items such as the essay examination, résumé, personal statement, and oral report. In these chapters, you'll notice how down-to-earth and action oriented genres can be. They do bona fide work.

And that is how genres differ from the *strategies of writing* presented in Chapter 27, such as description, division, comparison, classification, and definition. ○ These techniques are essential tools of writing, but they apply across a full range of genres. In writing a report or argument, you might need to illustrate a point, offer a description, or draw a comparison to make ideas stand out. But you would rarely just describe or compare or illustrate without making some larger point represented by a genre.

understand
evaluation p. 106

develop a draft
p. 398

Know how to use genres.   Many people think of genres chiefly in terms of their structures of organization. Naturally, when writing a book review or a psychology term paper, it makes sense to study examples of the genre, noting what elements go where. That's a useful first step.

But to understand a genre well, you must also recognize its typical aims, audiences, styles of language, special features, and characteristic media. Reports, for example, often rely on tables and graphs; a research paper always needs reliable sources and careful documentation; and arguments deploy lots of examples and evidence. Such matters are covered in the "Genres" and "Special Assignments" chapters in this book (see Chapters 1–18). Once you grasp the way genres work, you won't be intimidated by any of them.

Appreciate that genres change.   Genres in almost every medium always change: Consider how the vampire movie has evolved from Bela Lugosi's 1931 *Dracula* to today's *Twilight* series. Genres of writing typically alter in response to the needs of audiences and institutions. But we are probably more aware than ever of such evolution today because of the speed of technological developments.

Consider how personal communications have been transformed, moving from paper to e-mail to text message to Twitter feed, each new medium creating its own expectations and etiquette. In working with such rapidly changing technologies, you are actually learning how genres arise and evolve. So pay attention.

Name	Time	Artist	Album	Genre
☑ Believe Me Natalie	5:07	The Killers	Hot Fuss	Alternative
☑ 'A vucchella	3:16	Anton Guadagno, L...	Luciano Pavarotti –...	Classical
☑ Getting Better	2:48	The Beatles	Sgt. Pepper's Lonel...	Rock
☑ One More Night	2:25	Bob Dylan	Nashville Skyline	Folk
☑ I Will Find You	1:51	Clannad	The Last Of The M...	Soundtrack
☑ Losing Touch	4:15	The Killers	Day & Age	Alternative...

You may recognize the term *genre* from iTunes, where it heads the column labeling the types of music you download. What musical genres from your iTunes list probably wouldn't be found on this baby boomer's iPod?

Thesis 26

A *thesis* is a statement in which a writer affirms or defends the specific idea that will focus or organize a paper. Typically, the thesis appears in an opening paragraph or section, but it may also emerge as the paper unfolds. In some cases, it may not be stated in classic form until the very conclusion. A thesis can be complex enough to require several sentences to explain, or a single sentence might suffice. But a thesis will be in the writing somewhere.

Offering a thesis is a move as necessary and, eventually, as instinctive to a writer as stepping on a clutch before shifting used to be to drivers. No thesis, no forward motion.

How do you write and frame a thesis? Consider the following advice.

Write a complete sentence. Phrases can identify topic areas, even intriguing ones, but they don't make the assertions or claims that provoke thinking and require support. Sentences do. ○ None of the following phrases comes close to providing direction for a paper.

> Polygamy in the United States
>
> Reasons for global warming
>
> Economist Steven D. Levitt's controversial theory about declining crime rates

develop a
statement

Make a significant claim or assertion. *Significant* here means that the notion provokes discussion or inquiry. Give readers substance or controversy—in other words, a reason to spend time with your writing.

> Until communities recognize that polygamy persists in parts of the United States, girls and young women will continue to be exploited by the practice.
>
> Global warming won't stop until industrial nations either lower their standards of living or admit the need for more nuclear power.

Write a declarative sentence, not a question. Questions may focus attention, but they are not assertions. So, while you might use a question to introduce a topic, don't rely on it to state your claim. A humdrum question acting as a thesis can provoke simplistic responses. There's always the danger, too, that in offering your thesis as a question, you invite strong reactions from readers—and not the ones you want. But introduce an idea as a statement and you gain more control. There is one exception to this guideline: Provocative questions can often help structure personal and exploratory writing.

Expect your thesis to mature. Your initial thesis will likely grow more complicated as you learn more about your subject. That's natural. But avoid the misconception that a thesis is a statement that breaks a subject into three parts. Theses that follow this pattern too often read like shopping lists, with only remote connections between the ideas presented. Just putting the claims in such a tri-part statement into a relationship often makes for a more compelling thesis. The items in dark red type do that job in the second example below.

ORGINAL THESIS

Crime in the United States has declined because more people are in prison, the population is growing older, and DNA testing has made it harder to get away with murder.

REVISED THESIS

It is **much more likely** that crime in the United States has declined because more people are in prison **than because** the population is growing older **or** DNA testing has made it harder to get away with murder.

Introduce a thesis early in a project.   This sound guideline is especially applicable to academic projects and term papers. Instructors will usually want to know up front what the point of a paper will be, especially in reports and some arguments. Whether phrased as a single sentence or several, a thesis typically follows an introductory paragraph or two. Here's the thesis (highlighted in yellow) of Andrew Kleinfeld and Judith Kleinfeld's essay "Go Ahead, Call Us Cowboys," following an opening paragraph that offers a context for their claim.

> Everywhere, Americans are called *cowboys*. On foreign tongues, the reference to America's Western rural laborers is an insult. Cowboys, we are told, plundered the earth, arrogantly rode roughshod over neighbors, and were addicted to mindless violence. So some of us hang our heads in shame. We shouldn't. The cowboy is in fact our Homeric hero, an archetype that sticks because there's truth in it.

Or state a thesis late in a project.   In high school, you may have heard that the thesis statement is *always* the last sentence in the first paragraph. That may be so in conventional five-paragraph essays, but you'll rarely be asked to follow so predictable a pattern in college or elsewhere.

In fact, it is not unusual, especially in some arguments, for a paper to build toward a thesis—and that statement may not appear until the final paragraph or sentence. ⵔ Such a strategy makes sense when a claim might not be convincing or rhetorically effective if stated baldly at the opening of the piece. Bret Stephens uses this strategy in an essay entitled "Just Like Stalingrad" to debunk frequent comparisons between former President George W. Bush and either Hitler or Stalin. Stephens's real concern turns out to be not these exaggerated comparisons themselves but rather what happens to language when it is abused by sloppy writers. The final two paragraphs of his essay summarize this case and, arguably, lead up to a thesis in the very last sentence of the essay—more rhetorically convincing there because it comes as something of a surprise.

> Care for language is more than a concern for purity. When one describes President Bush as a fascist, what words remain for real fascists? When one describes Fallujah as Stalingrad-like, how can we express, in the words that remain to the language, what Stalingrad was like?

understand
argument p. 72

> George Orwell wrote that the English language "becomes ugly and inaccurate because our thoughts are foolish, but the slovenliness of our language makes it easier for us to have foolish thoughts." In taking care with language, we take care of ourselves.
>
> – *Wall Street Journal*, June 23, 2004

Write a thesis to fit your audience and purpose.   Almost everything you write will have a purpose and a point (see the following table), but not

Type of Assignment	Thesis or Point
Narratives	Usually implied, not stated. (See thesis example on p. 9.)
Reports	Thesis usually previews material or explains its purpose. (See thesis example on p. 66.)
Arguments	Thesis makes an explicit and arguable claim. (See thesis example on p. 76.)
Evaluations	Thesis makes an explicit claim of value based on criteria of evaluation. (See thesis example on p. 127.)
Causal analyses	Thesis asserts or denies an explanatory or causal relationship, based on an analysis of evidence. (See thesis example on p. 141.)
Proposals	Thesis offers a proposal for action. (See thesis example on p. 181.)
Literary analyses	Thesis explains the point of the analysis. (See thesis example on p. 209.)
Rhetorical analyses	Thesis explains the point of the analysis. (See thesis example on p. 265.)
Essay examinations	Thesis previews the entire answer, like a mini-outline. (See thesis example on p. 288.)
Position papers	Thesis makes specific assertion about reading or issue raised in class. (See thesis example on p. 293.)
Annotated bibliographies	Each item may include a statement that describes or evaluates a source. (See example on p. 298.)
Synthesis papers	Thesis summarizes and paraphrases different sources on a specific topic. (See thesis example on p. 306.)
E-mails	Subject line may function as thesis or title. (See thesis example on p. 313.)
Business letters	Thesis states the intention for writing. (See thesis example on p. 320.)
Résumés	"Career objective" may function as a thesis. (See thesis example on p. 328.)
Personal statements	May state an explicit purpose or thesis or lead readers to inferences about qualifications. (See thesis example on p. 333.)
Lab reports	Thesis describes purpose of experiment. (See thesis example on p. 339.)
Oral reports	Introduction or preview slide describes purpose. (See thesis example on p. 350.)

every piece will have a formal thesis. In professional and scientific writing, readers want to know your claim immediately. For persuasive and exploratory writing, you might prefer to keep readers intrigued or have them track the path of your thinking, and delay the thesis until later.

Your Turn   Transform two or three of the following song titles into full-blown thesis statements that might be suitable in an academic paper or newspaper op-ed piece. If these titles don't inspire you, start with several song, album, or movie titles of your own choosing. Be sure that your theses are full, declarative sentences that make a significant assertion.

"Taxman"	"Lost in the Supermarket"
"Shark in the Water"	"Times Like These"
"Rain Is a Good Thing"	"Bleed American"
"Share the Ride"	"Especially in Michigan"
"I Don't Want Control of You"	"We Are Nowhere and It's Now"
"Waiting on the World to Change"	"I Turn My Camera On"
"All You Fascists"	"Someone Else's Problem"
"Concrete and Barbed Wire"	"Let the Idiot Speak"
"The Times They Are A-Changin' "	"Be True to Your School"

27 Strategies

develop a
draft

If *genres* represent forms of writing that serve specific aims and audiences, ○ then *strategies* describe patterns of writing that work across genres and are useful in many situations. This chapter looks at some of these essential tools, such as description, division, classification, definition, and comparison/contrast. It's true that you may sometimes write "descriptions" for their own sake, or "compare and contrast" just for the heck of it. But mostly you'll use these modes of writing while working within other genres.

Use description to set a scene.   Descriptions, which use language to recreate physical characteristics, can be impressive enough to stand on their own. But you'll often need descriptive passages to support other kinds of writing — perhaps a sentence to set the scene in a narrative or many paragraphs to bring a historical period alive in a term paper. Writers adapt descriptions to particular situations. In an explanation of an apparatus in a lab report, the language might be cold and technical, but in an opening chapter of a novel, the description would likely be richer and more connotative, as in the following paragraph.

> *Malpais*, translated literally from the Spanish, means "bad country." In New Mexico, it signifies specifically those great expanses of lava flow which make black patches on the map of the state. The malpais of the Checkerboard country lies just below Mount Taylor, having been produced by the same volcanic

choose a genre
p. 390

fault that, a millennium earlier, had thrust the mountain fifteen thousand feet into the sky. Now the mountain has worn down to a less spectacular eleven thousand feet and relatively modern eruptions from cracks at its base have sent successive floods of melted basalt flowing southward for forty miles to fill the long valley between Cebolleta Mesa and the Zuni Mountains.

—Tony Hillerman, *People of Darkness*

Descriptions always involve selection. Just as a photographer carefully frames a subject, you have to decide which elements (visual, aural, tactile, and so on) in a scene will convey the situation most accurately, efficiently, and memorably and then turn them into words. Think nouns first, then modifiers. Adjectives and adverbs are essential, but it's easy to ruin a description by overdressing the scene. Be specific, concrete, and honest. ○

A smart procedure is to write down everything in a descriptive passage that you want to include, and then edit out any words or phrases that are not essential. Be careful, too, to build the scene in a way that a reader can follow, providing clear directions for the eyes and mind. The following paragraph is from an argument about music and identity that uses a variety of techniques to describe the fans of punk rock; note that the passage focuses as much on sound as sight, which is appropriate when dealing with music.

Few genres showcase the unifying power of music better than punk. Punk surfaced in the mid-1970s as a form of anticulture and quickly swelled to epic influence. Finding multitudes of fans worldwide in a matter of years, bands like the Ramones and the Clash offered a fast, brash, and unforgiving sound that sonically "scoffed" at usual genre conventions. And their fans began mimicking that desire to separate from the current culture. The type of person you would associate with punk music didn't exist, so fans re-created themselves to personify the ideas the music portrays. Much like the loud, careless, and in-your-face fury of the power chords that punk music hurls at listeners, "punks," as they were labeled, began doing everything "loudly." They used their bodies as canvases for tattoos and piercings, while wearing their clothes down to the threads to refuse the "establishment's" idea of a member of society. And the effect back then was the same as it is today. Visually, this style connects listeners to the music and each other; when a punk sees one of his own (or hears him listening to punk music), the sense of kindred identity between the two is

improve your
sentences p. 444

unmistakable. And the way punks act, the jobs they take, and the items they consume all follow suit. Ironically, the music style that aimed to go against culture created an entirely new one.

– Jeremy Burchard

> **Your Turn**   Write a paragraph of about 200–250 words describing something or someone you love. This is a tough assignment because it calls for you to choose details that will convey a sentiment to readers that they won't initially share. If you can find a focus for the description, perhaps even a thesis, your job will be easier.

Use division to divide a subject.   This strategy of writing is so common you might not notice it in action. A division involves no more than breaking a subject into its major components or enumerating its parts. In a report for an art history class, you might use division to study a famous cathedral by listing and describing its major architectural features, one by one: facade, nave, towers, windows, and so on. Or in a sports column on the Big Ten's NCAA football championship prospects, you could just run through its roster of twelve teams. That's a reasonable structure for a review, given the topic.

Division also puts ideas into logical relationships that make them easier for readers to understand and use. The challenge comes when a subject doesn't break apart as neatly as a tangerine. Then you have to decide which parts are essential and which are subordinate. Divisions of this sort are more than mechanical exercises: They require your clear understanding of a subject. For example, in organizing a Web site for your school or college, you'd probably start by deciding which components of the school merit top-tier placement on the home page. ○ Such a decision will shape the entire project. (See the two examples on the next page.)

learn media
conventions p. 577

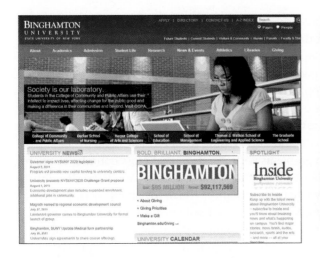

> **Your Turn**   As a strategy of writing (or organization), just how common is division? Look for examples of division in the texts you use or encounter during one day and keep a list. Then compare your list with those compiled by others. Which items on your list are straightforward examples of division and which shade into classification? (See the next strategy.) Does the difference matter?

Use classification to sort objects or ideas by consistent principles.

Classification breaks subjects into parts not by separating objects, but by clustering them according to meaningful or useful principles. Just think of all the ways that people can be classified:

By body type: endomorph, ectomorph, mesomorph

By hair color: black, brown, blond, red, gray, other

By weight: underweight, normal, overweight, obese

By sexual orientation: straight, bisexual, gay/lesbian, transgender

By race: black, Asian, white, other

By religion: Hindu, Buddhist, Muslim, Christian, Jew, other, no religion

Ideally, a principle of classification should apply to every member of the general class studied (in this case, people), and there would be no overlap among the resulting groups. But almost all useful efforts to classify complex phenomena—whether people, things, or ideas—have holes, gaps, or overlaps. Classifying people by religious beliefs, for instance, usually means mentioning the major groups and then lumping tens of millions of other people in a convenient category called "other."

Even scientists who organize everything from natural elements to species of birds run into problems with creatures that cross boundaries (plant or animal?) or discoveries that upset familiar categories. You'll wrestle with such problems routinely when, for instance, you argue about social policy: How do notions such as gay marriage or school vouchers fit into conventional classifications of "marriage" or "public education"? At some point, principles of classification evolve or change to maintain their explanatory power, because that's the rationale for any classification: to organize information accurately and perceptively.

> **Your Turn**   Not all classifications are equally important or useful. Begin with a large general category with which you are quite familiar: It might be sports franchises, politicians, horror movies, video games, cheeses, dogs, or some other topic. Next come up with three principles of division that you believe people less knowledgeable about your subject than you might find useful in understanding it better. Then, for fun, come up with three pointless or frivolous principles of division. For example, it might be important to classify politicians by education, political orientation, or region; it might be less useful to group them by hair color, weight, or their tastes in popular music. Or would it? Discuss your schemes of classification with your classmates.

Use definition to clarify meaning.   Definitions don't appear in dictionaries only. Like other strategies in this chapter, they occur in many genres. A definition might become the subject of a scientific report (what is a planet?), the bone of contention in a legal argument (how does the statute define *life*?), or the framework for a cultural analysis (can a comic book be a serious novel?). In all such cases, writers need to know how to construct valid definitions.

Though definitions come in various forms, the classic dictionary definition is based on principles of classification discussed in the previous section. Typically a term is defined first by placing it in a general class. Then its distinguishing features or characteristics are enumerated, separating it from other members of the larger class. You can see the principle operating in this comic paragraph, which first fits "dorks" into the general class of "somebody," that is to say, a *person*, and then claims two distinguishing characteristics.

> It's important to define what I truly mean by "dork," just so he or she doesn't get casually lumped in with "losers," "burnouts" and "lone psychopath bullies." To me, the dork is somebody **who didn't fit in at school** and who **therefore sought consolation in a particular field** – computers, "Star Trek," theater, heavy metal, medieval war reenactments, fantasy, sports trivia, even isolation sports like cross-country and ice skating.
>
> – Ian R. Williams, "Twilight of the Dorks?" *Salon.com*, October 23, 2003

In much writing, definitions become crucial when a question is raised about whether a particular object does or does not meet the criteria to join a particular group. You engage in this kind of debate when you argue about what is or isn't a sport, a punk band, a progressive piece of legislation, a loyal Democrat, an act of terrorism, and so on. In outline form, the structure of such a discussion looks like this:

Defined group:

– General class

– Distinguishing characteristic 1

– Distinguishing characteristic 2 . . .

Controversial term

– **Is/is not in the general class**

– **Does/does not share characteristic 1**

– **Does/does not share characteristic 2** . . .

Controversial term is/is not in the defined group

> **Your Turn**   Write a short argument in which you use a definition to determine whether someone or something does or does not deserve to be identified with a particular term. A classic example of such an argument, now settled by a federal court, is whether "cheerleading" is a "sport." (It's not.) Find a subject of your own, perhaps drawing from actual discussions or debates you have had with friends.

Use comparison and contrast to show similarity and difference.

We seem to think better when we place ideas or objects side-by-side. So it's not surprising that comparisons and contrasts play a role in all sorts of writing, especially reports, arguments, and analyses. Paragraphs are routinely organized to show how things are alike or different.

> The late 1960s and early 1970s were a time of cultural conflict, a battle between what I have called the beautiful people and the dutiful people. While Manhattan glitterati thronged Leonard Bernstein's apartment to celebrate the murderous Black Panthers, ordinary people in the outer boroughs and the far-flung suburbs of New Jersey like Hamilton Township were going to work, raising their families, and teaching their children to obey lawful authority and work their way up in the world.
>
> – Michael Barone, "The Beautiful People vs. the Dutiful People,"
> *U.S. News & World Report*, January 16, 2006

Much larger projects can be built on similar structures of comparison and/or contrast.

To keep extended comparisons on track, the simplest structure is to evaluate one subject at a time, running through its features completely before moving on to the next. Let's say you decided to contrast economic conditions in France and Germany. Here's how such a paper might look in a scratch outline if you focused on the countries one at a time. ○

France and Germany: An Economic Report Card
I. France
    A. Rate of growth
    B. Unemployment rate
    C. Productivity

order ideas
p. 408

      D. Gross national product
      E. Debt
  II. Germany
      A. Rate of growth
      B. Unemployment rate
      C. Productivity
      D. Gross national product
      E. Debt

The disadvantage of evaluating subjects one at a time is that actual comparisons, for example, of rates of employment in the outline above, might appear pages apart. So in some cases, you might prefer a comparison-contrast structure that looks at features point by point. O

France and Germany: An Economic Report Card
  I. Rate of growth
      A. France
      B. Germany
  II. Unemployment rate
      A. France
      B. Germany
 III. Productivity
      A. France
      B. Germany
 IV. Gross national product
      A. France
      B. Germany
  V. Debt
      A. France
      B. Germany

Your Turn   Often, the most interesting and fiercely argued contrasts are to be found between things that appear to be quite similar, for example, senators from the same political party, or high-end cameras, or competing top shelf sports teams. Write a short comparison involving closely paired items that you know well. Use the piece to illuminate the differences for readers who might not care much about the differences. Show them why they might be wrong.

---

understand evaluation
p. 106

28 Organization

shape your
work

To describe the organization of their projects, writers often use metaphors or other figures of speech. They visualize the elements of their work linked by chains, frames, patterns, or even skeletons. Such structural concepts help writers keep their emerging ideas on track, giving them shape and consistency. Effective organization also makes life easier for readers who come fresh to any paper or project, wondering how its words and ideas will fit together.

In Parts 1 and 2, you'll find specific suggestions for structuring a wide variety of writing genres. The following general advice will help you organize your work.

Examine model documents.   Many types of writing are highly conventional—which simply means that they follow predictable patterns and formulas. So study the structure of several examples of any new genre you're expected to compose. Some structural elements are immediately obvious, such as headings or introductory and concluding sections. But look for more subtle moves too—for example, many editorials first describe a problem, then blame someone for it, and finally make a comment or offer a comparison. Working with models of a genre will point your project in the right direction.

Sketch out a plan or sequence.   Even if you are brainstorming, starting with a rough plan helps give a project direction and purpose. A scratch (or informal) outline or similar device puts your initial ideas on paper, suggests relationships between them (sequence, similarity, difference), and perhaps hints at flaws or omissions. Just as important, creating a structure makes a writing project suddenly seem more doable because you've broken a complex task into smaller, more manageable parts.

Visualize structure when appropriate.   Technology can make it easier to organize your project. Consider how deftly you can move the slides in a PowerPoint project until you find the most effective order. Pen and paper can work just as well for visualizing the relationships between elements in a project, whether you prepare an outline to separate divergent features in a comparison/contrast piece or notecards to map the administrative structure of a complex organization. Seeing these items can point to ways of organizing everything from a paper to a Web site. ○

Provide clear steps or signals for readers.   Just because you know how the parts of your paper or project fit together, don't assume readers will. You have to give them cues—which come in various forms, including titles, headings, captions, and, especially, transitional words and phrases. For example, in a narrative you might include transitional words to mark the passage of time (*next, then, before, afterward*). Or if you organize a project according to a principle of magnitude, you might give readers signals that clearly show a change from *best* to *worst*, *cheapest* to *most expensive, most common species* to *endangered*. And if you are writing to inform or report, you might also rely heavily on visuals to help make your point. ○

Deliver on your commitments.   This is a basic principle of organization. If, for example, you promise in an introductory paragraph to offer two reasons in support of a claim, you need to offer two clearly identifiable reasons in that paper or readers will feel that they missed something. But commitments are broader than that: Narratives ordinarily lead somewhere, perhaps to a climax; editorials offer opinions; proposals offer and defend new ideas; evaluations make judgments. You can depart from these structural expectations, but you should do so knowing what readers expect and anticipating how they might react to your straying from the formula.

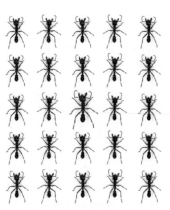

Your ideas won't march in rows like these ants, so you'll need a plan for your work.

think visually
p. 592

order ideas
p. 408

29 Outlines

Despite what you may believe, outlines are designed to make writing easier, not harder, as they help you put ideas in manageable form. And you'll feel more confident when you begin with a plan. The trick is to start simple and let outlines evolve to fit your needs.

order ideas

Begin with scratch outlines.   Many writers prefer working first with scratch, or informal, outlines—the verbal equivalent of the clever mechanical idea hurriedly sketched on a cocktail napkin.

In fact, the analogy is especially apt because good ideas often do evolve from simple, sometimes crude, notions that begin to make sense only when seen on paper. Both the Internet and the structure of the DNA molecule began with the visual equivalents of scratch outlines.

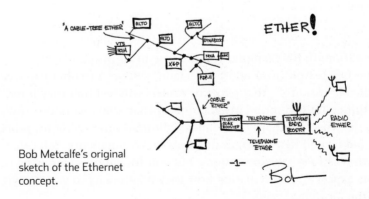

Bob Metcalfe's original sketch of the Ethernet concept.

List key ideas.   Write down your preliminary thoughts so you can see exactly what they are, eliminating any that obviously overlap. Keep these notes brief but specific, using words and phrases rather than complete sentences. Your initial scratch outline will likely resemble a mildly edited brainstorming list, like the one that follows.

<u>Fuel-efficient vehicles</u>
Hybrids
Electric cars haven't worked well
Europeans prefer diesels
Strengths and weaknesses
Costs might be high
Mechanically reliable?

Once you have ideas, begin applying the three principles that make outlining such a powerful tool of organization: *relationship, subordination,* and *sequence*.

Look for relationships.   Examine the initial items on your list and try grouping *like* with *like*—or look for opposites and contrasts. Experiment with various arrangements or clusters. In the brief scratch outline above, for example, you might decide that the items fall into two distinct categories. The three types of fuel-efficient cars are obviously related, while the remaining items represent aspects of these vehicles.

Hybrids	Strengths
Electric cars	Weaknesses
Diesels	Costs
	Reliability

Subordinate ideas.   Outlines are built on this principle of subordination or hierarchy: You are systematically dividing a subject into topics and subtopics. So some ideas belong not only grouped with others but also under them—that is to say, they belong to a smaller subset within a larger set.

For instance, looking again at those simple groupings of fuel-efficient vehicles, you could argue that *cost* and *reliability* are items that fit better

under either *strengths* or *weaknesses*. They are aspects of these larger categories. So you remove them from the outline for the moment.

You might notice, too, that your notes so far suggest a comparison/
contrast structure for your project. (See "Use comparison and contrast to show
similarity and difference" on p. 405 of Chapter 27, "Strategies.") Deciding to
replace *strengths* and *weaknesses* with the slightly more aggressive terms
advantages and *disadvantages*, you sketch out a rather more complex outline.

> Fuel-efficient vehicles
> Advantages
>   Hybrids
>   Electric cars
>   Diesels
> Disadvantages
>   Hybrids
>   Electric cars
>   Diesels

Decide on a sequence.   Now that you've moved from an initial list of
ideas to a basic design, consider the order in which to present the material.
You might arrange the items chronologically or by magnitude. Or your order
might be determined rhetorically—by how you want readers to respond.

Let's say you drive a Prius and have done enough research to believe that
hybrids represent the best option for saving on fuel costs. So you arrange the
paper to end on that note, understanding that readers are most likely to
remember what they read last. Reading the end of your paper, the audience
will focus on the advantages of gas-electric hybrid vehicles.

> A. Disadvantages of fuel-efficient vehicles
>   1. Electrics
>   2. Diesels
>   3. Gas-electric hybrids
> B. Advantages of fuel-efficient vehicles
>   1. Electrics
>   2. Diesels
>   3. Gas-electric hybrids

Move up to a formal outline.   You may be required to submit a formal outline with your final paper. By adhering to the following outline conventions, you can ferret out weaknesses in your thinking. ○

● Align the headings at every level (see example).

● Present at least two items at every heading level (I, A, and 1). If you can't find a second item to match the first in a new level of heads, perhaps the new level isn't needed.

● Present all items (except the thesis) as complete and parallel statements (not questions), properly punctuated.

● Place a topic sentence above the outline, underlined or italicized. That topic sentence sitting up top may keep you from wandering off-subject.

Thesis: <u>Though all fuel-efficient vehicles have technological strengths and weaknesses, hybrids currently represent the best option for drivers today</u>.

I. Currently available fuel-efficient vehicles have different technological problems.
    A. Electric vehicles lack versatility.
       1. Their batteries limit them to about one hundred miles before recharging.
       2. Their batteries are heavy, expensive, and slow to charge.
    B. Diesel vehicles can be truck-like.
       1. Their emissions are hard to clean up.
       2. Their fuel is smelly and toxic.
       3. Diesel fuel can be expensive.
    C. Gas-electric hybrids are technologically risky.
       1. They are heavy.
       2. Their dual propulsion systems (gas and electric) are complex.
II. Fuel-efficient vehicles have significant strengths.
    A. Electric vehicles are simple and civilized machines.
       1. They emit no measurable pollution where they are used.
       2. Their motors are almost silent and free of vibration.
    B. Diesels are robust vehicles suitable for all road conditions.
       1. Their engines are based on well-proven and strong technology.
       2. They burn fuel efficiently.
    C. Gas-electric hybrids combine advantages of other fuel-efficient vehicles.
       1. They work like electric vehicles in the city.
       2. They are as strong as diesels on the highway.
       3. They combine well-proven electric and internal-combustion technologies.

The fully electric Nissan Leaf has a range of one hundred miles per charge, but needs up to eight hours to charge.

develop a statement
p. 393

30 Paragraphs

develop ideas

Paragraphs are a practical invention, created to make long continuous blocks of writing easier to read by dividing them up. Because they give writers a physical way to shape ideas and transmit them to readers, paragraphs are a powerful tool. You've heard many rules and definitions over the years, but the fact is that paragraphs exist to help you develop and structure your ideas. Here are some helpful ways to think about them.

Make sure paragraphs lead somewhere.   Sometimes you'll use a straightforward topic sentence to state your point and introduce a claim that the rest of your paragraph will develop. ○ But, just as often, you may wait until the concluding sentences to make your point, or you may weave a key idea into the fabric of the entire paragraph (as in the first paragraph of the example that follows). Whatever your strategy, all paragraphs should do significant work: introduce a subject, move a narrative forward, offer a new argument or claim, provide support for a claim already made, contradict another point, amplify an idea, furnish more examples, even bring discussion to an end. It has to do *something* that readers see as purposeful and connected to what comes before and after.

For instance, reviewing the third album of the rock band Coldplay, music critic Jon Pareles leads his readers through an opening paragraph demanding enough to try any rocker's patience. What's he doing here? But then he delivers his death-blow in a second, much shorter, paragraph. Suddenly, you have no

develop a statement
p. 393

doubt where Pareles stands—and probably want to read the entire review, even if you like the band.

> There's nothing wrong with self-pity. As a spur to songwriting, it's right up there with lust, anger, and greed, and probably better than the remaining deadly sins. There's nothing wrong, either, with striving for musical grandeur, using every bit of skill and studio illusion to create a sound large enough to get lost in. Male sensitivity, a quality that's under siege in a pop culture full of unrepentant bullying and machismo, shouldn't be dismissed out of hand, no matter how risible it can be in practice. And building a sound on the lessons of past bands is virtually unavoidable.
>
> But put them all together and they add up to Coldplay, the most insufferable band of the decade.
>
> – "The Case Against Coldplay," *New York Times*, June 5, 2005

Develop ideas adequately.   Instructors who insist that paragraphs run a minimum number of sentences (say 6–10) are usually just tired of students who don't back up claims with details and evidence. ⭕ In fact, most writers don't count sentences when they build paragraphs. Instead, they develop a sense for paragraph length, matching the swell of their ideas to the habits of their intended readers.

Consider the following paragraph, which describes the last moments of the final Apollo moon mission in December 1972. The paragraph might be reduced to a single sentence: *All that remained of the 363-foot* Apollo 17 *launch vehicle was a 9-foot capsule recovered in the ocean.* But what would be lost? The pleasure of the full paragraph resides in the details the writer musters to support the final sentence, which contains his point.

> A powerful Sikorsky Sea King helicopter, already hovering nearby as they [the *Apollo 17* crew] hit the water, retrieved the astronauts and brought them to the carrier, where the spacecraft was recovered shortly later. The recovery crew saw not a gleaming instrument of exotic perfection, but a blasted, torn, and ragged survivor, its titanic strength utterly exhausted, a husk now a shell. The capsule they hauled out of the ocean was all that remained of the *Apollo 17* Saturn V. The journey had spent, incinerated, smashed, or blistered into atoms every other part of the colossal, 363-foot white rocket, leaving only this burnt and brutalized 9-foot capsule. A great shining army had set out over the horizon, and a

understand
argument p. 72

lone squadron had returned, savaged beyond recognition, collapsing into the arms of its rescuers, dead. Such was the price of reaching for another world.

–David West Reynolds, *Apollo: The Epic Journey to the Moon*

Organize paragraphs logically.   It would be surprising if paragraphs didn't borrow structural strategies used by full essays: thesis and support, division, classification, comparison/contrast. But it's ideas that drive the shape of paragraphs, not patterns of organization. Most writers don't pause to wonder whether their next paragraph should follow a narrative or cause-effect plan. They just write it, making sure it makes a point and offers sufficient evidence to keep readers engaged.

In fact, individual paragraphs in any longer piece can be organized many different ways. And because paragraphs are relatively short, you usually see their patterns unfold right before your eyes. The following two passages are from an essay by Jon Katz entitled "Do Dogs Think?" The paragraphs within them use structures Katz needs at that given moment.

Narrative paragraph describes changes in Blue's behavior.

Blue, Heather's normally affectionate and obedient Rottweiler, began tearing up the house shortly after Heather went back to work as an accountant after several years at home. The contents of the trash cans were strewn all over the house. A favorite comforter was destroyed. Then Blue began peeing all over Heather's expensive new living-room carpet and systematically ripped through cables and electrical wires.

Katz uses *causal* pattern to explore Blue's behavioral problem.

Lots of dogs get nervous when they don't know what's expected of them, and when they get anxious, they can also grow restless. Blue hadn't had to occupy time alone before. Dogs can get unnerved by this. They bark, chew, scratch, destroy. Getting yelled at and punished later doesn't help: The dog probably knows it's doing something wrong, but it has no idea what. Since there's nobody around to correct behaviors when the dog is alone, how could the dog know which behavior is the problem? Which action was wrong?

A simple *statement-proof* structure organizes this paragraph.

I don't believe that dogs act out of spite or that they can plot retribution, though countless dog owners swear otherwise. To punish or deceive requires the perpetrator to understand that his victim or object has a particular point of view and to consciously work to manipulate or thwart it. That requires mental processes dogs don't have.

Why will Clementine come instantly if she's looking at me, but not if she's sniffing deer droppings? Is it because she's being stubborn or, as many people tell me, going through "adolescence"? Or because, when following her keen predatory instincts, she simply doesn't hear me? Should my response be to tug at her leash or yell? Maybe I should be sure we've established eye contact before I give her a command, or better yet, offer a liver treat as an alternative to whatever's distracting her. But how do I establish eye contact when her nose is buried? Can I cluck or bark? Use a whistle or hoot like an owl?

    I've found that coughing, of all things, fascinates her, catches her attention, and makes her head swivel, after which she responds. If you walk with us, you will hear me clearing my throat repeatedly. What can I say? It works. She looks at me, comes to me, gets rewarded.

– *Slate.com*, October 6, 2005

> The paragraphs in this passage together follow a *problem-solution* structure common in *proposal* arguments.

Design paragraphs for readability.   Paragraph breaks work best when they coincide with shifts or divisions within the writing itself. Readers understand that your thoughts have moved in some new direction. But paragraphs are often at the mercy of a text's physical environment as well. When you read a news items on the Web, the short paragraphs used in these single-column stories look fine. But hit the "print this article" link and the text suddenly sprawls across the screen, becoming difficult to read.

    The point? You can manipulate the length and shape of paragraphs to suit the environment in which your words will appear.

Use paragraphs to manage transitions.   Paragraphs often furnish direction in a paper. An opening paragraph can be used to set the scene in a narrative or to preview the content in a report. ○ You might occasionally use very brief paragraphs—sometimes just a sentence or two long—to punctuate a piece by drawing attention to a turn in your thinking or offering a strong judgment. You've likely seen paragraphs that consist of nothing more than an indignant "Nonsense!" or a sarcastic "Nuts" or "Go figure." There's always a risk in penning a paragraph with so much attitude, but it's an option when the occasion calls for it. In longer papers, you might need full transitional paragraphs to summarize what has already been covered or to point the project in new directions.

shape a beginning
p. 420

31

Transitions

connect ideas

What exactly makes words, sentences, and ideas flow from paragraph to paragraph as fluidly as Michael Phelps slipping through the water at the Beijing Olympics? *Transitional words and phrases*, many writers would reply—thinking of words such as *and, but, however, neither . . . nor, first . . . second . . . third,* and so on. Placed where readers need them, these connecting words make a paper read smoothly. But they are only part of the story.

Almost any successful piece of writing is held together by more devices than most writers can consciously juggle. Fortunately, a few of the devices—such as connections between pronouns and their referents—almost take care of themselves. Here are some guidelines for making smooth transitions between ideas in paragraphs and sections of your writing.

Common Transitions

Connection or Consequence	Contrast	Correlation	Sequence or Time	Indication
and	but	if . . . then	first . . . second	this
or	yet	either . . . or	and then	that
so	however	from . . . to	initially	there
therefore	nevertheless		subsequently	for instance
moreover	on the contrary		before	for example
consequently	despite		after	in this case
hence	still		until	
	although		next	
			in conclusion	

Use appropriate transitional words and phrases.   There's nothing complicated or arcane about them: You'll recognize every word in any list of transitions. But be aware that they have different functions and uses, with subtle differences even between words as close in meaning as *but* and *yet*.

Transitional words are often found at the beginnings of sentences and paragraphs, simply because that's the place where readers expect a little guidance. There are no rules, per se, for positioning transitions—though they can be set off from the rest of the sentence with commas.

Use the right word or phrase to show time or sequence.   Readers often need specific words or phrases to help keep events in order. Such expressions can simply mark off stages: *first, second, third*. Or they might help readers keep track of more complicated passages of time.

Use sentence structure to connect ideas.   When you build sentences with similar structures, readers will infer that the ideas in them are related. Devices you can use to make this kind of linkage include *parallelism* ○ and *repetition*.

making a list?
p. 629

In the following example, the first three paragraphs of James P. Gannon's "America's Quiet Anger," you can see both strategies at work, setting up an emotional argument that continues in this pattern for another three paragraphs. Parallel items are highlighted.

> There is a quiet anger boiling in America.
> It is the anger of millions of hard-working citizens who pay their bills, send in their income taxes, maintain their homes and repay their mortgage loans—and see their government reward those who do not.
> It is the anger of small town and Middle American folks who have never been to Manhattan, who put their savings in a community bank and borrow from a local credit union, who watch Washington lawmakers and presidents of both parties hand billions in taxpayer bailouts to the reckless Wall Street titans who brought down the economy in 2008.
>
> — *American Spectator*, March 20, 2010

Pay attention to nouns and pronouns.   Understated transitions in a piece can occur between pronouns and their antecedents, but make sure the relationships between the nouns and pronouns are clear. ○ And, fortunately, readers usually don't mind encountering a pronoun over and over—except maybe *I*. Note how effortlessly Adam Nicolson moves between *George Abbot, he*, and *man* in the following paragraph from *God's Secretaries* (2003), in which he describes one of the men responsible for the King James translation of the Bible:

> George Abbot was perhaps the ugliest of them all, a morose, intemperate man, whose portraits exude a sullen rage. Even in death, he was portrayed on his tomb in Holy Trinity, Guilford, as a man of immense weight, with heavy, wrinkled brow and coldly open, staring eyes. He looks like a bruiser, a man of such conviction and seriousness that anyone would think twice about crossing him. What was it that made George Abbot so angry?

Use synonyms.   Simply by repeating a noun from sentence to sentence, you make an obvious and logical connection within a paper—whether you

help with common
errors p. 600

are naming an object, an idea, or a person. To avoid monotony, vary terms you have to use frequently. But don't strain with archaic or inappropriate synonyms that will distract the reader.

Note the sensible variants on the word *trailer* in the following paragraph.

> Hype and hysteria have always been a part of movie advertising, but the frenzy of film trailers today follows a visual style first introduced by music videos in the 1980s. The quick cut is everything, accompanied by a deafening soundtrack. Next time you go to a film, study the three or four previews that precede the main feature. How are these teasers constructed? What are their common features? What emotions or reactions do they raise in you? What might trailers say about the expectations of audiences today?

Use physical devices for transitions.   You know all the ways movies manage transitions between scenes, from quick cuts to various kinds of dissolves. Writing has fewer visual techniques to mark transitions, but they are important. Titles and headings in lab reports, for instance, let your reader know precisely when you are moving from "Methods" to "Results" to "Discussion." O In books, you'll encounter chapter breaks as well as divisions within chapters, sometimes marked by asterisks or perhaps a blank space. Seeing these markers, readers expect that the narration is changing in some way. Even the numbers in a list or shaded boxes in a magazine can be effective transitional devices, moving readers from one place to another.

Read a draft aloud to locate weak transitions. The best way to test your transitions in a paper or project may be to listen to yourself. As you read, mark every point in the paper where you pause, stumble, or find yourself adding a transitional word or phrase not in the original text. Record even the smallest bobble because tiny slips have a way of cascading into bigger problems.

understand lab
reports p. 336

32 Introductions

shape a
beginning

An introduction has to grab and hold a reader's attention, but that's not all. It also must introduce a topic, a writer, and a purpose. Like the music over a film's opening credits, an introduction tells readers what to expect. Any doubts about where the following opening lines are heading?

> Normal people don't like today's computers. Most loathe them because they can't fully understand their absurd complexity and arcane conventions. That's why the iPad will kill today's computers, just like the latter killed computers running with punchcards and command lines.
>
> —Jesus Diaz, "iPad Is the Future," *Gizmodo*, April 2010

> At a liquidation sale, every day is Black Friday. Customers hover outside the store before it opens like vultures waiting for a dying animal to become a fresh carcass.
>
> —Michael Nance, "Everything Must Go," May 2010

Of course, you will want to write introductions that fit your projects. In some cases a single line may be enough—as in an e-mail request for information. ○ A paragraph can provide all the push you need to get a short paper rolling. In a senior thesis or book, a preface or an entire chapter can set the stage for your project. Realize, too, that in longer projects, you'll write what amounts to an introduction for every new section or major division.

understand e-mail
p. 310

What should your introductory paragraphs accomplish? The following are some options.

Announce your project. In academic papers, introductions typically declare a subject directly and indicate how it will be developed. Quite often, an introductory paragraph or section leads directly to a thesis statement or a hypothesis. ○ This is a pattern you can use in many situations.

> In her novel *Wuthering Heights* (1847), Emily Brontë presents the story of the families of Wuthering Heights and Thrushcross Grange through the seemingly impartial perspective of Nelly Dean, a servant who grows up with the families. Upon closer inspection, however, it becomes apparent that Nelly acts as much more than a bystander in the tragic events taking place around her. In her status as an outsider with influence over the families, Nelly strikingly resembles the Byronic hero Heathcliff and competes with him for power. Although the author depicts Heathcliff as the more overt gothic hero, Brontë allows the reader to infer from Nelly's story her true character and role in the family. The author draws a parallel between Nelly Dean and Heathcliff in their relationships to the Earnshaw family, in their similar roles as tortured heroes, and in their competition for power within their adoptive families.
>
> —Manasi Deshpande, "Servant and Stranger: Nelly and Heathcliff in *Wuthering Heights*"

Paper opens by identifying its general topic or theme.

Detailed thesis states what paper will prove.

Preview your project. Sometimes you'll have to use an introductory section to set up the material to follow, helping readers to understand why an issue deserves their attention. You might, for example, present an anecdote, describe a trend, or point to some change or development readers may not have noticed. Then you can explore its significance or implications. In the following example, Gabriela Montell, a writer for *The Chronicle of Higher Education*, first describes a research study so she can then explain why she is interested in whether looks matter for college professors.

develop a statement
p. 393

News article opens by getting readers interested in research study.

Researchers identified and study described in sufficient, but limited, detail.

Professors aren't known for fussing about their looks, but the results of a new study suggest they may have to if they want better teaching evaluations.

Daniel Hamermesh, a professor of economics at the University of Texas at Austin, and Amy Parker, one of his students, found that attractive professors consistently outscore their less comely colleagues by a significant margin on student evaluations of teaching. The findings, they say, raise serious questions about the use of student evaluations as a valid measure of teaching quality.

In their study, Mr. Hamermesh and Ms. Parker asked students to look at photographs of ninety-four professors and rate their beauty. Then they compared those ratings to the average student evaluation scores for the courses taught by those professors. The two found that the professors who had been rated among the most beautiful scored a point higher than those rated least beautiful (that's a substantial difference, since student evaluations don't generally vary by much).

Full story will examine implications of study for educators.

While it's not news that beauty trumps brains in many quarters, you would think that the ivory tower would be relatively exempt from such shallowness.

– "Do Good Looks Equal Good Evaluations?" October 15, 2003

Provide background information.   Decide what your readers need to know about a subject and then fill in the blanks. Provide too little background information on a subject and readers may find the remainder of the project confusing. Supply too much context and you lose fans quickly: Readers may assume that the paper has nothing new to offer them or may simply grow impatient.

And yet, even when readers know a subject well, you still need, especially in academic papers, to answer basic questions about the project or topic—*who, what, where, when, how,* and *why.* Name names in your introduction, offer accurate titles, furnish dates, and explain what your subject is. Imagine readers from just slightly outside your target audience who might not instantly recall, for instance, that Shakespeare wrote a play titled *Henry V* or that the *Deepwater Horizon* oil rig exploded in the Gulf of Mexico on April 20, 2010.

Catch the attention of readers.   Give them a reason to enter your text. You can invite them any number of ways—with a compelling incident or amusing story, with a recitation of surprising or intriguing facts, with a dramatic question, with a provocative description or quotation. For visual texts (like a brochure or poster), a cover, masthead, or headline can lead readers inside the project.

Naturally, any opening has to be in sync with the material that follows—not outrageously emotional if the argument is sober, not lighthearted and comic if the paper has a serious theme. It is hard to imagine a reader even modestly interested in history not being caught by the opening paragraph of Barbara Tuchman's *The First Salute* (1998):

> White puffs of gun smoke over a turquoise sea followed by the boom of cannon rose from an unassuming fort on the diminutive Dutch island of St. Eustatius in the West Indies on November 16, 1776. The guns of Fort Orange on St. Eustatius were returning the ritual salute on entering a foreign port of an American vessel, the *Andrew Doria*, as she came up the roadstead, flying at her mast the red-and-white-striped flag of the Continental Congress. In its responding salute the small voice of St. Eustatius was the first officially to greet the largest event of the century—the entry into the society of nations of a new Atlantic state destined to change the direction of history.

Set a tone.   Introductory material sends readers all sorts of signals, some of them almost subliminal. Make noticeable errors in grammar and usage in an opening section and you immediately lose credibility with your readers.

More typically, though, readers use your opening material to determine whether they belong to the audience you are addressing. A paper beginning with highly technical language signals that the territory is open to specialists only, while a more personal or colloquial style welcomes a broader audience. ○

Follow any required formulas.   Many genres of writing define how you may enter a subject. This is especially the case for technical material (lab reports, research articles, scholarly essays) and highly conventional genres

refine your tone
p. 432

such as business letters, job-application letters, and even e-mail. Quite often, these conventions are simple: A business letter opens with a formal salutation; a job letter announces that you are applying for a specific announced position. You cannot ignore these details without raising eyebrows and doubts. To get such introductions right, review models of the genre and follow them.

Write an introduction when you're ready.   The opening of a project— especially of longer efforts such as research papers and theses—can be notoriously difficult to compose. If you are blocked at the outset of a project, plunge directly into the body of the paper and see where things go. You can even write the opening section last. No one will know.

Similarly, if you write your introduction first, review it when you come to the end of the paper—and revise as necessary. ○ Sometimes, the promises you made at the beginning aren't the same ones you delivered on. When that's the case, recast the opening to reflect the paper's new content or revise the body of the paper to conform to important commitments made in the introduction.

Your Turn   Examine the opening paragraphs in several chapters of this section of *How to Write Anything* (Chapters 25–34). What strategies do you notice? How do the chapter openers differ? Do you find any of the chapters more successful than others? Why?

---

revise and edit
p. 452

Conclusions

Composing introductions carries all the trepidations of asking for a first date. So conclusions should be much easier, right? By the time you write a conclusion, you've established a relationship with readers, provided necessary background, laid down arguments, and discussed important issues. All that remains is the verbal equivalent of a good-night kiss . . . Okay, maybe conclusions aren't that simple.

shape an ending

Like introductions, conclusions serve different purposes and audiences. A brief e-mail or memo may need no more sign-off than a simple closing: *regards, best, later.* A senior thesis, however, could require a whole chapter to wrap things up. Here are some of the options when writing conclusions.

Summarize your points, then connect them. In reports and arguments, use the concluding section to recap what you've covered and tie your major points together. The following is the systematic conclusion of a college report on a childhood developmental disorder, cri du chat syndrome (CDCS). Note that this summary paragraph also leads where many other scientific and scholarly articles do: to a call for additional research.

> Though research on CDCS remains far from abundant, existing studies prescribe early and ongoing intervention by a team of specialists, including speech-language pathologists,

Major point

Major point

physical and occupational therapists, various medical and educational professionals, and parents. Such intervention has been shown to allow individuals with CDCS to live happy, long, and full lives. The research, however, indicates that the syndrome affects all aspects of a child's development and should therefore be taken quite seriously. Most children require numerous medical interventions, including surgery (especially to correct heart defects), feeding tubes, body braces, and repeated treatment of infections. Currently, the best attempts are being made to help young children with CDCS reach developmental milestones earlier, communicate effectively, and function as independently as possible. However, as the authors of the aforementioned studies suggest, much more research is needed to clarify the causes of varying degrees of disability, to identify effective and innovative treatments/interventions (especially in the area of education), and to individualize intervention plans.

Conclusion ties together main points made in paper, using transitional words and phrases.

—Marissa Dahlstrom, "Developmental Disorders: Cri du Chat Syndrome"

Reveal your point.   In some writing, including many arguments, you may not want to disclose your key point until the very end, following a convincing presentation of claims and evidence. ○ The paper unfolds a bit like a mystery, keeping readers on edge, eager to discover your point. You don't open with a thesis, nor do you tip your hand completely until the conclusion.

Here, for example, are the concluding paragraphs of an article in which Andrew Sullivan has been guiding readers through a city he argues has grown more self-absorbed and alienated because of technologies like the Internet and iPod. In his conclusion, Sullivan raises important questions that lead toward his chief belief that we need to turn outward again to enrich our lives.

> We become masters of our own interests [thanks to technology], more connected to people like us over the Internet, more instantly in touch with anything we want, need, or think we want and think we need. Ever tried a Stairmaster in silence? But what are we missing? That hilarious shard of an overheard conversation that stays with you all day; the child whose chatter on the pavement takes you back to your early memories;

birdsong; weather; accents; the laughter of others. And those thoughts
that come not by filling your head with selected diversion, but by allowing
your mind to wander aimlessly through the regular background noise of
human and mechanical life.

External stimulation can crowd out the interior mind. Even the boredom
that we flee has its uses. We are forced to find our own means to overcome it.

And so we enrich our life from within, rather than from white wires. It's
hard to give up, though, isn't it?

Not so long ago I was on a trip and realized I had left my iPod behind.
Panic. But then something else. I noticed the rhythms of others again, the
sound of the airplane, the opinions of the taxi driver, the small social cues
that had been obscured before. I noticed how others related to each other.
And I felt just a little bit connected again and a little more aware.

Try it. There's a world out there. And it has a soundtrack all its own.

—"Society Is Dead: We Have Retreated into the iWorld," *New York Times*

> Details give argument power: Plugged in, we're missing a lot.

> Sullivan anticipates readers' objections and acknowledges his own weakness.

> Final anecdote drives home key point.

> Three short concluding sentences punctuate the essay.

Finish dramatically.   Arguments, personal narratives, and many other
kinds of writing often call for conclusions that will influence readers and
maybe change their opinions. Since final paragraphs are what many readers
remember, it makes sense that they be powerfully written. Here's the conclusion of a lengthy personal essay by Shane McNamee on gay marriage that
leads up to a poignant political appeal.

Forget for the moment the rainbow flags and pink triangles. Gay pride is
not about being homosexual; it's about the integrity and courage it takes to
be honest with yourself and your loved ones. It's about spending life with
whomever you want and not worrying what the government or the neighbors think. Let's protect that truth, not some rigid view of sexual orientation
or marriage. Keep gay marriage out of your church if you like, but if you
value monogamy as I do, give me an alternative that doesn't involve
dishonesty or a life of loneliness. Many upstanding gay citizens yearn for
recognition of their loving, committed relationships. Unless you enjoy being
lied to and are ready to send your gay friends and family on a Trail of
Queers to Massachusetts or Canada—where gay marriage is legal—then
consider letting them live as they wish.

—"Protecting What Really Matters"

> Deliberate repetition focuses readers on serious point.

> Conclusion makes direct appeal to readers, addressed as *you*.

> Final sentence appeals emotionally through both images and language.

34 Titles

Titles may not strike you as an important aspect of writing, but they can be. Sometimes the struggle to find a good title helps a writer shape a piece and define its main point. Of course, a proper title tells readers what a paper is about and makes finding the document later easier.

name your work

Use titles to focus documents. A too-broad title early on in a project is a sure sign that you have yet to find a workable subject. If all you have is "Sea Battles in World War II" or "Children in America," expect to do more reading and research. If no title comes to mind at all, you don't have a subject. ○ You're still exploring ideas.

Titles for academic papers need only be descriptive. Consider these items culled at random from one issue of the *Stanford Undergraduate Research Journal* (Spring 2008). As you might guess, scientific papers aimed at a knowledgeable audience of specialists have highly technical titles. Titles in the social sciences and liberal arts are slightly less intimidating, but just as focused on providing information about their subjects.

> "Molecular and Morphological Characterization of Two Species of Sea Cucumber, *Parastichopus parvimensis* and *Parastichopus californicus*, in Monterey, CA"
>
> — Christine O'Connell, Alison J. Haupt, Stephen R. Palumbi

develop a statement
p. 393

"Justifiers of the British Opium Trade: Arguments by Parliament, Traders, and the *Times* Leading Up to the Opium War"

– Christine Su

"The Incongruence of the Schopenhauerian Ending in Wagner's *Götterdämmerung*"

– James Locus

Create searchable titles.   For academic or professional papers, a title should make sense standing on its own and out of context. That way if the paper winds up in someone's bibliography or in an online database, readers know what your subject is. Your title should also include keywords by which it might be searched in a database or online.

"Rethinking the Threat of Domestic Terrorism"

If you must be clever or allusive, follow the cute title with a colon and an explanatory subtitle.

"'Out, Damn'd Spot!': Images of Conscience and Remorse in Shakespeare's *Macbeth*"

"Out, Damn'd Spot: Housebreaking Your Puppy"

Avoid whimsical or suggestive titles.   A bad title will haunt you like a silly screen name. At this point you may not worry about publication, but documents take on a life of their own when uploaded to the Web or listed on a résumé. Any document posted where the public can search for it online needs a levelheaded title, especially when you approach the job market.

Capitalize and punctuate titles carefully.   The guidelines for capitalizing titles vary between disciplines. See Chapters 49 and 50 for the MLA and APA guidelines, or consult the style manual for your discipline.

Your titles should avoid all caps, boldface, underscoring, and, with some exceptions, italics (titles within titles and foreign terms may be italicized; see examples above). For Web sites, newsletters, PowerPoint presentations, and so on, you can be bolder graphically. O

Titles tell readers what to expect.

think visually
p. 592

Style

Need help with revising and editing? See page 450. / Need help with common errors? See page 600.

35

High, Middle, and Low Style

define your
style/refine
your tone

We all have an ear for the way words work in sentences and paragraphs, for the distinctive melding of voice, tone, rhythm, and texture some call *style*. You might not be able to explain exactly why one paragraph sparkles and another is flat as day-old soda, but you know when writing feels energetic, precise, and clear or stodgy, lifeless, and plodding. Choices you make about sentence type, sentence length, vocabulary, pronouns, and punctuation *do* create distinctive verbal styles—which may or may not fit particular types of writing. ○

In fact, there are as many styles of writing as of dress. In most cases, language that is clear, active, and economical will do the job. But even such a bedrock style has variations. Since the time of the ancient Greeks, writers have imagined a "high" or formal style at one end of a scale and a "low" or colloquial style at the other, bracketing a just-right porridge in the middle. Style is more complex than that, but keeping the full range in mind reveals some of your options.

High, middle, and low styles of weddings: formal and traditional, less formal, and totally informal.

432

improve your
sentences p. 444

Use high style for formal, scientific, and scholarly writing. You will find high style in professional journals, scholarly books, legal briefs, formal addresses, many editorials, some types of technical writing, and some wedding invitations. Use it yourself when a lot is at stake—in a scholarship application, for example, or a job letter, term paper, or thesis. High style is signaled by some combination of the following features—all of which can vary.

- Serious or professional subjects
- Knowledgeable or professional audiences
- Dominant third-person (*he, she, it, they*) or impersonal point of view
- Relatively complex and self-consciously patterned sentences (that display *parallelism, balance, repetition*), often in the passive voice
- Professional vocabulary, often abstract and technical
- No contractions, colloquial expressions, or nonstandard forms
- Conventional grammar and punctuation; standard document design
- Formal documentation, when required, often with notes and a bibliography

The following example is from a scholarly journal. The article uses a formal scientific style, appropriate when an expert in a field is writing for an audience of his or her peers.

Temperament is a construct closely related to personality. In human research, temperament has been defined by some researchers as the inherited, early appearing tendencies that continue throughout life and serve as the foundation for personality (A. H. Buss, 1995; Goldsmith et al., 1987). Although this definition is not adopted uniformly by human researchers (McCrae et al., 2000), animal researchers agree even less about how to define temperament (Budaev, 2000). In some cases, the word *temperament* appears to be used purely to avoid using the word *personality*, which some animal researchers associate with anthropomorphism. Thus, to ensure that my review captured all potentially relevant reports, I searched for studies that examined either personality or temperament.

—Sam D. Gosling, "From Mice to Men: What Can We Learn About Personality from Animal Research?" *Psychological Bulletin*

Technical terms introduced and defined.

Sources documented.

Perspective generally impersonal—though *I* is used.

The following *New York Times* editorial also uses a formal style. This is common when dealing with serious political or social issues.

Tone of first paragraph is sober and direct.

Haiti, founded two centuries ago by ex-slaves who fought to regain their freedom, has again become a hub of human trafficking.

Key term is defined.

Today, tens of thousands of Haitian children live lives of modern-day bondage. Under the system known as *restavek*, a Creole word meaning "stay with," these children work for wealthier families in exchange for education and shelter. They frequently end up cruelly overworked, physically or sexually abused, and without access to education.

Vocabulary is fairly abstract.

The most effective way to root out this deeply oppressive but deeply ingrained system would be to attack the conditions that sustain it—chiefly, impoverished, environmentally unsustainable agriculture and a severe shortage of rural schools.

This is an area in which America can and should help. Washington has been quick to respond to political turmoil in Haiti, with its accompanying fears of uncontrollable refugee flows. But the frenzied flurries of international crisis management that follow typically leave no lasting results.

Borrows technical language of diplomacy and government.

A wiser, more promising alternative would be to help create long-term economic options by improving access to schools and creating sustainable agriculture. Meanwhile, the United States should work with nongovernmental organizations to battle the resigned acceptance by many Haitians of the restavek system. They could, for example, help local radio stations broadcast programs of open dialogue about how damaging the system is, and include restavek survivors or human-rights experts.

Voice throughout is that of a serious institution, not an individual.

The primary responsibility for eliminating the restavek system lies with the Haitian people and their government. After years of political crisis, there is a new democratically elected government. Eradicating the restavek system should be one of its top priorities, combining law enforcement efforts with attacks on the root social and economic causes.

Tone of final paragraph is more emotional than rest of editorial.

The former slaves who won Haiti's freedom two hundred years ago dreamed of something better for their children than restavek bondage. The time is overdue for helping those dreams become reality.

—"The Lost Children of Haiti," *New York Times*

Use middle style for personal, argumentative, and some academic writing. This style, perhaps the most common, falls between the extremes. It is the language of journalism, popular books and magazines, professional memos and nonscientific reports, instructional guides and manuals, and most commercial Web sites. Use this style in position papers, letters to the editor, personal statements, and business e-mails and memos—even in some business and professional work, once you are comfortable with the people to whom you are writing. Middle style doesn't so much claim features of its own as walk a path between formal and everyday language. It may combine some of the following characteristics:

- Full range of topics, from serious to humorous
- General audiences
- Range of perspectives, including first (*I*) and second (*you*) person points of view
- More often a human rather than an institutional voice
- Sentences in active voice that are varied in complexity and length
- General vocabulary, more specific than abstract, with concrete nouns and action verbs and with unfamiliar terms or concepts defined
- Informal expressions, some dialogue, slang, and contractions
- Conventional grammar and reasonably correct formats
- Informal documentation, usually without notes

In the following article for the online magazine *Slate.com*, Joel Waldfogel, a professor of business and public policy, explains recent research in his field to a general audience—people who are not experts in either business or public policy.

It is well-documented that short people earn less money than tall people do. To be clear, pay does not vary lockstep by height. If your friend is taller than you are, then it's nearly a coin toss whether she earns more. But if you compare two large groups of people who are similar in every respect but height, the average pay for the taller group will be higher. Each additional inch of height adds roughly 2 percent to average annual earnings, for both men and women. So, if the average heights of our hypothetical groups

Expressions are casual.

Readers are addressed familiarly as *you*, and an example is offered to clarify the causal relationship.

were 6 feet and 5 feet 7 inches, the average pay difference between them would be 10 percent.

But why? One possibility is height discrimination in favor of the tall. A second involves adolescence. A few years ago, Nicola Persico and Andrew Postlewaite of the University of Pennsylvania and Dan Silverman of the University of Michigan discovered that adult earnings are more sharply related to height at age sixteen than to adult height—suggesting, scarily, that the high-school social order determined the adult economic order. For boys at least, height at sixteen affects things like social and athletic success—scoring chicks and baskets or, as the authors put it, "participation in clubs and athletics." And maybe those things affect later earning power.

That wasn't likely to make short people feel good, but the latest explanation is worse. In a new study, Anne Case and Christina Paxson, both of Princeton University, find that tall people earn more, on average, because they're smarter, on average. Yikes.

–Joel Waldfogel, "Short End," *Slate.com*

Next, in this excerpt from an article that appeared in the popular magazine *Psychology Today*, Ellen McGrath uses a conversational middle style to present scientific information to a general audience.

Families often inherit a negative thinking style that carries the germ of depression. Typically it is a legacy passed from one generation to the next, a pattern of pessimism invoked to protect loved ones from disappointment or stress. But in fact, negative thinking patterns do just the opposite, eroding the mental health of all exposed.

When Dad consistently expresses his disappointment in Josh for bringing home a B minus in chemistry although all the other grades are A's, he is exhibiting a kind of cognitive distortion that children learn to deploy on themselves—a mental filtering that screens out positive experience from consideration.

Or perhaps the father envisions catastrophe, seeing such grades as foreclosing the possibility of a top college, thus dooming his son's future. It is their repetition over time that gives these events power to shape a person's belief system.

–Ellen McGrath, "Is Depression Contagious?" *Psychology Today*

Transition between paragraphs reads like spoken English: easy and natural.

Sources cited, but not documented.

Highlights difference between his informality and high style of scholars.

A surprisingly informal expression ends the paragraph.

Vocabulary is sophisticated but not technical.

Familiar example (fictional son is even named) illustrates technical term: *cognitive distortion.*

Phrase following dash offers further clarification helpful to educated, but nonexpert, readers.

Use a low style for personal, informal, and even playful writing.
Don't think of "low" here in a negative sense: A colloquial or informal style is
fine on occasions when you want or need to sound more at ease and open. Low
style can be right for your personal e-mails and instant messaging, of course,
as well as in many blogs, advertisements, magazines trying to be hip, personal
narratives, and humor writing. Low style has many of the following features:

- Everyday or off-the-wall subjects, often humorous or parodic
- In-group or specialized readers
- Highly personal and idiosyncratic points of view; lots of *I, me, you, us,*
  and dialogue
- Shorter sentences and irregular constructions, especially fragments
- Vocabulary from pop culture and the street—idiomatic, allusive, and
  obscure to outsiders
- Colloquial expressions resembling speech
- Unconventional grammar and mechanics and alternative formats
- No systematic acknowledgment of sources

Note the relaxed style this former college instructor uses in her blog.

TUESDAY, JANUARY 03, 2006

Dumpster diving

Stuff I've found in or near the dumpsters after the college kids move out of
our apartment complex between semesters:

- Brand new HP printer, all cords still attached
- Tall oak computer-printer stand on wheels
- Blank computer discs and CD-ROMs
- China tea set
- Funky 1950s plates and saucers, left in a box beside the garbage bin
- Unopened bottle of semi-expensive champagne (still in my fridge)
- Nearly full bottles of expensive shampoos and conditioners
- Leather camera bag
- Replacement car antenna, still in unopened package
- Framed movie posters

Stuff and *kids* immediately
signal casual tone—as
does the sentence
fragment.

Highly personal
parenthetical remark—and
slangy *fridge*.

"Really made out bigtime"
is deliberately low, echoing
student chatter.

Pause marked by ellipsis.

Article omitted at
beginning of sentence
makes advice seem casual.

One of my students told me about one of the rare perks of being a resident assistant in the dorm. She really made out bigtime with stuff left behind. One girl moved out and left all the dresser drawers loaded with clothes (and not by accident . . . she just didn't want to pack the stuff). Lots of students abandon bicycles, stereos, VCRs, TVs, sofas, and futons. Best days for scavenging are during final exams and right after.

> **Your Turn**   Over the next day, look for three pieces of writing that seem to you to represent examples of high, middle, and low style. Then study several paragraphs or a section of each in detail, paying attention to the features listed in the checklists for the three styles. How well do the pieces actually conform to the descriptions of high, middle, and low style? Where would you place your three examples on a continuum that moves from high to low? Do the pieces share some stylistic features? Do you find any variations of style within the individual passages you examined?

The very serious story told in the *9/11 Commission Report* was retold in *The 9/11 Report: A Graphic Adaptation* (p. 439). Creators Sid Jacobson and Ernie Colón use the colloquial visual style of a comic book to make the formidable data and conclusions of a government report accessible to a wider audience. ○

choose a genre
p. 390

Panels combine verbal and visual elements to tell a story.

Political figures become characters in a real-life drama.

Sounds (*Shoom!*) are represented visually—as in superhero tales.

Real images (the photograph on the left) are sometimes juxtaposed with cartoon panels as part of the collage.

36 Inclusive and Culturally Sensitive Style

respect your
readers

Writers in school or business today need to remember how small and tightly connected the world has become and how readily people may be offended. When you compose any document electronically (including a Word file), it may sail quickly around the Web. You can't make every reader in this potential audience happy, but you can at least write respectfully, accurately, and, yes, honestly. Language that is both inclusive and culturally sensitive can and should have these qualities.

Avoid expressions that stereotype genders.   Largely purged from contemporary English usage are job titles that suggest that they are occupied exclusively by men or women. Gone are *poetess* and *stewardess, policeman* and *congressman, postman* and *woman scientist.* When referring to professions, even those still dominated by one gender or another, avoid using a gendered pronoun.

Don't strain sense to be politically correct. *Nun* and *NFL quarterback* are still gendered, as are *witch* and *warlock* — and *surrogate mother.* Here are some easy solutions.

STEREOTYPED   The postman came up the walk.

INCLUSIVE   The letter carrier came up the walk.

STEREOTYPED   Among all her other tasks, a nurse must also stay up-to-date on her medical education.

INCLUSIVE   Among all their other tasks, nurses must also stay up-to-date on their medical education.

Outdated Terms	Alternatives
postman	letter carrier, postal worker
mankind	humankind, people, humans
congressman	congressional representative
chairman	chair
policewoman	police officer
stewardess	flight attendant
actress, poetess	actor, poet
fireman	firefighter

Avoid expressions that stereotype races, ethnic groups, or religious groups.   Deliberate racial slurs these days tend to be rare in professional writing. But it is still not unusual to find clueless writers (and politicians) noting how "hardworking," "articulate," "athletic," "well-groomed," or "ambitious" members of minority and religious groups are. The praise rings hollow because it draws on old and brutal stereotypes. You have an obligation to learn the history and nature of such ethnic caricatures and grow beyond them. It's part of your education, no matter what group or groups you belong to.

Refer to people and groups by the expressions used in serious publications, understanding that almost all racial and ethnic terms are contested: *African American, black* (or *Black*), *Negro, people of color, Asian American, Hispanic, Mexican American, Cuban American, Native American, Indian, Inuit, Anglo, white* (or *White*). Even the ancient group of American Indians once called Anasazi now go by the more culturally and historically accurate Native Puebloans. While shifts of this sort may seem fussy or politically correct to some, it costs little to address people as they prefer, acknowledging both their humanity and our differences.

Be aware, too, that being part of an ethnic or racial group usually gives you license to say things about the group not open to outsiders. Chris Rock and Margaret Cho can joke about topics Jay Leno can't touch, using epithets that would cost the *Tonight Show* host his job. In academic and professional settings, show similar discretion in your language — though not in your treatment of serious subjects. Sensitivities of language should not become an excuse for avoiding open debate, nor a weapon to chill it. In the following table are suggestions for inclusive, culturally sensitive terms.

Outdated Terms	Alternatives
Eskimo	Inuit
Oriental	Asian American (better to specify country of origin)
Hispanic	Specify: Mexican, Cuban, Nicaraguan, and so on
Negro (acceptable to some)	African American, black
colored	people of color
a gay, the gays	gay, lesbian, gays and lesbians
cancer victim	cancer survivor
boys, girls (to refer to adults)	men, women
woman doctor	doctor
male nurse	nurse

Treat all people with respect. This policy makes sense in all writing. Some slights may not be intended—against the elderly, for example. But writing that someone drives *like an old woman* manages to offend two groups. In other cases, you might mistakenly think that most readers share your prejudices or narrow vision when describing members of campus groups, religious groups, the military, gays and lesbians, athletes, and so on. You know the derogatory terms and references well enough, and you should avoid them if for no other reason than the golden rule. Everyone is a member of some group that has at one time or another been mocked or stereotyped. So writing that is respectful will itself be treated with respect.

Avoid sensational language. It happens every semester. One or more students ask the instructor whether it's okay to use four-letter words in their papers. Some instructors tolerate expletives in personal narratives, but it is difficult to make a case for them in academic reports, research papers, or position papers unless they are part of quoted material—as they may be in writing about contemporary literature or song lyrics.

Certain kinds of writing do effectively push the limits of their audience or, rather, appreciate that their readers might occasionally enjoy seeing a subject justly skewered by a few well-chosen words. You'll see this gleeful meanness in book, movie, or music reviews, for example. ○ The following paragraph is from Richard Corliss's review of M. Night Shyamalan's fantasy epic, *The Last Airbender*, a film set in ancient China, which had been criticized for not casting enough ethnic Asians. Note that Corliss avoids offensive language, but he doesn't mince words either.

> You can relax, bloggers. The dearth of racially appropriate casting in the U.S. simply means that fewer Asians were humiliated by appearing in what is surely the worst botch of a fantasy epic since Ralph Bakshi's animated desecration of *The Lord of the Rings* back in 1978. The actors who didn't get to be in *The Last Airbender* are like the passengers who arrived too late to catch the final flight of the *Hindenburg*.
>
> –"*The Last Airbender:* Worst Movie Epic Ever?" *Time*, July 2, 2010

Your Turn   Write a paragraph or two about any pet peeve you may have with language use. Your problem may address a serious issue like insensitivities in naming your ethnicity, community, or beliefs. Or you may just be tired of a friend insisting that you describe Sweetie Pie as your "animal companion" rather than use that demeaning and hegemonic term "pet." You'll surely want to share your paragraph and also read what others have written.

understand
evaluation p. 106

37

Vigorous, Clear, Economical Style

Ordinarily, tips and tricks don't do much to enhance your skills as a writer. But a few guidelines, applied sensibly, can improve your sentences and paragraphs noticeably—and upgrade your credibility as a writer. You sound more professional and confident when every word and phrase pulls its weight.

Always consider the big picture in applying the following tips: Work with whole pages and paragraphs, not just individual sentences. Remember, too, that these are guidelines, not rules. Ignore them when your good sense suggests a better alternative.

Use strong, concrete subjects and objects.   Scholar Richard Lanham famously advised writers troubled by tangled sentences to ask, "Who is kicking who?" That's a memorable way of suggesting that readers shouldn't have to puzzle over what they read.

Lower the level of generality to add interest. Nouns should be as specific as possible so that sentences create images for readers.

ABSTRACT	SPECIFIC
bird	roadrunner
cactus	prickly pear
animal	coyote

Most readers can more readily imagine *students* than *constituencies*; they can picture a *school*, not an *academic institution*. A wordy sentence can seem almost hopeless until you start translating phrases like "current fiscal pressures" into everyday English.

WORDY   All of the separate constituencies at this academic institution
         must be invited to participate in the decision making process under
         the current fiscal pressures we face.

BETTER   Faculty, students, and staff at this school must all have a say
         during this current budget crunch.

Avoid clumsy noun phrases.   It's too easy to build massive noun phrases that sound impressive but give readers fits, especially as they accumulate in sentence after sentence. You can spot such phrases by various markers:

- Strings of prepositional phrases
- Verbs turned into nouns via endings such as *-ation* (*implement* becomes *implementation*)
- Lots of articles (*the*, *a*)
- Lots of heavily modified verbals

Such expressions are not always inaccurate or wrong, just tedious. They make your reader work hard for no reason. They are remarkably easy to pare down once you notice them.

WORDY   members of the student body at Arizona State

BETTER   students at Arizona State

WORDY   the manufacturing of products made up of steel

BETTER   making steel products

WORDY   the prioritization of decisions for policies of the student government

BETTER   the student government's priorities

Avoid sentences with long windups.   Get to the point quickly. The more stuff you pile up ahead of the main verb, the more readers have to remember. Most people today prefer sentences that put any lengthy modifying phrases and clauses *after* the verb. The following sentence from the Internal Revenue Service Web site keeps you waiting too long for a verb. It's easy to fix.

> Don't use words too big for the subject. Don't say "infinitely" when you mean "very"; otherwise you'll have no word left when you want to talk about something really infinite.

–C. S. Lewis

ORIGINAL   A new scam e-mail that appears to be a solicitation from the IRS and the U.S. government for charitable contributions to victims of the recent Southern California wildfires has been making the rounds.

REVISED   A new scam e-mail making the rounds asks for charitable contributions to victims of the recent Southern California wildfires. Though it appears to be from the IRS and the U.S. government, it is a fake.

Use action verbs when possible.   Verbs get as tangled up as nouns if you lose track of the action. Cut through the clutter.

WORDY VERB PHRASE   We must make a decision soon.

BETTER   We must decide soon.

WORDY VERB PHRASE   Students are reliant on credit cards.

BETTER   Students rely on credit cards.

WORDY VERB PHRASE   Engineers proceeded to reinforce the levee.

BETTER   Engineers reinforced the levee.

Avoid strings of prepositional phrases.   Prepositional phrases consist of a preposition and its object, which may take modifiers: *under* the spreading chestnut tree; *between* you and me; *in* the line *of* duty. You can't write without prepositional phrases. But use more than two or, rarely, three in a row and they drain the energy from your sentences. Try moving the prepositions or turning them into more compact modifiers. Sometimes you can alter the verb to eliminate a preposition, or it might be necessary to revise the sentence even more substantially.

TOO MANY PHRASES   We stood in line at the observatory on the top of a hill in the mountains to look in a huge telescope at the moons of Saturn.

BETTER   We lined up at the mountaintop observatory to view Saturn's moons through a huge telescope.

Don't repeat key words close together.   You can often improve the style of a passage just by making sure you haven't used a particular word or phrase too often—unless you repeat it deliberately for effect (*government of the people, by the people, for the people*). Your sentences will sound fresher after you have eliminated unintentional and pointless repetition.

This is a guideline to apply sensibly: Sometimes to be clear, especially in technical writing, you must repeat key nouns and verbs sentence after sentence.

> The *New Horizons* payload is incredibly power efficient, with the instruments collectively drawing only about 28 watts. The payload consists of three optical instruments, two plasma instruments, a dust sensor, and a radio science receiver/radiometer.
>
> —NASA, "*New Horizons* Spacecraft Ready for Flight"

Avoid doublings.   In speech, we tend to repeat ourselves or say things two or three different ways to be sure listeners get the point. Such repetitions are natural, even appreciated. But in writing, the habit of doubling can be irritating. And it is very much a habit, backed by a long literary tradition comfortable with pairings such as *home and hearth, friend and colleague, tried and true, clean and sober, neat and tidy,* and so on.

Often, writers will add an extra noun or two to be sure they have covered the bases: *colleges and universities, books and articles, ideas and opinions*. There may be good reasons for a second (or third) item. But not infrequently, the doubling is just extra baggage that slows down the train. Leave it at the station.

Turn clauses into more direct modifiers.   If you are fond of *that, which,* and *who* clauses, be sure you need them. You can sometimes save a word or two by pulling the modifiers out of the clause and moving them ahead of the words they embellish. Or you may be able to tighten a sentence just by cutting *that, which,* or *who*.

WORDY   Our football coach, who is nationally renowned, expected a raise.

BETTER   Our nationally renowned football coach expected a raise.

WORDY   Our football coach, who is nationally renowned and already rich, still expected a raise.

BETTER   Our football coach, nationally renowned and already rich, still expected a raise.

Cut introductory expressions such as *it is* and *there is/are* when you can.   Such expressions, called *expletives*, are just part of the way we say some things: *It is going to rain today. There is a tide in the affairs of men.* Some expletives are fine, but don't let them stand in for clearer and more specific subjects. Revise as necessary. But don't let an expletive substitute for a clearer expression.

WORDY   It is necessary that we reform the housing policies.

BETTER   We need to reform the housing policies.

WORDY   There were many incentives offered by the company to its sales force.

BETTER   The company offered its sales force many incentives.

Vary your sentence lengths and structures.   Sentences, like music, have rhythm. If all your sentences run about the same length or rarely vary from a predictable subject-verb-object pattern readers will grow bored without knowing why. Every so often, surprise them with a really short statement. Or begin with a longer-than-usual introductory phrase. Or try compound subjects or verbs, or attach a series of parallel modifiers to the verb or object. Or let a sentence roll toward a grand conclusion, as in the following example.

> [Carl] Newman is a singing encyclopedia of pop power. He has identified, cultured, and cloned the most buoyant elements of his favorite Squeeze, Raspberries, Supertramp, and Sparks records, and he's pretty pathological about making sure there's something unpredictable and catchy happening in a New Pornographers song every couple of seconds — a stereo flurry of *ooohs*, an extra beat or two bubbling up unexpectedly.
>
> — Douglas Wolk, "Something to Talk About," *Spin*

Listen to what you have written.   Read everything that matters aloud at least once. Then fix the words or phrases that cause you to pause or stumble. This is a great way to find problem spots. If you can't unravel your own writing, a reader won't be able to either. Better yet, persuade a friend or roommate to read your draft to you and take notes.

Cut a first draft by 25 percent — or more.   If you tend to be wordy, try to cut your first drafts by at least one-quarter. Put all your thoughts down on the page when drafting a paper. But when editing, cut every unnecessary expression. Think of it as a competition. However, don't eliminate any important ideas and facts. If possible, ask an honest friend to read your work and point out where you might tighten your language.

> I believe more in the scissors than I do in the pencil.

— Truman Capote

If you ~~are aware that you~~ tend to ~~say more than you need to in your writing,~~ *be wordy,*
then ~~get in the habit of~~ try~~ing~~ to cut ~~the~~ *your* first drafts ~~that you have written~~ by at least one-quarter. ~~There may be good reasons for you to~~ put all your thoughts ~~and ideas~~ down on the page when ~~you are in the process of~~ drafting a paper ~~or project.~~ But when ~~you are in the process of~~ editing, ~~you should be sure to~~ cut every unnecessary ~~word that is not needed or necessary. You may find it advantageous to~~ *expression.* Think of it as a competition ~~or a game. In making your cuts, it is important that you~~ *However,* don't eliminate any important ideas ~~that may be essential or~~ *and* facts ~~that may be important.~~ If ~~you find it~~ possible, ~~you might consider~~ ask~~ing~~ an honest friend ~~whom you trust~~ to read your ~~writing~~ *work* and ~~ask them to~~ point out ~~those places in your writing~~ where you might ~~make~~ *tighten* your language ~~tighter.~~

> **Your Turn**   Even if you think your prose is as stingy as Lean Cuisine, take a first draft you have written and try the 25 percent challenge. Count the words in the original version (or let your software do it for you) and then pare away until you come in under quota. And, while you are at it, turn abstract nouns and strung-out verbs into livelier expressions and eliminate long windups and boring chains of prepositional phrases. When you are done, read the revised version aloud — and then revise one more time.

Revising & Editing

Need style help? See page 430. / Need help with common errors? See page 600.

38 Revising Your Own Work

revise
and edit

How much time should you spend revising a draft? Decide this based on the importance of the document and the time available to complete it. A job-application letter, résumé, or term paper had better be perfect. But you shouldn't send even an e-mail without a quick review, if only to make certain you're sending it to the right people and that your tone is appropriate. Errors might not bother you, but don't assume that other readers are just as easygoing. Given a choice, a well-edited piece always trumps sloppy work.

How you revise your work is a different matter. Some people edit line by line, perfecting every sentence before moving on to the next. Others write whole drafts quickly and then revise, and others combine these methods.

In most cases, it makes sense to draft a project fairly quickly and then edit it. Why? Because revising is hierarchical: Some issues matter more to your work than others. You might spend hours on a draft, getting each comma right and deleting every word not pulling its weight. But then you read the whole thing and you get that sinking feeling: The paper doesn't meet the assignment or is aimed at the wrong audience. So you trash paragraph after carefully edited paragraph and reorganize many of your ideas. Maybe you even start from scratch.

Wouldn't it have been better to discover those big problems early on, before you put in so many hours polishing the punctuation? With major projects, consider revising and editing sequentially, starting with the big issues like content and organization. Think of *revising* as making sweeping changes, and *editing* as finessing the details.

Revise to see the big picture.   When you revise, be willing to overhaul your whole project. Of course, you'll need a draft first and it should be a real one with actual words on the page, not just good intentions. With media projects such as a Web site or blog, you might work with a site plan and page designs. O But nothing beats a prototype to test a project. Revisions at this top level may require wholesale rewrites of the paper, even starting over. Whatever it takes.

- **Does the project meet the assignment?** You really can get so wrapped up in a paper that you forget the original assignment. If you received an assignment sheet, go back and measure your draft by its requirements. If it asks for a report and you have argued, prepare for major revisions. Review, too, any requirements set for length or use of sources.

- **Does the project reach its intended audience?** Who will read your paper? Are your tone and the level of vocabulary right for these people? What kinds of sources have you used? You'll have to revise heavily if your project won't work for the assigned or intended audience.

- **Does the project do justice to its subject?** This is a tough question to address and you may want to get another reader's input. It might also help to review a successful model of the assignment before you revise your paper. Look for such work in magazines, newspapers, and text-books. Or ask your instructor or a writing-center staff member to suggest examples. How well does yours compare? Be certain you treat your subject intelligently and thoroughly and have included all the parts required. (These requirements obviously vary from assignment to assignment.) If you find some sections of the paper wanting, admit it and fix the problems.

Edit to make the paper flow.   There are different opinions as to what *flow* means when applied to writing, but it's a good thing. Once you are confident that you've met the major requirements of an assignment, check how

think visually
p. 592

well you have coordinated all its various elements. Editing to improve flow takes time and can produce valuable changes in a paper. It's the stage that gets skipped in more hurried forms of communication.

- **Does the organization work for the reader?** You may understand how a project fits together, but is that structure clear to readers? If your paper needs a thesis, does it have one that readers can identify readily and will find challenging? Do your paragraphs develop coherent points? Pay particular attention to the opening sentences in those paragraphs: They must both connect to what you just wrote and preview the upcoming material.

- **Does the paper have smooth and frequent transitions?** Transitional words and phrases support the overall organization. They are road signs to help keep readers on track. Make sure transitions appear not only at the beginning of paragraphs but also throughout the project. To navigate media projects, readers need other devices, from the captions and boxes on brochures to headings and links on Web sites. ○

- **Is the paper readable?** Once you've got the basics in place, especially a sound organization, you can tinker to your heart's content with the language, varying sentence structures, choosing words to achieve the level of style you want, and paring away clumsy verbiage (which almost rhymes with *garbage*). Review the chapters on style and apply those suggestions to the paper at this stage.

Edit to get the details right.   Most people are perfectionists when it comes to things that matter to them, but have a hard time understanding the obsessions of others. In preparing your paper, you may wonder who cares whether a page number is in the right place, a figure is correctly captioned, or a title is italicized. You'd be surprised.

When editing a paper, nothing clears your mind as much as putting a draft aside for a few days and then looking at it with fresh eyes. You will be amazed at all the changes you will want to make. But you have to plan ahead to take advantage of this unsurpassed editing technique. Wait until the last minute to complete a project and you lose that opportunity.

- **Is the format correct right down to the details?** Many academic and professional projects follow templates from which you cannot vary. In

○

connect ideas
p. 416

fact, you may be expected to learn these requirements as a condition for entering a profession or major. So if you are asked to prepare a paper in Modern Language Association (MLA) or American Psychological Association (APA) style, for instance, invest the few minutes it takes to get details right for titles, margins, headings, and page number formats. ○ Give similar attention to the formats for lab reports, e-mails, Web sites, and so on. You'll look like a pro if you do.

● **Are the grammar and mechanics right?** Word-processing programs offer a surprising amount of help in these areas. But use this assistance only as a first line of defense, not as a replacement for carefully rereading every word yourself. Even then, you still have to pay close attention to errors you make habitually. You know what they are. ○

● **Is the spelling correct?** Spell-checkers pick up some obvious gaffes but may not be any help with proper nouns or other special items—such as your professor's last name. They also don't catch correctly spelled words that simply aren't the ones you meant to use: *the* instead of *then*, *rein* instead of *reign*, and so on.

> **Your Turn**   Advice about revising can sound abstract, but the process is a real one you engage in regularly—or should. In a discussion with your colleagues (or in a paragraph or two), describe your habits of revision. Explore questions such as the following:
>
> - Do you revise as you write, or do you prefer to wait until you have a full draft?
> - How willing are you to make big changes in a draft?
> - Have you ever been embarrassed or hurt by what seemed like minor errors?
> - Do you know your specific areas of weakness, and how do you address them?
> - Do you allow yourself enough time to give your projects a close second look? Should you?
> - Have you ever had a surprising success with a paper you wrote at the last minute and turned in almost unrevised?

understand citation
styles p. 501

help with common
errors p. 600

39

Peer Editing

comment/
peer review/
proofread

Many people get nervous when asked to play editor, though such requests come all the time: "Read this for me?" Either they don't want to offend a colleague with their criticisms, or they have doubts about their own abilities. These are predictable reactions, but you need to get beyond them.

Your job in peer editing drafts is not to criticize other writers, but to help them. And you will accomplish that best by approaching any draft honestly, from the perspective of a typical reader. You may not grasp all the finer points of grammar, but you will know if a paper is boring, confusing, or unconvincing. Writers need this response: You really do have the expertise to give a classmate worthwhile feedback about issues that require attention.

And yet most peer editors in college or professional situations edit only minimally. They focus on tiny matters, such as misspellings or commas, and ignore arguments that completely lack evidence or paragraphs dull enough to kill small mammals. Frankly, spelling and punctuation errors are just easy to circle. It's much tougher to suggest that whole pages need to be redone or that a colleague should do better research. But there's nothing charitable about ignoring these deeper issues when a writer's grade or career may be on the line. So what should you do?

First, before you edit any project, agree on the ground rules for making comments. It is very easy to annotate electronic drafts since you won't have to touch or change the original file. But writers may be more protective of paper copies of their work. Always ask whether you may write comments on a paper and then make sure that your handwriting is legible and your remarks signed or initialed.

Peer edit the same way you revise your own work.   As suggested in Chapter 38, pay attention to global issues first. ○ Examine the purpose, audience, and subject matter of the project before dealing with its sentence structure, grammar, or mechanics. Deal with these major issues in a thoughtful and supportive written comment at the end of the paper. Use marginal comments and proofreading symbols (see p. 460) to highlight mechanical problems. But don't correct these items. Leave it to the writer to figure out what is wrong.

Be specific in identifying problems or opportunities.   For instance, it doesn't help a writer to read "organization is confusing." Instead, point to places in the draft that went off track. If one sentence or paragraph exemplifies a particular problem—or strength—highlight it in some fashion and mention it in the final comment. Nothing helps a writer less than vague complaints or cheerleading:

> *You did a real good job though I'm not sure you supported your thesis.*

It's far better to write something like the following:

> *Your thesis on the opening page is clear and challenging, but by the second page, you have forgotten what you are trying to prove. The paragraphs there don't seem tied to the original claim, nor do I find enough evidence to support the points you do make. Restructure these opening pages?*

Too tough? Not at all. The editor takes the paper seriously enough to explain why it's not working.

Offer suggestions for improvement.   You soften criticism when you follow it up with reasonable suggestions or strategies for revision. It's fine, too, to direct writers to resources they might use, from more authoritative

> No passion in the world is equal to the passion to alter someone else's draft.

—H. G. Wells

revise and edit
p. 452

sources to better software. Avoid the tendency, however, to revise the paper for your colleague or to redesign it to suit your own interests and opinions.

Praise what is genuinely good in the paper.   An editor can easily overlook what's working well in a paper, and yet a writer needs that information as much as any pertinent criticism. Find something good to say, too, even about a paper that mostly doesn't work. You'll encourage the writer who may be facing some lengthy revisions. But don't make an issue of it. Writers will know immediately if you are scraping bottom to find something worthy of praise.

Use proofreading symbols.   Proofreading marks may seem fussy or impersonal, but they can be a useful way of quickly highlighting some basic errors or omissions. Here are some you might want to remember and use when editing a paper draft.

sp	Word misspelled (not a standard mark, but useful)
✗	Check for error here (not a standard mark)
ᵧ	Delete marked item
⌒	Close up space
⋀	Insert word or phrase
⋀̯	Insert comma
ᵛ ᵛ	Insert quotation marks
☰	Capitalize
⊙	Insert period
∽	Transpose or reverse the items marked
¶	Begin new paragraph
#	Insert or open up space
(ital)	Italicize word or phrase

        how   *s*
It is amazing much of our day-to-day lives now depend on increasingly

SP (seemless) kinds of communication, our cell phones talking to our PDAs,

drawing e-mails from the air, sharing texts with each other, down loading

images, and taking pictures. Our communications now seem infinitely

layered a real-life *Alice in Wonderland* experience Messages don't begin

or end somewhere; they are part of a magical stream of information that

extends the reach of human intelligence, to make us all connected to

anything we want.

Keep comments tactful.   Treat another writer's work the way you'd
like to have your own efforts treated. Slips in writing can be embarrassing
enough without an editor tweeting about them.

Your Turn   Anderson Cooper of CNN reported on a teacher in North Carolina
suspended without pay for two weeks for writing "Loser" on a sixth-grader's
papers. Apparently the student wasn't offended because the teacher was
known to be a "jokester," but administrators were. Did they overreact with
the suspension (without pay), or should teachers and editors show discretion
when commenting on something as personal as writing? Is there any room
for sarcasm when peer editing? Make the case, one way or the other, in an
exploratory paragraph.

How to... Insert a comment in a Word document

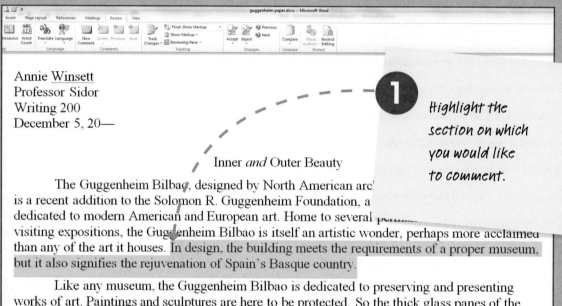

1 Highlight the section on which you would like to comment.

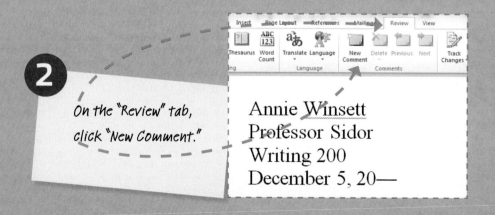

2 On the "Review" tab, click "New Comment."

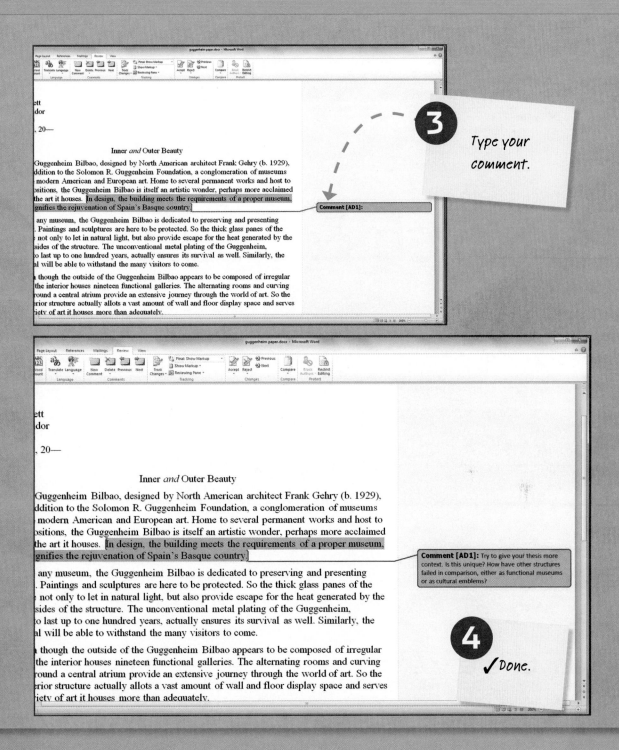

Research & Sources

7

40 Beginning Your Research

plan a project

Research can be part of any writing project. Creative writers spend long hours in a library gathering details about historical periods or contemporary events. Authors of reports conduct surveys and studies to confirm what they believe about a topic. And people engaged in arguments (ideally, at least) consult dozens of professional sources to be sure their claims are accurate and supported. ○

When doing research, you find out what is already known about a topic. For humanities courses, this involves examining a wide range of books, articles, and Web sources. In the social and natural sciences, you may also perform experiments or do field research to create and share new knowledge about a topic.

So where do you begin your research project and how do you keep from being swamped by the sheer quantity of information available? You need smart research strategies.

Know your assignment. Begin by reviewing the assignment sheet for a term paper or research project, when one is provided, and be sure you understand the kinds of research the paper requires. For a one-page position paper related to a class discussion, you might use only the reference section of the library and your textbook. An argument about current events will likely send you to newspapers, magazines, and Web sites, while a full-length term paper will draw on academic books and journals for support. (For details and advice on a wide variety of assignments, refer to Parts 1 and 2.)

choose a genre p. 390

Come up with a plan.   Research takes time. You have to find sources, read them, record your findings, and then write about them. Most research projects also require full documentation and some type of formal presentation, either as a research paper or, perhaps, an oral report. This stuff cannot be scammed the night before. You can avoid mayhem by preparing a calendar that links specific tasks to specific dates. Simply creating the schedule (and you should keep it *simple*) might even jump-start your actual research. At a minimum, record important due dates in your day planner. Here's a basic schedule for a research paper with three deadlines.

Research is formalized curiosity. It is poking and prying with a purpose.

—Zora Neale Hurston

Schedule: Research Paper

February 20: Topic proposal due
___ Explore and select a topic
___ Do preliminary library/Web research
___ Define a thesis or hypothesis
___ Prepare an annotated bibliography

March 26: First draft due
___ Read, summarize, paraphrase, and synthesize sources
___ Organize the paper

April 16: Final draft due
___ Get peer feedback on draft
___ Revise the project
___ Check documentation
___ Edit the project

Find a manageable topic.   Keep in mind that any topic and thesis for a research project should present you with a reasonable problem to solve. (For advice on finding and developing topics, see Part 3.) Look for an idea or a question you can handle realistically within the scope of the assignment and the time available, and with the resources available to you.

When asked to submit a ten- or twenty-page term paper, some writers panic, thinking they need a topic broad or general enough to fill up all these blank pages. But the opposite is true. You will have more success finding helpful sources if you break off small but intriguing parts of much larger subjects.

> *not* Military Aircraft, *but* The Development of Jet Fighters in World War II
>
> *not* The History of Punk Rock, *but* The Influence of 1970s Punk Rock on Nirvana
>
> *not* Developmental Disorders in Children, *but* Cri du Chat Syndrome

Read widely at first to find a general subject; then narrow it down to a specific topic. Brainstorm this topic to come up with focused questions you might ask in your preliminary research. By the end of this early stage of the research process, your goal is to have turned a topic idea or phrase into a claim at least one full sentence long. ○

In the natural and social sciences, topics sometimes evolve from research problems already on the table in various fields. Presented with this research agenda in a course, you ordinarily begin with a "review of the literature" to determine what others have published on this issue in the major journals and what represents state-of-the-art thinking in the field. Then create an experiment in which your research question—offered as a claim called a *hypothesis*—either confirms the direction of ongoing work in the field or perhaps advances or changes it. In basic science courses, get plenty of advice from your instructor about formulating workable research questions and hypotheses.

Seek professional help.   During your preliminary research phase, you'll quickly discover that not all sources are equal. ○ They differ in purpose, method, media, audience, and authority. Until you get your legs as a researcher, never hesitate to ask questions about research tools and strategies: Get recommendations about the best available journals, books, and authors from teachers and reference librarians. Ask them which publishers, institutions, and experts carry the most intellectual weight in their fields. If your topic is highly specialized, plan to spend additional time tracking down sources outside of your own library.

develop a statement
p. 393

find reliable sources
p. 482

Distinguish between primary and secondary sources.   This basic distinction is worth keeping in mind as you approach a new subject and project: A *primary source* is a document that provides an eyewitness account of an event or phenomenon; a *secondary source* is a step or two removed, an article or book that interprets or reports on events and phenomena described in primary sources. The famous Zapruder film of the John F. Kennedy assassination in Dallas (November 22, 1963) is a memorable primary historical document; the many books or articles that draw on the film to comment on the assassination are secondary sources. Both types of sources are useful to you as a researcher.

Use primary sources when doing research that breaks new ground. Primary sources represent raw data—letters, journals, newspaper accounts, official documents, laws, court opinions, statistics, research reports, audio and video recordings, and so on. Working with primary materials, you generate your own ideas about a subject, free of anyone else's opinions or explanations. Or you can review the actual evidence others have used to make prior claims and arguments, perhaps reinterpreting their findings, correcting them, or bringing a new perspective to the subject.

Use secondary sources to learn what others have discovered or said about a subject. In many fields, you spend most of your time reviewing secondary materials, especially when researching areas of knowledge new to you. Secondary sources include scholarly books and articles, encyclopedias,

Web sites featuring government resources, such as Thomas or FedStats, and corporate annual reports provide primary material for analysis.

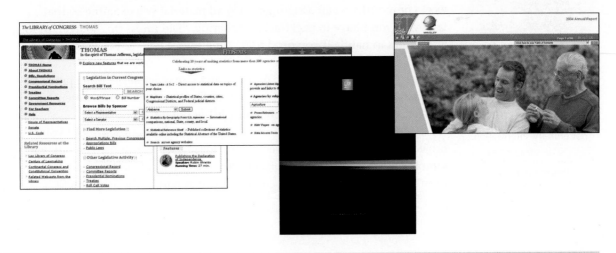

magazine pieces, and many Web sites. In academic assignments, you may find yourself moving easily between different kinds of materials, first reading a primary text like *Hamlet* and then reading various commentaries on it.

Record every source you examine.   Most writers and researchers download or photocopy sources rather than examine original copies in a library and take notes. However you plan on working, *you must* accurately record every source you encounter right from the start, gathering the following information:

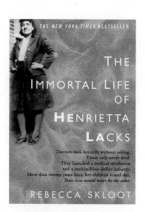

- Authors, editors, translators, sponsors (of Web sites), or other major contributors
- Titles, subtitles, edition numbers, and volumes
- Publication information, including places of publication and publishers (for books); titles of magazines and journals, as well as volume and page numbers; dates of publication and access (the latter for online materials)
- Page numbers, URLs, electronic pathways, keywords, or other locators

You'll need these details later to document your sources.

It might seem obsessive to collect basic bibliographic data on books and articles you know you are unlikely to use. But when you expect to spend weeks or months on an assignment, log all material you examine so that later you won't have to backtrack, wondering, "Did I miss this source?" A log also comes in handy if you need to revisit a source later in your research.

Books and magazines often provide secondary, not primary, information.

(*Nature* cover reprinted by permission from Macmillan Publishers Ltd.: NATURE, © January 2008.)

Prepare a topic proposal.   Your instructor may request a topic proposal. Typically, this includes a topic idea, a draft thesis or hypothesis, potential sources, your intended approach, and a list of potential problems.

Remember that such proposals are written to get feedback about your project's feasibility, and that even a good idea raises questions. The following sample proposal for a short project is directed chiefly at classmates, who must respond via electronic discussion board as part of the assignment.

Eades 1

Micah Eades

Professor Kurtz

English 201

March 20, 20--

Causal Analysis Proposal: Awkward Atmospheres

People don't like going to the doctor's office. You wait in an office room decorated from the 1980s reading *Highlights* or last year's *Field & Stream* and listen to patients in the next room talking about the details of their proctology exam. Since I am planning a future as a primary care physician, I don't want people to dread coming to see me.

My paper will propose that patient dissatisfaction with visits to their physicians may not be due entirely to fear of upcoming medical examinations but rather to the unwelcoming atmosphere of most waiting and treatment rooms. More specifically, I will examine the negative effect that noise, poor interior design, and unsympathetic staff attitudes may have on patient comfort. I will propose that these factors have a much larger impact on patient well-being than previously expected. Additionally, I will propose possible remedies and ways to change these negative perceptions.

My biggest problem may be finding concrete evidence for my claims. For evidence, I do intend to cite the relatively few clinical studies that have been conducted on patient satisfaction and atmosphere. My audience will be a tough crowd: doctors who have neither an awareness of the problems I describe nor much desire to improve the ambience of their offices.

Title indicates that proposal responds to a specific assignment.

Opening paragraph offers a rationale for subject choice.

Describes planned content and structure of paper.

Has done enough research to know that literature on subject is not extensive.

Paper will be directed to a specific audience.

41 Finding Print and Online Sources

refine your search

When beginning an academic research project, whether a brief report or a full term paper or thesis, you'll likely turn to three resources: local and school libraries, informational databases and indexes, and the Internet.

At the library are books, journals, and newspapers and other printed materials in a collection overseen by librarians to preserve information and support research. Often, the help of these librarians is necessary to locate and evaluate sources.

Also at a library or among its online resources are databases and indexes with electronic access to abstracts or full-text versions of up-to-date research materials in professional journals, magazines, and newspaper archives. Your library or school purchases licenses to allow you to use these password-protected resources—services such as *EBSCOhost, InfoTrac*, and *LexisNexis*.

And, of course, you can find endless streams of information online simply by exploring the Web, using search engines such as Google and Bing to locate data. Information on the Web varies hugely in quality, but covers just about every subject imaginable.

Whether working in a physical library, within a library catalog or an electronic database, or at home on your computer or mobile device, you need to know how to use the full capacity of research tools designed to search large bodies of information.

Learn to navigate the library catalog.   All but the smallest or most specialized libraries now organize their collections electronically. Be sure you know how the electronic catalog works: It tells you if the library has an item you need, where it is on the shelves, and whether it has been checked out. You can search for most items by author, title, subject, keywords, and even call number.

Pay special attention to the terms or keywords used to index an item you've located in an electronic catalog. You can then use those terms to search for similar materials—an important way of generating leads on a topic.

In addition to author, title, and publication information, the full entry for an item in a library catalog will also include subject headings. These terms may suggest additional avenues of research.

Locate research guides.   Another excellent option for starting an academic project is to use research sites prepared by libraries or universities to help researchers working in specific fields. Check to see whether your institution has developed such materials. Or simply search the phrase "library research guides" on the Web. Such sites identify resources both within and outside of academic institutions and may also give you suggestions for topic ideas or research areas. Use these guides carefully, since they may contain links to sites that libraries and schools cannot vouch for entirely. Some of the university-based materials may be restricted to students at the particular schools. But, even then, they may identify resources you can access through your own institution. The charts on pages 474 and 477 may help you identify databases for your subject.

You will probably begin your search with one or more multidisciplinary databases such as *LexisNexis Academic, Academic OneFile,* or *Academic Search Premier.* These resources cover a wide range of materials, including newspapers, respected magazines, and some professional journals. Most libraries

Research Guides and Databases	
Institution	**Subject Guides at**
Columbia University Library	www.columbia.edu/cu/lweb/eresources
New York Public Library	http://www.nypl.org/collections/ nypl-recommendations/research-guides
University of Chicago	http://guides.lib.uchicago.edu/home
University of Virginia	www.lib.virginia.edu/resguide.html
Electronic Books	www.lib.utexas.edu/books/etext.html
Infomine	http://infomine.ucr.edu
The Internet Public Library	www.ipl.org
Library of Congress Research and Reference Services	http://www.loc.gov/rr/

subscribe to one or more such information services, and these can be searched using keywords.

But for more in-depth work, focus on the databases within your specific discipline. There are, in fact, hundreds of such databases and tools, far too many to list here. Look for databases that present current materials at a level you can understand: Some online resources may be too specific or technical for your project. When working with a database for the first time, review the Help section or page to find the most efficient way to conduct your searches. Librarians, too, can offer professional advice on refining your search techniques.

Identify the best reference tools for your needs.   For encyclopedias, almanacs, historical records, maps, and so on, head to the reference section of your library and ask the librarian to direct you to the appropriate items.

Quite often, for instance, you'll need to trace the biographical facts of important people—dates of birth, countries of origin, schools attended, career paths, and so on. For current newsmakers, you might find enough fairly reliable data from a Web search or a Wikipedia entry. But to get the most accurate information on historical figures, consult more authoritative library tools such as the *Oxford Dictionary of National Biography* (focusing on the United Kingdom) or the *Dictionary of American Biography*. The British work is available in an up-to-date online version. Libraries also have more specialized biographical resources, both in print and online. Ask about them.

When you need information from old newspapers, you'll need more ingenuity. Libraries don't store newspapers, so local and selected national papers will be available only on microfilm. Just as limiting, few older papers are indexed. So, unless you know the approximate date of an event, you may have a tough time finding a story in the microfilmed copies of newspapers. Fortunately, both the *New York Times* and *Wall Street Journal* are indexed and available on microfilm in most major libraries. You'll also find older magazines on microfilm. These may be indexed (up to 1982) in print bibliographies such as the *Readers' Guide to Periodical Literature*. Ask a librarian for help.

When your library doesn't have the material you need, ask the librarian if it's possible to acquire the material from another facility through interlibrary loan. The loan process may take time, but if you plan ahead, you can get any reasonable item.

Use online sources intelligently.   Browsing the Web daily to check the sports scores and surf your favorite blogs and Web sites is a completely different matter than using the Web for research. Thanks to exhaustive search engines like Google and Bing, you can find facts on just about any subject—often too much information. And the quality of the results you turn up in a Web search will be uneven. Hits are generally returned by popularity, not reliability.

Improve your online research the same way you learn to navigate a library's academic databases: Study the Help screens that accompany the Web browser. Most offer advanced search options to help you turn up fewer and more pertinent materials.

Google's Help screen provides tips on how to search the Internet.

© 2011 Google

But you also need to exercise care with Web sources. Be certain you know who is responsible for the material (for instance, a government agency, a congressional office, a news service, a corporation), who is posting it, who is the author of the material or sponsor of the Web site, what the date of publication is, and so on. ○ A site's information is often skewed by those who pay its bills or run it; it can also be outdated, if no one regularly updates the site.

Keep current with Web developments too. Web companies such as Google are making more books and journal articles both searchable and available through their sites. Although these and other projects to broaden access to scholarly information do raise questions about copyright and the ownership of intellectual property, you should certainly take time to explore these tools as they become available.

For instance, a tool such as Google Scholar will direct you to academic sources and scholarly papers on a subject—exactly the kind of material you would want to use in a term paper or report. As an experiment, you might compare the hits you get on a topic with a regular Google search with those that turn up when you select the Scholar option. You'll quickly notice that the Scholar items are more serious and technical—and also more difficult to access. In some cases, you may see only an abstract of a journal article or the first page of the item. Yet the sources you locate may be worth a trip to the library to retrieve in their entirety.

find reliable sources
p. 482

Resources to Consult When Conducting Research			
Source	**What It Provides**	**Usefulness in Academic Research**	**Where to Find It**
Scholarly Books	Fully documented and detailed primary research and analyses by scholars	Highly useful if not too high-level or technical	Library, Google Scholar
Scholarly Journals	Carefully documented primary research by scientists and scholars	Highly useful if not too high-level or technical	Library, databases
Newspapers	Accounts of current events	Useful as starting point	Library, microfilm, databases (*LexisNexis*), Internet
Magazines	Wide topic range, usually based on secondary research; written for popular audience	Useful if magazine has serious reputation	Libraries, newsstands, databases (*EBSCOhost*, *InfoTrac*), Internet
Encyclopedias (General or Discipline-Specific)	Brief articles	Useful as a starting point	Libraries, Internet
Wikipedia	Open-source encyclopedia: entries written/edited by online contributors	Not considered reliable for academic projects	Internet: www.wikipedia.org
Special Collections	Materials such as maps, paintings, artifacts, etc.	Highly useful for specialized projects	Libraries, museums; images available via Internet
Government, Academic, or Organization Web Sites	Vast data compilations of varying quality, some of it reviewed	Highly useful	Internet sites with URLs ending in *.gov, .edu,* or *.org*
Commercial Web Sites	Information on many subjects; quality varies	Useful if possible biases are known	Internet sites
Blogs	Controlled, often highly partisan discussions of specialized topics	Useful when affiliated with reputable sources such as newspapers	Internet
Personal Web Sites	Often idiosyncratic information	Rarely useful; content varies widely	Internet

42 Doing Field Research

interview and observe

While most research you do will be built on the work of others—that is, their books, articles, and fact-finding—you can strike out on your own in many situations. For instance, you might interview people with experiences or information related to the subject you're exploring. ○ Or you could support a claim by carefully observing and recording how people actually behave or think.

Field research is done in many ways and with different tools and media.

ask for help p. 379

Interview people with unique knowledge of your subject.   When considering whether an interview makes sense for your project, ask yourself the important question, "What do I expect to learn from the interviewee?" If the information you seek is readily available online or in print, don't waste everyone's time going through with an interview. If, on the other hand, this person provides a fresh perspective on your topic, a personal interview may make an excellent contribution to your research.

Interviews can be written or spoken. Written interviews, whether by e-mail or letter, allow you to keep questions and answers focused and provide a written record of your interviewee's exact words. But spoken interviews, both in person and on the phone, allow in-depth discussion of a topic and may lead to more memorable quotes or deeper insights. Be flexible in setting up the type of interview most convenient for your subject. For interviews, keep the following suggestions in mind:

- Request an interview formally by phone, confirming it with a follow-up e-mail.

- Give your subjects a compelling reason for meeting or corresponding with you; briefly explain your research project and why their knowledge or experience is important to your work.

- Let potential interviewees know how you chose them as subjects. If possible, provide a personal reference—a professor or administrator who can vouch for you.

- Prepare a set of thoughtful and relevant interview questions to encourage your subject to elaborate. Don't try to wing it in an interview.

- Think about how to phrase questions to open up the interview. Avoid questions that can be answered in one word, such as, *Did you enjoy your years in Asia?* Instead, ask, *What did you enjoy most about the decade you spent in Tokyo?*

- Start the interview by thanking the interviewee for his or her time and providing a brief reminder of your research project.

- Keep a written record of material you wish to quote. If necessary, confirm the exact wording with your interviewee.

- End the interview by again expressing your thanks.

- Follow up on the interview with a thank-you note or e-mail and, if the interviewee's contributions were substantial, send him or her a copy of the research paper.

- In your paper, give full credit to any people interviewed by properly documenting the information they provided. ○

If you conduct your interview in writing, request a response by a certain date—one or two weeks is reasonable for ten questions. Refer to Chapter 13 for e-mail etiquette and Chapter 14 for guidelines on writing business letters.

For telephone interviews, call from a place with good reception, where you will not be interrupted. Your cell phone should be fully charged or plugged in.

For an interview conducted in person, arrive at the predetermined meeting place on time and dressed professionally. If you wish to tape-record the interview, be sure to ask permission first.

> **Your Turn**   Prepare a full set of questions you would use to interview a classmate about some *academic* issue—for example, his or her study habits, method for writing papers, or career objectives. Think about how you would sequence the questions, how you would follow up on the possible replies (if the interview were oral), and how you might avoid one-word replies that would give you little material for a report based on the interview. Write down your questions and then pair up with a classmate for a set of mutual interviews.
>
> When you are done, write a one-page report based on what you learn and share the results with classmates.

Make careful and verifiable observations.   In writing either reports or arguments, especially those that focus on a specific local group or community, you might find yourself lacking enough data to move your claims beyond mere opinion. The point of systematic observation is to provide a clear, reliable, and verifiable way of studying a narrowly defined activity or phenomenon.

For example, an anecdote or a few random examples may not be enough to persuade administrators that the open meeting rooms in the student union are not being used efficiently. But you could probably construct a systematic observation of these facilities, showing exactly how many student groups use them, and on what basis, over a given period of time. This kind

understand citation
styles p. 501

of evidence carries far more weight than mere opinion because your readers can study exactly how you conducted your observations and accept or challenge your results.

Some situations can't be counted or measured as readily as the one described above. If, for example, you wanted to compare the various meeting rooms to determine whether those with windows facilitated more productive discussions than rooms without, your observations would need to be more qualitative. For example, to record whether meeting participants appeared alert or distracted, you might describe the tone of their voices and the general mood of the room. Numbers should figure in this observation as well; for instance, you could track how many people participated in the discussion or the number of tasks accomplished during the meeting.

To avoid bias in their observations, many researchers use double-column notebooks. In one column, they record the physical details of their observation as objectively as possible—descriptions, sounds, countable data, weather, time, circumstances, activity, and so on. In the second column, they record their interpretations and commentaries on the data.

In addition to careful and objective note-taking techniques, devices such as cameras, video recorders, and tape recorders provide reliable backup evidence about an event. Also, having more than one witness observe a situation can help verify your findings.

Learn more about fieldwork.   In those disciplines or college majors that use fieldwork, you will find guides or manuals to explain the details of such research procedures. You will also discover that fieldwork comes in many varieties, from naturalist observations and case studies to time studies and market research.

OBSERVABLE DATA	COMMENTARY
9/12/11 2 P.M. Meeting of Entertainment Committee Room MUB210 (no windows) 91 degrees outside Air conditioning broken People appear quiet, tired, hot	Heat and lack of a/c probably making everyone miserable.

A double-column notebook entry.

43 Evaluating Sources

find reliable
sources

In Chapter 41, you were steered in the direction of the best possible print and online sources for your research. But the fact is, all sources, no matter how prestigious, have strengths and weaknesses, biases and limitations. Even the most well-intentioned librarians have their prejudices. So evaluating sources is simply a routine and unavoidable part of any careful research process. Here are some strategies to use when making your own judgments about potential sources.

Preview source materials for their key features and strategies.   Give any source a quick once-over, looking for clues to its aim, content, and structure. Begin with the title and subtitle, taking seriously its key terms and qualifiers. A good title tells what a piece is—and is not—about. For many scholarly articles, the subtitle (which typically follows a colon) describes the substance of the argument.

Then scan the introduction (in a book) or abstract (in an article). From these items, you should be able to quickly grasp what the source covers, what its methods are, and what the author hopes to prove or accomplish.

Inspect the table of contents in a book or the headings in an article methodically, using them to grasp the overall structure of the work or to find specific information. Briefly review charts, tables, and illustrations, too, to discover what they offer. If a book has an index—and a serious book should—look for the key terms or subjects you are researching to see how well they are covered.

If the work appears promising, read its final section or chapter. Knowing how the source concludes gives considerable insight into its value for your research. Finally, look over the bibliography. The list of sources indicates how thorough the author has been and, not incidentally, points you to other materials you might want to examine.

Check who published or produced the source.   In general, books published by presses associated with colleges and universities (Harvard, Oxford, Stanford, etc.) are reputable sources for college papers. So are articles from professional journals described as *refereed* or *peer-reviewed*. These terms are used for journals in which the articles have been impartially evaluated by panels of experts prior to publication.

You can also usually rely on material from reputable commercial publishers and from established institutions and agencies. The *New York Times, Wall Street Journal*, CNN, Random House, Simon & Schuster, and the U.S. government make their ample share of mistakes, of course, but are generally considered to be more reliable than blogs or personal Web sites. But you always need to be cautious.

Check who wrote the work.   Ordinarily, you should cite authorities on your topic. Look for authors who are mentioned frequently and favorably within a field or whose works appear regularly in notes or bibliographies. Get familiar with these names.

The Web makes it possible to review the careers of many authors whom you might not recognize. Search for their names online to confirm that they are professional experts or reputable journalists. Avoid citing authors working too far beyond their areas of professional expertise. Celebrities especially like to cross boundaries, sometimes mistaking their passion for an issue for genuine mastery of the subject.

Consider the audience for a source.   What passes for adequate information in the general marketplace of ideas may not cut it when you're doing academic research. Many widely read books and articles that popularize a

You can learn a lot about a source by previewing a few basic elements.

ACADEMIC
PRESS

Available online at www.sciencedirect.com

Journal of Research in Personality 36 (2002) 607–614

JOURNAL OF
RESEARCH IN
PERSONALITY

www.academicpress.com

Brief report

Are we barking up the right tree? Evaluating a comparative approach to personality

Samuel D. Gosling [*] and Simine Vazire

Department of Psychology, University of Texas, Austin, TX, USA

Playful title nonetheless fits: Article is about animals.

Abstract

Animal studies can enrich the field of human personality psychology by addressing questions that are difficult or impossible to address with human studies alone. However, the benefits of a comparative approach to personality cannot be reaped until the tenability of the personality construct has been established in animals. Using criteria established in the wake of the person–situation debate (Kenrick & Funder, 1988), the authors evaluate the status of personality traits in animals. The animal literature provides strong evidence that personality does exist in animals. That is, personality ratings of animals: (a) show strong levels of interobserver agreement, (b) show evidence of validity in terms of predicting behaviors and real-world outcomes, and (c) do not merely reflect the implicit theories of observers projected onto animals. Although much work remains to be done, the preliminary groundwork has been laid for a comparative approach to personality.

Abstract previews entire article.

Introduction

Personality characteristics have been examined in a broad range of non-human species including chimpanzees, rhesus monkeys, ferrets, hyenas, rats,

Headings throughout signal this is a research article.

[*] Corresponding author. Fax: 1-512- 471-5935.
E-mail address: gosling@psy.utexas.edu (S.D. Gosling).

0092-6566/02/$ - see front matter © 2002 Elsevier Science (USA). All rights reserved.
PII: S0092-6566(02)00511-1

608   *Brief report / Journal of Research in Personality 36 (2002) 607 614*

sheep, rhinoceros, hedgehogs, zebra finches, garter snakes, guppies, and oc-
topuses (for a full review, see Gosling, 2001). Such research is important because animal studies can be used to tackle questions that are difficult or
impossible to address with human studies alone. By reaping the benefits
of animal research, a comparative approach to personality can enrich the
field of human personality psychology, providing unique opportunities to
examine the biological, genetic, and environmental bases of personality,
and to study personality development, personality-health links, and personality perception. However, all of these benefits hinge on the tenability of the
personality construct in non-human animals. Thus, the purpose of the present paper is to address a key question in the animal domain: is personality
real? That is, do personality traits reflect real properties of individuals or are
they fictions in the minds of perceivers?

   Thirty years ago, the question of the reality of personality occupied the
attention of human-personality researchers, so our evaluation of the comparative approach to personality draws on the lessons learned in the human domain. Mischel's (1968) influential critique of research on human
personality was the first of a series of direct challenges to the assumptions
that personality exists and predicts meaningful real-world behaviors. Based
on a review of the personality literature, Mischel (1968) pointed to the lack
of evidence that individuals' behaviors are consistent across situations (Mischel & Peake, 1982). Over the next two decades, personality researchers
garnered substantial empirical evidence to counter the critiques of personality. In an important article, Kenrick and Funder (1988) carefully analyzed the various arguments that had been leveled against personality
and summarized the theoretical and empirical work refuting these arguments.

   The recent appearance of studies of animal personality has elicited renewed debate about the status of personality traits. Gosling, Lilienfeld,
and Marino (in press) proposed that the conditions put forward by Kenrick
and Funder (1988) to evaluate the idea of human personality can be mobi-
lized in the service of evaluating the idea of animal personality. Gosling et
al. (in press) used these criteria to evaluate research on personality in non-
human primates. In the present paper, we extend their analysis to the broader field of comparative psychology, considering research on nonhuman
animals from several species and taxa. Kenrick and Funder's paper delin-
eates three major criteria that must be met to establish the existence of personality traits: (1) assessments by independent observers must agree with
one another; (2) these assessments must predict behaviors and real-world
outcomes; and (3) observer ratings must be shown to reflect genuine attributes of the individuals rated, not merely the observers' implicit theories
about how personality traits covary. Drawing on evidence from the animal-
behavior literature, we evaluate whether these three criteria have been met
with respect to animal personality.

Point of this brief study is
defined at end of opening
paragraph.

This page reviews literature
on studies of animal
personality. ◯

Matt Damon shared his thoughts on President Obama at an interview about Damon's film *The Adjustment Bureau.* He may be one of your favorite actors, but don't cite him as a political expert in a research paper.

subject—such as climate change or problems with health-care costs—may, in fact, be based on more technical scholarly books and articles. For academic projects, rely primarily on those scholarly works themselves, even if you were inspired to choose a subject by reading respectable nonfiction. Glossy magazines shouldn't play a role in your research either, though the lines can get blurry. *People, O, Rolling Stone*, or *Spin* might be important in writing about popular culture or music, but not for much else. Similarly, Wikipedia is invaluable for a quick introduction to a subject, but don't cite it as an authority in an academic paper.

Establish how current a source is.   Scholarly work doesn't come with an expiration date, but you should base your research on the latest information. For fields in which research builds on previous work, the date of publication may even be highlighted by its system of documentation. Copyright pages, on the back of the title page, list the date of publication.

Check the source's documentation.   All serious scholarly and scientific research is documented. Claims are based on solid evidence backed up by formal notes, data are packed into charts and tables, and there will be a bibliography at the end. All of this is done so that readers can verify the claims an author makes.

In a news story, journalists may establish the credibility of their information by identifying their sources or, at a minimum, attributing their findings to reliable unnamed sources—and usually more than one. The authors of serious magazine pieces don't use footnotes and bibliographies either, but they, too, credit their major sources somewhere in the work. No serious claim should be left hanging. ⭘

For your own academic projects, avoid authors and sources with undocumented assertions. Sometimes you have to trust authors when they are writing about personal experiences or working as field reporters, but let readers know when your claims are based on uncorroborated personal accounts.

think critically
p. 372

Annotating Sources

44

Once you locate trustworthy sources, review them to identify the best ideas and most convincing evidence for your project. During this process of careful and critical reading, you annotate, sum-marize, ○ synthesize, ○ and paraphrase ○ your sources, in effect creating the notes you need to compose your paper.

Annotate sources to understand them.   Examine impor-tant sources closely enough to understand not only what they say but also how they reached their conclusions or compiled their data. In a sense, you have to become an expert on the sources you cite. To assist your analysis, you'll want to mark key texts with appropriate tools—notes in the margins, Post-it notes, electronic comments, and so forth. Simply making such comments will draw you deeper into a text and make you think about it more.

Read sources to identify claims.   Begin by noting and highlighting any specific claims, themes, or thesis statements a writer offers early in a text. Then pay attention to the way these ideas recur within the work, especially near the conclusion. At a minimum, decide whether a writer has made reasonable claims, developed them consistently, and delivered on promised evi-dence. In the example on pages 488–90 claims and reasons are highlighted in yellow.

Read sources to understand assumptions.   Finding and annotating the assumptions in a source can be *much* trickier than

analyze
claims and
evidence/
take notes

487

locating claims. Highlight any assumptions stated outright in the source; they will be rare. More often, you have to infer the writer's assumptions, put them in your own words, and perhaps record them in marginal notes. Identifying controversial or debatable assumptions is particularly important. For instance, if a writer makes the claim that *America needs tighter border security to prevent terrorist attacks,* you draw the inference that the writer believes that terrorism is caused by people crossing inadequately patrolled borders. Is that assumption accurate? Should the writer explain or defend it? Raise such questions. The one key assumption in the example that follows is highlighted in orange.

Read sources to find evidence.   Look for evidence that authors use to support both their claims and their assumptions. Evidence can come in the form of data, examples, illustrations, or logical inferences. Since evidentiary sections make up the bulk of most academic materials you read, highlight only the key items—especially any facts or materials you intend to cite in your own project. Make sure no crucial point goes unsupported; if you find one, make a note of it. In the following example, key evidence is highlighted in blue.

Record your personal reactions to source material.   When reading multiple sources, you'll want a record of what you appreciated or objected to in them. To be certain you don't later mistake your personal comments for observations *from* the source, use first person or pose questions as you respond. Use personal annotations, too, to draw connections to other source materials you have read. In the following example, personal reactions appear on the left.

SANITY 101

Parents of adolescents usually strive for an aura of calm and reason. But just two words can trigger irrational behavior in parent and child alike: "college admissions."

It's not an unreasonable response, actually, given the list of exasperating questions facing parents seeking to maximize their children's prospects: Do I tutor my child to boost college admissions test scores? Do I rely on the school

CLAIM AND REASON:
Fear of college admissions procedures is key point in editorial.

admissions counselor or hire a private adviser? Do I hire a professional editor to shape my child's college essay?

EVIDENCE:
Specific concerns support initial claim. They are the issues troubling parents most.

The price tags behind those decisions drive up the angst. A testing tutor "guaranteeing" a 200-point score boost on the SAT admissions test will charge roughly $2,400. Hiring a private college counselor can cost from $1,300 to $10,000. And hiring an essay editor can cost between $60 and $1,800. Wealthy suburbs are particularly lucrative for the college prep industry. Less affluent families are left with even greater reason to fret: Their children face an unfair disadvantage.

CLAIM

EVIDENCE

READER'S REACTION:
Why don't colleges realize how unfair their admissions policies might be to poorer applicants?

Now, private employers are stepping in to help out.

CLAIM

In a front-page article on Tuesday, *USA Today*'s education reporter Mary Beth Marklein revealed a range of counseling packages that companies are offering parents of college applicants, from brown-bag discussion lunches to Web-based programs that manage the entire admissions process.

EVIDENCE

It's thoughtful of the employers, but it shouldn't be necessary.

READER'S REACTION:
Might there be a parallel here to out-of-control sports programs? Why are schools so poorly administered?

Thanks to overanxious parents, aggressive college admissions officials and hustling college prep entrepreneurs, the admissions system has spun out of control. And the colleges have done little to restore sanity.

CLAIM:
This assertion, midway through editorial, may in fact be its thesis.

EVIDENCE

Take just one example, the "early decision" process in which seniors apply to a college by November 1 and promise to attend if admitted.

Early decision induces students to cram demanding courses into their junior year so they will appear on the application record. That makes an already stressful year for students and parents even more so. Plus, students must commit to a college long before they are ready. The real advantages of early decision go to colleges, which gain more control over their student mix and rise in national rankings by raising their acceptance rates.

Parents and students can combat the stress factor by keeping a few key facts in mind. While it's true that the very top colleges are ruthlessly selective—both Harvard and Yale accept slightly less than 10 percent of applicants—most colleges are barely selective. Of the 1,400 four-year colleges in the United States, only about 100 are very selective, and they aren't right for every student. Among the other 1,300, an acceptance rate of about 85 percent is more the norm.

And the best part of all: Many of those 1,300 colleges are more interested in educating your child than burnishing their rankings on lists of the "top" institutions. So the next time you hear the words "college admissions," don't instantly open your wallet. First, take a deep breath.

—Editorial/Opinion, *USA Today*, January 19, 2006

CLAIM AND REASON:
Parents are worrying too much.

EVIDENCE:
Statistics offer reasons not to fear college admissions procedures.

ASSUMPTION:
Change "are" to "should be" and you have the assumption underlying this entire argument.

Your Turn   With a classmate, exchange a draft of papers you are developing. Then read your colleague's paper as outlined in this chapter, imagining how you might use it as a source. First highlight major claims and reasons offered by the author; then identify any key assumptions in the paper. Bracket those sections of the project that primarily offer evidence. Finally, offer your personal reactions to various parts of the paper.

You might use highlighting pens of different colors to separate claims/reasons from assumptions and evidence, as in the sample essay.

Summarizing Sources

Once you determine that specific articles, books, and other texts deserve closer attention and you have read them critically—with an eye toward using their insights and data in your project—you're ready to summarize the material, putting ideas you've found into your own words. These brief summaries or fuller paraphrases can become the springboard for composing your paper. ○

sum up ideas

Use a summary to recap what a writer has said.   Look carefully for the main point and build your summary on it, making sure that this statement *does* reflect the actual content of the source, not your opinion of it. Be certain that the summary is *entirely* in your own words. Include the author and title of the work, too, so you can easily cite it later. The following is one summary of the *USA Today* editorial reprinted on pages 488–90, with all the required citation information:

> In "Sanity 101," the editors of *USA Today* (January 19, 2006) criticize current college admission practices, which, they argue, make students and parents alike fear that getting into an appropriate school is harder than it really is.
>
> Source: "Sanity 101." Editorial. *USA Today* 19 Jan. 2006: 10A. Print.

restate ideas
p. 494

Be sure your summary is accurate and complete.   Even when a source makes several points, moves in contradictory directions, or offers a complex conclusion, your job is simply to describe what the material does. Don't embellish the material or blur the distinction between the source's words and yours. Include all bibliographical information (title, author, and date) from the source. The following summary of "Sanity 101" shows what can go wrong if you are not careful.

Omits title/source. Opening claim is not in editorial.

Editorial actually makes opposite point.

Summary improperly uses source's exact words. Might lead to inadvertent plagiarism later on.

> According to *USA Today*, most students get into the colleges they want. But admission into most colleges is so tough that many parents blow a fortune on tutors and counselors so that their kids can win early admission. But the paper's advice to parents is don't instantly open your wallet. First, take a deep breath.

Use a summary to record your take on a source.   In addition to reporting the contents of the material accurately, note also how the source might (or might not) contribute to your paper. But make certain that your comments won't be confused with claims made in the summarized article itself. The following are two acceptable sample summaries for "Sanity 101."

> In "Sanity 101," *USA Today* (January 19, 2006) describes the efforts of college applicants and parents to deal with the progressively more competitive admissions policies of elite institutions. The editorial claims that most schools, however, are far less selective. The article includes a reference to another *USA Today* piece by Mary Beth Marklein on the support some companies offer employees to assist them with college admissions issues.
>
> Source: "Sanity 101." Editorial. *USA Today* 19 Jan. 2006: 10A. Print.

> In an editorial (January 19, 2006) entitled "Sanity 101," *USA Today* counsels parents against worrying too much about hypercompetitive current college admission practices. In reality only a small percentage of schools are highly selective about admissions. The editorial doesn't provide the schools' side of the issue.
>
> Source: "Sanity 101." Editorial. *USA Today* 19 Jan. 2006: 10A. Print.

Prepare a summary to provide a useful record of a source.   After
reading a research source, you may decide that all you need is a brief description of it—the gist of it—recorded either on a card or in an electronic file
(with complete bibliographic data). Such a summary reminds you that you
have, in fact, seen and reviewed the source, which can be no small comfort
when developing projects that stretch over several weeks or months. After
you've examined dozens and dozens of sources, it's easy to forget what exactly you've already read.

Use summaries to prepare an annotated bibliography.   In an
annotated bibliography, brief summaries are provided for every item in an
alphabetical list of sources. These summaries help readers understand the
content and scope of materials. For more about annotated bibliographies, see
Chapter 11. O

> **Your Turn**   Practice writing summaries by pairing up with a classmate and
> finding (probably online) a newspaper or blog page with a variety of opinion-
> oriented articles. For instance, check out the "Opinion" page in the *New York
> Times* or the home page of *Arts & Letters Daily* or the *Huffington Post*.
>   Agree on three or four pieces that both of you will summarize separately.
> Then write the paired summaries, being careful to identify the items, describe
> them accurately, and separate your recaps from any comments you make about
> the material you have read. When you are done, compare your summaries.
> Discuss their accuracy and make certain that neither of you has inadvertently
> borrowed language from the original articles.

understand annotated
bibliographies p. 296

46 Paraphrasing Sources

restate ideas

Paraphrases provide more complete records of the sources you examine than do summaries. ○ Like a summary, a paraphrase recaps a source's main point, but it also tracks the reasons and important evidence supporting that conclusion. Paraphrase any materials you expect to use extensively in a project. Then consider how the research materials you have gathered work in relationship to each other.

Identify the key claims and structure of the source. Determine the main points made by the article, chapter, or text, and study how the work organizes information to support its claims. ○ Then be sure your paraphrase follows the same structure as the source. For example, your paraphrase will likely be arranged sequentially when a work has a story to tell, be arranged by topic when you're dealing with reported information, or be structured logically when you take notes from arguments or editorials.

Track the source faithfully. A paraphrase should follow the reasoning of the source, moving through it succinctly but remaining faithful to its organization, tone, and, to some extent, style. In effect, you are preparing an abstract of the material, complete and readable in itself. So take compact and sensible notes, adapting the paraphrase to your needs—understanding that some materials will be more valuable for your project than others. ○

494

sum up ideas
p. 491

think critically
p. 372

take notes
p. 487

Record key pieces of evidence.   Thanks to photocopies and downloaded files, you don't usually have to copy data laboriously into your notes—and you probably shouldn't. (The chances of error greatly multiply whenever you copy information by hand.) But be certain that your paraphrase does record the reasons supporting all major claims in the source, as well as key evidence and facts. Key evidence proves a point or seals the deal. Also, keep track of page numbers for the important data so you can cite this material directly from your notes.

Be certain your notes are entirely in your own words.   If you borrow the language of sources as you paraphrase them, you'll likely slip into plagiarism when you compose your paper. Deliberately or not, you could find yourself copying phrases or sentences from the sources into your project.

When you are confident that you've paraphrased sources correctly, never borrowing their language, you may then safely transfer those notes directly into your project—giving the original writers due credit. In effect, you've begun to compose your own paper whenever you write competent paraphrases.

The following is a paraphrase of "Sanity 101," the complete, fully annotated text of which appears in Chapter 44 (pp. 488–90). Compare the paraphrase here to the summaries of the article that appear in Chapter 45 (pp. 491–92).

> In an editorial entitled "Sanity 101" (January 19, 2006), the editors of *USA Today* worry that many fearful parents are resorting to costly measures to help assure their child's college admission, some hiring private counselors and tutors that poorer families can't afford. Companies now even offer college admission assistance as part of employees' job packages. Colleges themselves are to blame for the hysteria, in part because of "early admission" practices that benefit them more than students. But parents and students should consider the facts. Only a handful of colleges are truly selective; most have acceptance rates near 85 percent. In addition, most schools care more about students than about their own rankings.

Avoid misleading or inaccurate paraphrasing.   Your notes won't be worth much if your paraphrases of sources distort the content of what you read. Don't rearrange the information, give it a spin you might prefer, or offer your own opinions on a subject. Make it clear, too, whenever your comments focus just on particular sections or chapters of a source, rather than on the entire piece. That way, you won't misread your notes months later and give readers a wrong impression about an article or book. The following is a paraphrase of "Sanity 101" that gets almost everything wrong.

Opening sentences follow language of editorial too closely, and also distort structure of editorial.

Paraphrase shifts tone, becoming much more colloquial than editorial.

Paraphrase borrows words and phrases too freely from original.

Paraphrase offers opinion on subject, its criticism of colleges going beyond original editorial.

Parents of teens usually try to be reasonable, the editors of *USA Today* complained on January 19, 2006. But the words "college admission" can make both child and parent irrational. The response is not unreasonable, given all the irritating questions facing parents seeking to improve their children's prospects. But the fact is that just a few colleges are highly selective. Most of the four-year schools in the country have acceptance rates of 85 percent. So high school students and parents should just chill and not blow their wallets on extra expenses. Rely on the school admissions counselor; don't hire a private adviser or professional editor to shape your child's college essay. A testing tutor might charge $2,400; a private college counselor can cost from $1,300 to $10,000. This is unfair to poorer families too, especially when companies start offering special admissions services to their employees. As always, the colleges are to blame, with their pushy "early admissions" programs, which make them look good in rankings but just screw their students.

Use your paraphrases to synthesize sources.   If you are asked to prepare a literature review or synthesis paper on a subject, begin that work by carefully summarizing and paraphrasing a range of reputable sources. For much more about synthesis and synthesis papers, see Chapter 12. ○

> **Your Turn**   Practice writing paraphrases by pairing up with a classmate and choosing a full essay to paraphrase from Part 1 of this book.
>   Write your paraphrases of the agreed-upon essay separately, just as if you intended to cite the piece later in a report, research paper, or argument yourself. When both of you are done, compare your paraphrases. What did you identify as the main point(s) or thesis of the piece? What kind of structure did the article follow: for example, narrative, report, comparison/contrast, argument, and so on? What evidence or details from the article did you include in your paraphrases? How did your paraphrases compare in length?
>   Discuss the differences. How might you account for them?

understand synthesis
papers p. 300

Integrating Sources into Your Work

When you integrate sources effectively into your work, you give readers information they need to identify paraphrased or quoted items and to understand how they may have been edited for clarity or accuracy.

Cue the reader in some way whenever you introduce borrowed material, whether it is summarized, paraphrased, or quoted directly. Readers *always* need to be able to distinguish between your ideas and those you've obtained from other authors. So you must provide a signal whenever source material is introduced. Think of it as framing this material to set it off from your own words. Framing also enables you to offer an explanation or context for borrowed material, giving it the weight and power you believe it should have.

Often, all that's required for a frame is a brief signal phrase that identifies the author, title, or source you are drawing on.

President Obama explained at a press conference that ". . .

According to a report in *Scientific American*, . . .

. . . ," said the former CEO of General Electric, arguing that ". . .

In *Blink*, author Malcolm Gladwell makes some odd claims. For example, he . . .

avoid plagiarism/ use quotations

MLA and APA Style

The examples in this section follow MLA (Modern Language Association) style, covered in Chapter 49. For information on APA (American Psychological Association) style, see Chapter 50.

At other times you'll need a clause or a complete sentence or more to incorporate borrowed material into a paper. Your frame can introduce, interrupt, follow, or even surround the words or ideas taken from sources, but be sure that your signal phrases are grammatical and lead naturally into the material.

Select an appropriate "verb of attribution" to frame borrowed material.   Note that source material is often introduced or framed by a "verb of attribution" or "signal verb." These verbs influence what readers think of borrowed ideas or quoted material.

Use more neutral signal verbs in reports, and descriptive or even biased terms in arguments. Note that, by MLA convention, verbs of attribution are usually in the present tense when talking about current work or ideas. (In APA, these verbs are generally in the past or present perfect tense.)

Verbs of Attribution		
Neutral	**Descriptive**	**Biased**
adds	acknowledges	admits
explains	argues	charges
finds	asserts	confesses
notes	believes	confuses
offers	claims	derides
observes	confirms	disputes
says	disagrees	evades
shows	responds	impugns
states	reveals	pretends
writes	suggests	smears

Use ellipsis marks [. . .] to shorten a lengthy quotation.   When quoting a source in your paper, it's not necessary to use every word or sentence, as long as the cuts you make don't distort the meaning of the original material. An ellipsis mark, formed from three spaced periods, shows where words, phrases, full sentences, or more have been removed from a quotation. The mark doesn't replace punctuation within a sentence. Thus, you might see a period or a comma immediately followed by an ellipsis mark.

ORIGINAL PASSAGE

Although gift giving has been a pillar of Hopi society, trade has also flourished in Hopi towns since prehistory, with a network that extended from the Great Plains to the Pacific Coast, and from the Great Basin, centered on present-day Nevada and Utah, to the Valley of Mexico. Manufactured goods, raw materials, and gems drove the trade, supplemented by exotic items such as parrots. The Hopis were producers as well, manufacturing large quantities of cotton cloth and ceramics for the trade. To this day, interhousehold trade and barter, especially for items of traditional manufacture for ceremonial use (such as basketry, bows, cloth, moccasins, pottery, and rattles), remain vigorous.

Highlighting shows words to be deleted when passage is quoted.

–Peter M. Whiteley, "Ties That Bind: Hopi Gift Culture and Its First Encounter with the United States," *Natural History*, November 2004, p. 26

PASSAGE WITH ELLIPSES

Whiteley has characterized the practice this way:
> Although gift giving has been a pillar of Hopi society, trade has also flourished in Hopi towns since prehistory. . . . Manufactured goods, raw materials, and gems drove the trade, supplemented by exotic items such as parrots. The Hopis were producers as well, manufacturing large quantities of cotton cloth and ceramics for the trade. To this day, interhousehold trade and barter, especially for items of traditional manufacture for ceremonial use, . . . remain vigorous. (26)

Ellipses show where words have been deleted.

Use brackets [ ] to insert explanatory material into a quotation.

By convention, readers understand that the bracketed words are not part of the original material.

Writing in the *London Review of Books* (January 26, 2006), John Lancaster describes the fears of publishers: "At the moment Google says they have no intention of providing access to this content [scanned books still under copyright]; but why should anybody believe them?"

Use ellipsis marks, brackets, and other devices to make quoted materials suit the grammar of your sentences. Sometimes, the structure of sentences you want to quote won't quite match the grammar, tense, or perspectives of your own surrounding prose. If necessary, cut up a quoted passage to slip appropriate sections into your own sentences, adding bracketed changes or explanations to smooth the transition.

ORIGINAL PASSAGE

Words to be quoted are highlighted.

Among Chandler's most charming sights are the business-casual dads joining their wives and kids for lunch in the mall food court. The food isn't the point, let alone whether it's from Subway or Dairy Queen. The restaurants merely provide the props and setting for the family time. When those kids grow up, they'll remember the food court as happily as an older generation recalls the diners and motels of Route 66 – not because of the businesses' innate appeal but because of the memories they evoke.

–Virginia Postrel, "In Defense of Chain Stores," *Atlantic Monthly*, December 2006

MATERIAL AS QUOTED

Words quoted from source are highlighted.

People who dislike chain stores should ponder the small-town America that cultural critic Virginia Postrel describes, one where "business-casual dads [join] their wives and kids for lunch in the mall food court," a place that future generations of kids will remember "as happily as an older generation recalls the diners and motels of Route 66."

Use [sic] to signal an obvious error in quoted material. You don't want readers to blame a mistake on you, and yet you are obligated to reproduce a quotation exactly — including blunders in the original. You can highlight an error by putting *sic* (the Latin word for "thus") in brackets immediately following the mistake. The device says, in effect, that this is the way you found it.

The late Senator Edward Kennedy once took Supreme Court nominee Samuel Alito to task for his record: "In an era when America is still too divided by race and riches, Judge Alioto [sic] has not written one single opinion on the merits in favor of a person of color alleging race discrimination on the job."

Documenting Sources 48

Required to document your research paper? It seems simple in theory: List your sources and note where and how you use them. But the practice can be intimidating. For one thing, you have to follow rules for everything from capitalizing titles to captioning images. For another, documentation systems differ between fields. What worked for a Shakespeare paper won't transfer to your psychology research project. Bummer. What do you need to do?

Understand the point of documentation. Documentation systems differ to serve the writers and researchers who use them. Modern Language Association (MLA) documentation, which you probably know from composition and literature classes, highlights author names, books, and article titles, and assumes that writers will be quoting a lot—as literature scholars do. American Psychological Association (APA) documentation, gospel in psychology and social sciences, focuses on publication dates because scholars in these fields value the latest research. Council of Science Editors (CSE) documentation, used in the hard sciences, provides predictably detailed advice for handling formulas and numbers.

So systems of documentation aren't arbitrary. Their rules simply anticipate problems researchers face when dealing with sources.

Understand what you accomplish through documentation. First, you clearly identify the sources you have used. In a world awash with information, readers really do need to have reliable information about titles, authors, data, media of publication, and so on.

understand
citation
styles

By citing your sources, you certify the quality of your research and, in turn, receive credit for your labor. You also provide evidence for your claims. A shrewd reader or instructor can tell a lot from your bibliography alone.

Finally, when you document a paper, you encourage readers to follow up on your work. When you've done a good job, serious readers will want to know more about your subject. Both your citations and your bibliography enable them to take the next step in their research.

Style Guides Used in Various Disciplines

Field or Discipline	Documentation and Style Guides
Anthropology	*Chicago Manual of Style* (16th ed., 2010)
Biology	*Scientific Style and Format: The CSE Manual for Authors, Editors, and Publishers* (7th ed., 2006)
Business and management	*The Business Style Handbook: An A-to-Z Guide for Writing on the Job* (2002)
Chemistry	*The ACS Style Guide: Effective Communication of Scientific Information* (3rd ed., 2006)
Earth sciences	*Geowriting: A Guide to Writing, Editing, and Printing in Earth Science* (5th ed., 1995)
Engineering	Varies by area; *IEEE Standards Style Manual* (online)
Federal government	*United States Government Printing Office Manual* (30th ed., 2008)
History	*Chicago Manual of Style* (16th ed., 2010)
Humanities	*MLA Handbook for Writers of Research Papers* (7th ed., 2009)
Journalism	*The Associated Press Stylebook and Briefing on Media Law* (2011); *UPI Stylebook and Guide to Newswriting* (4th ed., 2004)
Law	*The Bluebook: A Uniform System of Citation* (19th ed., 2010)
Mathematics	*A Manual for Authors of Mathematical Papers* (8th ed., 1990)
Music	*Writing about Music: An Introductory Guide* (4th ed., 2008)
Nursing	*Writing for Publication in Nursing* (2nd ed., 2010)
Political science	*The Style Manual for Political Science* (2006)
Psychology	*Publication Manual of the American Psychological Association* (6th ed., 2010)
Sociology	*ASA Style Guide* (4th ed., 2010)

MLA Documentation and Format

The style of the Modern Language Association (MLA) is used in many humanities disciplines. For complete details about MLA style, consult the *MLA Handbook for Writers of Research Papers*, 7th ed. (2009). The basic details for documenting sources and formatting research papers in MLA style are presented below.

Document sources according to convention.   When you use sources in a research paper, you are required to cite the source, letting readers know that the information has been borrowed from somewhere else, and showing them how to find the original material if they would like to study it further. An MLA-style citation includes two parts: a brief in-text citation and a more detailed works cited entry to be included in a list at of the end of your paper.

In-text citations must include the author's name as well as the number of the page where the borrowed material can be found. The author's name (shaded in orange) is generally included in the signal phrase that introduces the passage, and the page number (shaded in yellow) is included in parentheses after the borrowed text.

> Frazier points out that the Wetherill-sponsored expedition to explore Chaco Canyon was roundly criticized (43).

Alternatively, the author's name can be included in parentheses along with the page number.

> The Wetherill-sponsored expedition to explore Chaco Canyon was roundly criticized (Frazier 43).

cite in MLA

At the end of the paper, in the works cited list, a more detailed citation includes the author's name as well as the title (shaded in green) and publication information about the source (shaded in blue).

Frazier, Kendrick. *People of Chaco: A Canyon and Its Culture.* Rev. ed. New York: Norton, 1999. Print.

Both in-text citations and works cited entries can vary greatly depending on the type of source cited (book, periodical, Web site, etc.). The following pages give specific examples of how to cite a wide range of sources in MLA style.

Directory of MLA In-Text Citations

1. Author named in signal phrase 505
2. Author named in parentheses 505
3. With block quotations 505
4. Two or three authors 506
5. Four or more authors 506
6. Group, corporate, or government author 506
7. Two or more works by the same author 506
8. Authors with same last name 507
9. Unidentified author 507
10. Multivolume work 507
11. Work in an anthology 507
12. Entry in a reference book 507
13. Literary work 508
14. Sacred work 508
15. Entire work 509
16. Secondary source 509
17. No page numbers 509
18. Multiple sources in the same citation 509

MLA in-text citation

1. Author Named in Signal Phrase

Include the author's name in the signal phrase that introduces the borrowed material. Follow the borrowed material with the page number of the source in parentheses. Note that the period comes after the parentheses. For a source without an author, see item 9; for a source without a page number, see item 17.

> According to Seabrook, "astronomy was a vital and practical form of knowledge" for the ancient Greeks (98).

2. Author Named in Parentheses

Follow the borrowed material with the author and page number of the source in parentheses, and end with a period. For a source without an author, see item 9; for a source without a page number, see item 17.

> For the ancient Greeks, "astronomy was a vital and practical form of knowledge" (Seabrook 98).

Note: Most of the examples below follow the style of item 1, but naming the author in parentheses (as shown in item 2) is also acceptable.

3. With Block Quotations

For quotations of four or more lines, MLA requires that you set off the borrowed material indented one inch from the left-hand margin. Include the author's name in the introductory text (or in the parentheses at the end). End the block quotation with the page number(s) in parentheses, *after* the end punctuation of the quoted material.

> Jake Page, writing in *American History*, underscores the significance of the well-organized Pueblo revolt:
>
> > Although their victory proved temporary, in the history of Indian-white relations in North America the Pueblo Indians were the only Native Americans to successfully oust European invaders from their territory. . . . Apart from the Pueblos, only the Seminoles were able to retain some of their homeland for any length of time, by waging war from the swamps of the Florida Everglades. (36)

4. Two or Three Authors

If your source has two or three authors, include all of their names in either the signal phrase or parentheses.

> Muhlheim and Heusser assert that the story "analyzes how crucially our actions are shaped by the society . . . in which we live" (29).

> According to some experts, "Children fear adult attempts to fix their social lives" (Thompson, Grace, and Cohen 8).

5. Four or More Authors

If your source has four or more authors, list the first author's name followed by "et al." (meaning "and others") in the signal phrase or parentheses.

> Hansen et al. estimate that the amount of fish caught and sold illegally worldwide is between 10 and 30 percent (974).

6. Group, Corporate, or Government Author

Treat the name of the group, corporation, or government agency just as you would any other author, including the name in either the signal phrase or the parentheses.

> The United States Environmental Protection Agency states that if a public water supply contains dangerous amounts of lead, the municipality is required to educate the public about the problems associated with lead in drinking water (3).

7. Two or More Works by the Same Author

If your paper includes two or more works by the same author, add a brief version of the works' titles (shaded in green) in parentheses to help readers locate the right source.

> Mills suggests that new assessments of older archaeological work, not new discoveries in the field, are revising the history of Chaco Canyon ("Recent Research" 66). She argues, for example, that new analysis of public spaces can teach us about the ritual of feasting in the Puebloan Southwest (Mills, "Performing the Feast" 211).

8. Authors with Same Last Name

If your paper includes two or more sources whose authors have the same last name, include a first initial with the last name in either the signal phrase or the parentheses.

> According to T. Smith, "as much as 60 percent of the computers sold in India are unbranded and made by local assemblers at about a third of the price of overseas brands" (12).

9. Unidentified Author

If the author of your work is unknown, include a brief title of the work in parentheses.

> The amount of protein that tilapia provides when eaten exceeds the amount that it consumes when alive, making it a sustainable fish ("Dream Fish" 26).

10. Multivolume Work

If you cite material from more than one volume of a multivolume work, include in the parentheses the volume number followed by a colon before the page number. (See also item 11, on p. 515, for including multivolume works in your works cited list.)

> Odekon defines *access-to-enterprise zones* as "geographic areas in which taxes and government regulations are lowered or eliminated as a way to stimulate business activity and create jobs" (1: 2).

11. Work in an Anthology

Include the author of the work in the signal phrase or parentheses. There is no need to refer to the editor of the anthology in the in-text citation; this and other details will be included in the works cited list at the end of your paper.

> Vonnegut suggests that *Hamlet* is considered such a masterpiece because "Shakespeare told us the truth, and [writers] so rarely tell us the truth" (354).

12. Entry in a Reference Book

In the signal phrase, include the author of the entry you are referring to, if there is an author. In the parentheses following the in-text citation, include the title of the entry and the page number(s) on which the entry appears.

> Willis points out that the Empire State Building, 1,250 feet tall and built in just over one year, was a record-breaking feat of engineering ("Empire State Building" 375-76).

For reference entries with no author (such as dictionaries), simply include the name of the article or entry in quotation marks along with the page reference in parentheses.

> *Black* is defined as a color "producing or reflecting comparatively little light and having no predominant hue" ("Black" 143).

13. Literary Work

Include as much information as possible to help readers locate your borrowed material. For classic novels, which are available in many editions, include the page number, followed by a semicolon, and additional information such as book ("bk."), volume ("vol."), or chapter ("ch.") numbers.

> At the climax of Brontë's *Jane Eyre*, Jane fears that her wedding is doomed, and her description of the chestnut tree that has been struck by lightning is ominous: "it stood up, black and riven: the trunk, split down the center, gaped ghastly" (274; vol. 2, ch. 25).

For classic poems and plays, include division numbers such as act, scene, and line numbers; do not include page numbers. Separate all numbers with periods. Use arabic (1, 2, 3, etc.) numerals instead of roman (I, II, III, etc.) unless your instructor prefers otherwise.

> In Homer's epic poem *The Iliad,* Agamemnon admits that he has been wrong to fight with Achilles, but he blames Zeus, whom he says "has given me bitterness, who drives me into unprofitable abuse and quarrels" (2.375-76).

14. Sacred Work

Instead of page numbers, include book, chapter, and verse numbers when citing material from sacred texts.

> Jesus' association with the sun is undeniable in this familiar passage from the Bible: "I am the light of the world. Whoever follows me will not walk in darkness, but will have the light of life" (John 8.12).

15. Entire Work

When referring to an entire work, there is no need to include page numbers in parentheses; simply include the author's name(s) in the signal phrase.

> Boyer and Nissenbaum argue that the witchcraft trials persisted because of the unique social and political environment that existed in Salem in 1692.

16. Secondary Source

To cite a source you found within another source, include the name of the original author in the signal phrase. In the parentheses, include the term "qtd. in" and give the author of the source where you found the quote, along with the page number. Note that your works cited entry for this material will be listed under the secondary source name (Pollan) rather than the original writer (Howard).

> Writing in 1943, Howard asserted that "artificial manures lead inevitably to artificial nutrition, artificial food, artificial animals, and finally to artificial men and women" (qtd. in Pollan 148).

17. No Page Numbers

If the work you are citing has no page numbers, include only the author's name (or the brief title, if there is no author) for your in-text citation.

> Gorman reported that in early 2007, hunger-striking enemy combatants at Guantanamo Bay were force-fed.

18. Multiple Sources in the Same Citation

If one statement in your paper can be attributed to multiple sources, alphabetically list all the authors with page numbers, separated by semicolons.

> Most historians agree that the Puritan religion played a significant role in the hysteria surrounding the Salem witchcraft trials (Karlsen 14; Norton 22; Reis 145).

Directory of MLA Works Cited Entries

General Guidelines for MLA Works Cited Entries

AUTHOR NAMES

- Authors listed at the start of an entry should be listed last name first and should end with a period.

- Subsequent author names, or the names of authors or editors listed in the middle of the entry, should be listed first name first.

DATES

- Dates should be formatted day month year: 27 May 2007.

- Use abbreviations for all months except for May, June, and July, which are short enough to spell out: Jan., Feb., Mar., Apr., Aug., Sept., Oct., Nov., Dec. (Months should always be spelled out in the text of your paper.)

TITLES

- Titles of long works—such as books, plays, periodicals, entire Web sites, and films—should be italicized. (Underlining is an acceptable alternative to italics, but note that whichever format you choose, you should be consistent throughout your paper.)

- Titles of short works—such as essays, articles, poems, and songs— should be placed in quotation marks.

PUBLICATION INFORMATION

- Include only the city name.

- Abbreviate familiar words such as "University" ("U") and "Press" ("P") in the publisher's name. Leave out terms such as "Inc." and "Corp."

- Include the medium of publication for each entry ("Print," "Web," "DVD," "Radio," etc.).

MLA works cited entries

AUTHOR INFORMATION

1. Single Author

> Author's Last Name, First Name. *Book Title*. Publication City: Publisher, Year of Publication. Medium.

> Will, George. *Men at Work: The Craft of Baseball*. New York: Macmillan, 1990. Print.

2. Two or Three Authors

List the authors in the order shown on the title page.

> First Author's Last Name, First Name, and Second Author's First Name Last Name. *Book Title*. Publication City: Publisher, Year of Publication. Medium.

> Mortenson, Greg, and David Oliver Relin. *Three Cups of Tea: One Man's Mission to Promote Peace . . . One School at a Time*. New York: Penguin, 2007. Print.

> Clark, Ricky, George W. Knepper, and Ellice Ronsheim. *Quilts in Community: Ohio's Traditions*. Nashville: Rutledge, 1991. Print.

3. Four or More Authors

When a source has four or more authors, list only the name of the first author (last name first), followed by a comma and the Latin term "et al." (meaning "and others").

> First Author's Last Name, First Name, et al. *Book Title*. Publication City: Publisher, Year of Publication. Medium.

> Roark, James L., et al. *The American Promise: A History of the United States*. 4th ed. Boston: Bedford, 2009. Print.

4. Corporate Author

If a group or corporation rather than a person appears to be the author, include that name as the work's author in your list of works cited.

Name of Corporation. *Book Title.* Publication City: Publisher, Year of
  Publication. Medium.

Congressional Quarterly. *Presidential Elections: 1789-2004.* Washington:
  CQ, 2005. Print.

5. Unidentified Author

If the author of a work is unknown, begin the works cited entry with the title of the work.

Note that in the example given, "The New York Times" is not italicized because it is a title within a title (see item 19).

Book Title. Publication City: Publisher, Year of Publication. Medium.

The New York Times *Guide to Essential Knowledge: A Desk
  Reference for the Curious Mind.* New York: St. Martin's, 2004.
  Print.

6. Multiple Works by the Same Author

To cite two or more works by the same author in your list of works cited, organize the works alphabetically by title (ignoring introductory articles such as *The* and *A*). Include the author's name only for the first entry; for subsequent entries, type three hyphens followed by a period in place of the author's name.

Author's Last Name, First Name. *Title of Work.* Publication City:
  Publisher, Year of Publication. Medium.

---. *Title of Work.* Publication City: Publisher, Year of Publication.
  Medium.

Friedman, Thomas L. *The Lexus and the Olive Tree: Understanding
  Globalization.* New York: Farrar, 1999. Print.

---. *The World Is Flat: A Brief History of the Twenty-First Century.*
  New York: Farrar, 2005. Print.

BOOKS

7. Book: Basic Format

The example here is the basic format for a book with one author. For author variations, see items 1–6. For more information on the treatment of authors, dates, titles, and publication information, see the box on page 511. After listing the author's name, include the title (and subtitle, if any) of the book, italicized. Next give the publication city, publisher's name, and year. End with the medium of publication.

> Author's Last Name, First Name. *Book Title: Book Subtitle*. Publication
>   City: Publisher, Publication Year. Medium.

> Mah, Adeline Yen. *Falling Leaves: The True Story of an Unwanted
>   Chinese Daughter*. New York: Wiley, 1997. Print.

8. Author and Editor

Include the author's name first if you are referring to the text itself. If, however, you are citing material written by the editor, include the editor's name first, followed by a comma and "ed."

> Author's Last Name, First Name. *Book Title*. Year of Original Publication.
>   Ed. Editor's First Name Last Name. Publication City: Publisher, Year
>   of Publication. Medium.

> Editor's Last Name, First Name, ed. *Book Title*. Year of Original
>   Publication. By Author's First Name Last Name. Publication City:
>   Publisher, Year of Publication. Medium.

> Dickens, Charles. *Great Expectations*. 1861. Ed. Janice Carlisle. Boston:
>   Bedford, 1996. Print.

> Carlisle, Janice, ed. *Great Expectations*. 1861. By Charles Dickens.
>   Boston: Bedford, 1996. Print.

9. Edited Collection

> Editor's Last Name, First Name, ed. *Book Title*. Publication City: Publisher,
>   Year of Publication. Medium.

> Abbott, Megan, ed. *A Hell of a Woman: An Anthology of Female Noir*.
>   Houston: Busted Flush, 2007. Print.

10. Work in an Anthology or a Collection

Author's Last Name, First Name. "Title of Work." *Book Title.* Ed. Editor's
First Name Last Name. Publication City: Publisher, Year of Publication.
Page Numbers of Work. Medium.

Okpewho, Isidore. "The Cousins of Uncle Remus." *The Black Columbiad:
Defining Moments in African American Literature and Culture.* Ed.
Werner Sollors and Maria Diedrich. Cambridge: Harvard UP, 1994.
15-27. Print.

11. Multivolume Work

To cite one volume of a multivolume work, include the volume number after
the title. Including the volume number in your list of works cited means that
you do not need to list it in your in-text citation. To cite two or more
volumes, include the number of volumes after the title. In this case, you
would need to include the specific volume number in each of your in-text
citations for this source.

Author or Editor's Last Name, First Name. *Title of Work.* Vol. Number.
Publication City: Publisher, Year of Publication. Medium.

Odekon, Mehmet, ed. *Encyclopedia of World Poverty.* Vol. 2. Thousand
Oaks: Sage, 2006. Print.

Author or Editor's Last Name, First Name. *Title of Work.* Number of vols.
Publication City: Publisher, Year of Publication. Medium.

Odekon, Mehmet, ed. *Encyclopedia of World Poverty.* 3 vols. Thousand
Oaks: Sage, 2006. Print.

12. Part of a Series

After the title of the book, include the series title and number (if any) from
the title page.

Author or Editor's Last Name, First Name. *Title of Work.* Title and Number
of Series. Publication City: Publisher, Year of Publication. Medium.

Dixon, Kelly J. *Boomtown Saloons: Archaeology and History in Virginia
City.* Wilbur S. Shepperson Ser. in Nevada Hist. Reno: U of Nevada
P, 2005. Print.

How to...
Cite from a book (MLA)

BOOK COVER

TITLE PAGE

Andrews McMeel Publishing, LLC
Kansas City · Sydney · London

1 author

2 book title and subtitle

3 city of publication and publisher

> When a publisher lists more than one city, use the first one.

COPYRIGHT PAGE

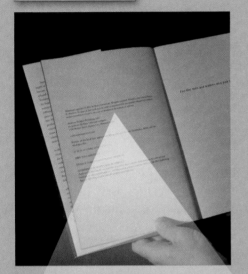

Tomatoland copyright © 2011 by Barry Estabrook.

QUOTED PAGE

145

4 year of publication

5 page number

6 medium

MLA in-text citation

Describing his vision for the new tomato breed, the seed company owner explained, "We were going to start with roadside growers and chefs. People who were interested in good flavor and good quality" (Estabrook 145).

1 **5**

1 **2**

MLA works cited entry

Estabrook, Barry. *Tomatoland: How Modern Industrial Agriculture Destroyed*

3 **4** **6**

Our Most Alluring Fruit. Kansas City: Andrews McMeel, 2011. Print.

13. Republished Book

If the book you are citing was previously published, include the original publication date after the title. If the new publication includes additional text, such as an introduction, include that, along with the name of its author, before the current publication information.

> Author's Last Name, First Name. *Title of Work.* Original Year of
>   Publication. New Material Author's First Name Last Name.
>   Publication City: Publisher, Year of Publication. Medium.

> Twain, Mark. *Life on the Mississippi.* 1883. Introd. Justin Kaplan.
>   New York: Penguin, 2001. Print.

14. Later Edition

Include the edition number as a numeral with letters ("2nd," "3rd," "4th," etc.) followed by "ed." after the book's title. If the edition is listed on the title page as "Revised," without a number, include "Rev. ed." after the title of the book.

> Author(s). *Title of Work.* Number ed. Publication City: Publisher, Year of
>   Publication. Medium.

> Hartt, Frederick, and David G. Wilkins. *History of Italian Renaissance
>   Art: Painting, Sculpture, Architecture.* 4th ed. New York: Abrams,
>   2006. Print.

15. Sacred Work

Include the title of the work as it is shown on the title page. If there is an editor or a translator listed, include the name after the title with either "Ed." or "Trans."

> *Title of Work.* Editor or Translator. Publication City: Publisher, Year of
>   Publication. Medium.

> *The New American Bible.* New York: Catholic Book, 1987. Print.

> *The Qur'an: A New Translation.* Trans. M. A. S. Abdel Haleem.
>   New York: Oxford UP, 2004. Print.

16. Translation

Original Author's Last Name, First Name. *Title of Work.* Trans. Translator's First Name Last Name. Publication City: Publisher, Year of Publication. Medium.

Fasce, Ferdinando. *An American Family: The Great War and Corporate Culture in America.* Trans. Ian Harvey. Columbus: Ohio State UP, 2002. Print.

17. Article in a Reference Book

If there is no article author, begin with the title of the article.

Article Author's Last Name, First Name. "Title of Article." *Book Title.* Publication City: Publisher, Year of Publication. Medium.

Lutzger, Michael A. "Peace Movements." *The Encyclopedia of New York City.* New Haven: Yale UP, 1995. Print.

"The History of the National Anthem." *The World Almanac and Book of Facts 2004.* New York: World Almanac, 2004. Print.

18. Introduction, Preface, Foreword, or Afterword

Book Part Author's Last Name, First Name. Name of Book Part. *Book Title.* Ed. Book Author or Editor's First Name Last Name. Publication City: Publisher, Year of Publication. Page Numbers. Medium.

Groening, Matt. Introduction. *Best American Nonrequired Reading 2006.* Ed. Dave Eggers. Boston: Houghton, 2006. xi-xvii. Print.

19. Title within a Title

If a book's title includes the title of another long work (play, book, or periodical) within it, do not italicize the internal title.

Author's Last Name, First Name. *Book Title* Title within Title. Publication City: Publisher, Year of Publication. Medium.

Norris, Margot. *A Companion to James Joyce's* Ulysses. Boston: Bedford, 1998. Print.

PERIODICALS

20. Article in a Scholarly Journal

List the author(s) first, then include the article title, the journal title (in italics), the volume number, the issue number, the publication year, the page numbers, and the publication medium.

> Author's Last Name, First Name. "Title of Article." *Title of Journal* Volume Number.Issue Number (Year of Publication): Page Numbers. Medium.

> Burt, Stephen, et al. "Does Poetry Have a Social Function?" *Poetry* 189.4 (2007): 297-309. Print.

21. Article in a Scholarly Journal with No Volume Number

Follow the format for scholarly journals (as shown in item 20), but list only the issue number before the year of publication.

> Author's Last Name, First Name. "Title of Article." *Title of Journal* Issue Number (Year of Publication): Page Numbers. Medium.

> Lee, Christopher. "Enacting the Asian Canadian." *Canadian Literature* 199 (2008): 6-27. Print.

22. Magazine Article

Include the date of publication rather than volume and issue numbers. (See abbreviation rules in the box on p. 511.) If page numbers are not consecutive, add "+" after the initial page.

> Author's Last Name, First Name. "Title of Article." *Title of Magazine* Date of Publication: Page Numbers. Medium.

> Fredenburg, Peter. "Mekong Harvests: Balancing Shrimp and Rice Farming in Vietnam." *World and I* Mar. 2002: 204+. Print.

23. Newspaper Article

If a specific edition is listed on the newspaper's masthead, such as "Late Edition" or "National Edition," include an abbreviation of this after the date. If page numbers are not consecutive, add "+" after the initial page.

Author's Last Name, First Name. "Title of Article." *Title of Newspaper* Date
of Publication: Page Numbers. Medium.

Smith, Stephen. "Taunting May Affect Health of Obese Youths."
Boston Globe 11 July 2007: A1+. Print.

Author's Last Name, First Name. "Title of Article." *Title of Newspaper* Date
of Publication, Spec. ed.: Page Numbers. Medium.

Rohde, David. "Taliban Push Poppy Production to a Record Again."
New York Times 26 Aug. 2007, natl. ed.: 3. Print.

If a newspaper numbers each section individually, without attaching
letters to the page numbers, include the section number in your citation.

Author's Last Name, First Name. "Title of Article." *Title of Newspaper* Date
of Publication, sec. Section Number: Page Numbers. Medium.

Bowley, Graham. "Keeping Up with the Windsors." *New York Times*
15 July 2007, sec. 3: 1+. Print.

24. Editorial

For a newspaper editorial, do not include an author, but do include the word
"Editorial," followed by a period, after the title of the article.

"Title of Article." Editorial. *Title of Newspaper* Date of Publication: Page
Number(s). Medium.

"Living on Iraq Time." Editorial. *New York Times* 28 May 2007: A15.
Print.

25. Letter to the Editor

Letter Writer's Last Name, First Name. Letter. *Title of Newspaper* Date of
Publication: Page Number. Medium.

Zita, Ken. Letter. *Financial Times* 16 Aug. 2006: 8. Print.

26. Unsigned Article

"Title of Article." *Title of Newspaper* Date of Publication: Page Number. Medium.

"Justice Probes Lenders." *Washington Post* 26 July 2007: DO2. Print.

MAGAZINE COVER

March 2010

ARTICLE

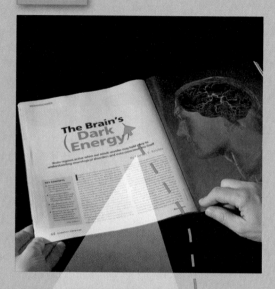

By Marcus E. Raichle

1 magazine title   **2** publication date   **3** author   **4** article title

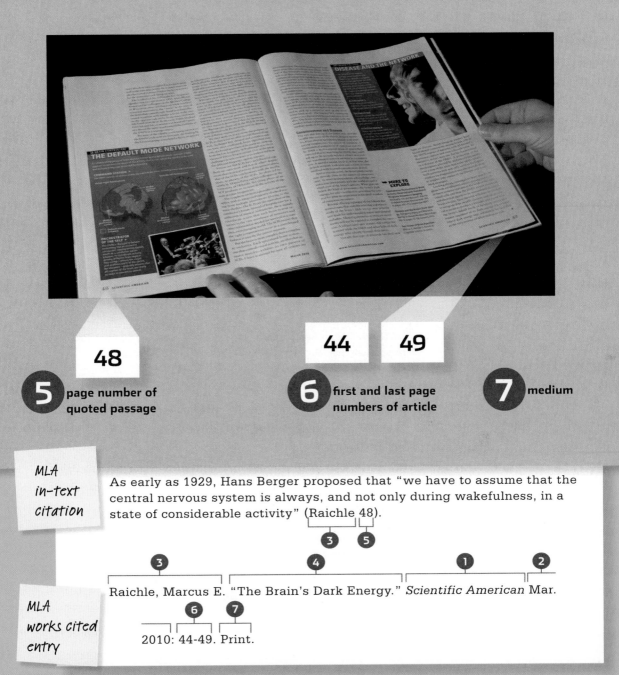

48

5 page number of quoted passage

44 **49**

6 first and last page numbers of article

7 medium

MLA in-text citation

As early as 1929, Hans Berger proposed that "we have to assume that the central nervous system is always, and not only during wakefulness, in a state of considerable activity" (Raichle 48).

3 **5**

3 **4** **1** **2**

Raichle, Marcus E. "The Brain's Dark Energy." *Scientific American* Mar.

MLA works cited entry

6 **7**

2010: 44-49. Print.

27. Review

Add "Rev. of" before the title of the work being reviewed.

> Review Author's Last Name, First Name. "Title of Review." Rev. of *Title of Work Being Reviewed*, by Author of Work Being Reviewed First Name Last Name. *Title of Publication in Which Review Appears* Volume.Issue (Year of Publication): Page Numbers. Medium.

> Levin, Yuval. "Diagnosis and Cure." Rev. of *Sick: The Untold Story of America's Health-Care Crisis and the People Who Pay the Price*, by Jonathan Cohn. *Commentary* 124.1 (2007): 80-82. Print.

ELECTRONIC SOURCES

28. Short Work from a Web Site

> Short Work Author's Last Name, First Name. "Title of Short Work." *Title of Web Site.* Name of Sponsoring Organization, Date of Publication or Most Recent Update. Medium. Date of Access.

> McFee, Gord. "Why 'Revisionism' Isn't." *The Holocaust History Project.* Holocaust Hist. Project, 15 May 1999. Web. 10 Sept. 2011.

29. Entire Web Site

> Short Work Author's Last Name, First Name. *Title of Web Site.* Name of Sponsoring Organization, Date of Publication or Most Recent Update. Medium. Date of Access.

> Myers, Robert, et al. *Exploring the Environment.* Wheeling Jesuit U, 28 Apr. 2005. Web. 12 Sept. 2007.

30. Entire blog (Weblog)

Include any of the following elements that are available. If there is no publisher or sponsoring organization, use the abbreviation "N.p."

> Blog Author's Last Name, First Name. *Title of Blog.* Name of Sponsoring Organization (if any), Date of Most Recent Post. Medium. Date of Access.

> Sellers, Heather. *Word after Word.* N.p., 26 Aug. 2011. Web. 14 Sep. 2011.

31. Entry in a blog (Weblog)

Entry Author's Last Name, First Name. "Title of Blog Entry." *Title of Blog.* Name of Sponsoring Organization (if any), Date of Entry. Medium. Date of Access.

Sellers, Heather. "East Coast." *Word after Word.* N.p., 7 Nov. 2007. Web. 30 Jan. 2008.

32. Online Book

Book Author's Last Name, First Name. *Title of Book.* Book Publication City: Book Publisher, Book Publication Year. *Title of Web Site.* Medium. Date of Access.

Riis, Jacob. *How the Other Half Lives.* New York: Scribner's, 1890. *Bartleby.com: Great Books Online.* Web. 6 Nov. 2010.

33. Work from a Library Subscription Service (such as *InfoTrac* or *FirstSearch*)

Follow the format for periodical articles as shown in items 20–27, above. If page numbers are not available, use the abbreviation "n. pag." End the citation with the database name (in italics), the publication medium ("Web"), and the date of access.

Article Author(s). "Title of Article." *Title of Periodical* Volume Number.Issue Number (Year of Publication): Page Numbers. *Name of Database.* Medium. Date of Access.

Cotugna, Nancy, and Connie Vickery. "Educating Early Childhood Teachers about Nutrition: A Collaborative Venture." *Childhood Education* 83.4 (2007): 194-98. *Academic OneFile.* Web. 10 July 2011.

TOP OF WEB PAGE

1 Web site title

2 article title

JAD ABUMRAD and
ROBERT KRULWICH

3 author

August 17, 2010

4 update date

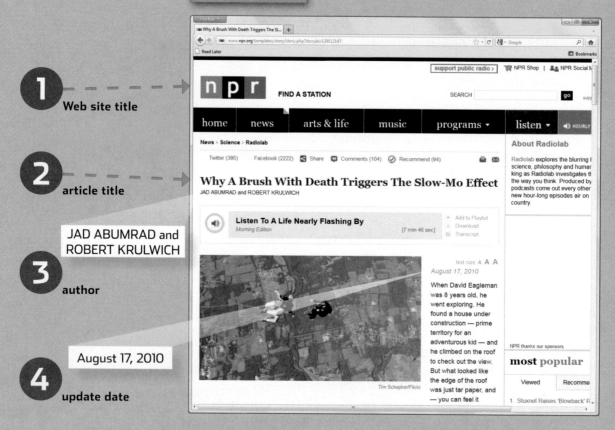

BOTTOM OF WEB PAGE

7 medium

Copyright 2011 NPR

5 Web site sponsor

August 25, 2011

6 date of access

MLA in-text citation

Dr. Eagleman suggests that moments of near-death panic prompt the brain to form memories of otherwise-ignored stimuli, and "when you read that back out, the experience feels like it must have taken a very long time" (Abumrad and Krulwich).

3

---

3   **2**

MLA works cited entry

Abumrad, Jad, and Robert Krulwich. "Why a Brush with Death Triggers the

1 **5** **4** **7** **6**

Slow-Mo Effect." *NPR*. NPR, 17 Aug. 2010. Web. 25 Aug. 2011.

How to...
Cite from a database (MLA)

5 volume and issue number

6 publication date

7 name of database

DATABASE SCREEN

1 journal title

2 article title

3 author

4 page numbers

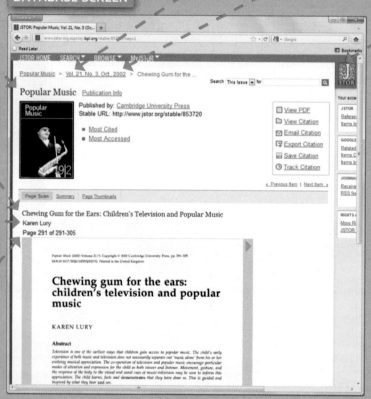

Most databases have a way to download the journal article, often as a PDF.

PDF VIEW

Use the PDF to double-check your citation elements. If you print the PDF, the medium is still Web, not print.

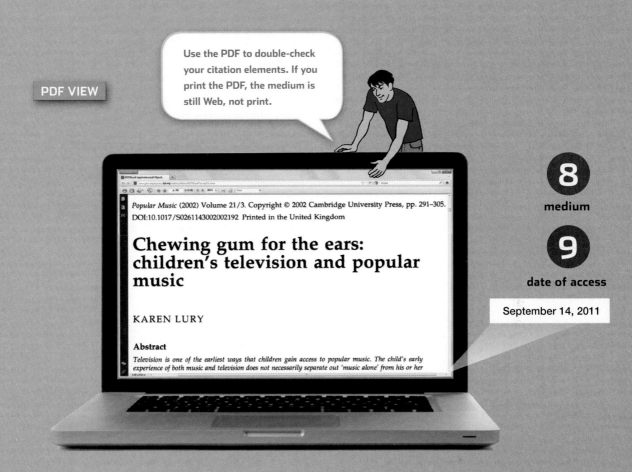

8
medium

9
date of access

September 14, 2011

Popular Music (2002) Volume 21/3. Copyright © 2002 Cambridge University Press, pp. 291–305.
DOI:10.1017/S0261143002002192 Printed in the United Kingdom

Chewing gum for the ears: children's television and popular music

KAREN LURY

Abstract

Television is one of the earliest ways that children gain access to popular music. The child's early experience of both music and television does not necessarily separate out 'music alone' from his or her

MLA in-text citation

Children accept even nonsensical lyrics as legitimate musical expression, and one researcher calls their tolerance "a mode of engagement carried productively into the adult's experience of popular songs" (Lury 300).

3 **4**

3 **2**

Lury, Karen. "Chewing Gum for the Ears: Children's Television and

MLA works cited entry

1 **5** **6** **4** **7**

Popular Music." *Popular Music* 21.3 (2002): 291-305. *JSTOR*.

8 **9**

Web. 14 Sept. 2011.

34. Work from an Online Periodical

Follow the format for periodical articles as shown in items 20–27, above, listing the Web site name, in italics, as the periodical title. For articles in scholarly journals, include page numbers (or the abbreviation "n. pag." if page numbers are unavailable). End the citation with the publication medium ("Web") and the date of access.

> Journal Article Author(s). "Title of Article." *Title of Online Journal* Volume Number.Issue Number (Year of Publication): Page Numbers (or "n. pag."). Medium. Date of Access.

> Arora, Vibha, and Justin Scott-Coe. "Fieldwork and Interdisciplinary Research." *Reconstruction* 9.1 (2009): n. pag. Web. 13 Apr. 2009.

For articles appearing in online magazines and newspapers, list the publisher's name after the online periodical title. Page numbers are not required for nonscholarly articles published online.

> Magazine or Newspaper Article Author(s). "Title of Article." *Title of Online Periodical.* Periodical Publisher, Publication Date. Medium. Date of Access.

> Gogoi, Pallavi. "The Trouble with Business Ethics." *BusinessWeek.* McGraw, 25 June 2007. Web. 3 Oct. 2011.

35. Online Posting

> Post Author's Last Name, First Name. "Title (or Subject) of Post." *Title of Message Board.* Date of Post. Medium. Date of Access.

> Winkleman, Tallulah. "Reducing Your Food Miles." *Farm Folk City Folk Bulletin.* 13 July 2007. Web. 10 Sept. 2010.

36. E-mail

> E-mail Author's Last Name, First Name. "Subject of E-mail." Message to the author (or Name of Recipient). Date Sent. Medium.

> Gingrich, Newt. "Drill here. Drill now." Message to the author. 20 May 2008. E-mail.

37. CD-ROM

CD-ROM Author's (if any) Last Name, First Name. *Title of CD-ROM.*
    Publication City: Publisher, Publication Year. Medium.

History through Art: The Twentieth Century. San Jose: Fogware,
    2001. CD-ROM.

38. Podcast

For downloaded podcasts, include the file type, such as "MP3 file," as the
medium. If the file type is unknown, use the term "MP3 file."

"Title of Podcast." Names and Function of Pertinent Individual(s). *Title
    of Web Site.* Name of Sponsoring Organization, Date of Publication.
    Medium.

"Capping Pollution at the Source." Prod. Lester Graham. *The Environment
    Report.* Nature Conservancy, 31 July 2006. MP3 file.

For podcasts that were listened to directly from the host Web site, list "Web"
as the medium and include an access date at the end.

39. Entry in a Wiki

Wiki content is continually edited by its users, so there is no author to cite.

"Title of Entry." *Title of Wiki.* Name of Sponsoring Organization, Date of
    Publication or Most Recent Update. Medium. Date of Access.

"Emo." *Wikipedia.* Wikimedia Foundation, 24 June 2008. Web.
    2 Feb. 2009.

OTHER

40. Dissertation

For unpublished dissertations, put the title in quotation marks.

Author's Last Name, First Name. "Dissertation Title." Diss. Name of
    University, Year. Medium.

Mooney, John Alfonso. "Shadows of Dominion: White Men and Power
    in Slavery, War, and the New South." Diss. U of Virginia, 2007.
    Print.

If the dissertation is published as a book, italicize the title and include the publication information.

> Author's Last Name, First Name. *Dissertation Title*. Diss. Name of
> University, Year. Publication City: Publisher, Publication Year. Medium.

> Beetham, Christopher A. *Echoes of Scripture in the Letter of Paul to the
> Colossians*. Diss. Wheaton Coll. Graduate School, 2005. Boston:
> Brill, 2008. Print.

41. Published Conference Proceedings

List the editor(s) name(s), followed by "ed." or "eds." and italicize the title of the proceedings. Before the conference information, add "Proc. of" and follow with the conference title, dates, and location.

> Editor(s), ed(s). *Title of Proceedings*. Proc. of Conference Title, Conference
> Date, Conference Location. Publication City: Publisher, Year. Medium.

> Westfahl, G., and George Slusser, eds. *Nursery Realms: Children in
> the World of Science Fiction, Fantasy, and Horror*. Proc. of J. Lloyd
> Eaton Conf. on Science Fiction and Fantasy Lit., Jan. 1999, U of
> California, Riverside. Athens: U of Georgia P, 1999. Print.

42. Government Document

Begin by listing the government (usually a country or state) that issued the document, and then list the specific department or agency. Most U.S. government documents are published by the Washington-based Government Printing Office (GPO).

> Government. Department or Agency. *Title of Document*. Publication City:
> Publisher, Date of Publication. Medium.

> United States. Dept. of Labor. *Summary Data from the Consumer Price
> Index News Release*. Washington: GPO, Oct. 2006. Print.

43. Pamphlet

> *Pamphlet Title*. Publication City: Publisher, Year of Publication. Medium.

> *50 Ways to Be Water Smart*. West Palm Beach: South Florida Water
> Management Dist., 2006. Print.

44. Letter (Personal and Published)

For personal letters that you received, give the name of the letter writer followed by the description "Letter to the author." For publication medium, list "TS" ("typescript") for typed letters or "MS" ("manuscript") for handwritten letters. For e-mail, see item 36.

Letter Writer's Last Name, First Name. Letter to the author. Date of Letter. Medium.

Nader, Ralph. Letter to the author. 15 Oct. 2010. TS.

For published letters, list the letter writer as well as the recipient.

Letter Writer's Last Name, First Name. Letter to First Name Last Name. Date of Letter. *Title of Book.* Ed. Editor's First Name Last Name. Publication City: Publisher, Year. Medium.

Lincoln, Abraham. Letter to T. J. Pickett. 16 Apr. 1859. *Wit & Wisdom of Abraham Lincoln: As Reflected in His Letters and Speeches.* Ed. H. Jack Lang. Mechanicsburg: Stackpole, 2006. Print.

45. Legal Source

List the names of laws or acts (with no underlining or quotation marks), followed by the Public Law number and the date. Also give the Statutes at Large cataloging number and the medium. For other legal sources, refer to *The Bluebook: A Uniform System of Citation*, 19th ed. (Cambridge: Harvard Law Review Assn., 2010).

Title of Law. Pub. L. number. Stat. number. Date of Enactment. Medium.

No Child Left Behind Act of 2001. Pub. L. 107-110. Stat. 1425. 8 Jan. 2002. Print.

46. Lecture or Public Address

For the medium, describe the type of speech ("Reading," "Address," "Lecture," etc.).

Speaker's Last Name, First Name. "Title of Speech." Name of Sponsoring Institution. Location of Speech. Date of Speech. Medium.

Wallace, David Foster. "Kenyon Commencement Speech." Kenyon College. Gambier. 21 May 2005. Address.

47. Interview

For published or broadcast interviews, give the title (if any), followed by the publication or broadcast information for the source that aired or published the interview. If there is no title, use "Interview" followed by a period.

> Interviewee's Last Name, First Name. "Title of Interview." *Book, Periodical, Web Site, or Program Title.* Publication or Broadcast Information (see specific entry for guidance). Medium.

> Rushdie, Salman. "Humanism and the Territory of Novelists." *Humanist* 67.4 (2007): 19-21. Print.

> Roth, Philip. Interview. *Fresh Air*. Natl. Public Radio. WQCS, Fort Pierce. 18 May 2006. Radio.

For interviews that you conduct yourself, include the name of the interviewee, interview type ("Personal interview," "E-mail interview," "Telephone interview," etc.), and date.

> Dean, Howard. E-mail interview. 3 May 2011.

48. Television or Radio Program

If you access an archived show online, include the access date after the medium.

> "Episode Title." *Program Title. or Series Title.* Network. Local Channel's Call Letters, City (if any). Air Date. Medium. Date of Access.

> "Poirot: Murder on the Orient Express." *Masterpiece*. PBS. WGBH, Boston. 22 May 2011. Television.

> "Past Deals Come Back to Haunt UAW." *Marketplace Morning Report*. Amer. Public Media. 29 June 2007. Web. 2 Nov. 2007.

49. Film or Video Recording

If you accessed the film via videocassette or DVD, include the distributor name and release date.

> *Film Title.* Dir. Director's First Name Last Name. Original Release Date. Distributor, Release Date of Recording. Medium.

> *Rear Window*. Dir. Alfred Hitchcock. 1954. Universal, 2001. DVD.

To highlight a particular individual's performance or contribution, begin with that person's name, followed by a descriptive label (for example, "perf." or "chor.").

> Stewart, James, perf. *Rear Window*. Dir. Alfred Hitchcock. 1954.
>   Universal, 2001. DVD.

50. Sound Recording

Performer's Last Name, First Name or Band's Name. "Title of Song." *Title of Album*. Record Label, Year. Medium.

> Thomas, Irma. "Time Is on My Side." *Live: Simply the Best*. Rounder,
>   1991. CD.

51. Musical Composition

Long works such as operas, ballets, and named symphonies should be italicized. Additional information, such as key or movement, may be added at the end.

Composer's Last Name, First Name. *Title of Long Work*. Artists' names. Orchestra. Conductor. Manufacturer, Date. Medium.

> Mozart, Wolfgang Amadeus. *Le nozze di Figaro*. Perf. Alfred Poel,
>   Cesare Siepi, Fernando Corena, and Hilde Gueden. Vienna
>   Philharmonic Orchestra. Cond. Erich Kleiber. Decca, 1955. LP.

> Beethoven, Ludwig van. Sonata no. 16 in G major, op. 31. Perf. John
>   O'Connor. Telarc, 1990. CD.

52. Live Performance

Performance Title. By Author Name. Dir. Director Name. Perf. Performer Name(s). Theater or Venue Name, City. Date of Performance. Medium.

> *How to Succeed in Business without Really Trying*. By Frank Loesser.
>   Dir. Rob Ashford. Perf. Daniel Radcliffe and John Larroquette. Al
>   Hirschfeld Theatre, New York. 26 Mar. 2011. Performance.

53. Work of Art

Artist's Last Name, First Name. *Title of Artwork.* Date. Institution, City.

Sargent, John Singer. *The Daughters of Edward Darley Boit.* 1882.
    Museum of Fine Arts, Boston.

A publication medium is required only for reproduced works, such as in
books or online. For works accessed on the Web, include an access date.

Kapoor, Anish. *Ishi's Light.* 2003. Tate Mod., London. *Tate Online.* Web.
    4 Oct. 2007.

54. Map or Chart

Title of Map. Map. Publication City: Publisher Name, Year. Medium.

Northwest Territories and Yukon Territory. Map. Vancouver: Intl.
    Travel Maps, 1998. Print.

If you accessed the map online, include an access date.

Cambodia. Map. *Google Maps.* 2009. Web. 15 April 2009.

55. Cartoon or Comic Strip

Artist's Last Name, First Name. "Cartoon Title" (if given). Cartoon. *Title of
    Periodical* Date: Page Number. Medium.

Chast, Roz. "National Everything Awareness Day." Cartoon. *New
    Yorker* 3 Sept. 2007: 107. Print.

56. Advertisement

Product Name. Advertisement. *Title of Periodical* Date: Section Number:
    Page Number(s). Medium.

Louis Vuitton. Advertisement. *New York Times* 22 July 2007, sec. 9: 8-9.
    Print.

If you accessed the advertisement online, include an access date.

Dodge Journey. Advertisement. Dodge YouTube Channel 10 Sept. 2011.
    Web.

Format an MLA paper correctly.   You can now find software to format your academic papers in MLA style, but the key alignments for such documents are usually simple enough for you to manage on your own.

- Set up a header on the right-hand side of each page, one-half inch from the top. The header should include your last name and the page number.

- In the upper left on the first—or title—page, include your name, the instructor's name, the course title and/or number, and the date.

- Center the title above the first line of text.

- Use one-inch margins on all sides of the paper.

- Double-space the entire paper (including your name and course information, the title, and any block quotations).

- Indent paragraphs one-half inch.

- Use block quotations for quoted material of four or more lines. Indent block quotations one inch from the left margin.

- Do not include a separate title page unless your instructor requires one.

- When you document using MLA style, you'll need to create an alphabetically arranged works cited page at the end of the paper so that readers have a convenient list of all the books, articles, and other data you have used.

Miller 1

Student's name, instructor's name, course title, and date appear in upper-left corner.

Melissa Miller

Professor Spahr

English 112

November 23, 20--

Center the title.

Distinguishing the *Other* in Two Works by Tolstoy

The Cossacks and the Chechens are two very different peoples; they share neither language nor religion. The Cossacks are Russian-speaking Christians, while the Chechens speak a Caucasian language and follow Islam. Certainly, Leo Tolstoy (1828-1910) knew these facts, since he spent a significant length of time in the Caucasus. However, it is difficult to distinguish them as different peoples in Tolstoy's work. The Cossacks in Tolstoy's novel of the same name (1863) and the Chechens in his story "A Prisoner in the Caucasus" (1872) share so many cultural and ethnic features—appearance, reverence for warriors and horses, their behavior—that they appear to be the same people. As a result, their deep cultural differences all but disappear to Tolstoy and his European readers.

One-inch margin on all sides of page.

Double-space all elements on title page.

From Tolstoy's descriptions of the Cossacks and the Chechens, they appear identical: Both groups are dark in complexion, wear *beshmets*, and are wild. The Cossack men have black beards and Maryanka has black eyes (*Cossacks* 30, 55), while Dina has black hair and a face like her father's, "the dark man" ("Prisoner" 316). In addition to the black, both groups are red in countenance: Uncle Yeroshka is "cinnamon-colored" (*Cossacks* 60), Maryanka is sunburned (93), and Kazi

Half-inch indent for new paragraph.

Source and page number appear in parentheses.

Works Cited

Said, Edward W. *Orientalism*. New York: Vintage, 1976. Print.

Tolstoy, Leo. *The Cossacks*. New York: Scribner's, 1899. Print.

---. "A Prisoner in the Caucasus." *Walk in the Light and Twenty-three Tales*. Maryknoll: Orbis, 2003. 78. Print.

"Works Cited" centered at top of page.

Entire page is double-spaced: no extra spaces between entries.

Begins on separate page.

Entries arranged alphabetically.

Second and subsequent lines of entries indent five spaces or one-half inch.

50 APA Documentation and Format

APA (American Psychological Association) style is used in many social science disciplines. For full details about APA style and documentation, consult the *Publication Manual of the American Psychological Association*, 6th ed. (2010). The basic details for documenting sources and formatting research papers in APA style are presented below.

Document sources according to convention.   When you use sources in a research paper, you are required to cite the source, letting readers know that the information has been borrowed from somewhere else and showing them how to find the original material if they would like to study it further. Like MLA style, APA includes two parts: a brief in-text citation and a more detailed reference entry.

In-text citations should include the author's name, the year the material was published, and the page number(s) that the borrowed material can be found on. The author's name and year of publication are generally included in a signal phrase that introduces the passage, and the page number is included in parentheses after the borrowed text. Note that for APA style, the verb in the signal phrase should be in the past tense (*reported*, as in the example on p. 541) or present perfect tense (*has reported*).

> Millman (2007) reported that college students around the country are participating in Harry Potter discussion groups, sports activities, and even courses for college credit (p. A4).

Alternatively, the author's name and year can be included in parentheses with the page number.

> College students around the country are participating in Harry Potter discussion groups, sports activities, and even courses for college credit (Millman, 2007, p. A4).

The list of references at the end of the paper contains a more detailed citation that repeats the author's name and publication year and includes the title and additional publication information about the source. Inclusive page numbers are included for periodical articles and parts of books.

> Millman, S. (2007). Generation hex. *The Chronicle of Higher Education, 53*(46), A4.

Both in-text citations and reference entries can vary greatly depending on the type of source cited (book, periodical, Web site, etc.). The following pages give specific examples of how to cite a wide range of sources in APA style.

Directory of APA In-Text Citations

1. Author named in signal phrase 543
2. Author named in parentheses 543
3. With block quotations 543
4. Two authors 543
5. Three to five authors 544
6. Six or more authors 544
7. Group, corporate, or government author 544
8. Two or more works by the same author 545
9. Authors with the same last name 545
10. Unknown author 545
11. Personal communication 545
12. Electronic source 546
13. Musical recording 546
14. Secondary source 546
15. Multiple sources in same citation 546

General Guidelines for In-Text Citations in APA Style

AUTHOR NAMES

- Give last names only, unless two authors have the same last name (see item 9 on p. 545) or if the source is a personal communication (see item 11 on p. 545). In these cases, include the first initial before the last name ("J. Smith").

DATES

- Give only the year in the in-text citation. The one exception to this rule is personal communications, which should include a full date (see item 11 on p. 545).

- Months and days for periodical publications should not be given with the year in in-text citations; this information will be provided as needed in the reference entry at the end of your paper.

- If you have two or more works by the same author in the same year, see item 8 on page 545.

- If you can't locate a date for your source, include the abbreviation "n.d." (for "no date") in place of the date in parentheses.

TITLES

- Titles of works generally do not need to be given in in-text citations. Exceptions include works with no author and two or more works by the same author. See items 8 and 10 on page 545 for details.

PAGE NUMBERS

- Include page numbers whenever possible in parentheses after borrowed material. Put "p." (or "pp.") before the page number(s).

- When you have a range of pages, list the full first and last page numbers (for example, "311-324"). If the borrowed material isn't printed on consecutive pages, list all the pages it appears on (for example, "A1, A4-A6").

- If page numbers are not available, use section names and/or paragraph (written as "para.") numbers when available to help a reader locate a specific quotation. See items 7 and 12 on pages 544 and 546 for examples.

APA in-text citation

1. Author Named in Signal Phrase

Doyle (2005) asserted that "although some immigrants are a burden on the welfare system, as a group they pay far more in taxes than they receive in government benefits, such as public education and social services" (p. 25).

2. Author Named in Parentheses

"Although some immigrants are a burden on the welfare system, as a group they pay far more in taxes than they receive in government benefits, such as public education and social services" (Doyle, 2005, p. 25).

3. With Block Quotations

For excerpts of forty or more words, indent the quoted material one-half inch and include the page number at the end of the quotation after the end punctuation.

Pollan (2006) suggested that the prized marbled meat that results from feeding corn to cattle (ruminants) may not be good for us:

> Yet this corn-fed meat is demonstrably less healthy for us, since it contains more saturated fat and less omega-3 fatty acids than the meat of animals fed grass. A growing body of research suggests that many of the health problems associated with eating beef are really problems with corn-fed beef. . . . In the same way ruminants are ill adapted to eating corn, humans in turn may be poorly adapted to eating ruminants that eat corn. (p. 75)

4. Two Authors

Note that if you name the authors in the parentheses, connect them with an ampersand (&).

Sharpe and Young (2005) reported that new understandings about tooth development, along with advances in stem cell technology, have brought researchers closer to the possibility of producing replacement teeth from human tissue (p. 36).

New understandings about tooth development, along with advances in stem cell technology, have brought researchers closer to the possibility of producing replacement teeth from human tissue (Sharpe & Young, 2005, p. 36).

5. Three to Five Authors

The first time you cite a source with three to five authors, list all their names in either the signal phrase or parentheses. If you cite the same source again in your paper, use just the first author's name followed by "et al."

> Swain, Scahill, Lombroso, King, and Leckman (2007) pointed out that "[a]lthough no ideal treatment for tics has been established, randomized clinical trials have clarified the short-term benefits of a number of agents" (p. 947).

> Swain et al. (2007) claimed that "[m]any tics are often under partial voluntary control, evidenced by patients' capacity to suppress them for brief periods of time" (p. 948).

6. Six or More Authors

List the first author's name only, followed by "et al."

> Grossoehme et al. (2007) examined the disparity between the number of pediatricians who claim that religion and spirituality are important factors in treating patients and those who actually use religion and spirituality in their practice (p. 968).

7. Group, Corporate, or Government Author

> The resolution called on the United States to ban all forms of torture in interrogation procedures (American Psychological Association [APA], 2007, para. 1). It also reasserted "the organization's absolute opposition to all forms of torture and abuse, regardless of circumstance" (APA, 2007, para. 5).

8. Two or More Works by the Same Author

To see reference list entries for these sources, see item 6 on page 550.

> Shermer (2005a) has reported that false acupuncture (in placebo experiments) is as effective as true acupuncture (p. 30).

> Shermer (2005b) has observed that psychics rely on vague and flattering statements, such as "You are wise in the ways of the world, a wisdom gained through hard experience rather than book learning," to earn the trust of their clients (p. 6).

9. Authors with the Same Last Name

Distinguish the authors by including initials of their first names.

> M. Dunn (2003) argued that, in fact, the opposite may be true (p. 5).

10. Unknown Author

Identify the item by its title. However, if the author is actually listed as "Anonymous," treat this term as the author in your citation.

> Tilapia provides more protein when eaten than it consumes when alive, making it a sustainable fish ("Dream Fish," 2007, 26).

> The book *Go Ask Alice* (Anonymous, 1971) portrayed the fictional life of a teenager who is destroyed by her addiction to drugs.

11. Personal Communication

If you cite personal letters or e-mails or your own interviews for your research paper, cite these as personal communication in your in-text citation, including the author of the material (with first initial), the term "personal communication," and the date. Personal communications should not be included in your reference list.

> One instructor has argued that it is important to "make peer review a lot more than a proofreading/grammar/mechanics exercise" (J. Bone, personal communication, July 27, 2007).

To include the author of a personal communication in the signal phrase, use the following format:

> J. Bone (personal communication, July 27, 2007) has argued that it is important to "make peer review a lot more than a proofreading/grammar/mechanics exercise."

12. Electronic Source

If page numbers are not given, use section names or paragraph numbers to help your readers track down the source.

> A recent report showed that, in 2006, "59 percent of KIPP fifth graders outperformed their local districts in reading, and 74 percent did so in mathematics" ("Charter Schools/Choice," 2007, para. 4).

13. Musical Recording

> In an ironic twist, Mick Jagger sings backup on the song "You're So Vain" (Simon, 1972, track 3).

14. Secondary Source

Include the name of the original author in the signal phrase. In the parentheses, add "as cited in," and give the author of the quoted material along with the date and page number. Note that your end-of-paper reference entry for this material will be listed under the secondary source name (Pollan) rather than the original writer (Howard).

> Writing in 1943, Howard asserted that "artificial manures lead inevitably to artificial nutrition, artificial food, artificial animals, and finally to artificial men and women" (as cited in Pollan, 2006, p. 148).

15. Multiple Sources in Same Citation

If one statement in your paper can be attributed to multiple sources, alphabetically list all the authors with dates, separated by semicolons.

> Most historians agree that the Puritan religion played a significant role in the hysteria surrounding the Salem witchcraft trials (Karlsen, 1998; Norton, 2002; Reis, 1997).

Directory of APA Reference Entries

General Guidelines for Reference Entries in APA Style

AUTHOR NAMES

- When an author's name appears *before* the title of the work, list it by last name followed by a comma and first initial followed by a period. (Middle initials may also be included.)

- If an author, editor, or other name is listed *after* the title, then the initial(s) precede the last name (see examples on pp. 000).

- When multiple authors are listed, their names should be separated by commas, and an ampersand (&) should precede the final author.

DATES

- For scholarly journals, include only the year (2007).

- For monthly magazines, include the year followed by a comma and the month (2007, May).

- For newspapers and weekly magazines, include the year, followed by a comma and the month and the day (2007, May 27).

- Access dates for electronic documents use the month-day-year format: "Retrieved May 27, 2007."

- Months should not be abbreviated.

- If a date is not available, use "n.d." (for "no date") in parentheses.

TITLES

- Titles of periodicals should be italicized, and all major words capitalized (*Psychology Today*; *Journal of Archaeological Research*).

- Titles of books, Web sites, and other nonperiodical long works should be italicized. Capitalize the first word of the title (and subtitle, if any) and proper nouns only (*Legacy of ashes: The history of the CIA*).

- For short works such as essays, articles, and chapters, capitalize the first word of the title (and subtitle, if any) and proper nouns only (The black sites: A rare look inside the CIA's secret interrogation program).

PAGE NUMBERS

- Reference entries for periodical articles and sections of books should include the range of pages: "245-257." For material in parentheses, include the abbreviation "p." or "pp." before the page numbers ("pp. A4-A5").

- If the pages are not continuous, list all the pages separated by commas: "245, 249, 301-306."

APA reference entries

AUTHOR INFORMATION

1. One Author

> Chopra, A. (2007). *King of Bollywood: Shah Rukh Khan and the seductive world of Indian cinema*. New York, NY: Warner Books.

2. Two Authors

> Johnson, M. E., & Vickers, C. (2005). *Threading the generations: A Mississippi family's quilt legacy*. Jackson, MS: University Press of Mississippi.

3. Three or More Authors

List every author up to and including seven; for a work with eight or more authors, give the first six names followed by three ellipsis dots and the last author's name.

> Thompson, M., Grace, C. O., & Cohen, L. J. (2001). *Best friends, worst enemies: Understanding the social lives of children*. New York, NY: Ballantine Books.

> Vitiello, B., Brent, D. A., Greenhill, L. L., Emslie, G., Wells, K., Walkup, J. T., . . . Zelazny, J. (2009). Depressive symptoms and clinical status during the treatment of adolescent suicide attempters (TASA) study. *Journal of the American Academy of Child & Adolescent Psychiatry, 48*, 997-1004.

4. Group, Corporate, or Government Author

In many cases, the group name is the same as the publisher. Instead of repeating the group name, use the term "Author" for the publisher's name.

> Society for the Protection of the Rights of the Child. (2003). *The state of Pakistan's children 2002*. Islamabad, Pakistan: Author.

5. Unidentified Author

If the author is listed on the work as "Anonymous," list that in your reference entry, alphabetizing accordingly. Otherwise, start with and alphabetize by title.

> Anonymous. (1971). *Go ask Alice*. New York, NY: Simon & Schuster.

> Dream fish. (2007, July/August). *Eating Well, 6*, 26-30.

6. Multiple Works by the Same Author

> Shermer, M. (2003). I knew you would say that [Review of the book *Intuition: Its powers and perils*]. *Skeptic, 10*(1), 92-94.

> Shermer, M. (2005a, August). Full of holes: The curious case of acupuncture. *Scientific American, 293*(2), 30.

> Shermer, M. (2005b). *Science friction.* New York, NY: Henry Holt, 6.

BOOKS

7. Book: Basic Format

> Author. (Publication Year). *Book title: Book subtitle.* Publication City, State (abbreviated) or Country of Publication: Publisher.

> Mah, A. Y. (1997). *Falling leaves: The true story of an unwanted Chinese daughter.* New York, NY: John Wiley & Sons.

8. Author and Editor

> Author. (Publication Year). *Book title: Book subtitle* (Editor's Initial(s). Editor's Last Name, Ed.). Publication City, State (abbreviated) or Country of Publication: Publisher.

> Faulkner, W. (2004). *Essays, speeches, and public letters* (J. B. Meriwether, Ed.). New York, NY: Modern Library.

9. Work in an Anthology or a Collection

Begin with the author and date of the short work and include the title as you would a periodical title (no quotations and minimal capitalization). Then list "In" and the editor's first initial and last name followed by "Ed." in parentheses. Next give the anthology title and page numbers in parentheses. End with the publication information. If an anthology has two editors, connect them with an ampersand (&) and use "Eds."

> Author. (Publication Year). Title of short work. In Editor's First Initial. Editor's Last Name (Ed.), *Title of anthology* (pp. Page Numbers). Publication City, State (abbreviated) or Country of Publication: Publisher.

Plimpton, G. (2002). Final twist of the drama. In N. Dawidoff (Ed.),
   Baseball: A literary anthology (pp. 457-475). New York, NY: Library
   of America.

For more than two editors, connect them with commas and an ampersand.
For large editorial boards, give the name of the lead editor followed by "et al."

J. Smith, L. Hoey, & R. Burns (Eds.)

N. Mallen et al. (Eds.)

10. Edited Collection

Editor. (Ed.). (Publication Year). *Book title: Book subtitle.* Publication
   City, State (abbreviated) or Country of Publication: Publisher.

Danquah, M. N. (Ed.). (2000). *Becoming American: Personal essays by
   first generation immigrant women.* New York, NY: Hyperion.

11. Multivolume Work

Author(s) or Editor(s) (Eds.). (Year of Publication). *Book title: Book
   subtitle* (Vols. volume numbers). Publication City, State (abbreviated)
   or Country of Publication: Publisher.

Lindahl, C., MacNamara, J., & Lindow, J. (Eds.). (2000). *Medieval folklore:
   An encyclopedia of myths, legends, tales, beliefs, and customs*
   (Vols. 1-2). Santa Barbara, CA: ABC-CLIO.

12. Later Edition

In parentheses include the edition type (such as "Rev." for "Revised" or
"Abr." for "Abridged") or number ("2nd," "3rd," "4th," etc.) as shown on the
title page, along with the abbreviation "ed." after the book title.

Author. (Publication Year). *Book title* (Edition Type or Number ed.). Publication
   City, State (abbreviated) or Country of Publication: Publisher.

Handlin, D. P. (2004). *American architecture* (2nd ed.). London, England:
   Thames and Hudson.

13. Translation

List the translator's initial, last name, and "Trans." in parentheses after the title. After the publication information, list "Original work published" and year in parentheses. Note that the period is omitted after the final parenthesis.

> Author. (Publication Year of Translation). *Book title* (Translator Initial(s). Last Name, Trans.). Publication City, State (abbreviated) or Country of Publication: Publisher. (Original work published Year)

> Camus, A. (1988). *The stranger* (M. Ward, Trans.). New York, NY: Knopf. (Original work published 1942)

14. Article in a Reference Book

> Article Author. (Publication Year). Article title. In Initial(s). Last Name of Editor (Ed.), *Reference book title* (pp. Page Numbers). Publication City, State (abbreviated) or Country of Publication: Publisher.

> Schwartz, J. (1995). Brownstones. In K. T. Jackson (Ed.), *Encyclopedia of New York City* (pp. 162-163). New Haven, CT: Yale University Press.

If a reference book entry has no author, begin with the title of the article.

> Article title. (Publication Year). In *Book title*. Publication City, State (abbreviated) or Country of Publication: Publisher.

> The history of the national anthem. (2004). In *The world almanac and book of facts 2004*. New York, NY: World Almanac Books.

PERIODICALS

15. Article in a Journal Paginated by Volume

> Article Author. (Publication Year). Title of article. *Title of Journal, Volume Number*, Page Numbers.

> Harwood, J. (2004). Relational, role, and social identity as expressed in grandparents' personal Web sites. *Communication Studies, 55*, 300-318.

16. Article in a Journal Paginated by Issue

> Article Author. (Publication Year). Title of article. *Title of Journal, Volume Number*(Issue Number), Page Numbers.

Clancy, S., & Simpson, L. (2002). Literacy learning for indigenous
    students: Setting a research agenda. *Australian Journal of
    Language and Literacy, 25*(2), 47-64.

17. Magazine Article

Article Author. (Publication Year, Month). Title of article. *Title of Magazine,
    Volume Number*(Issue Number), Page Number(s).

Murrel, J. (2007, July). In the year of the storm: The topography of
    resurrection in New Orleans. *Harper's Magazine, 315*(7), 35-52.

18. Newspaper Article

Article Author. (Publication Year, Month Day). Title of article. *Title of
    Newspaper,* p. Page Number.

Dempsey, J. (2007, August 26). Germans ease curbs on skilled labor
    from Eastern Europe. *The New York Times,* p. 8.

19. Letter to the Editor

Include "Letter to the editor" in brackets after the letter title (if any) and
before the period.

Author. (Publication Year, Month Day). Title of letter [Letter to the editor].
    Title of Newspaper, p. Page Number.

Miller, E. D. (2007, August 29). It is the sworn duty of law officers to
    uphold the law [Letter to the editor]. *The Stuart News,* p. A6.

20. Review

After the review title (if any), include in brackets "Review of the" and the
medium of the work being reviewed ("book," "film," "CD," etc.), followed by
the title of the work in italics. If the reviewed work is a book, include the
author's name after a comma; if it's a film or other media, include the year of
release.

Author Name. (Publication Year, Month Day). Title of review [Review of the
    book *Book title,* by Author Name]. *Title of Periodical, Volume Number,*
    Page Number.

Adams, L. (2007, July 15). The way west [Review of the book *Shadow
    of the Silk Road,* by C. Thubron]. *The New York Times Book
    Review, 1,* 10.

ELECTRONIC SOURCES

21. Article with a DOI

A DOI (digital object identifier) is a unique number assigned to specific content, such as a journal article. Include the DOI but not the database name or URL. Note that there is no period after the DOI.

> Thibedeau, H. (2009). Safer toys coming, but not with Santa Claus. *Canadian Medical Association Journal, 181*, E111-E112. doi:10.1503/cmaj.109-3003

22. Article without a DOI

Give the exact URL or the URL for the journal's home page if access requires a subscription. Do not give the database name. Note that there is no period after the URL.

> Moyo, J. (2009). Academic freedom and human rights in Zimbabwe. *Social Research, 76*, 611-614. Retrieved from http://www.socres.org/

23. Article in Internet-Only Periodical

An article published exclusively online is unlikely to have page numbers.

> Clark-Flory, T. (2007, August 31). Do we teach children to fear men? *Salon .com.* Retrieved from http://www.salon.com/mwt/broadsheet /2007/08/31/men/index.html

24. Multipage Web Site

Include a retrieval date before the URL if the material is likely to be changed or updated or if it lacks a set publication date. Do not add a period at the end of the entry.

> Web Site Author or Sponsor. (Date of Most Recent Update). *Title of Web site.* Retrieved date, from URL

> Annie E. Casey Foundation. (2007). *Kids count.* Retrieved September 9, 2007, from http://www.aecf.org/MajorInitiatives/KIDSCOUNT.aspx

> Hartmann, D., Gerteis, J., & Edgell, P. (2007). *American Mosaic Project.* Retrieved from http://www.soc.umn.edu/research/amp/

25. Part of a Web Site

Short Work Author. (Date of Most Recent Update). Title of short work. *Title of Web site.* Retrieved date, from URL

Taylor, W., Jr. (2005, November 16). A time to be thankful. *The Hopi Tribe Web site.* Retrieved from http://www.hopi.nsn.us/view_article .asp?id=116&cat=3

26. Online Posting

Post Author. (Year, Month Day of post). Title of post [Description of post]. Retrieved from URL

Winkleman, T. (2007, July 13). Reducing your food miles [Online forum comment]. Retrieved from http://tech.groups.yahoo.com/group /FFCFBulletin/message/220

27. Computer Software

If the software has an author or editor, the reference begins with that.

Title of software [Computer software]. (Publication Year). Publication City, State (abbreviated) or Country of Publication: Publisher.

History through art: The twentieth century [Computer software]. (2001). San Jose, CA: Fogware.

28. Entry in a blog (Weblog)

Sellers, H. (2008, June 21). Re: East Coast [Web log post]. Retrieved from http://heathersellers.com/blog/index.php

29. Podcast

Graham, L. (Producer). (2006, July 31). Capping pollution at the source. [Audio podcast]. *The environment report.* Retrieved from http://www.environmentreport.org/story.php3?story_id=3102

30. Entry in a Wiki

Article title. Posting date (if any). Retrieved date, from URL

Emo. (n.d.). Retrieved June 24, 2008, from http://en.wikipedia.org/wiki /Emo

Cite from a Web site (APA)

2 publisher of report
(if not named as author)

1 publication
date

3 report
number

4 title of online
report

5 author

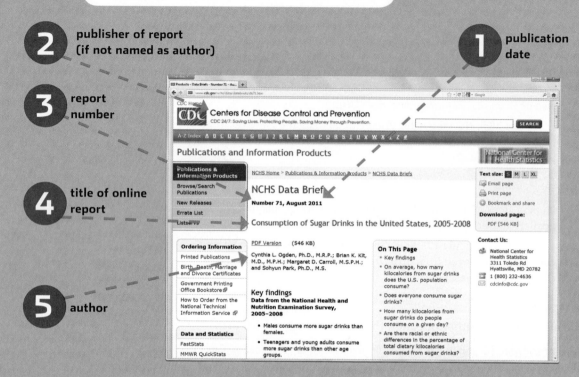

If you cite a source with three or more authors
more than once in text, only list all of the authors
the first time. Subsequent times only need the
first author's last name, like this: (Ogden et al.).

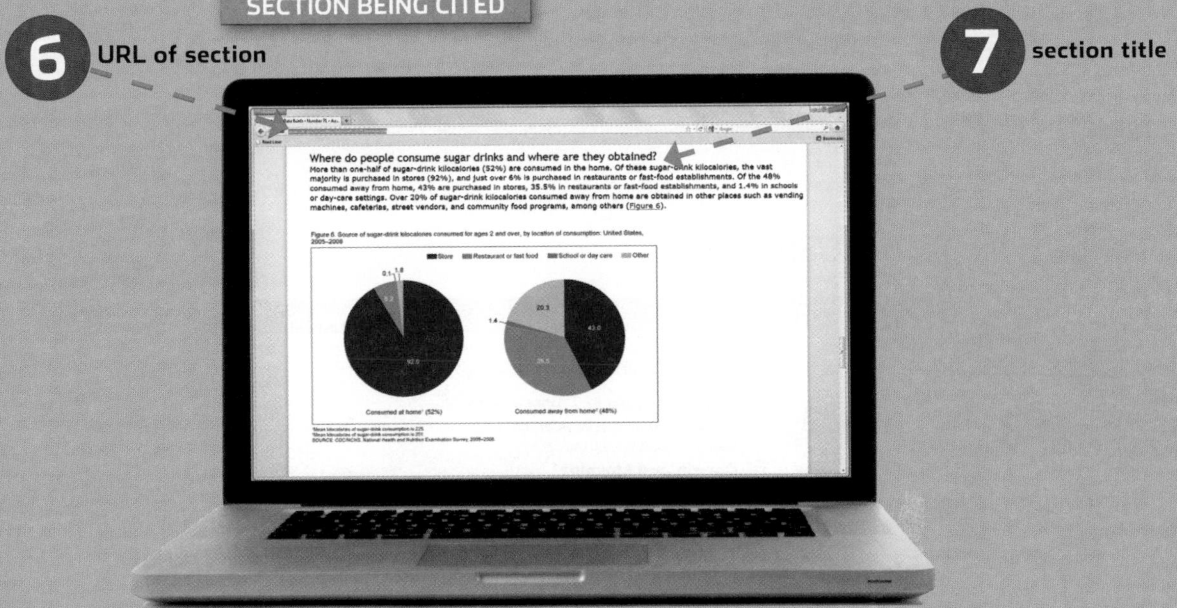

SECTION BEING CITED

6 URL of section

7 section title

Where do people consume sugar drinks and where are they obtained?
More than one-half of sugar-drink kilocalories (52%) are consumed in the home. Of these sugar-drink kilocalories, the vast majority is purchased in stores (92%), and just over 6% is purchased in restaurants or fast-food establishments. Of the 48% consumed away from home, 43% are purchased in stores, 35.5% in restaurants or fast-food establishments, and 1.4% in schools or day-care settings. Over 20% of sugar-drink kilocalories consumed away from home are obtained in other places such as vending machines, cafeterias, street vendors, and community food programs, among others (Figure 6).

Figure 6. Source of sugar-drink kilocalories consumed for ages 2 and over, by location of consumption: United States, 2005-2008

APA in-text citation

A nutrition survey of U.S. behavior between 2005 and 2008 found that an overwhelming 92% of sugar-drink kilocalories consumed outside the home were from drinks purchased in stores, not restaurants (Ogden, Kit, Carroll, & Park, 2011).

APA references list entry

Ogden, C. L., Kit, B. K., Carroll, M. D., & Park S. (2011, August). Where do people consume sugar drinks and where are they obtained? In *Consumption of sugar drinks in the United States, 2005-2008* (NCHS Data Brief No. 71). Retrieved from Centers for Disease Control and Prevention website: http://www.cdc.gov/nchs/data/databriefs/db71.htm#people

How to...
Cite from a database (APA)

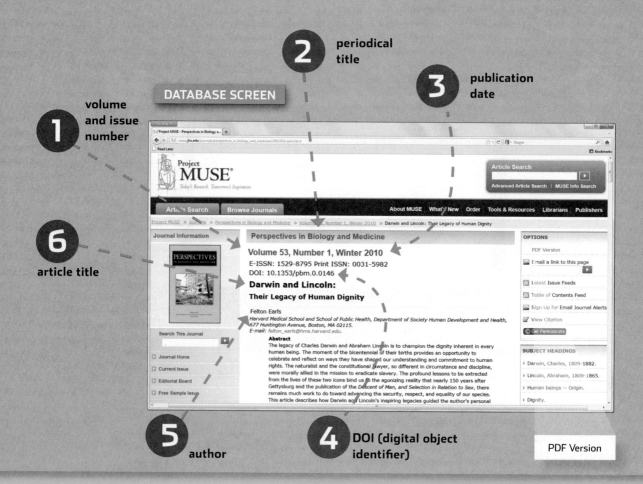

DATABASE SCREEN

1 volume and issue number

2 periodical title

3 publication date

6 article title

5 author

4 DOI (digital object identifier)

PDF Version

If you're reading an article in an Internet browser and aren't sure where to find the information you need, try viewing the article as a PDF, which usually shows what originally appeared in the print journal.

PDF VIEW (FIRST PAGE)

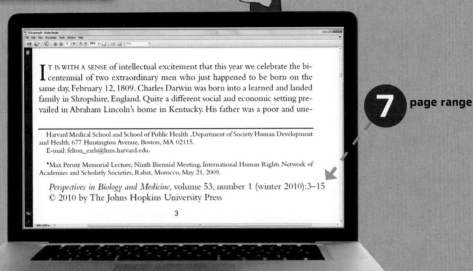

I T IS WITH A SENSE of intellectual excitement that this year we celebrate the bicentennial of two extraordinary men who just happened to be born on the same day, February 12, 1809. Charles Darwin was born into a learned and landed family in Shropshire, England. Quite a different social and economic setting prevailed in Abraham Lincoln's home in Kentucky. His father was a poor and une-

Harvard Medical School and School of Public Health , Department of Society Human Development and Health, 677 Huntington Avenue, Boston, MA 02115.
E-mail: felton_earls@hms.harvard.edu.

*Max Perutz Memorial Lecture, Ninth Biennial Meeting, International Human Rights Network of Academies and Scholarly Societies, Rabat, Morocco, May 21, 2009.

Perspectives in Biology and Medicine, volume 53, number 1 (winter 2010):3–15
© 2010 by The Johns Hopkins University Press

3

7 page range

APA in-text citation

It's important to note the contributions of Darwin and Lincoln to modern conceptions of human rights, "particularly the beliefs that scientists are free to pursue knowledge, no matter how different from or risky to the prevailing wisdom, and that one of the responsibilities of modern governments is to protect this right to rationality and critical inquiry" (Earls, 2010, 4).

5   3   7

5   3   6

APA references list entry

Earls, F. (2010, Winter). Darwin and Lincoln: Their legacy of human dignity.

2   1   7   4

Perspectives in Biology and Medicine, 53(1), 3-15. doi:10.1353/pbm.0.0146

OTHER

31. Group, Corporate, or Government Document

List the group or agency as the author, and include any identifying numbers. Many federal agencies' works are published by the U.S. Government Printing Office. If the group is also the publisher, use the word "Author" rather than repeating the group name at the end of the entry.

> Name of Group, Corporation, or Government Agency. (Publication Year). *Title of document* (Identifying number, if any). Publication City, State (abbreviated) or Country of Publication: Publisher.

> U.S. Department of Health and Human Services. (1995). *Disability among older persons: United States and Canada* (HE 20.6209:5/8). Washington, DC: U.S. Government Printing Office.

> Florida Department of Elder Affairs. (2006). *Making choices: A guide to end-of-life planning.* Tallahassee, FL: Author.

32. Published Conference Proceedings

> Editor(s). (Eds.). (Publication Year). *Proceedings of the Conference Name: Book title.* Publication City, State (abbreviated) or Country of Publication: Publisher.

> Bourguignon, F., Pleskovic, B., & Van Der Gaag, J. (Eds.). (2006). *Proceedings of the Annual World Bank Conference on Development Economics 2006: Securing development in an unstable world.* Washington, DC: World Bank.

33. Dissertation Abstract

For dissertations abstracted in *Dissertation Abstracts International*, include the author's name, date, and dissertation title. Then include the volume, issue, and page number. If you access the dissertation from an electronic database, identify the type of work ("Doctoral dissertation") before giving the database name and any identifying number. If you retrieve the abstract from the Web, include the name of the institution in the parentheses, and then give the URL.

Author. (Year of Publication). *Title of dissertation. Dissertation Abstracts International, Volume Number*(Issue Number), Page Number.

Berger, M. A. (2000). *The impact of organized sports participation on self-esteem in middle school children. Dissertation Abstracts International, 60*(11), 5762B.

Berger, M. A. (2000). *The impact of organized sports participation on self-esteem in middle school children* (Doctoral dissertation). Available from ProQuest Dissertations and Theses database. (730241441)

Berger, M. A. (2000). *The impact of organized sports participation on self-esteem in middle school children* (Doctoral dissertation. Pace University). Retrieved from http://digitalcommons.pace.edu /dissertations/AAI9950745/

34. Film

Writer(s), Producer(s), Director(s). (Release year). *Film title* [Motion picture]. Country of Origin: Movie Studio.

Haggis, P. (Writer/Director/Producer), & Moresco, B. (Writer/Producer). (2004). *Crash* [Motion picture]. United States: Lions Gate Films.

35. Television Program

Writer(s). Producer(s), Director(s). (Year of Release). Title of episode [Television series episode]. In Producer Initials. Last Name (Producer), *Title of series*. City, State (abbreviated) or Country of Publication: Broadcast Company.

Hochman, G. & Collins, M. (Writers), & Wolfinger, K. (Director). (2004). Ancient refuge in the Holy Land [Television series episode]. In P. S. Apsell (Producer), *NOVA*. Boston, MA: WGBH.

36. Musical Recording

Writer. (Copyright Year). Title of song [Recorded by Artist Name]. On *Album title* [Recording medium]. City of Recording, State (abbreviated) or Country of Publication: Record Label. (Recording Year).

Cornell, C. (1991). Rusty cage [Recorded by J. Cash]. On *Unchained* [CD]. Burbank, CA: American Recordings. (1994).

Format an APA paper correctly.   The following guidelines will help you prepare a manuscript using APA style.

- Set up a header on each page, one-half inch from the top. The header should include a brief title (shortened to no more than fifty characters) in all capital letters and should align left. Page numbers should appear in the upper right corner.

- Margins should be set at one inch on all sides of the paper.

- Check with your instructor to see if a title page is preferred. If so, at the top of the page, you need the short title you'll use in your header, in all capital letters, preceded by the words "Running head" and a colon. The page number appears on the far right. Next, the full title of your paper, your name, and your affiliation (or school) appear in the middle of the page, centered.

- If you include an abstract for your paper, put it on a separate page, immediately following the title page.

- All lines of text (including the title page, abstract, block quotations, and the list of references) should be double-spaced.

- Indent the first lines of paragraphs one-half inch or five spaces.

- Use block quotations for quoted material of four or more lines. Indent block quotations one inch from the left margin.

- When you document a paper using APA style, you'll need to create an alphabetically arranged references page at the end of the project so that readers have a convenient list of all the books, articles, and other data you have used in the paper or project.

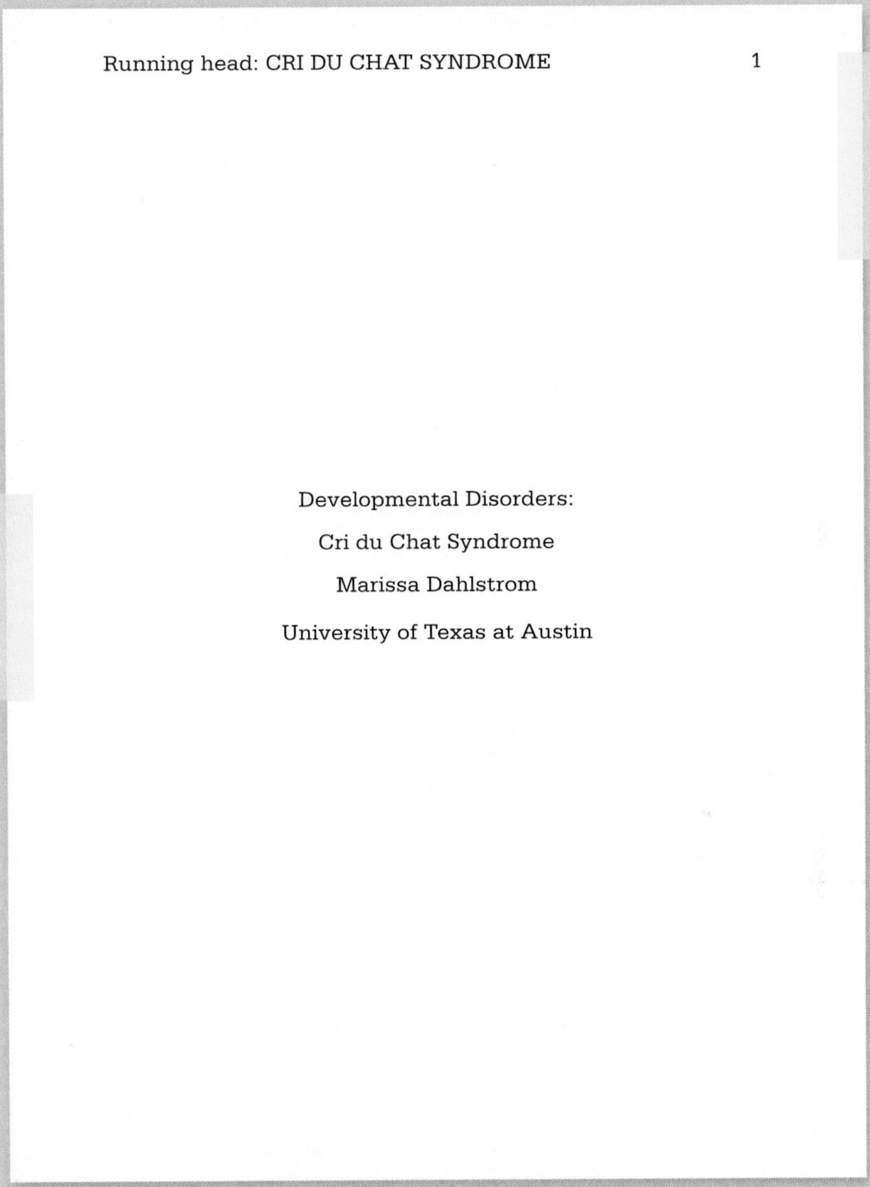

Running head: CRI DU CHAT SYNDROME   1

Short title in all capitals is aligned left. Arabic numerals used for page numbers.

Developmental Disorders:

Cri du Chat Syndrome

Marissa Dahlstrom

University of Texas at Austin

Full title, writer's name, and affiliation are all centered in middle of page.

CRI DU CHAT SYNDROME   2

Developmental Disorders: Cri du Chat Syndrome

Developmental disorders pose a serious threat to young children. However, early detection, treatment, and intervention often allow a child to lead a fulfilling life. To detect a problem at the beginning of life, medical professionals and caregivers must recognize normal development as well as potential warning signs. Research provides this knowledge. In most cases, research also allows for accurate diagnosis and effective intervention. Such is the case with cri du chat syndrome (CDCS), also commonly known as cat cry syndrome, 5p-syndrome, and 5p-minus syndrome.

Cri du chat syndrome, a fairly rare genetic disorder first identified in 1963 by Dr. Jerome Lejeune, affects between 1 in 15,000 to 1 in 50,000 live births (Campbell, Carlin, Justen, & Baird, 2004). The syndrome is caused by partial deletion of chromosome number 5, specifically the portion labeled as 5p; hence the alternative name for the disorder (Five P-Minus Society). While the exact cause of the deletion is unknown, it is likely that "the majority of cases are due to spontaneous loss . . . during development of an egg or sperm. A minority of cases result from one parent carrying a rearrangement of chromosome 5 called a translocation" (Sondheimer, 2005). The deletion leads to many different symptoms and outcomes. Perhaps the most noted characteristic of children affected by this syndrome—a high-pitched cry resembling the mewing of a cat—explains Lejeune's choice of the name *cri du chat* syndrome. Pediatric nurse Mary Kugler writes that the cry is caused by "problems with the larynx and nervous system" (2006). Other symptoms, characteristics,

Center the title

This paper does not include an abstract; check with your instructor to find out whether an abstract is required.

The authors' names and publication date appear in parentheses.

A signal phrase including author's name introduces quotation, so only the date appears in parentheses.

CRI DU CHAT SYNDROME   6

References

Campbell, D., Carlin M., Justen, J., III, & Baird, S. (2004).

    Cri-du-chat syndrome: A topical overview. Retrieved from

    http://www.fivepminus.org/online.htm

Denny, M., Marchand-Martella, N., Martella, R., Reilly, J. R., &

    Reilly, J. F. (2000). Using parent-delivered graduated

    guidance to teach functional living skills to a child with cri

    du chat syndrome. *Education & Treatment of Children,*

    23(4), 441.

Five P-Minus Society. (n.d.). *About 5P-syndrome.* Retrieved

    from http://www.fivepminus.org/about.htm

Kugler, M. (2006). Cri-du-chat syndrome: Distinctive kitten-

    like cry in infancy. Retrieved from http://rarediseases.

    about.com/cs/criduchatsynd/a/010704.htm

McClean, P. (1997). Genomic analysis: *In situ* hybridization.

    Retrieved from http://www.ndsu.nodak.edu/instruct

    /mcclean/plsc431/genomic/genomic2.htm

Sarimski, K. (2003). Early play behavior in children with

    5p-syndrome. *Journal of Intellectual Disability Research,*

    47(2), 113-120.

Sondheimer, N. (2005). Cri du chat syndrome. In *MedlinePlus*

    medical encyclopedia. Retrieved from http://www.nlm

    .nih.gov/medlineplus/ency/article/001593.htm

Media & Design

part eight

51

Understanding Digital Media

go
multimodal

Schools, businesses, and professional organizations are finding innovative uses for new media tools and services such as blogs, wikis, digital video, web-mapping software, social networks, and more. The resulting texts—often spun from Web 2.0 interactive media technologies—represent genres much in flux. And yet they already play a role in many classrooms. You are employing new media if you contribute to a college service project hosted on a blog, schedule study sessions with classmates via Facebook, or use slide software to spiff up a report to the student government.

Plotting Flickr and Tweet locations in Europe produces this luminous map of the continent, suggesting the sweep of new media activity.

Choose a media format based on what you hope to accomplish.
A decision to compose with digital tools or to work in an environment
such as Facebook or Flickr should be based on what these new media offer
you. An electronic tool may support your project in ways that conventional
printed texts simply cannot—and that's the reason to select it. Various
media writing options are described in the following table.

Format	Elements	Purpose	Software Technology/Tools
Blogs	Topic-driven online discussion postings; interactive; text; images; video; links	Create communities (fan, political, academic); distribute news and information	Blogger; Moveable Type; Tumblr; WordPress
Web sites	Web-based information site; text; images; video; links; interactive posts	Compile and distribute information; establish presence on Web; sell merchandise, etc.	Dreamweaver; Drupal; WordPress
Wikis	Collaboratively authored linked texts and posts; Web-based; information; text; images; data	Create and edit collaborative documents based on community expertise; distribute and share information	DokuWiki; MediaWiki; Tiki Wiki
Podcasts	Digital file-based audio or (sometimes) video recording; downloadable; voice; music; episodic	Distribute mainly audio texts; document or archive audio texts and performances	Audacity; GarageBand
Maps	Interactive image maps; text; data; images	Give spatial or geographical dimension to data or texts; help users locate or visualize information	iMapBuilder; Google Earth; Google Maps
Video	Recorded images; live-action images; enhanced slides; animation; sound; music	Record events; provide visual documentation; create presentations; furnish instructions, etc.	Animoto; Camtasia; iMovie; Microsoft Movie Maker; Soundslides; Xtranormal
Remixes and mashups	Combined media; sampling; music; sound; images; video	Juxtapose or combine existing texts to create new perspectives; examine media conventions; explore new genres and texts	Audacity; Mixcraft

Use blogs to create communities.   Blogs are moderated online discussions hosted by groups or individuals that typically focus on topics such as politics, news, sports, technology, and entertainment. They integrate individual postings, comments, images, videos, and lots of links; the busiest blogs are constantly updated, archived, and searchable.

Some college courses now use blogs to spur discussion of class materials, to distribute information, and to document research activities. An instructor may set up a site for a class or make the creation of a blog a course project. If blogging is part of a course assignment, understand the ground rules. Instructors often require a defined number of postings/comments of a specific length. Participate regularly by reading and commenting on other students' blogs or blog posts; by making substantive comments of your own on the assigned topic; and by contributing relevant images, videos, and links.

Keep your postings focused and title them descriptively; respond to others by commenting substantively on their ideas, asking pertinent questions, and suggesting links. Postings should be academic in style. Avoid the vitriol you may encounter on national sites: Remember that anyone—from your mother to a future employer—might read your remarks.

Create Web sites to share information.   Not long ago, building Web sites was at the leading edge of technological savvy in the classroom. Today, blogs, wikis, and social networks are more efficient vehicles for many types of online communication. Still, Web sites remain essential because of their

capacity to organize large amounts of text and information online. A Web site you create for a course might report research findings or provide a portal to information on a complex topic.

Public School is a Web site hosted by a small regional group of artists who are eager to showcase good design and talk about their own work. Note its use of school-themed design elements.

When creating a site with multiple pages, plan early on how to organize that information; the structure will depend on your purpose and audience. A simple site with sequential information (e.g., a photo essay) might lead readers through items one by one. More complicated sites may require a complex, hierarchical structure, with materials organized around careful topic divisions. The more comprehensive the site, the more deliberately you will need to map out its structure, allowing for easy navigation and growth.

Use wikis to collaborate with others.   If you have ever opened Wikipedia, you know what a wiki does: It enables a group to collaborate on the development of an ongoing online project—from a comprehensive encyclopedia to focused databases on just about any imaginable topic. Such an effort combines the knowledge of all its contributors, ideally making the whole greater than its parts. But the project also shares its contributors' weaknesses. A resource such as Wikipedia demonstrates the scope of potential projects, but must be used with caution.

In academic courses, wikis have many applications. Instructors may ask class members to publish articles on an existing wiki—in which case you should read the site guidelines, examine its existing entries and templates, and then post your item. More likely you will use wiki software to develop a collaborative project for the course itself—bringing together research on a specific academic topic such as a historical event or a work of literature. A wiki might even be used for a service project in which participants gather useful information about nutrition, jobs, or arts opportunities for specific communities.

As always with electronic projects, you need to learn the software—which will involve not only uploading material to the wiki but also editing and developing texts that classmates have already placed there. If the assignment allows, parcel out wiki responsibilities to capitalize on the strengths of individual participants.

Make podcasts to share audio files.   Podcasts are convenient downloadable audio or video files you can review on various devices from MP3 players to iPads. Often published in series, podcasts are an inexpensive way to share music, information, or media broadcasts.

Audio podcasts might be a way of sharing interviews you've made as part of a sociology project, an efficient method for explaining a complex procedure in an engineering course, or a tool for teaching or learning language skills. Depending on the intended audience, academic podcasts usually need to be scripted and edited.

Producing a podcast is a two-step process. First you must record the podcast; then you need to upload it to a Web site for distribution. Software such as GarageBand can do both.

Use maps to position ideas.   You use mapping services such as Google Maps whenever you search online for a restaurant, store, or hotel. The service quickly provides maps and directions to available facilities, often embellished with links, information, and images. Not surprisingly, Google

Maps, the related Google Earth, and other mapping software are also finding classroom applications, as shown on these pages.

Multimedia maps also make it possible to display information such as economic trends, movements of people, climate data, and other variables

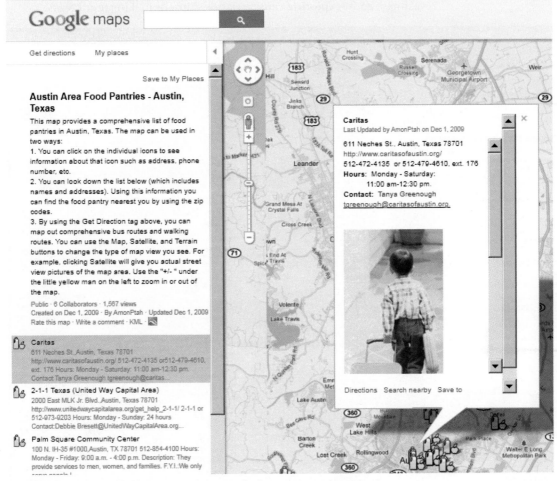

(Copyright © Google. Sean McCarthy's Writing in Digital Environments class.)

Students in a course called Writing in Digital Environments produced this Google Maps project to show where food pantries serve the community of Austin.

graphically and dynamically, using color, text, images, and video/audio clips to emphasize movement and change across space and time. Even literary texts can be mapped so that scholars or readers may track events or characters as they move in real or imaginary landscapes. Mapping thus becomes a vehicle for reporting and sharing information, telling personal stories, revealing trends, exploring causal relationships, or making arguments.

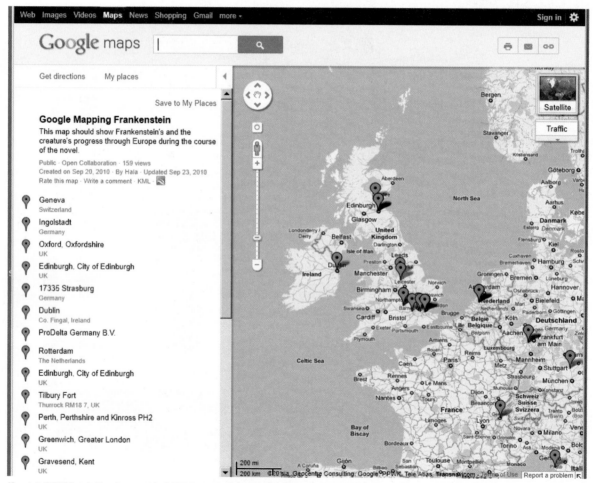

(Copyright © 2011 Google. Map data copyright © 2010 Europa Technologies, PPWK, Tele Atlas. Hala Herbly.)

English instructor Hala Herbly asked students to map the movements across Europe of the monster from Mary Shelley's novel *Frankenstein*.

Make "movies" to show and tell.   Digital video is a medium that is easy and cheap to use. A video or cell phone camera can film any subject—from smart kitties to stupid boyfriends. Many simple items go viral on YouTube: Has anyone *not* seen "Charlie Bit Me"? But there are sophisticated ways to shape video narratives into worthwhile "small screen" presentations.

In a course assignment, you might be asked to develop a video that tells a story or makes an argument. Consider what you'd like to accomplish and then match your goals to available software resources. If you want to film an event, do interviews, or tell a story with actors, you need conventional software such as Microsoft Movie Maker or iMovie. With this software you can edit and mix digital scenes, refine the sound, add special effects, titles, and captioning, and so on. Such options enable you to achieve specific visual and rhetorical effects. If your subject is better served by animation, software such as Xtranormal gives you different choices.

You can construct nonnarrative kinds of video writing by combining text, film clips, still photos, and music. Software such as Animoto, Soundslides, or Camtasia provides the frameworks for such projects. If you have a concept, you can turn it into a clip and then upload it to a blog, presentation software, or Web sites with enormous audiences such as YouTube, Flickr, or Metacafe. To upload materials to Web sites, you'll establish an account and then follow the instructions for sending files.

Try remixes and mashups to create something new.   Combining media in unexpected ways may expose surprising relationships between vastly different kinds of texts. Already common in commercial music, design, and advertising, projects of this kind are now appearing in academic fields across various disciplines.

Mashups build texts by sampling and combining materials that may be poles apart, sometimes from within the same genre (in the movie *300*, does Leonidas channel the cartoon superhero Batman?) and sometimes across genres and media (do Walt Whitman's poems really work in Levi's Jeans "Go Forth" campaign?).

Such creative juxtapositions redefine what writing and composition mean: Just as DJs have been remixing music for decades, surprising audiences with unanticipated convergences, your own ideas and stories can be repurposed and reenergized through a "remix."

For instance, you could take a traditional argumentative essay and add photos, video, and art. Or you could transform it into a video or give it its own Facebook page, profile, and posts. You see this kind of remix in the music industry whenever artists take songs and develop them into videos or films.

Alternatively, a remix might allow you to illustrate your own ideas by references to other texts; for instance, you could fuse scenes from your favorite movies to explore a political position—just as a producer such as Kanye West samples from other songs to create the beat or the background for new songs. Mashups often take this form of sampling to the extreme, putting together disparate genres—as Danger Mouse did with the *Grey Album,* remixing the Beatles' *White Album* and Jay-Z's *Black Album.* Texts can also be remixed collaboratively: You can take your ideas, stories, or arguments and put them into conversation with those of your peers.

Part of the pleasure of this type of composing is in discovering new angles and ideas as you move texts around and recombine them. It is important, however, to develop creative strategies for citation when you are remixing: Keep track of everything you borrow and give creative credit wherever it is due.

Your Turn   Most of the software programs mentioned in this chapter have Web sites that describe their features, and some, such as Xtranormal, even include sample projects. Explore one or two of these programs online to learn about their capabilities. Then describe a new media project you would like to create using the software.

Digital Elements 52

Every day, you navigate an amazing variety of media, from video games and phone apps to e-readers and social networking sites, to name but a few. Yet creating academic or professional texts that use media effectively can be a challenge if you aren't familiar with some of the conventions, tools, or opportunities for introducing images, audio, and video. This chapter covers some of the basics.

learn media
conventions

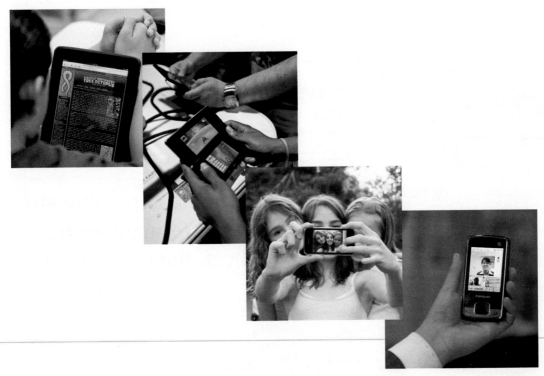

577

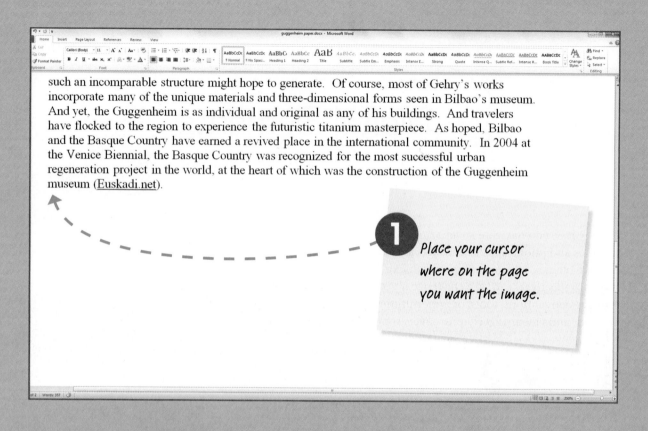

such an incomparable structure might hope to generate. Of course, most of Gehry's works incorporate many of the unique materials and three-dimensional forms seen in Bilbao's museum. And yet, the Guggenheim is as individual and original as any of his buildings. And travelers have flocked to the region to experience the futuristic titanium masterpiece. As hoped, Bilbao and the Basque Country have earned a revived place in the international community. In 2004 at the Venice Biennial, the Basque Country was recognized for the most successful urban regeneration project in the world, at the heart of which was the construction of the Guggenheim museum (Euskadi.net).

1 Place your cursor where on the page you want the image.

2 On the "Insert" tab, click "Picture."

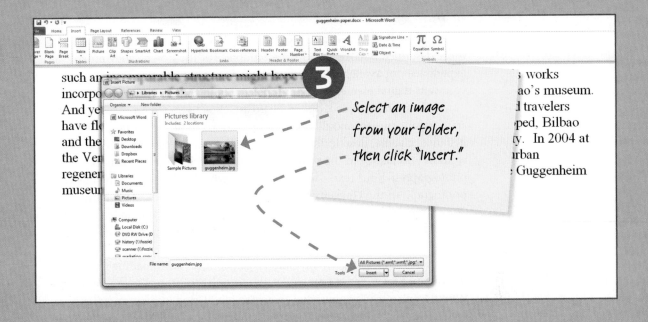

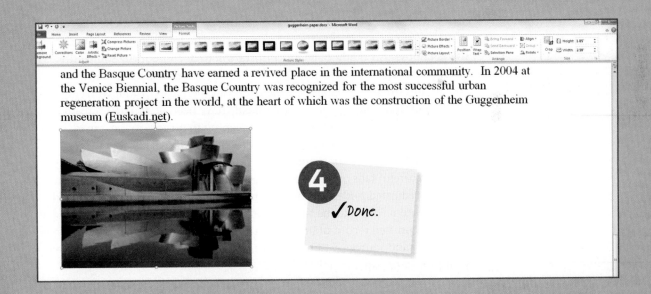

Have good reasons for using new media.   New media projects such as those described in Chapter 51 have rationales of their own: They provide an experience not available in conventional documents. But in academic work, you want digital elements to be purposeful, not mere eye candy or bling.

A photograph, video, or audio clip attached to an electronic version of an academic project should do what printed words alone cannot. For instance, a verbal description of the style of a Frank Gehry building probably wouldn't do justice to the subject. Readers would likely benefit from seeing a photograph in your text—which is exactly why Annie Winsett includes the photograph of the Guggenheim Bilbao in her report on page 67. Similarly, an oral report on Winston Churchill would appropriately include an audio file enabling the audience to hear clips from the British prime minister's famous wartime radio broadcasts of 1940.

On the other hand, what would be gained from downloading images of the current secretaries of state or defense into a report for a government class? Who doesn't already know what they look like? Using unnecessary digital embellishments contributes to clutter, the media equivalent of wordiness. ○

Download and save digital elements.   Most digital files on the Web can be saved on your computer simply by control clicking (or right clicking) on them and then transferring them to an appropriate location on your finder. If you choose this method, be *extremely careful* to document the source site; obtain permission if necessary. ○ You can also purchase whole libraries of clip art and stock photography, which you can then use without worrying about copyright infringement. Other media have been designated "creative commons" by their authors or owners, meaning that they can be reused and/or modified freely. Search for materials of this kind at sites such as <www.search.creativecommons.org>.

Keep careful tabs on the electronic content you collect for your project. Create a dedicated folder on your desktop, hard drive, or online archive and save each item with a name that will remind you where it came from. Keeping a printed record of images, with more detailed information about copyrights and sources, will be a great time-saver later, when you are putting your project or paper together.

improve your
sentences p. 444

understand citation
styles p. 501

Use tools to edit digital media.   Nonprint media texts often require as much revising and editing as traditional written ones. In fact, the tools for manipulating video, audio, and still-image files are among the most remarkable accomplishments of the digital revolution. If you are developing a podcast, an audio file can be tweaked a dozen ways using an audio editor like GarageBand or Audacity; such programs can also be used to create or refine musical clips. Comparable software is available for editing video clips.

You are apt to be familiar with tools for editing digital photographs. Even the simplest image-editing software enables users to adjust the tint, contrast, saturation, and sharpness of digital photographs. You might need to heighten the contrast of a PowerPoint image so that it projects better or adjust the tint in a portrait to purge the green from skin tones. Or you might use the cropping tool to select just the portion of an image you need for your project.

Image-editing software offers numerous options for enhancing picture files. Look for these options on palettes, toolbars, or dropdown menus.

Be aware, though, that when you enlarge a section of a larger digital image, it loses sharpness. And never crop an image in a way that distorts its meaning.

Sophisticated programs such as Photoshop allow you to do even more. Don't, however, tinker with the settings on professional photographs, even if you have permission to use them. Unless you have purchased the images from a stock photography library, or they are designated as "creative commons" material, they belong to someone else.

Use appropriate digital formats.   Working online, you quickly discover the various forms digital documents can take. Most of your academic work will be created in familiar word-processing, presentation, or spreadsheet software. Compatibility is rarely an issue today as you move your materials across computer platforms (PC to Mac) or download a presentation in a classroom for an oral report. Still, it never hurts to check ahead of time if, for example, you use Keynote or Prezi for a report rather than the more common PowerPoint.

Occasionally you need to save word-processing files in special formats. Sharing a file with someone using an older version of Word or Office may require saving a document in compatibility mode (.doc) rather than the now-standard .docx mode. Or moving across different applications may be easier if you use a plain text (.txt) or rich text format (.rtf)—in which case your document will lose some features, though the text will be preserved. When you want to share a document exactly as you wrote it and send it successfully across platforms, choose the .pdf mode. Files in .pdf form arrive exactly as you sent them, without any shifts in headings, alignments, or image locations; just as important, they cannot be easily altered.

Even if you have limited knowledge of differing image file formats (such as JPG, GIF, or TIFF), you probably understand that digital files come in varying sizes. The size of a digital-image file is directly related to the quality, or resolution, of the image. Attach a few high-resolution 14-megapixel photos to an e-mail and you'll clog the recipient's mailbox (or the e-mail will bounce back).

For most Web pages and online documents, compressed or lower-resolution images will be acceptable. On the other hand, if you intend to print an image—in a paper or brochure, for example—use the

At this size, the image downloaded from the Web is clear enough. But it would become distorted if you tried to enlarge it, because its resolution is too low.

highest-resolution image (the greatest number of pixels) available to assure maximum sharpness and quality.

Caption images correctly.   When using images or digital items in an academic paper, label, number, and caption them. Captions provide context for readers, so they know what an image, video, or audio file is and why they're considering it. If you also number your items (e.g., *Fig. 1.*), you can then direct readers to them unambiguously.

MLA and APA styles have different guidelines for captioning images and referring to them in the text, so consult the relevant guidebook before composing your captions. In general, however, captions should include the source of the image and any copyright and publication information. The photo on this page has not been previously published, but note that we still had to ask the photographer for permission to reprint.

Respect copyrights.   The images you find, whether online or in print, belong to someone. You cannot use someone else's property for commercial purposes—photographs, Web sites, brochures, posters, magazine articles, and so on—without permission. You may use a reasonable number of images in academic papers, but you must be careful not to go beyond "fair use," especially for any work you put online. Search the term "academic fair use" online for detailed guidelines.

Fig. 1. A boat ferries tourists from Zanzibar, Tanzania, to Prison Island, which was used as a quarantine station for yellow fever in the nineteenth century. (Courtesy Allie Goldstein.)

Tables, Graphs, and Infographics

display data

—Edward R. Tufte

Just as images and photographs are often the media of choice for conveying visual information, tables, graphs, and other "infographics" are essential tools for displaying numerical and statistical data. They take raw data and transform it into a story or picture readers can interpret.

Most such items are created in spreadsheet programs such as Excel that format charts and graphs and offer numerous design templates—though you will find basic graphics tools in Word and PowerPoint as well. More elaborate charts and graphs can be drawn with software such as Adobe Illustrator.

Creating effective tables and graphs is an art in itself, driven as always by purpose and audience. A table in a printed report that a reader will study can be rich in detail; a bar graph on screen for only a few moments must make its point quickly and memorably. Function always trumps appearance. Yet there's no question that handsome visual texts appeal to audiences. So spend the time necessary to design effective items. Use color to emphasize and clarify graphs, not just to decorate them. Label items clearly (avoiding symbols or keys that are hard to interpret), and don't add more detail than necessary.

In academic projects, be sure to label ("Fig.," "Table"), number, and caption your important graphic items, especially any that you mention in your text. Both MLA and APA style offer guidelines for handling labels; the APA rules are particularly detailed and specific.

Use tables to present statistical data. Tables can do all kinds of work. They are essential for organizing and recording information as it comes in, for example, daily weather events: temperature, precipitation, wind velocities, and so on. A table may also show trends or emphasize contrasts. In such cases, tables may make an argument (in a print ad, for example) or readers may be left to interpret complex data on their own—one of the pleasures of studying such material.

Tables typically consist of horizontal rows and vertical columns into which you drop data. The axes of the chart provide different and significant ways of presenting data, relating x to y: for example, in Table 1, lifetime earnings is connected to education level.

In designing a table, determine how many horizontal rows and vertical columns are needed, how to label them, and whether to use color or shading to enhance the readability of the data. Software will provide templates to suggest your options. Good tables can be very plain. In fact, many of the tables on federal government Web sites, though packed with information, are dirt simple and yet quite clear.

Table 1
Expected Lifetime Earnings Relative to High School Graduates, by Education Level

	Total Lifetime Earnings	Total Earnings Relative to High School Graduates	Present Value of Total Lifetime Earnings (3% Discount Rate)	Present Value Earnings Relative to HS Graduates (3% Discount Rate)
Not a High School Graduate	$941,370	0.74	$551,462	0.75
High School Graduate	1,266,730	1.00	738,609	1.00
Some College, No Degree	1,518,300	1.20	878,259	1.19
Associate Degree	1,620,730	1.28	943,181	1.28
Bachelor's Degree	2,054,380	1.62	1,189,836	1.61
Master's Degree	2,401,565	1.90	1,427,392	1.93
Doctoral Degree	3,073,240	2.43	1,748,716	2.37
Professional Degree	3,706,910	2.93	2,123,309	2.87
Bachelor's Degree or Higher	2,284,110	1.80	1,312,316	1.78

Sources: U.S. Census Bureau, 2006, PINC-03; calculations by the authors.

From College Board, *Education Pays: The Benefits of Higher Education for Individuals and Society*, 2007.

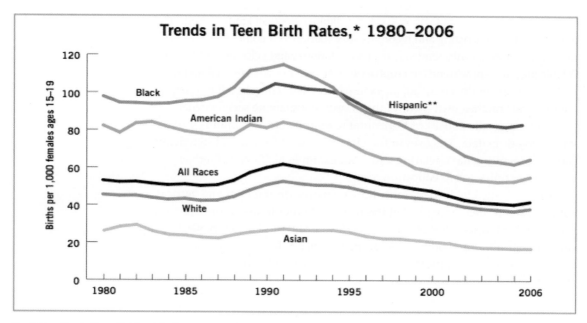

Fig. 1. Line Graph. From Children's Defense Fund, *The State of America's Children 2010* report.

Use line graphs to display changes or trends. Line graphs are dynamic images, visually plotting and connecting variables on horizontal *x*- and vertical *y*-axes so that readers can see how relationships change or trends emerge, usually over time. As such, line graphs often contribute to political or social arguments by tracking fluctuations in income, unemployment, educational attainment, stock prices, and so on.

Properly designed, line graphs are easy to read and informative, especially when just a single variable is presented. But it is possible to plot several items on an axis, complicating the line graph but increasing the amount of information it offers (see fig. 1).

Use bar and column graphs to plot relationships within sets of data. Column and bar graphs use rectangles to represent information either horizontally (bar graph) or vertically (column graph). In either form, these graphs emphasize differences and can show changes over time; they enable readers to grasp relationships that would otherwise take many words to explain. Bar and column graphs present data precisely, if their *x*- and *y*-axes are carefully drawn to scale. In Figure 2 , for example, a reader can determine the number of major tornadoes in any of more than fifty years and also note a slight trend toward fewer severe storms.

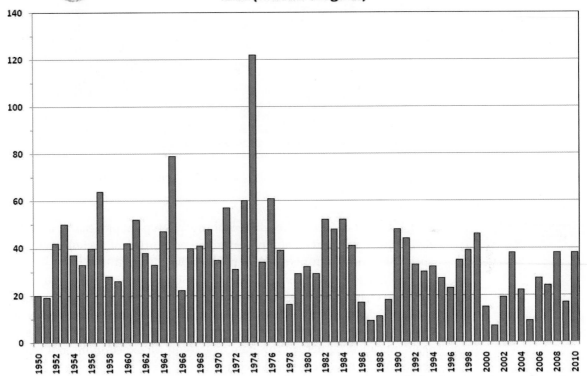

Number of Strong to Violent (EF3-EF5*)Tornadoes U.S. (March-August)

*Beginning in 2007, NOAA switched from the Fujita scale
to the Enhance Fujita scale for rating tornado strength.

Fig. 2. Number of Strong to Violent (EF3–EF5) Tornadoes. From NOAA Satellite and Information Service.

But it is easy to ask a single graphic image to do too much. For example, many readers probably find Figure 3 hard to interpret. Is the chart about the number of storms, their growing frequency, or their actual and adjusted costs? Storm effects in the background of the graphic just add to the clutter.

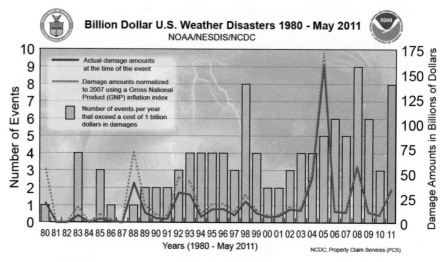

Fig. 3. Billion Dollar U.S. Weather Disasters 1980–2011. From NOAA Satellite and Information Service.

Use pie charts to display proportions.   A typical pie chart is a circle divided into segments that represent some proportion of a whole. While such charts do not display precise numbers well, they at least show which parts of a whole have greater or lesser significance. For instance, you could use a pie chart to depict the major categories of spending within the U.S. budget (defense, Social Security, Medicare, etc.). But since the segments in a typical pie chart need to total 100 percent, you would have to include a segment called "Other" in this item to account for expenditures not represented in the major categories (see fig. 4).

Pie-chart sections can be cut only so thin before they begin to lose clarity. If you wanted to use a pie chart to depict all significant federal outlays, you'd find yourself with thousands of slivers readers couldn't possibly distinguish. Better to transfer the data to a table, which could present each outlay in a separate row, page after page if necessary. A bar graph, too, might be able to handle more categories and translate data more effectively.

Use maps to display varying types of information.   Printed atlases or road maps deliver immense amounts of information, from the location and size of cities to the distances between them. But other kinds of data are now routinely laid atop geographic boundaries or displayed through technologies offered by services such as Google Maps. Everything from weather information to population movements (people, animals, plants) can be productively mapped.

Indeed, interactive technologies allow users to customize online maps to display just the information they want. The U.S. Bureau of Labor Statistics provides such a map to track employment statistics (see fig. 5). It is unlikely that you could produce a graphic this powerful, but it suggests options for presenting data.

Explore the possibilities of infographics.   People clearly enjoy using digital technologies to display information in groundbreaking ways. Under the rubric of "infographics," designers create data-driven visual texts about subjects from global warming to Halloween trends. One writer calls these focused presentations—freely combining charts, tables, timelines, maps, and other design elements—"visual essays." In some cases, infographics simply look like highly polished tables and charts (see fig. 6). But many presentations part ways with the academic conventions to tell livelier stories.

Various tools are available online to support the creation of infographics, including Many Eyes, Google Public Data Explorer, Wordle, and StatPlanet. For more about infographics and many examples, search the term online.

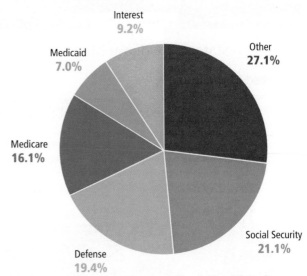

Federal Spending 2007
Actual fiscal year ended Oct. 31

Fig. 4. Fiscal Spending 2007. From Congressional Budget Office.

Fig. 5. Quarterly Census of Employment and Wages (QCEW) State and County Map. From U.S. Bureau of Labor Statistics, 2010.

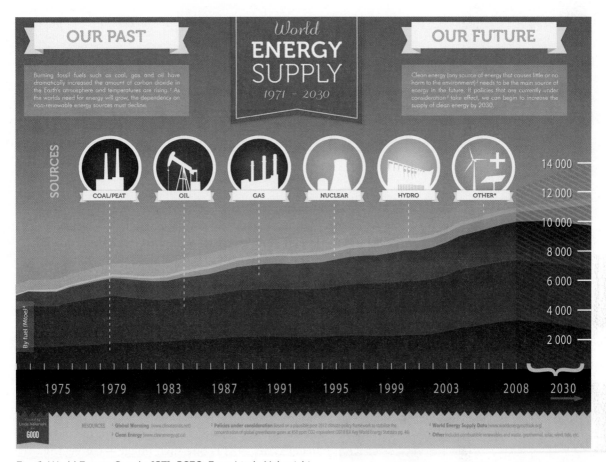

Fig. 6. World Energy Supply, 1971–2030. From Linda Nakanishi.

Your Turn   Examine Figure 6, "World Energy Supply," and then look online for additional examples of infographics. (They are readily available on sites such as VizWorld or Cool Infographics.) When you have sampled enough such items to have a sense of what the genre does, try to define the term "infographics" on your own. What do these charts have in common? What are their distinctive features?

54 Designing Print and Online Documents

think visually

Much advice about good visual design is common sense: You could guess that most academic and professional documents should look uncluttered, consistent, and balanced. But it is not always simple to translate abstract principles into practice. Nor are any visual qualities absolute. A balanced and consistent design is exactly what you want for research reports and government documents, but to create brochures or infographics, you may need more snap.

Understand the power of images. Most of us realize how powerful images can be, particularly when they perfectly capture a moment or make an argument that words alone struggle to express. The famous "Blue Marble" shot of the Earth taken by *Apollo 17* in 1972 is one such image—conveying both the wonder and fragility of our planet hanging in space. A very curious image of Osama bin Laden (see p. 593) had a similarly transformative (if much less memorable) impact in the summer of 2011, depicting, for our time, the banality of evil.

How do you diminish the ethos of an enemy like Osama bin Laden? Release a photo of him watching himself on TV. That's what the U.S. government did shortly after a team of Navy Seals killed the al-Qaeda leader in Pakistan in May 2011.

Visual texts can become potent tools in your own work. Use photographs to tell arresting stories or underscore important points. Videos can bring energy or provide visual evidence for an argument. And you can shape the visual elements of any page or screen—its colors, shapes, headings, type fonts, and so on—to make a text more appealing, focused, and accessible.

Keep page designs simple and uncluttered.   Simple doesn't mean a design should be simplistic, only that you shouldn't try to do more on a page than it (or your design skills) can handle. You want readers to find information they need, navigate your document without missteps, and grasp the structure of your project. Key information should stand out. If you keep the basic design uncomplicated, you can present lots of information without a page feeling cluttered.

Consider, for example, how cleverly Anthro Technology Furniture uses design cues as simple as *Step 1*, *Step 2*, and *Step 3* to guide consumers on a Web page through the complex process of configuring a workstation. Readers simply move left to right across a page, making specific choices. They don't feel overwhelmed by the options, even though the material is detailed.

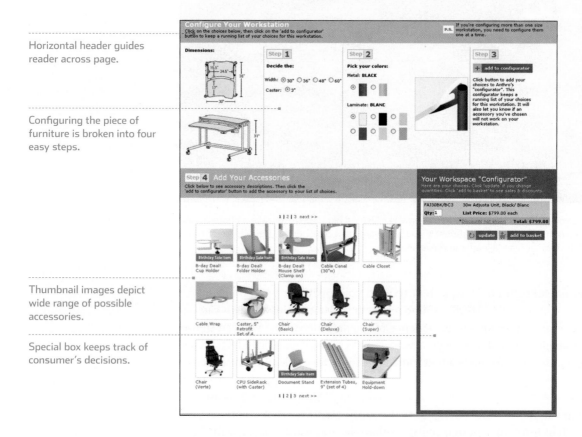

Horizontal header guides reader across page.

Configuring the piece of furniture is broken into four easy steps.

Thumbnail images depict wide range of possible accessories.

Special box keeps track of consumer's decisions.

Keep the design logical and consistent.   Readers need to be able to perceive the logic of a design quickly and then see those principles operating in elements throughout a document—especially on Web sites, in PowerPoint presentations, and in long papers.

Look to successful Web sites for models of logical and consistent design. Many sites build their pages around distinct horizontal and vertical columns that help readers locate information. A main menu generally appears near the top of the page, more detailed navigational links are usually found in a narrow side column, and featured stories often appear in wide columns in the center. To separate columns as well as individual items, the site designers use headlines, horizontal rules, images, or some combination of these devices. Handled well, pages are easy to navigate and thick with information, yet somehow seem uncluttered.

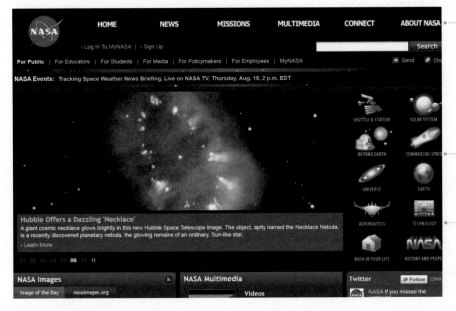

NASA home page

NASA's information-rich page has consistent horizontal orientation. The eye moves left to right to explore major options. Yet distinct horizontal sections also break the page into visually coherent segments.

Images are carefully aligned to convey information appealingly.

Full screen (not reproduced here) offers more than sixty links or options. Color scheme throughout the site is consistent: black, blue, and gray. Perhaps suggesting the vastness of space?

Keep the design balanced.   Think of balance as a dynamic term—what you hope to achieve *overall* in a design. You probably don't want many pages that, if split down the middle, would show mirror images. Strive for active designs, in which, for example, a large photograph on one side of a document is countered on the other by blocks of print and maybe several smaller images. The overall effect achieved is symmetry, even though the individual page elements may all differ in size and shape.

You can see conventional design principles at work on the front pages of most newspapers (print or online), where editors try to come up with a look that gives impact to the news. They have many elements to work with, including their paper's masthead, headlines of varying size, photographs and images, columns of copy, screened boxes, and much more. The pages of a newspaper can teach you a lot about design.

But you can learn, too, from the boundaries being pushed by designers of Web infographics (see Chapter 53), which use elaborate media effects to present information efficiently yet imaginatively. Unlike newspapers, magazines, or full Web sites, which must follow consistent specifications for page after page, a typical infographic focuses on a single theme or subject and chooses media tools best suited to the topic, whether graphs, flowcharts, maps, images, diagrams, or cutaways.

Use templates sensibly.   If you have the time and talent to design all of your own documents, that's terrific. But for many projects, you could do worse than to begin with the templates offered by many software products. The Project Gallery in Microsoft Office, for example, helps you create business letters, brochures, PowerPoint presentations, and more. It sets up a generic document, placing the document's margins, aligning key elements and graphics, and offering an array of customizations. No two projects based on the same template need look alike.

Colin Harman uses a simple Venn diagram to organize this infographic on design.

If you resist borrowing such materials from software, not wanting yet another part of your life packaged by corporate types, know that it is tough to design documents from scratch. Even if you intend to design an item yourself, consider examining a template to figure out how to assemble a complex document. Take what you learn from the model and then strike out on your own.

Front page of *The Plain Dealer*, March 29, 2011

To attract readers, a teaser for a sports story tops the simple masthead.

On the fold, a large image of President Obama dominates the page.

A full column with graphics in color summarizes the day's coverage and adds visual interest.

Local stories frame the page, their importance signaled by placement and headline size.

A story in a widened column is previewed by three parallel subheadings, adding variety to the design.

Why LeBron's game has changed; Cavs-Heat preview SPORTS

THE PLAIN DEALER

MORE THAN 1.3 MILLION READERS IN PRINT AND ON CLEVELAND.COM WEEKLY | 75¢ NEWSSTAND   56¢ HOME DELIVERY

TUESDAY, MARCH 29, 2011
★★★★

Cleveland to seek rate hikes of up to 82 percent for water

MARK GILLISPIE
Plain Dealer Reporter

The Cleveland Water Department wants to increase rates 82 percent over the next 4½ years for city residents and around 50 percent for suburban customers.

Mayor Frank Jackson's administration presented the proposed rates to City Council on Monday. The legislation is scheduled to be introduced Monday and is expected to draw criticism from suburban mayors who are angry about chronic billing and customer-service problems.

To address falling revenues and

declining consumption, the department proposes to make the bulk of the increase a fixed fee charged to all customers regardless of how much water they use.

The proposed increase calls for increasing the current 87 quarterly fee for residential customers to $18 starting July 1. It would remain at $18 next year and then increase $3 annually starting in 2013. Customers also would see increases in the amount charged for water use starting in 2012.

For many customers the water bills would probably kick in at the same time as increases in their sewer bills.

The regional sewer district, citing $3.3

billion in improvements required by the U.S. Environmental Protection Agency, wants to raise fees 75 percent by 2016. Average suburban residential customers would see their quarterly sewer bills go from $90 this year to $157 in 2016.

Cleveland's Water Department serves 1.3 million customers in 70 communities in five counties.

Jackson and his administration have said the water department needs to raise rates because of declining usage, higher costs and a requirement that its net revenues exceed the cost of its annual payments on $1.1 billion in debt.

Map inside
Check out the Cleveland Water Department's proposed rate hike for your community. A4

SEE WATER | A4

CRISIS IN COUNTY GOVERNMENT

Money manager charged with bribes

Dimora got Tiki hut, prosecutors say

PETER KROUSE
Plain Dealer Reporter

Money manager Charles Randazzo tried to bribe Jimmy Dimora with money for an artificial palm tree, prosecutors say, but what the then-Cuyahoga County commissioner really wanted was a Tiki hut.

And that's what he got, according to federal charges filed Monday against Randazzo, founder of Financial Network of America in Twinsburg, in connection with the ongoing public probe of corruption in county government.

Prosecutors claim Randazzo gave gifts to Dimora and then-County Auditor Frank Russo in exchange for their help getting Randazzo's company selected as a provider of deferred compensation services for county employees.

Randazzo plans to plead guilty, according to his attorney, Richard Weinberg. Russo has pleaded guilty to taking bribes and other crimes. Dimora is expected to contest 36 corruption-related crimes in a trial later this year.

Prosecutors state that between 2000 and 2009, Russo introduced Randazzo to a county employee with a connection to the payroll department and that helped Financial Network of America get in the door.

Also in 2004, Randazzo gave $1,079.14 each to Dimora and Russo toward the purchase of artificial palm trees for their backyards, according to the charges.

Two months later, Dimora voted in favor of Financial Network of America being added as a provider of deferred compensation services for the county. Deferred compensation is similar to a 401(k) retirement plan in that money is taken out of an employee's pay before taxes and invested in various ways.

The following spring, according to prosecutors, Dimora took the money for the palm tree and bought a Tiki hut instead.

SEE CRISIS | A4

OBAMA ON LIBYA

Not to act would have been 'a betrayal of who we are'

President Barack Obama said in a speech to the nation Monday night from the National Defense University in Washington that he had made good on his promise to limit U.S. military involvement against longtime Libyan leader Moammar Gadhafi's forces.

MANUEL BALCE CENETA | ASSOCIATED PRESS

Why we went in:
We had a moral imperative to stop Moammar Gadhafi's deadly advance

It won't expand:
With NATO's takeover we can quickly shift to a supporting role

When we'll leave:
The president offered no estimate of when the conflict might end

HELEN COOPER | *New York Times*

President Barack Obama defended the U.S.-led military assault in Libya on Monday, saying it was in the national interest of the United States to stop a potential massacre that would have "stained the conscience of the world." ¶ In his first major address since ordering U.S. airstrikes on the forces and artillery of Moammar Gadhafi nine days ago, Obama said the United States had the responsibility and the international backing to stop what he characterized as a looming genocide in the Libyan city of Benghazi. ¶ The president declared that the United States intervened in Libya to prevent a slaughter of civilians that would have stained the world's conscience and "been a betrayal of who we are" as Americans. ¶ But at the same time, he said, directing U.S. troops to forcibly remove Gadhafi from power would be a step too far and would "splinter" the international coalition that has moved against the Libyan government.

SEE OBAMA | A3

City bill would offer domestic partners health benefits

Measure has support, Cimperman says

PAT GALBINCEA
Plain Dealer Reporter

Cleveland Councilman Joe Cimperman says he has enough support for an ordinance he introduced Monday night that will give health care benefits to domestic partners of city employees.

But he said he also knows it will be a hard sell to those councilmen who oppose the plan.

About 120 unmarried couples are

on the city's domestic partner registry, which was first made available in May 2009. Those registering had to show they were sharing expenses on a long-term basis, such as a mortgage or utility bills, to ensure their authenticity.

The registry, which passed in late 2008 as a means of getting insurance, also created a stir. Soon after council adopted it 13-7, several local pastors, led by the Rev. C.J. Matthews of Mount Sinai Baptist Church, banded together to repeal it. They circulated petitions, needing to collect about 11,000 signatures to put the issue to a citywide vote.

But the effort fell way short of the goal.

Rev. Matthews did not return calls Monday.

The Rev. Marvin McMickle of Antioch Baptist Church in Cleveland, who said he is not fond of same-sex marriages, said he is not opposed to the domestic partners law that would give them health care benefits.

Registering does not guarantee any rights or mean a couple is legally married.

Cimperman said 10 council members are co-sponsoring the ordinance. He also said three others will vote for it, "so we have more than enough support to get this passed." He said Council President Martin J.

Swensey has agreed to the debate.

"But I always anticipate a hard sell," he said. "You take nothing for granted in the legislative process."

Council members were expected to assign the ordinance to at least one city committee, and Cimperman said as many as three — the finance, health and employment, and legislative committees — could consider its merits.

Cimperman said major firms like the Cleveland Clinic and Medical Mutual already offer health care to their domestic partner employees, and he said the city should follow suit.

SEE CITY | A4

Today's News

NATION&WORLD

Contaminated water leaking from Japanese reactor
Highly contaminated water is escaping from a damaged reactor at the crippled nuclear power plant in Japan and could soon leak into the ocean, the country's nuclear regulator warned. **Details, A4**

METRO

Changes made in SB 5 proposal
The latest version of Senate Bill 5 — a Republican-backed plan that would reduce collective bargaining rights — will be unveiled today with nearly a dozen changes, including modifications that could address concerns police and fire unions have raised. **Details, B1**

Promise progress: Gov. John Kasich promised to eliminate prevailing wage rules on public construction projects. PolitiFact Ohio puts the Kasich-O-Meter to work to see if the governor has made any strides toward that goal. **Details, B1**

PolitiFact Ohio

BUSINESS

MARVIN FONG | THE PLAIN DEALER

Boosting the West Side Market
A nonprofit group's report says the West Side Market needs significant repairs, swifter maintenance and better parking. And customers need to know that vendors will be open during posted hours. **Details, C1**

Goodrich jobs: A Goodrich Landing Gear factory in Cleveland may be in danger of closing, and city, county and state officials will meet with company executives this week. The city also wants to save 600 jobs here from a Goodrich facility in Canada. **Details, C1**

Big payday: Warren Buffett's $9 billion takeover of Lubrizol in Wickliffe will reward Chief Executive Officer James Hambrick with about $97 million in cash tied to his equity-based compensation. **Details, C1**

SPORTS

Players sweat out final cuts
Four players are fighting for the Indians' last three roster spots. Terry Pluto talks with them about what it feels like to sweat out the final cuts in Tribe camp. **Details, D1**

Kickoff rule backlash: One of the Browns' best special teams players isn't named Josh Cribbs is also against the new NFL rules on kickoffs. "It's football. You're gonna have collisions," Nick Sorensen says. **Details, D1**

Tribe essay contest: With the new Indians' season opening Friday, we asked readers to tell us their best memory of attending a game. Today, we present one of the five finalists, Matthew J. Kirlough of Valley City. **Details, D3**

HEALTH

Health reform's stickiest point
One of the big health care reform battles is over a single provision: that we must buy health insurance or pay a fine. Reporter Diane Suchetka explains what the law really says, and what it means to you. **Details, E1**

4-HOUR FORECAST

Full report: **B6** or cleveland.com/weather

6 a.m.	10 a.m.	2 p.m.	6	10	2 a.m.
21°	30°	37°	37°	30°	27°

Today: Chilly with sun mixing with clouds.
Precipitation: 0% morning, 5% afternoon.

To subscribe, call 1-888-559-7555

Coordinate your colors.   Your mother was right: Pay attention to colors and patterns when you dress and when you design color documents. To learn elementary principles of color coordination, try searching "color wheel" on the Web, but recognize that the subject is both complicated and more art than science. As an amateur, keep your design palettes relatively conventional and model your work on documents that you find particularly attractive.

For academic papers, the text is always black and the background is white. Color is fine in graphs and illustrations if the paper will be reviewed onscreen or printed in color. But be sure that no important elements are lost if the document is printed in black and white: A bar graph that relies on color to display differences might become unreadable. For Web sites and other projects, keep background colors light, if you use them at all, and maintain adequate contrast between text and background. Avoid either bright or pale fonts for passages of text.

Use headings if needed.   Readers appreciate headings as pathways through a text. In academic work, they should be descriptive rather than clever. If you have prepared a good scratch or topic outline, the major points may provide you with almost ready-made headings. ○ Like items in an outline, headings at the same level in a project should be roughly parallel in style. ○

A short paper (three to five pages) doesn't require much more than a title. For longer papers (ten to twenty pages), it's possible to use top-level items from your outline as headings. For some projects, especially in the sciences, you must use the headings you're given. This is especially true for lab reports and scientific articles, and you shouldn't vary from the template.

Choose appropriate fonts.   There are likely dozens or even hundreds of fonts to work with on your computer, but, as with most other design elements, simple is generally best. Here is some basic information to help you choose the best font for your needs.

Serif fonts, such as Century, show thin flares and embellishments (called serifs; circled in the illustration on p. 599) at the tops and bottoms of their

order ideas p. 408   help with common
                         errors p. 600

letters and characters. These fonts have a traditional look: Note the news-paper masthead on page 597. In contrast, *sans serif* fonts, such as Helvetica, lack the decorations of serif fonts. They are smoother and more contempo-rary. For an example, see "Why we went in:" page 597.

Serif fonts are more readable than sans serif for extended passages of writing, such as papers. Headings in a sans serif font often contrast well in a document using serif-font text. Some designers prefer sans serif fonts for Web sites and PowerPoint presentations, especially for headings and smaller items.

Display and decorative fonts are designed to attract attention. Avoid them for academic and professional writing, but you may want to explore their use when creating posters, brochures, or special PowerPoint presentations. Beyond the few words of a heading, display fonts are hard to read: Never use them for extended passages of writing.

For typical academic projects, all text, headings, and other elements—including the title—are set in one font size, either 10 or 12 point. The standard font is Times New Roman. In professional or business projects, such as résumés, newsletters, or PowerPoint slides, you'll need to vary type sizes to distinguish headings, captions, and headlines from other elements. Examine your pages carefully in the draft stage to see that there is a balance between the larger and smaller fonts. The impact of a résumé in particular can be diluted by headings that overwhelm the career data. Be careful, too, with smaller sizes. Some fonts look crowded (and strain eyesight) if they dip below 10 points.

Boldfaced items stand out clearly on a page but only if they are rare. Too many boldfaced headings close together and your page looks heavy and cluttered. Of course, you should not use boldface as the regular text through-out your project. If you want an emphatic font, find one that looks that way in its regular form.

Century

Century, a serif font.

Helvetica

Helvetica, a sans serif font.

Common Errors

part nine

55 Capitalization

Spring or
spring?

In principle, the guidelines for capitalizing seem straightforward. You surely know to capitalize most proper nouns (and the proper adjectives formed from them), book and movie titles, the first words of sentences, and so on. But the fact is that you make many judgment calls when capitalizing, some of which will require a dictionary. (Ask your instructor if he or she can advise you on a good one.) Here are just a few of the special cases that can complicate your editing.

Capitalize the names of ethnic, religious, and political groups.   The names of these groups are considered proper nouns. Nonspecific groups, however, are lowercase.

South Korean	Native Americans	native peoples
Buddhists	Muslims	true believers
Tea Party	Democrats	political parties
the Bay City Council		the city council

Capitalize modifiers formed from proper nouns.   In some cases, such as *french fry*, the expressions have become so common that the adjective does not need to be capitalized. When in doubt, consult a dictionary.

PROPER NOUN	PROPER NOUN USED AS MODIFIER
French	French thought
Navajo	Navajo rug
Jew	Jewish lore
American	American history

Capitalize all words in titles except prepositions, articles, or conjunctions.   This is the basic rule for the titles of books, movies, long poems, and so on.

Dickens and the Dream of Cinema

In the Company of Cheerful Ladies

The variations and exceptions to this general rule, however, are numerous. MLA style specifies that the first and last words in titles always be capitalized, including any articles or prepositions.

The Guide to National Parks of the Southwest

To the Lighthouse

Such Stuff as Dreams Are Made Of

APA style doesn't make that qualification, but does specify that all words longer than four letters be capitalized in titles—even prepositions.

A Walk Among the Tombstones

Sleeping Through the Night and Other Lies

In all major styles, any word following a colon (or, much rarer, a dash) in a title is capitalized, even an article or preposition:

True Blood: All Together Now

The Exile: An Outlander Graphic Novel

Finally, note that in APA style *documentation*—that is, within the notes and on the references page, titles are capitalized differently. Only the first word in most titles, any proper nouns or adjectives, and any word following a colon are capitalized. All other words are in lowercase:

Bat predation and the evolution of frog vocalizations in the neotropics

Human aging: Usual and successful

Take care with compass points, directions, and specific geo-graphical areas.   Points of the compass and simple directions are not capitalized when referring to general locations.

north	southwest
northern Ohio	eastern Canada
southern exposure	western horizons

But these same terms *are* capitalized when they refer to specific regions that are geographically, culturally, or politically significant (keep that dictionary handy!). Such terms are often preceded by the definite article, *the*.

the West	the Old South
the Third Coast	Southern California
Middle Eastern politics	the Western allies

Understand academic conventions.   Academic degrees are not capitalized, except when abbreviated.

bachelor of arts	doctor of medicine
MA	PhD

Specific course titles are capitalized, but they are lowercase when used as general subjects. Exception: Languages are always capitalized when referring to academic subjects.

Art History 101	Contemporary British Poetry
an art history course	an English literature paper

Capitalize months, days, holidays, and historical periods.   But don't capitalize the seasons.

January	winter
Monday	spring
Halloween	summer
the Enlightenment	fall

Apostrophes  56

Like gnats, apostrophes are small and irritating. They have two major functions: to signal that a noun is possessive and to indicate where letters have been left out in contractions. Apostrophes always need careful review.

Use apostrophes to form the possessive.   The basic rules for forming the possessive aren't complicated: For singular nouns, add 's to the end of the word:

> the wolf's lair
> the woman's portfolio
> IBM's profits
> Bush's foreign policy

Some possessives, while correct, look or sound awkward. In these cases, try an alternative:

ORIGINAL	REVISED
the class's photo	the class photo; the photo of the class
Bright Eyes's latest single	the latest single by Bright Eyes
in Kansas's budget	in the Kansas budget; in the budget of Kansas

it's or *its*?

For plural nouns that do not end in *s*, also add *'s* to the end of the word:

   men's shoes   the mice's cages   the geese's nemesis

For plural nouns that do end in *s*, add an apostrophe after that terminal *s*:

   the wolves' pups

   the Bushes' foreign policies

   three senators' votes

Use apostrophes in contractions.   An apostrophe in a contraction takes the place of missing letters. Edit carefully, keeping in mind that a spell-checker doesn't help you with such blunders. It catches only words that make no sense without apostrophes, such as *dont* or *Ive*.

DRAFT	Its a shame that its come to this.
CORRECTED	It's (It is) a shame that it's (it has) come to this.

DRAFT	Whose got the list of whose going on the trip?
CORRECTED	Who's (Who has) got the list of who's (who is) going on the trip?

Don't use apostrophes with possessive pronouns.   The following possessives do not take apostrophes: *its, whose, his, hers, ours, yours,* and *theirs.*

DRAFT	We photographed the tower at it's best angle.
CORRECTED	We photographed the tower at its best angle.

DRAFT	The book is her's, not his.
CORRECTED	The book is hers, not his.

DRAFT	Their's may be an Oscar-winning film, but our's is still better.
CORRECTED	Theirs may be an Oscar-winning film, but ours is still better.

There is, inevitably, an exception. Indefinite pronouns such as *everybody, anybody, nobody,* and so on do show possession via *'s.*

   The film was everybody's favorite.

   Why it was so successful is anybody's guess.

Commas 57

The comma has more uses than any other punctuation mark—uses that can often seem complex. The following guidelines will help you handle commas in academic writing.

Use a comma and a coordinating conjunction to join two independent clauses.   An independent clause can stand on its own as a sentence. To join two of them, you need both a coordinating conjunction *and* a comma. A comma alone is not enough.

> Fiona's car broke down. She had to walk two miles to the train station.
>
> Fiona's car broke down, so she had to walk two miles to the train station.

There are several key points to remember here. Be sure you truly have two independent clauses, and not just a compound subject or verb. Also, make certain to include both a comma and a coordinating conjunction (*and, but, for, nor, or, so, yet*). Leaving out the coordinating conjunction creates an error known as a comma splice (see p. 610).

Use a comma after an introductory word group.   Introductory word groups are descriptive phrases or clauses that open a

need to
connect
ideas?

sentence. Separate these introductions from the main part of the sentence with a comma.

> Within two years of getting a degree in journalism, Ishan was writing for the *Wall Street Journal*.

For very brief introductory phrases, the comma may be omitted, but it is not wrong to leave it in.

> After college I plan to join the Marines.
> After college, I plan to join the Marines.

Use commas with transitional words and phrases. Transitional expressions such as *however* and *for example* should be set off within a sentence by a pair of commas.

> These fans can be among the first, however, to clamor for a new stadium to boost their favorite franchise.

If a transitional word or phrase opens a sentence, it should be followed by a comma.

> Moreover, studies have shown that trans fats can lower the amount of good cholesterol found in the body.

Put commas around nonrestrictive (that is, nonessential) elements. You'll know that a word or phrase is functioning as a nonrestrictive modifier if you can remove it from the sentence without destroying the overall meaning of the sentence.

> Cicero, ancient Rome's greatest orator and lawyer, was a self-made man.
> Cicero was a self-made man.

The second sentence is less informative, but still makes sense. See also the guideline on page 609, "Do not use commas to set off restrictive elements."

Use commas to separate items in a series. Commas are necessary when you have three or more items in a series.

> American highways were once ruled by powerful muscle cars such as Mustangs, GTOs, and Camaros.

Do not use commas to separate compound verbs.   Don't confuse a true compound sentence (with two independent clauses) with a sentence that simply has two verbs.

> DRAFT   They rumbled through city streets, and smoked down drag strips.
>
> CORRECTED   They rumbled through city streets and smoked down drag strips.

They rumbled through city streets is an independent clause, but *and smoked down drag strips* is not, because it doesn't have a subject. To join the two verbs, use *and* with no comma. If you have three or more verbs, however, treat them as items in a series and do separate them with commas.

> Muscle cars guzzled gasoline, burned rubber, and drove parents crazy.

Do not use a comma between subject and verb.   Perhaps it's obvious why such commas don't work when you try one in a short sentence.

> Keeping focused, can be difficult.

When a subject gets long and complicated, you might be more tempted to insert the comma, but it would still be both unnecessary and wrong. The comma in the following sentence should be omitted.

> Keeping focused on driving while simultaneously trying to operate a cell phone, can be difficult.

Do not use commas to set off restrictive elements.   Phrases you cannot remove from a sentence without significantly altering meaning are called *restrictive* or *essential*. They are modifiers that provide information needed to understand the subject.

> Only nation that recognize a right to free speech and free press should be eligible for seats on international human rights commissions.
>
> Students who have a perfect attendance record will earn three points for class participation.

Delete the highlighted phrases in the above examples and you are left with sentences that are vague or confusing. Put commas around the phrases and you create the false impression that they could be removed.

58 Comma Splices, Run-ons, and Fragments

need a complete sentence?

The sentence errors marked most often in college writing are comma splices, run-ons, and fragments.

Identify comma splices and run-ons. A *comma splice* occurs when only a comma is used to join two independent clauses (an independent clause contains a complete subject and verb).

Identify a comma splice simply by reading the clauses on either side of a doubtful comma. If *both* clauses stand on their own as sentences (with their own subjects and verbs), it's a comma splice.

COMMA SPLICES
Officials at many elementary schools are trying to reduce childhood obesity on their campuses, research suggests that few of their strategies will work.

Some schools emphasize a need for more exercise, others have even gone so far as to reinstate recess.

A *run-on* sentence is similar to a comma splice, but it doesn't even include the comma to let readers take a break between independent clauses. The clauses bump together, confusing readers.

RUN-ON SENTENCES
Officials at many elementary schools are trying to reduce childhood obesity on their campuses research suggests that few of their strategies will work.

Some schools emphasize a need for more exercise others have even gone so far as to reinstate recess.

Fix comma splices and run-ons.   To fix comma splices and run-ons, you can include a comma and a coordinating conjunction after the first independent clause to join it with the second clause.

Common Coordinating
Conjunctions

and	or
but	so
for	yet
nor	

> Officials at many elementary schools are trying to reduce childhood obesity on their campuses, **but** research suggests that few of their strategies will work.

> Some schools emphasize a need for more exercise, **and** others have even gone so far as to reinstate recess.

Or you can use a semicolon to join the two clauses.

> Officials at many elementary schools are trying to reduce childhood obesity on their campuses; research suggests that few of their strategies will work.

> Some schools emphasize a need for more exercise; others have even gone so far as to reinstate recess.

Less frequently, colons or dashes may be used if the second clause summarizes or illustrates the main point of the first clause.

> Some schools have taken extreme measures: They have banned cookies, snacks, and other high-calorie foods from their vending machines.

Along with the semicolon (or colon or dash), you may wish to add a transitional word or phrase (such as *however* or *in fact*). If you do so, set off the transitional word or phrase with commas. O

> Officials at many elementary schools are trying to reduce childhood obesity on their campuses; research, **however,** suggests that few of their strategies will work.

> Some schools emphasize a need for more exercise—**in fact,** some have even gone so far as to reinstate recess.

You can also rewrite the sentence to make one of the clauses subordinate. Using a subordinating conjunction, revise so that one of the clauses in the sentence can no longer stand as a sentence on its own.

Common Subordinating
Conjunctions

after	once
although	since
as	that
because	though
before	unless
except	until
if	when

> **Although** officials at many elementary schools are trying to reduce childhood obesity on their campuses, research suggests that few of their strategies will work.

connect ideas
p. 416

Or use end punctuation to create two independent sentences.

> Officials at many elementary schools are trying to reduce childhood obesity on their campuses. Research suggests that few of their strategies will work.

Identify sentence fragments.   A sentence fragment is a word group that lacks a subject, verb, or possibly both. As such, it is not a complete sentence and is not appropriate for most academic and professional writing.

FRAGMENT   Climatologists see much physical evidence of climate change. **Especially in the receding of glaciers around the world.**

Fix sentence fragments in your work.   You have two options for fixing sentence fragments. Attach the fragment to a nearby sentence:

COMPLETE SENTENCE   Climatologists see much physical evidence of climate change, especially in the receding of glaciers around the world.

Turn the fragment into its own sentence:

COMPLETE SENTENCE   Climatologists see much physical evidence of climate change. They are especially concerned by the receding of glaciers around the world.

Watch for fragments in the following situations.   Often a fragment will follow a complete sentence and start with a subordinating conjunction.

FRAGMENT   Climate change seems to be the product of human activity. **Though some scientists believe sun cycles may explain the changing climate.**

COMPLETE SENTENCE   Climate change seems to be the product of human activity, though some scientists believe sun cycles may explain the changing climate.

Participles (such as *breaking, seeking, finding*) and infinitives (such as *to break, to seek, to find*) can also lead you into fragments.

FRAGMENT   Of course, many people welcome the warmer weather. Upsetting scientists who fear governments will not act until global warming becomes irreversible.

COMPLETE SENTENCE Of course, many people welcome the warmer weather. Their attitude upsets scientists who fear governments will not act until global warming becomes irreversible.

Use deliberate fragments only in appropriate situations. You'll find that fragments are common in advertising, fiction, and informal writing. In personal e-mail or on social networking sites, for example, expressions or clichés such as the following would likely be acceptable to your audience.

In your dreams. Excellent!

Not on your life. When pigs fly.

Subject/Verb Agreement

none are or
none is?

Verbs take many forms to express changing tenses, moods, and voices. To avoid common errors in choosing the correct verb form, follow these guidelines.

Be sure the verb agrees with its real subject.   It's tempting to link a verb to the nouns closest to it (in dark red below) instead of the subject, but that's a mistake.

DRAFT   Cameras and professional lenses that cost as much as a small **car** makes photography an expensive hobby.

CORRECTED   Cameras and professional lenses that cost as much as a small car make photography an expensive hobby.

DRAFT   Bottled water from convenience **stores** or **groceries** usually cost far more per ounce than gasoline.

CORRECTED   Bottled water from convenience stores or groceries usually costs far more per ounce than gasoline.

Some indefinite pronouns are exceptions to this rule. See the chart on page 615.

Indefinite Pronouns		
Singular	**Plural**	**Variable**
anybody	both	all
anyone	few	any
anything	many	more
each	others	most
everybody	several	none
everyone		some
everything		
nobody		
no one		
nothing		
one		
somebody		
someone		
something		

In most cases, treat multiple subjects joined by *and* as plural. But when a subject with *and* clearly expresses a single notion, that subject is singular.

> Hip-hop, rock, and country are dominant forms of popular music today. [subject is plural]

> Blues and folk have their fans too. [subject is plural]

> Peanut butter and jelly is the sandwich of choice in our house. [subject is singular]

> Rock and roll often strikes a political chord. [subject is singular]

When singular subjects are followed by expressions such as *along with,* *together with,* or *as well as,* the subjects may feel plural, but technically they remain singular.

DRAFT   Esperanza Spalding, as well as Drake, Justin Bieber, Florence & the Machine, and Mumford & Sons, were competing for Best New Artist at the 2011 Grammys.

CORRECTED   Esperanza Spalding, as well as Drake, Justin Bieber, Florence & the Machine, and Mumford & Sons, was competing for Best New Artist at the 2011 Grammys.

If the corrected version sounds awkward, try revising the sentence.

CORRECTED   Esperanza Spalding, Drake, Justin Bieber, Florence & the Machine, and Mumford & Sons were all competing for Best New Artist at the 2011 Grammys.

When compound subjects are linked by *either . . . or* or *neither . . . nor,* make the verb agree with the nearer part of the subject.   Knowing this rule will make you one person among a thousand.

Neither my sisters nor my mother is a fan of Kanye West.

When possible, put the plural part of the subject closer to the verb to make it sound less awkward.

Neither my mother nor my sisters are fans of Kanye West.

Confirm whether an indefinite pronoun is singular, plural, or variable.   Most indefinite pronouns are singular, but consult the chart on page 615 to double-check.

Everybody complains about politics, but nobody does much about it.

Each of the women expects a promotion.

Something needs to be done about the budget crisis.

A few indefinite pronouns are obviously plural: *both, few, many, others, several.*

Many complain about politics, but few do much about it.

And some indefinite pronouns shift in number, depending on the prepositional phrases that modify them.

> All of the votes **are** in the ballot box.
> All of the fruit **is** spoiled.

> Most of the rules **are** less complicated.
> Most of the globe **is** covered by oceans.

> None of the rules **makes** sense.
> On the Security Council, **none** but the Russians **favor** the resolution.

Be consistent with collective nouns.   Many of these words describing a group can be treated as either singular or plural: *band, class, jury, choir, group, committee.*

> The **jury seems** to resent the lawyer's playing to its emotions.
> The **jury seem** to resent the lawyer's playing to their emotions.

> The **band was** unhappy with its latest release.
> The **band were** unhappy with their latest release.

A basic principle is to be consistent throughout a passage. If *the band* is singular the first time you mention it, keep it that way for the remainder of the project. Be sensible too. If a sentence sounds odd to your ear, modify it:

AWKWARD   The **band were** unhappy with their latest release.
BETTER   The **members** of the band **were** unhappy with their latest release.

60 Irregular Verbs

Verbs are considered regular if they form the past and past participle—which you use to form various tenses—simply by adding -*d* or -*ed* to the base of the verb. Below are several regular verbs.

lie or *lay*?

Base Form	Past Tense	Past Participle
smile	smiled	smiled
accept	accepted	accepted
manage	managed	managed

Unfortunately, the most common verbs in English are irregular. The chart on page 619 lists some of them. When in doubt about the proper form of a verb, check a dictionary.

Base Form	Past Tense	Past Participle
be	was, were	been
become	became	become
break	broke	broken
buy	bought	bought
choose	chose	chosen
come	came	come
dive	dived, dove	dived
do	did	done
drink	drank	drunk
drive	drove	driven
eat	ate	eaten
get	got	gotten
give	gave	given
go	went	gone
have	had	had
lay (to put or place)	laid	laid
lie (to recline)	lay	lain
ride	rode	ridden
ring	rang, rung	rung
rise	rose	risen
see	saw	seen
set	set	set
shine	shone, shined	shone, shined
sing	sang, sung	sung
sink	sank, sunk	sunk
speak	spoke	spoken
swear	swore	sworn
throw	threw	thrown
wake	woke, waked	woken, waked
write	wrote	written

Pronoun/Antecedent Agreement

61

their or *his*
or *hers*?

You already know that pronouns take the place of nouns. Antecedents are the words pronouns refer to. Since pronouns in their many forms stand in for nouns, they also share some of the same markers, such as gender and number.

SINGULAR/FEMININE   The **nun** merely smiled because **she** had taken a vow of silence.

SINGULAR/MASCULINE   The **NASCAR champion** complained that **he** got little media attention.

SINGULAR/NEUTER   The **chess team** took **itself** too seriously.

PLURAL   **Members** of the chess team took **themselves** too seriously.

PLURAL   **They** seemed awfully subdued for **pro athletes**.

PLURAL   The **bridge and groom** wrote **their** own ditzy vows.

PLURAL   **Many** in the terminal resented searches of **their** luggage.

The basic rule for managing pronouns and antecedents couldn't be simpler: Make sure pronouns you select have the same number and gender as the words they stand for.

DRAFT   When a **student** spends too much time on sorority activities, **they** may suffer academically.

CORRECTED   When a **student** spends too much time on sorority activities, **she** may suffer academically.

620

As always, though, there are confusing cases and numerous exceptions. The following guidelines can help you avoid common problems.

Check the number of indefinite pronouns.   Some of the most common singular indefinite pronouns—especially *anybody, everybody, everyone*—may seem plural, but they should be treated as singular. (For the complete list of indefinite pronouns, see the chart on p. 615 in Chapter 59.)

DRAFT   Has **everybody** completed **their** assignment by now?

CORRECTED   Has **everybody** completed **his or her** assignment by now?

If using *his or her* sounds awkward, revise the sentence.

Have **all students** completed **their** assignments by now?

Correct sexist pronoun usage.   Using *his* alone (instead of *his or her*) to refer to an indefinite pronoun is considered sexist unless it clearly refers only to males. ○

Treat collective nouns consistently.   Collective nouns—such as *team, herd, congregation, mob*, and so on—can be treated as either singular or plural.

The Roman **legion** marched until **it** reached **its** camp in Gaul.

The Roman **legion** marched until **they** reached **their** camp in Gaul.

Just be consistent and sensible in your usage. Treat a collective noun the same way, as either singular or plural, throughout a paper or project. And don't hesitate to modify a sentence when even a correct usage sounds awkward.

AWKWARD   The **team** smiled as **it** received **its** championship jerseys.

BETTER   Members of the **team** smiled as **they** received **their** championship jerseys.

respect your readers
p. 440

62 Pronoun Reference

sure what *it* means?

A pronoun should refer back clearly to a noun or pronoun (its *antecedent*), usually the one nearest to it that matches it in number and, when necessary, gender.

> Consumers will buy a **Rolex** because **they** covet **its** snob appeal.
>
> Nancy Pelosi spoke instead of **Harry Reid** because **she** had more interest in the legislation than **he** did.

If connections between pronouns and antecedents wobble within a single sentence or longer passage, readers will struggle. The following guidelines can help you avoid three common problems.

Clarify confusing pronoun antecedents.   Revise sentences in which readers will find themselves wondering who is doing what to whom. Multiple revisions are usually possible, depending on how the confusing sentence could be interpreted.

CONFUSING	The batter collided with the first baseman, but he wasn't injured.
BETTER	The batter collided with the first baseman, who wasn't injured.
BETTER	The batter wasn't injured by his collision with the first baseman.

Make sure a pronoun has a plausible antecedent.   Sometimes the problem is that the antecedent doesn't actually exist—it is only implied. In these cases, either reconsider the antecedent/pronoun relationship or replace the pronoun with a noun.

CONFUSING   Grandmother had hip-replacement surgery two months ago, and it
              is already fully healed.

In the above sentence, the implied antecedent for *it* is *hip*, but the noun *hip* isn't in the sentence (*hip-replacement* is an adjective describing *surgery*).

BETTER   Grandmother had her hip replaced two months ago, and she is
              already fully healed.

BETTER   Grandmother had hip-replacement surgery two months ago, and her
              hip is already fully healed.

Be certain that the antecedent of *this, that,* or *which* isn't vague.
In the following example, a humble *this* is asked to shoulder the burden of a writer who hasn't quite figured out how to pull together all the ideas raised in the preceding sentence. What exactly might the antecedent for *this* be? It doesn't exist. To fix the problem, the writer needs to replace *this* with a more thoughtful analysis.

FINAL SENTENCE VAGUE

The university staff is underpaid, the labs are short on equipment, and campus maintenance is neglected. Moreover, we need two or three new parking garages to make up for the lots lost because of recent construction projects. Yet students cannot be expected to shoulder additional costs because tuition and fees are high already. This is a problem that must be solved.

FINAL SENTENCE CLARIFIED

How to fund both academic departments and infrastructure needs without increasing students' financial outlay is a problem that must be solved.

63 Pronoun Case

I or *me? who*
or *whom?*

In spoken English, you hear it when you run into a problem with pronoun case.

> "Let's just keep this matter between you and . . . *ummmm* . . . me."

> "To who . . . I mean, uh . . . whom does this letter go?"

> "Hector is more of a people person than her . . . than she is."

Like nouns, pronouns can be subjects, objects, or possessives, and their forms vary to show which case they express in a sentence.

Subjective Pronouns	Objective Pronouns	Possessive Pronouns
I	me	my, mine
you	you	your, yours
he, she, it	him, her, it	his, her, hers, its
we	us	our, ours
they	them	their, theirs
who	whom	whose

Unfortunately, determining case is the problem. Here are some strategies for dealing with these common situations.

Use the subjective case for pronouns that are subjects. When pronouns are the only subject in a clause, they rarely cause a problem. But double the subject, and there's trouble.

> Sara and . . . me . . . , or is it Sara and I wrote the report?

To make the right choice, try answering the question for one subject at a time. You quickly recognize that *Sara* wrote the report, and *I* did the same thing. So one possible revision is:

Sara and I wrote the report.

Or you can recast the sentence to avoid the difficulty in the first place.

We wrote the report.

Use the objective case for pronouns that are objects. Again, choosing one objective pronoun is generally obvious, but with two objects, the choice is less clear. How do you decide what to do in the following sentence?

The corporate attorney will represent both Geoff and I . . . Geoff and me?

Again, deal with one object at a time. Since the attorney will represent *me* and will also represent *Geoff*, a possible revision is:

The corporate attorney will represent Geoff and me.

Or, to be more concise:

The corporate attorney will represent us.

Use *whom* when appropriate. One simple pronoun choice brings many writers to their knees: *who* or *whom*. The rule, however, is the same as for other pronouns: Use the subjective case (*who*) for subjects and the objective case (*whom*) for objects. In some cases, the choice is obvious.

DRAFT   Whom wrote the report?
CORRECTED   Who wrote the report?

DRAFT   By who was the report written?
CORRECTED   By whom was the report written?

But this choice becomes tricky when you're dealing with subordinate clauses.

DRAFT   The shelter needs help from whomever can volunteer three hours per week.

The previous example may sound right because *whomever* immediately follows the preposition *from*. But, because the pronoun is the subject of a subordinate clause, it needs to be in the subjective case.

CORRECTED   The shelter needs help from whoever can volunteer three hours per week.

Finish comparisons to determine the right case.   Many times when writers make comparisons, they leave out some understood information.

> I've always thought John was more talented than Paul.
>
> (I've always thought John was more talented than Paul *was*.)

But leaving this information out can lead to confusion when it comes to choosing the correct pronoun case. Try the sentence, adding *him*.

DRAFT   I've always thought John was more talented than him.

              I've always thought John was more talented than him *was*.

CORRECTED   I've always thought John was more talented than he.

If it sounds strange to use the correct pronoun, complete the sentence.

CORRECTED   I've always thought John was more talented than he was.

Don't be misled by an appositive.   An *appositive* is a word or phrase that amplifies or renames a noun or pronoun. In the example below, *Americans* is the appositive. First, try reading the sentence without it.

DRAFT   Us Americans must defend our civil rights.

APPOSITIVE CUT   Us must defend our civil rights. [*Us* can't be a subject.]

CORRECTED   We Americans must defend our civil rights.

Note that when the pronoun is contained within the appositive, as in the examples below, the pronoun follows the case of the word or words it renames.

SUBJECTIVE   The bloggers who were still in the running, Lucy, Cali, and I, wrote all night trying to outdo each other.

OBJECTIVE   The site was dominated by the bloggers who were still in the running, Lucy, Cali, and me.

Misplaced and Dangling Modifiers

In general, modifiers need to be close and obviously connected to the words they modify. When they aren't, readers may become confused—or amused.

Position modifiers close to the words they modify.

are your
descriptions
clear?

MISPLACED   Layered like a wedding cake, Mrs. DeLeon unveiled her model for the parade float.

Mrs. DeLeon is not layered like a wedding cake; the model for the parade float is.

REVISED   Mrs. DeLeon unveiled her model for the parade float, which was layered like a wedding cake.

Place adverbs such as *only, almost, especially,* and *even* carefully.   If these modifiers are placed improperly, their purpose can be vague or ambiguous.

VAGUE   The speaker almost angered everyone in the room.

CLEARER   The speaker angered almost everyone in the room.

AMBIGUOUS   Joan only drove a stick shift.

CLEARER   Only Joan drove a stick shift.

CLEARER   Joan drove only a stick shift.

Don't allow a modifier to dangle.   A modifying word or phrase at the beginning of a sentence should be followed immediately by the subject it modifies. When it doesn't, the modifier is said to dangle.

DANGLING   **After picking me up at the airport,** San Francisco was introduced to me by my future business partner.

San Francisco didn't pick me up at the airport; my future business partner did. So *my future business partner* needs to be the subject of the sentence.

REVISED   **After picking me up at the airport,** my future business partner introduced me to San Francisco.

Parallelism

When items in sentences follow similar patterns of language, they are described as parallel. Parallel structure makes your writing easier to read and understand.

When possible, make compound items parallel.   Don't confuse your readers by requiring them to untangle subjects, verbs, modifiers, or other items that could easily be parallel.

making a list?

NOT PARALLEL	Becoming a lawyer and to write a novel are Leslie's goals.
PARALLEL	Becoming a lawyer and writing a novel are Leslie's goals.
NOT PARALLEL	The university will demolish its old stadium and bricks from it are being sold.
PARALLEL	The university will demolish its old stadium and sell the bricks.
NOT PARALLEL	The TV anchor reported the story thoroughly and with compassion.
PARALLEL	The TV anchor reported the story thoroughly and compassionately.

Keep items in a series parallel.   A series should consist of all nouns, all adjectives, all verbs, and so on.

NOT PARALLEL   She was a fine new teacher—eager, very patient, and gets her work done.

PARALLEL   She was a fine new teacher—eager, very patient, and conscientious.

NOT PARALLEL   We expected to rehabilitate the historic property, break even on the investment, and to earn the goodwill of the community.

PARALLEL   We expected to rehabilitate the historic property, to break even on the investment, and to earn the goodwill of the community.

PARALLEL   We expected to rehabilitate the historic property, break even on the investment, and earn the goodwill of the community.

Keep headings and lists parallel.   If you use headings to break up the text of a document, use a similar language pattern and design for all of them. It may help to type the headings out separately from the text to make sure you are keeping them parallel. Items in a printed list should be parallel as well.

Acknowledgments

Jane Austen. Dialogue from *Pride and Prejudice*.

Michael Barone. "The Beautiful People vs. The Dutiful People." From *Real Clear Politics*, January 16, 2006.

Sven Birkerts. "Reading in a Digital Age." From the *American Scholar*, Spring 2010. Reprinted by permission.

David R. Brower. "Let the River Run Through It." From *Sierra*, March/April 1997. Copyright © 1997. Reprinted by permission of The Estate of David R. Brower.

Robert Bruegmann. Excerpt from "How Sprawl Got a Bad Name." From *American Enterprise*, Volume 17, Issue 5, June 16, 2006, page 6. Copyright © 2006. Reprinted by permission of the author.

Frank Bruni. "Life in the Fast Food Lane." From the *New York Times*, May 24, 2006.

Nicholas Carr. "Does the Internet Make You Dumber?" From the *Wall Street Journal*, June 5, 2010.

Michael Chorost. "Rebuilt: How Becoming Part Computer Made Me More Human." Copyright © 2005, Houghton Mifflin Company.

Clive Cook. "John Kenneth Galbraith, Revisited." From *National Journal*, May 15, 2006.

Calvin Coolidge. "Address at the Celebration of the 150th Anniversary of the Declaration of Independence."

Richard Corliss. "*The Last Airbender*: Worst Movie Epic Ever?" From *Time*, July 2, 2010. Reprinted by permission of Time, Inc. in the formats of Text and Other Book via Copyright Clearance Center.

Ann Coulter. "Godless: The Church of Liberalism." Copyright © 2006 Random House, Inc.

Jesus Diaz. "iPad is the Future." From *Gizmodo*, April 2, 2010. Reprinted by permission of Gawker Media.

Emily Dickinson. "I felt a Funeral, in my Brain." From *The Poems of Emily Dickinson*, edited by Thomas H. Johnson, Cambridge, Mass: The Belknap Press of Harvard University Press. Copyright © 1951, 1955, 1979, 1983 by the President and Fellows of Harvard College. Reprinted by permission of the Publishers and the Trustees of Amherst College.

Maureen Dowd. "Live From Baghdad: More Dying." From the *New York Times*, May 31, 2006.

Ezra Dyer. "Relearning Performance Lingo for the Electric Era." From "On the Juice," *Automobile*, July 2010.

Roger Ebert. Excerpt from review of *The Lake House*. Posted on rogerebert.com, June 16, 2006. Reprinted by permission of the author.

Mark Edmundson. "The Pink Floyd Night School." From the *New York Times Op-Ed*, May 2, 2010.

Lynn Ehlers. " 'Play "Free Bird"!' "

Joseph Epstein. "Plagiary: It's Crawlin' All Over Me." Copyright © 2006 by Joseph Epstein. Originally appeared in the *Weekly Standard*, March 2006. Reprinted by permission of Georges Borchardt, Inc., on behalf of the author.

Verlyn Klinkenborg. "Further Thoughts of a Novice E-Main Text & Reader." From *Editorial Notebook, New York Times,* May 29, 2010.

Wade Lamb. "Plato's *Phaedrus*."

John Lancaster. "The Global Id." From the *London Review of Books,* Volume 28, Number 2, January 2006, page 26.

Laura Layton. "Uranus's Second Ring-Moon System." From *Astronomy,* December 2007, p. 29. Reproduced by permission. Copyright © 2007 Astronomy magazine, Kalmbach Publishing Co.

Donald Lazere. "A Core Curriculum for Civic Literacy." From the *Chronicle Review,* January 31, 2010. Reprinted by permission.

Elaine Liner. "Dumpster Diving." Copyright © 2006. Reprinted by permission of The Phantom Professor.

Nancy Linn. "Cover Letter."

"The Lost Children of Haiti." From the *New York Times,* September 5, 2006.

Kelli Marshall. "Show Musical Good, Paired Segments Better: *Glee*'s Unevenness Explained." From the academic forum of *FlowTV,* January 16, 2010. Reprinted by permission.

Ellen McGrath. "Is Depression Contagious?" From *Psychology Today,* July/August 2003.

Shane McNamee. "Synthesis of Luminol."

Gabriela Montell. "Do Good Looks Equal Good Evaluations?" From the *Chronicle of Higher Education,* October 15, 2003. Copyright © 2003. Reprinted by permission of The Chronicle of Higher Education.

James Morris. "My Favorite Wasteland." From *Wilson Quarterly,* Autumn 2005. Copyright © 2005. Reprinted by permission of the author.

Liza Mundy. "What's Really behind the Plunge in Teen Pregnancy?" From *Slate* May 3, 2006. Copyright © 2006. Reprinted by permission of the author.

Matthew James Nance. "Everything Must Go."

Matthew James Nance. "A Mockery of Justice."

Nation's Report Card. National Assessment of Educational Progress. www.nationsreportcard.gov.

Adam Nicholson. Excerpt from *God's Secretaries.* Copyright © 2003 HarperCollins Publishers, Inc.

Peggy Noonan. "Patriots Then and Now." From the *Wall Street Journal,* March 30, 2006. Copyright © 2006 by Dow Jones & Company, Inc. Reproduced with permission of Dow Jones & Company in the formats of Textbook and Other Book via Copyright Clearance Center.

Camille Paglia. "No Sex Please, We're Middle Class." From the *New York Times,* June 25, 2010.

Andrea Palladino. Résumé.

Pallettruth.com. "Asian Longhorned Beetles from Wood Pallets Invading NYC!"

John Pareles. "The Case against Coldplay." From the *New York Times,* June 5, 2005.

Miles Pequeno. "Check. Mate?"

Steven Pinker. "Mind over Mass Media." From the *New York Times Op-Ed,* June 11, 2010.

David Pogue. "Looking at the iPad from Two Angles." From the *New York Times*, March 31, 2010.

Virginia Postrel. "In Defense of Chain Stores." From the *Atlantic Monthly*, December 2006. Copyright © 2006. Reprinted by permission of the author.

Virginia Postrel. "Pop Psychology." From the *Atlantic Monthly*, December 2008. Reprinted by permission.

David West Reynolds. "Apollo: The Epic Journey to the Moon," page 210. Copyright 2002 Harcourt, Inc.

Matthew Robson. "How Teenagers Consume Media." From the *Guardian*, July 13, 2009. Reprinted by permission.

Richard Rodriguez. From *Hunger of Memory: The Education of Richard Rodriguez.* Copyright © 1982 by Richard Rodriguez. Reprinted by permission of David R. Godine, Publisher, Inc.

Heidi Rogers. "Triumph of the Lens."

Christina Rosen. "The Myth of Multitasking." From the *New Atlantis*, Spring 2008. Reprinted by permission.

Michael Ruse. "Science for Science Teachers." From the *Chronicle of Higher Education*, January 13, 2010.

John Ruszkiewicz. "Annual Big Bend Trip."

"Safe at Any Speed." From the *Wall Street Journal* by Editors, July 7, 2006. Copyright © 2006 by Dow Jones & Company, Inc. Reproduced with permission of Dow Jones & Company, Inc. in the formats Textbook and Other Book via copyright Clearance Center.

Terri Sagastume. "Presentation on Edenlawn Estates."

"Sanity 101." From *USA Today*, January 19, 2006. Reprinted with permission.

Marjane Satrapi. "The Veil" from *Persepolis: The Story of a Childhood*, translation copyright © 2003 by L'Association, Paris, France. Used by permission of Pantheon Books, an imprint of the Knopf Doubleday Publishing Group, a division of Random House LLC. All rights reserved.

Barrett Seaman. "How Bingeing Became the New College Sport." From *Time*, August 21, 2005. Copyright © 2005. Reprinted by permission of Time, Inc. in the formats of Text and Other Book via Copyright Clearance Center.

David Sedaris. "Advice on What to Write About, When I Was Teaching." From *January*, June 2000. Copyright © 2000 by David Sedaris. Reprinted by permission of Don Congdon Associates, Inc.

Clay Shirky. "Does the Internet Make You Smarter?" From the *Wall Street Journal*, June 4, 2010.

Kelsi Stayart. "Authentic Beauty in Morrison's *The Bluest Eye*."

Bret Stevens. "Just Like Stalingrad." From the *Wall Street Journal*, June 23, 2004.

Seth Stevenson. "Ad Report Card: Can Cougars Sell Cough Drops?" From *Slate.com*. Posted: Monday, November 9, 2009.

Ben Stewart. "Muscle Car Competition." From *Popular Mechanics*, March, 23, 2009.

Peter Suderman. "Don't Fear the E-Main Text & Reader." From *Reason*, March 23, 2010. Reprinted by permission of Reason magazine and reason.com.

Andrew Sullivan. "Society Is Dead: We Have Retreated into the iWorld." From *Times Online*, February 20, 2005. Copyright © 2005 by Andrew Sullivan. Reprinted with permission of The Wylie Agency, Inc.

Beth Teitell. "A Jacket of the People." From the *Boston Globe*, January 28, 2010.

Tyghe Trimble. "The Running Shoe Debate: How Barefoot Runners Are Shaping the Shoe Industry." From *Popular Mechanics*, December 18, 2009.

Barbara Tuchman. Excerpt from *The First Salute: A View of the American Revolution*. Copyright © 1989 Random House, Inc.

Michael Villaverde. "Application Essay for Academic Service Partnership Foundation Internship."

Katelyn Vincent. "Technology Time-out."

Joel Waldfogel. "Short End." From *Slate*, September 1, 2006.

Peter M. Whiteley. Excerpt from "Ties that Bind: Hopi Gift Culture and Its First Encounter with the United States." From *Natural History*, November 2004. Copyright © Natural History Magazine, Inc. 2004. Reprinted by permission.

George Will. "Let Cooler Heads Prevail." From the *Washington Post*, April 2, 2006.

George Will. "An Olympic Ego Trip." From the *Washington Post Op-Ed*, October 6, 2009.

Ian R. Williams. "Twilight of the Dorks." From *Salon.com*, October 29, 2003.

Annie Winsett. "Inner *and* Outer Beauty."

Douglas Wolk. "Something to Talk About." From *Spin*, August 2005. Copyright © 2005. Reprinted by permission of the author.

James Woods. "Acts of Devotion." From the *New York Times*, November 28, 2004.

Mike Wirth and Suzanne Cooper-Guasco. "How Our Laws Are Made."

Michael Yon. "An Army of Davids: How Markets and Technology Empower Ordinary People to Beat Big Media, Big Government, and Other Goliaths." Copyright © 2006 Nelson Current.

Cathy Young. "Duke's Sexist Sexual Misconduct Policy." From the *Boston Globe Op-Ed*, April 14, 2010.

Art credits (in order of appearance)

Page 5: Courtesy of StoryCorps.org an independent nonprofit whose mission is to record and collect stories of everyday Americans. www.storycorps.net.

Page 10: *Sun God*, 1983. Concrete structure, paint 413.4 x 177.2 x 118 inches. Stuart Collection, University of California, San Diego, California, USA.

Page 14: The Orange County Register/ZUMAPress.com.

Page 17: John J. Ruszkiewicz.

Page 20: Library of Congress, Prints & Photographs.

Page 21: Copyright © Bettmann/Corbis.

Page 22: Courtesy Sid Darion.

Page 45: (left) Frank Micelotta/Getty Images. (right) Copyright © 2011 by Consumers Union of U.S., Inc. Yonkers, NY 10703-1057, a nonprofit organization. Reprinted with permission from the February 2011 issue of *Consumer Reports* for educational purposes only. No commercial use or reproduction permitted. www .ConsumerReports.org.

Pages 47–48: NASA, ESA, and M. Showalter of the SETI Institute. Images courtesy of NASA Hubble site.

Page 50: Natural History Museum/The Image Works.

Page 57: Bob Daemmrich/The Image Works.

Page 65: Hugh Herr MIT Media Lab.

Page 67: Kenneth Garrett/Getty Images.

Page 73: Copyright © Estate of Ben Shahn/Licensed by VAGA, New York, NY. Photo copyright © Smithsonian American Art Museum, Washington, D.C./Art Resource, NY.

Page 74: Utah Department of Public Safety. Creative Director/Art Director: Ryan Anderson; Creative Director/Copywriter: Gary Sume; Account Supervisor: Peggy Lander; Agency: Richter7; Client: Utah Highway Safety Office, Derek Miller.

Page 80: (top) Ghislain & Marie David de Lossy/Getty Images. (bottom) Courtesy of Dr. Susan Farrell.

Page 84: Courtesy of Dr. Susan Farrell.

Page 85: Popperfoto/Getty Images.

Page 87: Jeff Foott/Getty Images.

Page 90: Bodo Marks/dpa/Landov.

Page 94: Courtesy of the Pima County Sheriff's Department.

Page 100: Marcus Maschwitz.

Page 104: Courtesy IfItWereMyHome.com/Copyright © 2011 Google, Europa Technologies, INEGI.

Page 107: Cover Photo from *Rolling Stone*, December, 27, 2010 © Rolling Stone LLC, 2005. All Rights Reserved. Reprinted by Permission.

Page 116: John J. Ruszkiewicz.

Page 118: www.CartoonStock.com.

Page 120: Andy Singer.

Page 122: (left) Photo by: Rob Rich/Everett Collection. (right) Linda Davids/Getty Images.

Page 126: Jeff Kay.

Page 127: Sara Krulwich/NYTimes/Redux Pictures.

Page 136: Courtesy of Insurance Institute for Highway Safety, http://www.iihs.org.

Page 139: Courtesy of the Environmental Protection Agency.

Page 144: Reprinted with permission of THE ONION. Copyright © 2010, by ONION, INC. www.theonion.com.

Page 148: Everett Collection.

Page 154: Mary Evans Picture Library/Everett Collection.

Page 156: From USA Today—© 2006 Gannet-USA Today. All rights reserved. Used by permission and protected by the Copyright Laws of the United States. The printing, copying, redistribution, or retransmission of this content without express written permission is prohibited.

Page 170: Bettmann/Corbis.

Page 171: John Springer Collection/Corbis.

Pages 172–73: Bettmann/Corbis.

Page 177: Courtesy of Denver Water.

Page 181: AP Photo/Israel Leal.

Page 183: By permission of Michael Ramirez and Creators Syndicate, Inc.

Page 186: Copyright © Corbis.

Page 191: HKS, Inc.

Page 204: plastics.com llc.

Page 207: Courtesy of Kayla Mohammadi. Reprinted with permission.

Page 217: (top) MIRAMAX/Kobal Collection/Jill Sabella. (bottom) HBO/Courtesy of Everett Collection.

Page 229: United Artist/Photofest.

Page 238: Copyright © 20th Century Fox/Everett Collection.

Pages 246–48: Library of Congress, Prints and Photographs Division, Washington, D.C.

Page 251: Courtesy of Joint Economic Committee.

Page 258: Used by permission of Deutsch, Inc. as agent for National Fluid Milk Processor Promotion Board.

Page 260: United States Navy (Courtesy of Navy Environmental Health Center).

Pages 271–72: Everett Collection.

Page 272: Mary Evans Picture Library/Copyright © 20th Century Fox/Everett Collection.

Page 280: Darren McCollester/Getty Images.

Page 285: Copyright © Bill Aron/PhotoEdit, Inc.

Page 286: Jim Zook/@ Images.com/Corbis.

Page 291: © George Steinmetz/Corbis.

Page 293: NSDAP/The Kobal Collection.

Page 297: Lauren Nicole/Getty Images.

Page 301: Copyright © 1993, Maggie Hopp photographer, Creative Time. Courtesy of Maira Kalman.

Page 303: (top to bottom) Will Vragovic/*St. Petersburg Times*/ ZUMA PRESS; Jackie Ricciardi/ *The Augusta Chronicle*/ ZUMA PRESS; ZUMA PRESS; Lannis Waters/ *The Palm Beach Post*/ZUMA PRESS.

Page 311: DILBERT Copyright © 2010 Scott Adams. Used By permission of UNIVERSAL UCLICK. All rights reserved.

Page 317: (left to right) Tim Graham/Getty Images; Copyright © Brigette M. Sullivan/PhotoEdit, Inc.

Page 319: Copyright © Gero Breloer/dpa/Corbis.

Page 325: Bob Daemmrich/The Image Works.

Page 327: Copyright © Hulton-Deutsch Collection/Corbis.

Page 331: Reproduced with permission from the American Council on Education.

Page 337: Copyright © Reuters/Christian Charisius/Landov.

Page 344: (left) A publication of The Council of Science Editors, www.councilscienceeditors.org. (right) *The ACS Style Guide: Effective Communication of Scientific Information, Third Edition* edited by Anne M. Coghill and Lorrin R. Garson (2006). By permission of Oxford University Press, Inc.

Page 347: Copyright © Hulton-Deutsch Collection/Corbis.

Pages 350–51: Microsoft.

Page 357: Courtesy of Jacob Bøtter.

Page 358: Library of Congress, Prints and Photographs Division, Washington, D.C.

Page 359: (top to bottom) Allie Goldstein; Sid Darion; Sid Darion.

Page 360: (left) Copyright © 2011 Google. (right) N.J. Schweitzer.

Page 361: (left) Wikipedia is a registered trademark of the Wikimedia Foundation. (right) Courtesy of National Institute of Justice, Department of Justice.

Page 362: NBC/Photofest. Copyright © Copyright NBC.

Page 363: Robert W. Ginn/Age Fotostock/Photolibrary.

Page 365: Used with permission from the American Library Association. www.ala.org.

Page 366: Copyright © Dick Dickinson.

Page 367: Harry Ransom Center, The University of Texas at Austin. *Ratner's Star* by Don DeLillo. Copyright © 1976 by Don DeLillo. *Players* by Don DeLillo. Copyright © 1977 by Don DeLillo. Used by permission of the Wallace Literary Agency, Inc. Used by permission of the David Foster Wallace Literary Trust.

Page 368: (top) Courtesy of Minnesota State University, Mankato. (bottom) Created by Stephen Von Worley.

Page 369: SOURCE: Census 2000 and 1960 Census Subject Reports, Migration Between State Economic Areas, Final Report PC(2)-2E, Washington, DC, 1967.

Page 370: U.S. Geological Survey.

Page 376: Copyright © Pat Brynes/The New Yorker Collection/www.cartoonbank.com.

Page 377: Copyright © Ariel Molvig/The New Yorker Collection/www.cartoonbank.com.

Page 381: Courtesy of University of Northern Carolina.

Page 385: Dan Burn-Forti/Getty Images.

Page 386: Library of Congress, Prints and Photographs Division, Washington, D.C.

Page 387: Peter Dazeley/Getty Images.

Page 391: (top to bottom) Copyright © Paramount Pictures/Photofest; Copyright © Paramount Pictures/Everett Collection; Copyright © Universal Pictures/Everett Collection; 20th Century Fox/Photofest.

Page 401: (left) Binghamton University, State University of New York. (right) Oklahoma State University.

Page 404: Adam Zyglis, The Buffalo News (blogs.buffalonews.com/adam-zyglis/).

Page 407: Gusto/Photo Researchers, Inc.

Page 408: Courtesy of PARC, Inc., a Xerox company.

Page 411: Jonathan Alcorn/ZUMA PRESS.

Page 416: Steve Terrill/Corbis.

Page 419: Simone End/Getty Images.

Page 421: Jeffrey Coolidge/Getty Images.

Page 429: (top to bottom) Photofest; Federal Emergency Management Agency/Ready Campaign; By permission. From *Merriam-Webster's Collegiate® Dictionary, 11th Edition* © 2013 by Merriam-Webster, Inc. (www.merriam-webster.com).

Page 432: (left to right) Michael Siluk/The Image Works; Andy Whale/Getty Images; UPI Photo/Landov.

Page 433: John Cole, www.politicalcartoons.com.

Page 439: Excerpt from *The 9/11 Report: A Graphic Adaptation* by Sid Jacobson and Ernie Colon. Copyright © 2006 by Castlebridge Enterprises, Inc. Reprinted by permission of Hill and Wang, a division of Farrar, Straus and Giroux, LLC.

Page 445: Photo by Arthur Strong Copyright © Ingrid Franzon.

Page 449: Library of Congress, Prints and Photographs Division, Washington, D.C.

Page 467: Library of Congress, Prints and Photographs Division, Washington, D.C.

Page 469: (left to right): Thomas/Library of Congress, http://thomas.loc.gov; FedStats, http://fedstats.gov; Courtesy of the Wm. Wrigley Jr. Company. Reprinted by permission; General Motors.

Page 470: (top) "Jacket cover," copyright © 2011 by Crown Publishers, an imprint of the Crown Publishing Group, a division of Random House, Inc., from *The Immortal Life of Henrietta Lacks*, by Rebecca Skloot. Used by permission of Crown Publishers, a division of Random House, Inc. (bottom) Reprinted by permission from Macmillan Publishers Ltd.: *Nature,* Copyright © January 2008.

Page 473: Chicago Public Library.

Page 476: Copyright © 2011 Google.

Page 478: (left to right) Topham/The Image Works; Topham/The Image Works; UPI/ Bill Greenblatt/Landov.

Pages 484–85: Sam Gosling.

Page 486: Associated Press/Matt Sayles.

Pages 516–17: *Tomatoland: How Modern Industrial Agriculture Destroyed Our Most Alluring Fruit* by Barry Estabrook. Published by Andrews McMeel.

Pages 522–23: Courtesy of *Scientific American*, a division of Nature America, Inc. All rights reserved.

Pages 526–27: "Why a Brush with Death Triggers the Slow-Mo Effect" by Jad Abumrad and Robert Krulwich, as posted on NPR and *Radiolab* August 7, 2010. Photo by Tim Schapker/Flickr.

Pages 528–29: Reprinted with permission of Cambridge University Press.

Pages 556–57: Centers for Disease Control and Prevention/National Center for Health Statistics.

Pages 558–59: "Darwin and Lincoln: Their Legacy of Human Dignity" by Felton Earls. *Perspectives in Biology and Medicine*, Volume 53, Number 1, Winter 2010. Project Muse, Johns Hopkins University Press.

Page 568: Eric Fischer.

Page 571: Public School, Family and Playlab, NASA's Ames Research Center.

Page 573: Copyright © Google. Sean McCarthy's Writing in Digital Environments class.

Page 574: Copyright © 2010 Google. Map data copyright © 2010 Europa Technologies, PPWK, Tele Atlas—Hala Herbley.

Page 577: (top to bottom) Lannis Waters/ *The Palm Beach Post*/ZUMA PRESS; Brian Cahn/ZUMA PRESS; Clarissa Leathy/ Cultura/ ZUMA PRESS; Bi Keqin/ Imaginechina/ ZUMA PRESS.

Page 582: Image from Airnow.gov.

Page 583: Allie Goldstein.

Page 584: Inge Druckrey.

Page 585: Source: *Education Pays*. Copyright © 2010 The College Board. www.collegeboard.org. Reproduced with permission.

Page 586: Children's Defense Fund.

Pages 587–88: National Oceanic and Atmospheric Administration and The Department of Commerce.

Page 589: Congressional Budget Office.

Page 590: U.S. Bureau of Labor Statistics.

Page 591: Linda Nakanishi.

Page 592: Science Source/Photo Researchers, Inc.

Page 593: Associated Press/Department of Defense.

Page 594: Courtesy of Anthro Corporation.

Page 595: NASA.

Page 596: Colin Harman, colinharman.com.

Page 597: The Plain Dealer/Landov.

Index